IMMIGRATION AND SETTLEMENT

IMMIGRATION AND SETTLEMENT

CHALLENGES, EXPERIENCES, AND OPPORTUNITIES

Edited by Harald Bauder

Canadian Scholars' Press Inc.

Toronto

Immigration and Settlement: Challenges, Experiences, and Opportunities
Edited by Harald Bauder

First published in 2012 by
Canadian Scholars' Press Inc.
180 Bloor Street West, Suite 801
Toronto, Ontario
M5S 2V6

www.cspi.org

Copyright © 2012 Harald Bauder, the contributing authors, and Canadian Scholars' Press Inc. All rights reserved. No part of this publication may be photocopied, reproduced, stored in a retrieval system, or transmitted, in any form or by any means, electronic, mechanical, or otherwise, without the written permission of Canadian Scholars' Press Inc., except for brief passages quoted for review purposes. In the case of photocopying, a licence may be obtained from Access Copyright: One Yonge Street, Suite 1900, Toronto, Ontario, M5E 1E5, (416) 868-1620, fax (416) 868-1621, toll-free 1-800-893-5777, www.accesscopyright.ca.

Every reasonable effort has been made to identify copyright holders. CSPI would be pleased to have any errors or omissions brought to its attention.

Canadian Scholars' Press Inc. gratefully acknowledges financial support for our publishing activities from the Government of Canada through the Canada Book Fund (CBF).

Library and Archives Canada Cataloguing in Publication
Immigration and settlement : challenges, experiences, and opportunities / [edited by] Harald Bauder.
ISBN 978-1-55130-405-2

1. Emigration and immigration—Textbooks. 2. Canada—Emigration and immigration—Textbooks. I. Bauder, Harald, 1969–

JV6035.I46 2012   304.8   C2011-907297-1

Text design by Aldo Fierro.
Cover design by Colleen Wormald.
Cover photo © Shutterstock/ Delmas Lehman

12 13 14 15 16   5 4 3 2 1

Printed and bound in Canada by Webcom

For Kenise Murphy Kilbride

who has been a driving force of immigration and settlement

studies in Toronto and beyond

TABLE OF CONTENTS

Preface ix
Acknowledgements xi
Contributors xii

INTRODUCTION 1

PART ONE: RIGHTS, STATE, CITIZENSHIP 5

Chapter 1: Human Rights and the Paradox of the City 7

Chapter 2: *Jus Domicile*: A Pathway to Citizenship for Temporary Foreign Workers? 21

Chapter 3: Race in Democratic Spaces: The Politics of Racial Embodiment in the City of Toronto 37

PART TWO: MIGRANTS AS LABOUR 55

Chapter 4: The Global City as Political Opportunity Structure for Immigrant Workers' Struggle: The Case of Domestic Worker Organizing in New York City 59

Chapter 5: Protecting Temporary Labour Migrants: An Emerging Role for Global Cities? 75

Chapter 6: Articulating the Self to the Engineering Market: Chinese Immigrants' Experiences from a Critical Transformative Learning Perspective 95

Chapter 7: Making a "Global" City: Racialization, Precariousness, and Regulation in the Toronto Taxi Industry 109

PART THREE: IDENTITIES AND COMMUNITIES 129

Chapter 8: Investigating Dimensions of Cross-National Marriages: A Case of Russian-Speaking Wives in Japan 131

Chapter 9: Recent Immigrants, Earlier Immigrants, and the Canadian-Born: Association with Collective Identities 147

Chapter 10: Religious and Secular Identities in a Plural Canada 171

Chapter 11: Moving Around the World: Russian Jews from Israel in Toronto 183

PART FOUR: HOUSING AND RESIDENTIAL CONTEXT 197

Chapter 12: Social Housing as a Tool for Ethnic Integration in Europe: A Critical View of the Italian Experience   199

Chapter 13: Hidden Homelessness in the Greater Toronto Area's Newcomer Communities: Signs, Symptoms, and Solutions   217

Chapter 14: Everyday Lives in Vertical Neighbourhoods: Exploring Bangladeshi Residential Spaces in Toronto   227

PART FIVE: EMERGING OPPORTUNITIES   247

Chapter 15: Creating and Channelling Refugee Political Activities: The Role of Refugee Organization Building Programs   249

Chapter 16: International Students as Immigrants   271

Chapter 17: The Settlement of Young Newcomer Children: Perspectives for Policy and Program Development   297

Copyright Acknowledgements   311

PREFACE

The publication of this book is linked to the establishment of the Ryerson Centre for Immigration and Settlement Studies (RCIS). This research centre is the brainchild of a group of enthusiastic members of the Faculty of Arts and Faculty of Community Services who saw the need for an institution that would facilitate cutting-edge research on immigration and settlement, and at the same time provide a service to the local community. By the time I arrived at Ryerson University in 2009, this group had reached out to colleagues throughout campus to collaboratively develop a concrete proposal for a university-wide research centre. This proposal was presented to the university administration in 2009 and approved by the Senate of Ryerson University in March of 2011.

According to the founding document, RCIS

> will be a global leader in the transdisciplinary exploration of international migration, integration, and diaspora and refugee studies. In addition to supporting research in these areas, the Centre's mission includes mentoring students, as well as consolidating Ryerson's reputation as the pre-eminent site of knowledge development and exchange with governments, community organizations, and other academics. (RCIS Senate Proposal 2011, 1)

Prior to Senate approval, a conference titled Migration and the Global City was organized as an event to announce the anticipated establishment of RCIS. In congruence with the vision for the institute, the objective of the conference was to bring together a wide range of participants, including academics and students from multiple disciplines, practitioners, community leaders, and policy-makers. In addition, the conference sought to link international contributors with participants who are firmly grounded in the immigration and settlement context of Toronto, Canada's main immigrant gateway and one of the world's most diverse cities. The conference took place in October 2010 and was a great success, with more than 100 paper presentations and 250 attendees from four continents.

Immigration and Settlement features a selection of some of the best papers presented at the conference. All conference presenters received an invitation to submit papers to be included in this volume. Of these submissions, papers were selected based on quality, scientific rigour, and/or accordance with the themes of the book. Given the variability in the nature of the contributions and the background and expertise of the authors, not a single yardstick could be applied to the assessment of quality of the papers. Rather they were judged based on their merit in the contexts of their own aims and perspectives. The selected papers meet the highest standards in this respect. Unfortunately, some excellent papers were not included due to the lack of thematic fit.

Rather than presenting the abstracts of the individual chapters separately, they were integrated in the editorial introductions of each of the five parts of this collection. In this way, these introductions represent a collective writing exercise involving the chapter authors (who provided original abstracts) and the editor (who assembled them into a coherent narrative).

This volume will be of interest to wide-ranging audiences, including academics, researchers, and students; policy-makers, NGOs, and settlement practitioners; and activists and community organizers. While its primary audience is in Canada, it will also be of interest to audiences in countries where Canada (Toronto in particular) serves as a point of interest and reference in matters of immigration and settlement. *Immigration and Settlement* is written for an interdisciplinary audience across the fields of international migration and settlement studies. Its accessible language makes it suitable for graduate and upper-level undergraduate teaching as well as an important resource for community and government. I hope that you, the reader, will find this collection inspiring and useful in gaining a deeper understanding of immigration and settlement.

Harald Bauder, Editor
Toronto, June 2011

ACKNOWLEDGEMENTS

The publication of this book is made possible by generous financial contributions from the Faculty of Arts and the Faculty of Community Services at Ryerson University. Mark Lovewell, the Interim Dean of the Faculty of Arts, and Usha George, the Dean of Community Services, deserve special mention for their encouragement and unwavering support. The affiliate faculty of the Graduate Program in Immigration and Settlement Studies (ISS) and RCIS provided a supportive and collegial environment in which this book project took shape.

This book benefited greatly from the counsel of an always available and diligent Editorial Advisory Board, consisting of John Shields, Myer Siemiatycki, and Vappu Tyyskä. An anonymous reviewer commented on the book, and individual chapters were further reviewed "internally" by the editor and other chapter authors.

Charity-Ann Hannan and ISS students Almara Enriquez, Lisa Deacon, and Kieu (Karen) Chung were highly committed and very competent editorial assistants. At the Canadian Scholars' Press Inc., thanks go to commissioning editor Lily Kalcevich and production manager Colleen Wormald. Paula Sarson was an extremely thorough copyeditor.

Finally, of note are the sponsors and organizers of the Migration and the Global City conference, held at Ryerson University in the fall of 2010, including the Office of the Provost, the Faculty of Arts and the Faculty of Community Services, the Graduate Program in Immigration and Settlement Studies (MA), Ted Rogers School of Management (all Ryerson University), and CERIS—The Ontario Metropolis Centre; an outstanding conference organizing committee consisting of Sedef Arat-Koç, Harald Bauder (chair), Morton Beiser, Laura Davies (CERIS Student Caucus representative), Marco Fiola, Grace-Edward Galabuzi, Sutama Ghosh, John Shields, Myer Siemiatycki, Sew Ming Tian (CERIS Student Caucus representative), and Vappu Tyyskä; the conference support team, consisting of Rita Plaskett and Stefanie Wolf of Agendum, and Mark Strongman of Effective Registration; and an exceptional team of volunteers.

CONTRIBUTORS

ALFREDO AGUSTONI has a PhD in Sociology and is senior researcher and aggregate professor of Urban and Environmental Sociology at the "G. d'Annunzio" Chieti-Pescara University. His research interests concern globalization, migrations and local communities, housing policies, and relations between energy and society. Recently he has co-published *Società urbane e convivenza interetnica* (Urban Societies and Inter-Ethnic Cohabitation) in 2009 and *Migrazioni, politiche urbane e abitative* (Migrations, Urban and Housing Policies) in 2011.

ALFREDO ALIETTI is senior researcher in Urban Sociology at the University of Ferrara, Italy. He has been involved in research at national and European levels on racism, inter-ethnic relations in urban setting, socio-spatial segregation and urban requalification of deprived areas. He has co-published *Metamorfosi del razzismo* (Metamorphosis of Racism) in 2005; and *Società urbane e convivenza interetnica* (Urban Societes and Inter-Ethnic Cohabitation) in 2009.

HANNAH ALLERDICE completed her doctoral degree in Political Science at Syracuse University. Her PhD thesis examined the impact of settlement policy on Sudanese refugee political activities. She currently lives in Washington DC.

SHANA ALMEIDA is currently a PhD candidate in the School of Social Work, York University. Her doctoral research engages with critical race and post-colonial studies to explore the racial logics of "diversity" discourse in the City of Toronto. She also worked in Toronto's municipal politics for six years, until mid-2009.

CARLY AUSTIN completed a master's degree in Immigration and Settlement Studies from Ryerson University. Her research interests include immigration policy, labour migration, and citizenship law. She currently works as a settlement officer for Citizenship and Immigration Canada.

HARALD BAUDER is Academic Director of the Ryerson Centre on Immigration and Settlement and an associate professor in the Graduate Program in Immigration and Settlement Studies and the Geography Department at Ryerson University. His recent books include *Labor Movement: How Migration Regulates Labor Markets* (2006) and *Immigration Dialectic: Imaging Community, Economy and Nation* (2011).

MARTINA BENZ has an MA in Political Science and Sociology from the Graduate School of North American Studies at the Free University in Berlin, Germany. Her research on domestic workers' struggles in New York City is part of her dissertation project on "Workers' Centers and Immigrant Organizing in the United States."

JUDITH A. COLBERT is a consultant based in Guelph, Ontario. She has written numerous reports and policy documents exploring service options for young newcomers and is principal author of requirements governing the provision of newcomer child care support funded by the Government of Canada. She is author of the book *Welcoming Newcomer Children* (2010).

ROBERTA CUCCA has a PhD in Sociology and is assistant professor at the Polytechnic of Milan, Italy. Her research interests focus on urban social inequalities and the social dimension of sustainability. She has co-published *Sviluppo economico e integrazione sociale. Il caso dei distretti industriali lombardi* (Economic Development and Social Integration: The Case of Industrial Districts in Lombardy) in 2010 and *Partecipare alla mobilità sostenibile. Politiche, strumenti e attori* (Participating in Sustainable Mobility: Policies, Tools and Actors) in 2009.

ERIKA GATES-GASSE was the Policy and Research Analyst at World Education Services when conducting the research for her chapter in this volume. Currently, she is the Policy and Research Coordinator at the Ontario Council of Agencies Serving Immigrants (OCASI). She has a BA in International Development and an MA in Public Policy and Administration.

SUTAMA GHOSH is an assistant professor in the Department of Geography at Ryerson University. Her research interests include migration and settlement experiences of newcomers in Canadian cities. In 2007 Ghosh's doctoral research won the Housing Studies Achievement Award from the Canada Mortgage and Housing Corporation (CMHC).

TARA GILKINSON is a research analyst at Citizenship and Immigration Canada's Research and Evaluation Branch and a teacher at Humber College. She holds a bachelor's degree in Sociology and Psychology and a master's degree in Immigration and Settlement Studies. Her current research focuses on the mental health and well-being outcomes of immigrants.

TAHIRA GONSALVES has a master's degree in Sociology and presently works for the Ontario provincial government. She has previously worked as a researcher in the international development sector and in social policy analysis. Her current areas of focus include the immigrant/newcomer and settlement sector, newcomers, mental health and religious identities.

S. GOPIKRISHNA is the Executive Director of the Scarborough Housing Help Centre (SHHC), a non-profit organization active in addressing housing needs of the residents of Scarborough and Markham. Gopikrishna's interest in "hidden homelessness" is informed by SHHC's priorities and his work on the Committee of Adjustment, City of Toronto, an adjudicative body mandated to grant relief from city bylaws.

LAURA HARRIS is a PhD candidate in Political Science at York University in Toronto, Ontario. Her dissertation examines issues of gender, reproduction, and nationalism, as well as human rights and international law.

VARVARA MUKHINA received a master's degree in the History of Asian and African Countries at Saint Petersburg State University, Russia, in 2007. She is now undertaking doctoral studies at Kumamoto University, Japan. Her research focuses on Russian-speaking wives in Japanese communities and the influence of migration on the marital life in cross-national marriages.

GENEVIÈVE SAUVÉ is Manager of Policy, Research, and Planning at the Strategic Management and Human Rights Branch, in the Citizenship and Heritage Sector of the Department of Canadian Heritage. She was previously a senior research analyst at Citizenship and Immigration Canada. Her research interests are focused on identity, belonging, and citizen engagement.

HONGXIA SHAN holds a doctoral degree in Adult Education from the University of Toronto. She specializes in immigrant studies, lifelong learning, qualitative research, and gender, race and class analysis. Her work has appeared in the *International Journal of Lifelong Education, Canadian Journal for the Study of Adult Education, Journal of Workplace Learning*, and other journals.

LEA SOIBELMAN is a registered social worker. She holds a Bachelor of Social Work from Tel Aviv University and a Master of Arts in Immigration and Settlement Studies from Ryerson University. She has extensive experience working with an immigrant population at JIAS (Jewish Immigrant Aid Services) Toronto.

APARNA SUNDAR is assistant professor in the Department of Politics and Public Administration at Ryerson University. Her research interests are broadly in the areas of social movements in the Global South, civil war in South Asia, working-class immigrant organizing in Toronto, and political ecology.

ETHEL TUNGOHAN is a PhD candidate in Political Science and the Collaborative Program in Women and Gender Studies at the University of Toronto. Her research examines the activist pursuits of temporary labour migrants. She is interested in social movement theory, critical race studies, and gender analysis.

INTRODUCTION

HARALD BAUDER

The world is becoming increasingly mobile. This mobility is apparent in countless ways. For example, the media have been flashing images of overcrowded boats in the Mediterranean Sea containing refugees fleeing Northern Africa in search of refuge in Europe from war, political oppression, and economic despair. Similarly, policymakers and lawmakers in Australia, Europe, and North America embrace mobility as a tool to boost national economies by attracting needed mobile "talent" in the form of highly skilled and educated migrants. Internet bloggers in the United States and parts of Europe have been zooming in on people who migrate in clandestine ways while their governments have constructed border fences to curb perceived floods of undesired migration. At the same time, sizable expatriate communities have formed in cities like Singapore and Dubai; Filipina nannies leave their own families to watch other people's children in Hong Kong and Vancouver; seasonal workers flock to Italy; Polish migrants work temporarily in the United Kingdom; and cosmopolitan elites circulate among Los Angeles, Mumbai, Paris, and other cities. While people are mobile, however, they are not detaching themselves from places and communities. Rather, they become temporarily or permanently attached to places and become members of local and national communities.

As the twenty-first century matures, international migration and the settlement of newcomers will transform nations, cities, and communities at an ever-accelerating pace. International migration and settlement are poised to become the defining political, economic, social, and cultural phenomena of our age. Migrants will claim political spaces and inclusion in political communities; they will provide labour power and skills that make economies globally competitive; they will shape the identities of societies; and they will present unprecedented opportunities to the communities in which they settle. At the same time, migrants will continue to generate political tensions, suffer from labour exploitation, be excluded from equal opportunities, and be seen as a threat to society. International migration and settlement are highly complex and deeply contradictory processes.

Although migration has become a global phenomenon and affects all parts of the world, nowhere are the trends and consequences of immigration and settlement better observable than in Canada, especially the country's main immigrant gateway city, Toronto. Many of the contemporary challenges, experiences, and opportunities of immigration and settlement converge in Toronto. As Paul Anisef and Michael Lanphier (2003) astutely observe in the title of an edited volume, Toronto resembles *The World in a City*. Its population is incredibly diverse in terms of ethnic origin, place of birth, languages spoken, and religious practice.

Such diversity is a key characteristic of today's global city. According to Saskia Sassen (2006), the economy and social structure of global cities are intricately linked to global migration flows—not only of people but also of capital and goods. As global capital flows converge at the stock markets and the banking sectors of Wall Street in New York and Bay Street in Toronto, a labour force of immigrants who work as janitors, maids, restaurant workers, taxi drivers, gardeners, and caretakers provide the necessary low-end labour to make these highly profitable economic centres function. Despite their economic importance, immigrants rarely receive their fair share of the value they help produce. Their wages tend to be lower than those of established residents, and they often reside in neglected and underserviced areas of the city, wedged between gentrified downtown areas and affluent suburbs (Young, Burke Wood, and Keil 2011). This coexistence between rich and poor, inclusion and exclusion, opportunity and despair are just some of the contradictions that characterize the study of migration.

Human mobility has been increasingly approached through the framework of networks. Most migrants are not abandoning their identities, social connections, and even the property they have acquired at the places where they lived before. Instead they are transnational actors operating within a "space of flows" (Castells 1989). These networks and flows penetrate various spatial scales, ranging from the apartment building, housing block, and neighbourhood, which frame migrants' social experience; to the city region, which defines their labour market; to the nation, which controls the borders and grants formal citizenship; and to the global scale, which frames all other scales. The ensuing social relations and identities are multi-faceted: a single person, for example, can simultaneously embrace identities as a Canadian citizen, an immigrant, a 1.5-generation Canadian, a Pakistani-Canadian, a "South Asian," a Torontonian, a "visible minority," and a citizen of the world. This book moves beyond existing conceptualizations of immigration and settlement as a "two-way" exchange between newcomers and a "host" society, and acknowledges the complexity of relations that characterize international migration and settlement.

The complex and contradictory nature of international migration and settlement is not something that can be reduced to a neat and simple theory or set of theories—nor should it be. There is no single approach to understanding migration, as Michael Samers (2010) has recently demonstrated. Even attempts to combine insights from various approaches will never achieve a point where migration and settlement will be perfectly understood. Rather, knowledge of migration and settlement processes will always depend on the observer's vantage point. Similarly, there will always be competing interests and motivations that shape migration and settlement practices. Rather than being examined through a particular theoretical approach or as a one-dimensional practice, international migration and settlement must be understood dialectically (e.g., Bauder 2011). Such a dialectical understanding embraces the inherent contradictions between numerous aspects of international migration, different experiences of settlement, and various geographical scales at which human mobility occurs. The chapters in this book present such a productive dialectical engagement between various aspects, perspectives, and scales of migration and settlement.

ORGANIZATION OF THE BOOK

With its conceptual and thematic diversity, the book offers a contextually grounded yet comprehensive understanding of international migration and settlement. The book is contextually grounded in that it links global, national, regional, and local scales. In particular, the recurrence of Canadian- and Toronto-based case studies provides an empirical thread weaving the chapters of the book together. The book, however, makes the important point that migration also occurs in other places, and that both international and Canadian perspectives are necessary to obtain a comprehensive picture of the challenges, experiences, and opportunities of international migration and settlement.

Some basic statistics illustrate the differences and linkages between various scales and help to contextualize some of the material presented in the following chapters. Of the global population of roughly 7 billion people, the International Organization for Migration (IOM 2010) estimates that 214 million people, or 3.1 percent, are international migrants. Generally, these numbers have been increasing over time; yet, the patterns of migration are highly unevenly distributed across regions of the world. Canada is among the countries that experience a net gain of immigration. According to Citizenship and Immigration Canada (2011), the country accepted more than 280,000 new immigrants in 2010—approximately two-thirds of these under the "economic class" in which immigrant selection occurred based on the anticipated economic benefits to Canada. An additional 182,000 foreign workers entered the country in the same year. According to the 2006 Census, roughly 20 percent of Canada's population is foreign-born. Within Canada, more than half of new Canadian immigrants settled in the Toronto area. As a result of this concentration, half of the population of the City of Toronto was foreign-born in 2006, and 47 percent were of non-European origin and belonged to a "visible minority" group (City of Toronto 2011).

The book is also comprehensive in that it approaches immigration and settlement from various aspects, which are organized into five thematic parts: (1) Rights, State, Citizenship; (2) Migrants as Labour; (3) Identities and Communities; (4) Housing and Residential Context; (5) and Emerging Opportunities. Each of the thematic parts consists of three or four chapters, which are arranged to offer an initial international perspective, followed by chapters that focus on Canada and/or Toronto. The structure of the book and its parts are intended to convey the multi-dimensionality of immigration and settlement, while highlighting the connections between aspects, perspective, and scales.

The individual chapters were written by emerging and established scholars and practitioners who contribute viewpoints from academia, policy-making, activism, and community service. In addition, they offer perspectives from multiple disciplines and cover theoretical, normative, and practice-oriented terrain. By integrating such thematic and conceptual diversity, the book aims to engage with and advance the dialectic of international migration and settlement studies.

REFERENCES

Anisef, P., and M. Lanphier, eds. 2003. *The World in a City*. Toronto: University of Toronto Press.

Bauder, H. 2011. *Immigration Dialectic: Imagining Community, Economy and Nation*. Toronto: University of Toronto Press.

Castells, M. 1989. *The Informational City: Information Technology, Economic Restructuring, and the Urban-Regional Process*. Oxford: Basil Blackwell.

Citizenship and Immigration Canada (CIC). 2011. "Fact and Figures, 2010." Accessed May 5, 2011. www.cic.gc.ca/english/resources/statistics/menu-fact.asp.

City of Toronto. 2011. "Census & Trends: 2006 Census Information." Accessed May 5, 2011. www.toronto.ca/demographics/reports.htm.

International Organization for Migration (IOM). 2010. "World Migration Report 2010—The Future of Migration: Building Capacities for Change." Geneva.

Samers, Michael. 2010. *Migration*. Oxon, UK: Routledge.

Sassen, S. 2006. *Cities in a World Economy*. 3rd ed. Thousand Oaks: Pine Forge Press.

Young, D., P. Burke Wood, and R. Keil, eds. 2011. *In-between Infrastructure: Urban Connectivity in an Age of Vulnerability*. Kelowna: Praxis (e)Press.

Part One

RIGHTS, STATE, CITIZENSHIP

The state plays a central role in immigration and settlement. For example, through immigration policy, the state selects people who are allowed to cross into its territory and thus become immigrants in the first place. In fact, the very notion of immigration would not make sense without the existence of a state. Once migrants enter a national territory, the state again frames the circumstances of their settlement, and their inclusion or exclusion. The state regulates populations and their mobility through mechanisms, such as citizenship and rights, and by framing policy and discourses about immigration and settlement. Part One examines these mechanisms and discourses.

In Chapter 1, Laura Harris explores the relationship between universal human rights, the city, and the state. Her chapter begins by outlining the groundwork for modern rights doctrines. In particular, it discusses the concepts of individual autonomy and rights as founded within nation-states. According to Immanuel Kant and Hannah Arendt, for rights doctrines to be effective they must be protected by the state; however, this relation between rights and the state is problematic when considering the case of refugees. Harris reflects upon modern theories of the state in contrast to notions of individual human rights and the rights of refugees. More specifically, Harris asks: must human rights be framed within a state system or can they exist at a scale below the nation-state, in the form of a city of refuge? By theorizing the possibility of a "city of refuge" as proposed by Jacques Derrida, Harris explores whether Arendt's paradox of human rights can be resolved at the urban scale. Although Harris's chapter is purely theoretical, the questions she raises about the urban, the state, and universal rights are highly applicable to discussions of migration and refuge in countries like Canada and cities like Toronto.

In Chapter 2, Carly Austin and Harald Bauder also conduct a theoretical thought experiment but apply their argument to the concrete case of Canada's Temporary Foreign Worker Program. In recent years, this program has grown dramatically and now exceeds in volume the country's permanent immigration program. While the Temporary Foreign Worker Program supplies needed labour to Canadian employers, it has failed to address issues of labour exploitation and social injustice. In their chapter, Austin and Bauder discuss contemporary theories of citizenship and explore whether the *jus domicile* principle of citizenship (i.e., citizenship based on residence, as opposed to birthplace or ancestry) can alleviate the problems and injustices associated with temporary labour migration. Taking into consideration existing federal and provincial policies, Austin and Bauder argue that *jus domicile* can provide a pathway to permanency and citizenship for temporary foreign residents in Canada. Similar to Chapter 1, this chapter contemplates whether rights and citizenship should be framed at urban, national, or other geographical scales.

In the final chapter of Part One, Shana Almeida focuses on the state at the urban scale, in particular the City of Toronto, and the local embodiment of the politics of race. Almeida examines the Plan of Action for the Elimination of Racism and Discrimination, which the Toronto City Council adopted in April 2003. This plan proposes to work proactively to remove barriers of racism and discrimination and vows to promote equitable participation of racial minorities and immigrants. Drawing on Sara Ahmed's liberal multiculturalism, Anthony Farley's race-pleasure concept, and David Theo Goldberg's "born again racism," and using Institutional Ethnography as a methodology, Almeida shows how this institutional document maintains ideological relations of rule and reifies the hegemonic state. The chapter also discusses the pervasiveness of "diversity discourse" and how this discourse commodifies racialized bodies, de-historicizes race, and de-races democracy. The chapter further highlights how a municipal policy document recirculates and sustains the problematic multicultural and racial rhetoric of Canada's nationalist agenda.

Chapter 1

HUMAN RIGHTS AND THE PARADOX OF THE CITY

LAURA HARRIS

INTRODUCTION

Emphasizing that stateless persons are the most vulnerable in the modern world, Hannah Arendt ([1951] 1994, 302) writes, "Without citizenship, a person loses all significance." Arendt did not mean that without a state a person ceases to be human, but rather that an individual without a state has nowhere to appeal to rights protection. This situation suggests that states are necessary elements of any successful human rights doctrine. Even if an individual were to appeal to a sense of universal human rights, without a state to physically protect those rights, violations would continue to occur. If one accepts that for human rights to be of force and effect they must be founded within a sovereign state, what options are there for refugee rights protection? As Hannah Arendt explains, in the eyes of the state, and even the international community at large, the stateless refugee or asylum seeker has lost all qualities which guarantee human rights.

In response to the continued presence of a growing number of refugees and the continued paradox of human rights as requiring state enforcement, Jacques Derrida (2000, 2001) in his works *Hospitality* and *Cosmopolitanism and Forgiveness* attempts to construct a new form of universal hospitality. Drawing upon his notion of universal hospitality, Derrida then proceeds to theorize the creation of "cities of refuge," which exist outside the modern nation-state system, as alternate spaces for refugee rights protection.

Within this chapter I will juxtapose Arendt's paradox of rights against Derrida's response via the notion of the city of refuge. To assess the ability or inability of Derrida's city of refuge to address the paradox of rights, I will conduct a thought experiment in which I theorize the creation of a city of refuge. To begin I will consider which elements of the nation-state are detrimental to the creation of universal hospitality, therefore deducing which elements are to be absent from the "city of refuge." As I work through the formation of a city as existing outside the nation-state, I will also consider the form that sovereignty has traditionally taken and what this will mean for the city of refuge. While this chapter outlines the theoretical relationship between sovereignty and citizenship, in Chapter 2 Carly Austin and Harald Bauder add further context by focusing on the case study of migrant labour. In this chapter I will also consider what role borders play in the maintenance of sovereign spaces for democratic recognition and participation. I argue that Derrida's city of refuge is unable to solve Arendt's paradox of rights because a borderless city of refuge, as conceived by Derrida, has removed the necessary bounded space for the functions of democratic citizenship and thus laws and rights. Derrida's cities of refuge lack a clear outline of what form sovereignty will take within the city; consequently, they are likely to resemble a world government, which Immanuel Kant ([1781–1797] 1991, 103) argues could turn into a "soulless despotism." To conclude this chapter, I will explain that rejecting Derrida's proposition of a city of refuge as a possible solution to Arendt's paradox of rights should not prompt us to give up on Derrida's idea entirely. As an alternative to a city of refuge, I consider the possibility for porous borders, as outlined by Seyla Benhabib (2002).

ARENDT'S PARADOX OF RIGHTS

In her work *On Totalitarianism*, Arendt is writing about the situation of the Jews in Nazi Germany who lost all rights at the hands of the Nazi regime. Arendt's (1994) discussion of rights and rightslessness is presented as a two-step argument. First, Arendt (1994, 275) explains that the "nation had conquered the state, national interest had priority over law long before Hitler could pronounce, 'Right is what is good for the German people.'" The second step in Arendt's argument is the notion that rights became based entirely on citizenship because there was no longer any place on Earth that had not already been claimed by either a nation or a nation-state, and therefore no place existed for the exercise of rights for the stateless. When speaking on the modern situation for stateless individuals, Arendt (1994, 297) explains: "The trouble is that this calamity arose not from any lack of civilization, backwardness or mere tyranny, but on the contrary, that it could not be repaired because there was no longer any 'uncivilized spot on Earth.'" If an individual is without citizenship, they must either find a new form of citizenship or they are forced to exist as a being that is unable to claim human rights. Arendt argues that we "become aware of the existence of a right to have rights ... and a right to belong to some kind of organized community, only when millions of people emerge who had lost and could not regain these rights because of the new global political situation [i.e., the emergence of the nation-state]" (296).

Seyla Benhabib (2002, 548) clarifies Arendt's notion of a "right to have rights" by explaining that the first use of the term "right" describes humanity's responsibility to recognize membership within the human community. The second use of the word "right" is built upon a prior claim to membership. Where Arendt believes that rights should be based on the first use of the word, as a common responsibility to humanity, she also recognizes that in the modern situation the term "right" has become dependent on membership within a specific community. Reflecting upon the complexity of rights discourse in the modern world, Arendt (1994, 297) argues that "the loss of home and political status have become identical with expulsion from humanity altogether." In light of this situation individuals must belong to some form of community within the larger realm of humanity in order to be considered political beings worthy of rights. When discussing Arendt's notion of the right to have rights, Benhabib asks: who is able to offer the recognition required to obtain a right to have rights? As Benhabib (2002) explains, for Arendt it is humanity's duty to protect human rights, but she is unsure if this is possible.

Returning to Arendt's discussion of the rightsless individuals in Europe during World War II, she explains that without a state to turn to for rights protection, the Jews of Europe faced unspeakable human rights violations. Arendt (1994, 268) remarks that "[the Jews] had lost those rights which had been thought of and defined as inalienable, the Rights of Man." When considering the *Declaration of the Rights of Man and the Citizen*, Arendt explains that the inalienable rights guaranteed by the *Declaration* were, "proclaimed to be 'inalienable,' irreducible and un-deducible from other rights or laws, [but] no authority was invoked for their establishment" (291). What is most striking about the *Rights of Man and the Citizen* itself is that the very title seems to suggest that for rights to exist in at least some capacity so, too, must citizenship. Arendt explains that during the Holocaust, the *Rights of Man* did not protect the Jews from persecution and murder because without a state to belong to people lost a crucial element to their humanness. She concludes that "[t]he world found nothing sacred in the abstract nakedness of being human" (299). In light of Arendt's work, it becomes clear that within the present nation-state system, although the invocation of rights may be essential for individual rights protection, the state or some form of state recognized community is equally necessary to upholding the very rights that require protection.

According to Arendt, the real travesty of the modern world is "[n]ot the loss of specific rights, then, but the loss of a community willing and able to guarantee any rights whatsoever" (297). What is most striking about Arendt's discussions of totalitarianism and the plight of refugees resulting from the global phenomena of the nation-state is her suggestions that the dilemma faced by worldwide refugees is a consequence of the formation of a global citizenry. For Arendt we have started to live in "one world," and consequently, "[t]he danger is that a global, universally interrelated civilization may produce barbarians from its own midst by forcing millions of people into conditions which, despite all appearances, are the conditions of savages"(302). Individuals are forced into the "conditions of savages" when rights become based solely on citizenship and thus stateless individuals are often considered to exist outside of humanity. In light of this statement, it would seem that for Arendt citizenship has become a necessary condition for humanness. Also, for Arendt a global citizenry is quite possibly even more dangerous than national citizenship.

DERRIDA'S CITY OF REFUGE

It is precisely the paradoxical relationship between the nation-state and rights, and the notion of a right to have rights that fuels Derrida's inquiry into the conception of hospitality and subsequently a "city of refuge" based upon universal hospitality. As a means of beginning his discussion of hospitality, Derrida considers Immanuel Kant's (1991) notion of a system of rights based on global hospitality. When discussing the three definitive articles for peace, which form the foundation for "Perpetual Peace," Kant explains that the third article is the expression of universal hospitality. Kant (1991, 449) writes:

> The Cosmopolitan of World Law shall be limited to conditions of universal hospitality. We are speaking in this as well as in the other articles not of philanthropy, but of law. Therefore hospitality means the right of a foreigner not to be treated with hostility when he arrives on the soil of another. The native may reject the foreigner if it can be done without his perishing, but as long as he stays peaceful, he must not treat him hostilely. It is not the right of becoming a permanent guest ... but it is the right to visit, which belongs to all men—the right belonging to all men to offer their society on an account of the common possession of the surface of the earth ... since it is a globe, they cannot disperse infinitely, but must tolerate each other. No man has a greater fundamental right to occupy a particular spot than any other.

For Kant hospitality is to be treated as a legal apparatus, which implies that it also requires an authority (typically a republican state) to enforce promises of hospitality. In addition, for Kant, hospitality is a temporary condition to be extended to foreigners; this in itself seems to limit the possibility for a situation of permanent hospitality and permanent residency. Although Kant argues that, "no man has a greater fundamental right to occupy a particular spot than any other," he maintains a distinction between foreigner and host suggesting that although initially all individuals have equal rights, once individuals occupy physical space they have a right over it. As Benhabib (2002, 551) explains, for Kant, "Hospitality is a right that belongs to all human beings insofar as we view them as potential participants in a world republic." Without membership, which allows for some form of democratic participation, for Kant, there can be no rights.

As part of a larger project for perpetual peace, Kant argues that the best political constitution is a republican one and therefore the goal of politics should be to create a world federation of republican states. Kant supports a project of a republican federation because he believes that only within a republican state can individuals, as citizens, be truly autonomous. According to Benhabib (2002), Kant is careful to clarify that he does not advocate for the creation of a world government; instead, he argues for a cosmopolitan citizenry where everyone is a member of a republican state. Kant argues that bounded communities are necessary for the proper exercise of citizenship. This is closely related to the issue of political representation, which will be discussed in greater detail later in this chapter.

In his discussion of Kant's third definitive article for peace, Derrida (2000) points to the opposition within the passage of the words hospitality and hostility, and illustrates that both words contain the "host" as their initial premise. The term "host" creates the first obstacle in Derrida's attempt to theorize a notion of universal hospitality that can be extended to all. For Derrida, a traditional conception of hospitality first requires that there is a host who extends hospitality to others, and second, the host must have the necessary authority over a home in order to offer hospitality.

Another critique of Kantian hospitality offered by Derrida (2001) is his argument that by defining hospitality as a law, Kant creates a situation in which the conditions for hospitality are dependent upon state sovereignty. The host must be sovereign over a property in order to invite the foreigner to visit. In his work on hospitality, it is Derrida's (2000, 6) goal to construct a universal hospitality because as long as we are unable to unconditionally welcome someone, "[w]e do not know what hospitality is." Derrida (2000, 8) explains that at present, "Hospitality is owed to the other as a stranger. But if one describes the other as a stranger one is already introducing the circles of conditionality that are family, nation, state and citizenship." A project which Derrida has later taken on in his work *On Cosmopolitanism and Forgiveness* is the creation of a "city of refuge," which encompasses his notion of universal hospitality.

Invoking the analogy of a doorway or threshold, Derrida (2000, 14) explains, "For there to be hospitality, there must be a door. But if there is a door; there is no longer hospitality." In other words, hospitality can only take place beyond hospitality. The city of refuge must therefore exist outside of traditional relationships of hospitality and it must not rely on an oppositional relationship between host and foreigner. Derrida begins his discussion of a city of refuge by describing the International Parliament of Writers and the cities of refuge they have sought to create in order to house persecuted writers. The Parliament of Writers, "Calls for the creation on autonomous cities of refuge, each as independent from the other and from the state as possible, but nevertheless, allied to each other according to forms of solidarity yet to be invented" (Derrida 2001, 4). It is Derrida's purpose in writing *On Cosmopolitanism* to take on this task of invention in which he theoretically "re-orients" the state and creates cities of refuge. It is not Derrida's purpose (nor is it the purpose of this chapter) to describe a concrete, pre-existing city of refuge. Rather, Derrida develops the theoretical construct "city of refuge" as a way of uncovering what a place of universal hospitality might look like.

For Derrida (2000, 6), the reason both he and the Parliament of Writers have turned to the city for a solution to the nation-state/rights paradox is that "[w]e have given up hope that the state might create a new image for the city." The nation-state is traditionally framed around strict notions of state sovereignty, rights based on citizenship, and a territorially defined space, all of which Derrida challenges. Derrida explains that although Arendt did not consider cities as a solution to the paradox of rights, he believes that the city could offer a place with new foundations for rights and a unique form of sovereignty, which could offer new possibilities for international law. Derrida (2001, 9) asks: "If the name and the identity of something like the city still has meaning, could it, when dealing with the related questions of hospitality and refuge, elevate itself above nation-states or at least free itself from them, in order to become … a free city?"

The most striking components of Derrida's city of refuge are its absence of clearly delineated borders and a sovereign authority or host. For Derrida, a city of pure hospitality would be open to all people at all times and therefore the existence of borders would nullify his project of creating perfect hospitality. In contrast to Derrida's borderless city and as a means of beginning my thought experiment, I will consider where sovereignty traditionally lies within the nation-state system. As a means of theorizing what the city might look like, I will consider where sovereignty might reside, if the present nation-state system were removed. I will also consider what elements of sovereignty Derrida opposes and how his city might function without borders or the presence of a sovereign authority. Furthermore, I will examine the desirability of creating a sovereign-less and borderless city as a safe haven for refugees.

THEORIZING SOVEREIGNTY

When theorizing the construction of a city of refuge, the first step might be to ask where has sovereignty traditionally existed and, subsequently, where will sovereignty lie within the city and what functions will it perform? By way of considering the historical forms that sovereignty has taken, I turn to the work of Benhabib (2007b) who explains that historically sovereignty has taken on two distinct forms: state sovereignty and popular sovereignty. One form of state sovereignty finds its origins in the work of Thomas Hobbes. In *Leviathan* ([1651] 1994) he argues that a sovereign authority in the form of a Leviathan is required to remove human beings from their natural state of anarchy. Hobbes (1994, 80) argues that the state of nature is a state of war of all against all and therefore it rationally follows that "every man has a right to everything, even to another's body." When people leave the state of nature and give up their right to everything (with the exception of preserving their lives) to the Leviathan, it becomes the Leviathan's role to provide human security that was absent in the state of nature. In removing the condition of war the Leviathan also controls the use of violence. In summation, for Hobbes sovereignty lies in the hands of the Leviathan, who obtained this authority from the citizens based on their desire for basic human security. This form of sovereignty involves very little citizen participation in governing as the citizens' only duty is to submit their individual right to everything to the authority of the sovereign who will in turn provide them with security. The citizens do not deliberate over which laws will be in effect within their state; instead it is the Leviathan who decides which laws are best suited to providing security and stability. With regard to international human security, the Leviathan is meant to rule over and create peace only for a limited population, under covenant to a single authority. The Leviathan does not create security or rights protection for all humans, but only for the Leviathan's own subjects.

In light of the crisis faced by refugees it is clear that a Hobbesian approach to sovereignty is precisely what Derrida argues *against*. It is the exclusionary practices of traditional state sovereignty that lead a refugee to be excluded from rights protections. The state sovereignty approach involves very little participation by the citizens.

In opposition to the state sovereignty model, the popular sovereignty is based in the work of Immanuel Kant, who argues that citizens are both the subjects as well as the authors of the law. Law, according to Kant (1991), is decided upon by all citizens with the interests of all citizens in mind. For Kant, laws must precede rights, which can only come into existence via legal processes. Kantian public rights are defined as "the sum total of those laws which require to be made universally public in order to produce a state of right" (137). Kant continues:

> Since the state takes the form of a union created by the common interest of everyone living in a state of right, it is called a *commonwealth*.... Within the general concept of public right, we must therefore include not only political right but also international right[;] ... these two concepts taken together necessarily lead to the idea of an *international political right* or a *cosmopolitan right*. (emphasis in original, 137)

For Kant ([1785] 2001), popular sovereignty implies that as rational beings, drawing upon the categorical imperative,[1] humans create laws that will be mutually beneficial. An important distinction to consider when discussing Kantian right and subsequently popular sovereignty is that rights, as they are understood by Kant, represent a most basic level of protection for human existence. Therefore, rights cannot exist without law (Kant 2001). When comparing state sovereignty and popular sovereignty it becomes clear that for both approaches, the state remains central: as the provider of human security in the case of the state sovereignty approach, and as the enforcer of law in the case of the popular sovereignty approach. In *On Cosmopolitanism and Forgiveness*, Derrida (2001, 22) explains that by framing hospitality in legalistic terms, "In the Kantian sense, hospitality, whether public or private, is dependent on and controlled by the law and the state police." In light of this statement we might ask how human security, sovereignty, and law can be constructed within the city of refuge. In the absence of a formal sovereign authority, who or what will be responsible for providing security and creating laws within the city of refuge? Without some form of sovereign authority, the city of refuge lacks a clear foundation for the creation of laws and subsequently for the protection of rights. I will now consider the role that territory traditionally plays in the formation of a political space.

SOVEREIGNTY AND TERRITORY

An element of sovereignty, which is traditionally considered to be foundational, is territoriality. Drawing on the symbolism of a doorway, Derrida seeks to remove the spatial element that separates host from foreigner. Derrida explains that as long as there is a door, there cannot be true hospitality as the person who owns the door has the power of hospitality or rejection (Derrida 2000, 14). Drawing upon Kantian temporary hospitality, Derrida (2000) explains that for a foreigner to visit there is often no door but instead a threshold. A door presents itself when the foreigner's stay is no longer temporary and becomes permanent. Derrida then argues for a place for refugees where the openness offered to temporary visitors is extended to those who might wish to stay permanently. For Derrida it is the physical presence of a door that creates the differentiation between host and foreigner accompanied by the fact that the host has sovereign authority over the place beyond the doorway. In order to create a city of refuge that removes the distinction between host and foreigner, the theoretical doorways or, on a larger scale, borders would have to be removed. In order for a city of refuge to offer unconditional hospitality, it would have to be borderless. Then it is necessary to ask: Should borders continue to exist and which functions could they potentially serve?

The various explanations for the creation and persistence of borders have been taken up in an interesting debate between Michael Walzer (1983) and Joseph Carens (1987). For Walzer, borders are necessary for human security. Without control over a specific territory, a state would be unable to offer exclusive protection to its citizens, who in turn owe a certain level of loyalty to their state. This relationship between citizens and sovereign is one of mutual duties and obligations.

In opposition to Walzer, Joseph Carens (1987) argues in *Aliens and Citizens* that there is little moral or practical reason for the maintenance of state borders and their resulting restrictions on immigration. Carens (1987) questions the arguments made by Walzer, that borders are necessary for national security, public order, and the maintenance of distinct communities. For Carens (1987), liberal theories of rights and citizenship assumed the context of the liberal state and are therefore ill-equipped to deal with questions of aliens. Carens explains that liberal theorists such as John Rawls appeal to liberal individuals because Rawls's writing speaks the individualistic language that modern society is accustomed to. Continued support of borders is actually a learned behaviour and lacks a moral basis. Carens's (1987, 269) support of open borders rests on the possibility that "[t]he general case for open borders is deeply rooted in the fundamental values of our tradition. No moral argument will seem acceptable to us, if it directly challenges the assumption of the equal moral worth of all individuals." In his conclusion, Carens does not remove the right for communities to distinguish between members and non-members. In fact Carens (1987, 271) argues, "People live in communities with bonds and bounds, but these may be of different kinds." Although Carens maintains the right for individuals to form bounded communities, he emphasizes that it would be liberal for communities to have closed territorial borders.

In light of Walzer's and Carens's debate over the liberal nature of open versus closed borders, it seems quite useful to consider the work of Seyla Benhabib who discusses the presence of borders. As a mediating presence between Walzer and Carens, Benhabib introduces elements of representation in her notion of *porous* borders. Benhabib (2007b, 25) poses an interesting challenge to state-centred approaches to sovereignty when she asks: "Can we still maintain the ideal of popular sovereignty and democratic rule if the state-centred model of sovereignty itself is becoming dysfunctional?" If sovereignty is becoming dysfunctional, Benhabib asks, "Does the twilight of state sovereignty mean the end of citizenship and democratic politics?" (28) This notion of a relationship between borders and democratic politics is essential to Benhabib's argument. Without some form of bounded space, Benhabib argues, democratic politics cannot function. In order for democracy to function, citizens must believe that they have the ability to actively participate in the formation of the laws that they are to be governed by; they must also feel that their sovereign leaders are accountable to the wishes of the citizenry. A bounded political space is necessary for democratic politics because it provides the necessary space for recognition and participation.

While Benhabib argues that some form of delineated space is necessary for democratic politics, she believes that a central question regarding human rights and refugees surrounds the issue of the definition of borders themselves. Benhabib asks if notions of borders only include strict territorial definitions, or if borders can instead be porous and constituted by a citizenry who shape them and not a physical space itself? If some form of political boundary is desirable, or even necessary, it seems pertinent to then consider how these boundaries should be delineated and what form sovereignty will take.

By removing the territorial requirement for a political community while maintaining some form of delineation of political space, Benhabib is reformulating Kantian popular sovereignty as not necessarily grounded in a territorial state. Benhabib (2007a, 448) explains that the "scope of democratic legitimacy needs to be circumscribed by the demos which has bounded itself as a people on a given territory [, therefore] an unbounded global political entity could not be a democratic one." While Benhabib argues that new cosmopolitan arenas for political action are being created, she does not argue, as Derrida does, that these new places are to be completely borderless. Benhabib rather argues that in some capacity borders remain necessary for democratic governance.

For Benhabib, new spaces for democratic-republican participation and more specifically new functions of citizenship have been created in the modern world. She explains that new urban activism, which includes citizens as well as non-citizens and members as well as non-members of urban activist groups, illustrates that political agency and participation are possible beyond the member/non-member divide (Benhabib 2007b). Furthermore Benhabib explains that new developments in international law and international human rights treaties are "creating new modalities for the exercise of [republican] federalism" (31).[2] Benhabib (2007b, 31) refers to the practice of laws operating across state boundaries as *democratic interactions*, which she defines as:

> complex processes of public argument, deliberation, and exchange through which universalist rights claims and principles are contested and contextualized, invoked and revoked, posited and positioned throughout legal and political institutions, as well as in the associations of civil society. Democratic interactions can take place in the "strong" public bodies of legislatures, the judiciary and the executive, as well as in the informal and "weak" publics of civil society associations and the media.

Democratic interactions describe the mechanism by which a new form of popular sovereignty is formed in which laws are created in the sphere of global politics and the authors of the law are the individuals who live within such communities.

For Kant, Arendt, and Benhabib alike, representation involves demarcation. Under a form of popular sovereignty in which citizens are authors and subjects of the law, citizens must also feel that their interests are being represented by the community to which they belong. For Benhabib (2007a, 449), popular sovereignty is not identical with territorial sovereignty: "Popular sovereignty means that all full members of the demos are entitled to have a voice in the articulation of the laws by which the demos governs itself." As Kant, Arendt, and Benhabib argue, the larger a polis grows, the more difficult it becomes to ensure that there is adequate representation of the citizenry's interests.

While Benhabib argues in favour of demarcation, she questions the notion that national borders are necessarily the only means to achieve this aim. Furthermore, while democratic governance involves the "demarcation of jurisdiction, it ought not to prohibit the flows of people across borders" (Benhabib 2007a, 448). Following the logic of popular sovereignty and demarcation based on jurisdiction and not territory, Benhabib (2007a, 448) argues that porous borders, in which all individuals are able to travel at will, are "intrinsic to the logic of democratic representation and thus to the exercise of public and private freedom." In other words, it would go against the logic of popular sovereignty to place restrictions on who can belong to a deliberative, democratic polis. Individuals may leave or join a community operating under the logic of popular sovereignty as long as they are willing to participate in the creation and maintenance of the sovereign structure.

While the territorial element of a sovereign group can be removed, the need to delineate between members and non-members must be maintained in order for a community to remain representative of its population. By way of illustrating forms of porous borders and modern popular sovereignty, Benhabib (2007b) explains that enforcement mechanisms for new forms of international law are found in the growing number of international judicial bodies such as the European Court of Human Rights and the International Criminal Court (ICC). These examples show that some form of international popular sovereignty has led individuals to join together in the common cause of creating a judicial body that exists outside of sovereign states. For Benhabib, what has changed then since 1951 when Arendt was writing is that the state is no longer the only viable enforcement for rights protection. For example, the ICC has been created to take the role of enforcement for violations of human rights out of the hands of states into the hands of an internationally recognized judicial body. While Benhabib cites the creation of the ICC and European Court of Human Rights as possible spaces for international law that moves beyond the nation-state system, nation-states must still agree to be subject to the laws of the ICC.

LOCATING SOVEREIGNTY: CITIES VERSUS GLOBAL GOVERNANCE

In light of Benhabib's discussion of porous borders, I now return to one of my original questions: where would sovereignty exist in a city of refuge? Both the city of refuge and a global state share the assumption that sovereignty would exist outside of the realm of nation-states, and thus operate outside of and independent of borders. For example, Derrida's city of refuge would exist without doorways or separation between host and foreigner, which suggests that it would be borderless. Despite the optimism that Derrida places in the city of refuge, it is necessary to consider his argument that Arendt did not discuss cities as solutions to the paradox of rights. I wonder if it could be possible that Arendt did not consider cities as solutions in the same way that she did not view a global government as a solution. Could Arendt have recognized the possibility that a city and a global government might resemble each other in many ways? Derrida (2001, 7–8) ponders the possibility of the city to "open up new horizons of possibility previously undreamt of by international state law," or free itself from them. If this is true, how then are the characteristics and goals of the city of refuge distinct from those of a world government? In order to outline the differences or similarities between cities of refuge and a world government, it is necessary to first reconsider how both Kant and Arendt foresaw a world government and what its downfalls would be. Further, one must consider just how cities of refuge differ from a world government or whether they are different at all.

In order to highlight the limitations and weaknesses of the complete openness of Derrida's cities, it is useful to turn to arguments put forth against global sovereignty by Kant, Arendt, Benhabib, and Étienne Balibar (2008). Below, I outline the downfalls of a global government as a way to illustrate some of the possible points of comparison between it and a city of refuge. I hope that by describing the weaknesses of the idea of global government, the limitations of a city of refuge will also be apparent. According to Kant, only within a system of separate republican states can rights be upheld without diminishing the force of the laws governing each state. Kant (1991, 113) argues, "The laws progressively lose their impact as government increases its range, and a soulless despotism … will finally lapse into anarchy." For Kant, the danger of a global state is found when considering the fact that as laws attempt to expand their reach, they subsequently lose their force.

Another argument against the creation of a global government comes from Arendt, who takes a critical approach to the nation-state system, and is equally opposed to a global government. For Arendt citizenship and public deliberation are necessary for human flourishing and these can only be practiced within delineated communities. Arendt (1994) argues that in order to avoid totalitarianism and tyranny, public space must be maintained for open discourse and this would not be possible under a world government. Yet another argument is developed by Étienne Balibar (2008, 553) who, drawing upon Gillies Deluze, suggests that a world government and the "complete suppression of state borders, far from producing a higher degree of freedom, would rather lead to a controlling sovereignty, whose practical form could be a monstrous global system of survey of individual moments and lives." Finally, Benhabib's (2007a) argument against a world government echoes that of Kant and Arendt, who propose that democratic governance requires a citizenry whose interests are represented by the laws of the polis.

In light of these three different arguments, it becomes clear that some form of border or delineation between individual communities and the global population are to be preferred over a global form of government and the absence of any borders. If the city of refuge remained borderless, it would not provide the necessary means for democratic participation in politics or representation for its citizens. While Benhabib maintains that some form of delineation between members and non-members of a community are necessary for representation and democratic participation, she questions the element of territoriality traditionally associated with statehood.

If the city of refuge remains borderless and without a clear program for sovereign authority it would contain the same contradictions inherent within a global government. The differences between a city of refuge and a global state seem to be based on issues of scale and not overall structure or content. As Kant argues, within a global government it would be nearly impossible to construct a governing body that would be representative of the population and thus able to construct the laws. Similarly, in a city of refuge, a clearly identifiable method of law creation would also be absent. In a global state, as well as in a city of refuge, citizens could become increasingly individualistic and therefore turn inward, focusing only on their private lives instead of choosing to participate in public deliberation and discourse. Finally, a borderless city of refuge—along with failing to offer a clear space for the creation of laws—would be unable to offer a space for the creation and maintenance of rights protection. As Arendt (1994, 297) explained, "Not the loss of specific rights, then, but the loss of a community willing and able to guarantee any rights whatsoever" is the real travesty of the modern world. Although Derrida's city of refuge presents a thought-provoking consideration of the relationship between the city and the nation-state, this city is unable to provide the type of community that Arendt argues is necessary for rights protection. As long as rights are founded in law (as they are today) a city of refuge will remain unable to solve Arendt's paradox of rights.

CONCLUSION

In light of the apparent inability of Derrida's city of refuge to solve Arendt's paradox, it seems possible to turn once again to Benhabib's proposal for porous borders as a viable alternative. Benhabib brings to light a notion that although some form of border may be necessary for democratic politics, first, these borders may not need to be territorially defined, and second, that democratic borders should be intrinsically porous. Therefore, under the project of porous borders and modern popular sovereignty, refugees should be able to enter a community and stay for as long as they choose, at will, as long as they are willing to participate in the democratic governance of the polis to which they belong. As decision making and sovereignty within the logic of popular sovereignty lie in the hands of the individuals who are affected by a law or practice, all those who are directly or indirectly affected by a law have the right to participate in its creation or abolishment, including those who are considered non-citizens.

As Benhabib (2007a) explains, the political domain which regulates popular sovereignty may be constantly changing and therefore boundaries themselves will also shift over time. If modern popular sovereignty is exemplified by the coming together of a group of individuals for the purpose of founding a system of laws which will be decided upon by all members, then the laws of popular sovereignty will be in a state of constant re-formulation and reinterpretation, if they are to remain representative of the people. Similarly, Étienne Balibar explains that democratic governance is something that is created by a collective group of people; it is not something that can be possessed or achieved. For Balibar (2008, 526), "Democracy is a permanent struggle for its own democratization and against its own reversal into oligarchy and monopoly of power." While porous borders constitute a separation between members and non-members (for the purpose of representation) these borders are not strictly formulated in the way territorial state boundaries are formed and instead they remain ever changing.

A solution to the paradox was not the goal of this chapter, instead my goal was to come to a better understanding of if and why delineated political spaces for citizenship remain necessary today. A next step could be to ask if spaces demarked by porous borders exist today, and if so are these spaces governed by modern forms of popular sovereignty as described by Benhabib?

ENDNOTES

1. The categorical imperative is described by Kant (2001, 185) as: "Man and generally any rational being *exists* as an end in himself, *not merely as a means* to be arbitrarily used by this or that will, but in all his actions, whether they concern himself or other rational beings, must always be regarded at the same time as an end."
2. Benhabib (2007b, 31) defines "'republican federalism' as the constitutionally structured reaggregation of the markers of sovereignty, in a set of interlocking institutions each responsible and accountable to the other."

REFERENCES

Arendt, H. (1951) 1994. *The Origins of Totalitarianism*. Orlando: Harcourt.

Balibar, É. 2008. "Historical Dilemmas of Democracy and Their Contemporary Relevance for Citizenship." *Rethinking Marxism* 20 (4): 522–538.

Benhabib, S. 2002. "Political Geographies in a Global World: Arendtian Reflections." *Social Research* 69 (2): 539–566.

———. 2007a. "Democratic Exclusions and Democratic Interactions." *European Journal of Political Theory* 6 (4): 445–462.

———. 2007b. "Twilight of Sovereignty or the Emergence of Cosmopolitan Norms? Rethinking Citizenship in Volatile Times." *Citizenship Studies* 11 (1): 19–36.

Carens, J. 1987. "Aliens and Citizens: The Case for Open Borders." *Review of Politics* 49: 251–273.

Derrida, J. 2000. "Hospitality." *Angelaki* 5 (3): 3–18.

———. 2001. *Cosmopolitanism and Forgiveness*. London: Routledge.

Hobbes, T. (1651) 1994. *Leviathan* Edited by Edwin Curley. Indianapolis: Hackett.

Kant, I. (1781–1797) 1991. *Kant's Political Writings*. Edited by Hans Reis. Cambridge: Cambridge University Press.

———. (1785) 2001."Fundamental Principles of the Metaphysics of Morals." In *Basic Writings of Kant*, edited by Allen W. Wood, 143–222. New York: Modern Library Classics.

Walzer, M. 1983. *Spheres of Justice: A Defence of Pluralism and Equality*. United States of America: Basic Books.

Chapter 2

JUS DOMICILE: A PATHWAY TO CITIZENSHIP FOR TEMPORARY FOREIGN WORKERS?

CARLY AUSTIN AND HARALD BAUDER

INTRODUCTION

Although industrialized countries increasingly depend on foreign migrant workers (Sassen 1998; Thomas 2010), these workers often lack permanent residency and access to citizenship, and the associated rights and entitlements which permanent residents and citizens can take for granted. At the same time, temporary foreign workers (TFWs) today are staying in the host country for longer periods and/or they are returning repeatedly. In Daniel Weinstock's (2008, 5) words, these countries have brought "great numbers of temporary workers in to occupy economic roles that nationals of these countries no longer wanted to perform, but without the intention of ever including them as full members, they have found themselves with communities of temporary economic migrants who were temporary in name only."

Canada, too, follows this practice (Fudge and MacPhail 2009). In recent years, it has accepted more temporary migrant labourers than permanent immigrants. The shift towards temporary migration to Canada has come with serious consequences, especially for the workers. Exploitation is widely documented and pathways to permanency are either complex or non-existent. While in the past, these migrants were promised membership in the national community, today most migrants are denied this opportunity. In this chapter, we discuss this situation within the context of citizenship.

The recent literature has challenged territorial conceptions of citizenship (Gustafson 2005). Notions of nested (Kivisto 2007; Kivisto and Faist 2007), transnational (Bauböck 1994), postnational (Soysal 1994), and stakeholder (Bauböck 1994) citizenships have emerged in response to the increasing mobility of populations and the geographical complexities of citizenship practices. By applying conceptual ideas of citizenship to the concrete case of Canada's Temporary Foreign Worker Program (TFWP), we seek to bridge the gap between theoretical scholarship and the practices of citizenship (Bloemraad et al. 2008). In particular, we explore the principle of *jus domicile* as an approach to improving stability, protection, and fairness for TFWs. In addition, like Laura Harris has done in Chapter 1 in the context of human rights, we ask about the geographical scale that should frame citizenship.

We first examine the literature on citizenship and contemporary configurations of citizenship practices. Second, we discuss principles of citizenship, including *jus domicile*. Third, we present an analysis of the TFWP. Fourth, we apply the *jus domicile* principle to the case of the TFWP. We conclude the chapter with a brief discussion.

CONFIGURING CONTEMPORARY CITIZENSHIP

The concept of citizenship can be traced back to the Greek city-state, the Roman Empire, feudal arrangements in medieval Europe, and the modern nation-state that emerged in the late eighteenth century. At the turn of the nineteenth century, citizenship began to be associated with certain economic, social, and educational rights, which supported citizens' civil and political standing (Castles and Davidson 2000). In the Introduction to T. H. Marshall's (1965) classic book on citizenship, Seymour Lipset (1965, x) illustrates how civil, political, and social aspects of modern citizenship evolved in the context of changing historical circumstances:

> The civil aspects of citizenship arose with the emergence of the bourgeoisie in the 18th century and involved a set of individual rights including liberty, freedom of speech, equality before the law, and the right to own property. Political rights, the access to the decision making process through participation in the choice of parliament by universal manhood suffrage, emerged in the 19th century and reflected in part the demands of the working classes for citizenship. Social rights, which include welfare, security, and education, have become a major component in the definition of citizenship in the 20th century.

Since Marshall published his work, the concept of citizenship has evolved further, based on changing material circumstances that have affected citizenship practices and the way scholars approach the concept of citizenship. International migration has led to the inclusion of cultural aspects into the concept of citizenship (Cohen 2009; Bloemraad et al. 2008). Multicultural citizenship, for example, is premised on the idea of group rights, whereby different ethno-racial groups exist together within a multicultural society and possess the right to be treated as full, equal, and respected participants in the political community (Kymlicka 1995). Multicultural citizenship, however, has also been criticized for perpetuating inequalities and maintaining structures of domination (Bloemraad et al. 2008; Bloemraad 2000; Young 1989; Kostakopoulou 2008).

Recent trends towards securitization (Wæver 1995; Burke 2002; Bigo 2002) have further led to the "thickening" of political belonging and the ethnicization of citizenship boundaries. As multicultural citizenship is thought to "gloss over" differences between ethno-racial groups, the notion of differentiated citizenship suggests that not all citizens are equal; some have different rights and entitlements within a society (Kostakopoulou 2008; Young 1989). This differentiation stems from increasing securitization and differential treatment of ethno-racial groups.

Contemporary geographies of citizenship are particularly problematic. Modern citizenship has been closely tied to the nation-state as the "natural" focal point of human welfare (Kostakopoulou 2008). However, with the increased mobility of people worldwide, citizenship tied to the nation-state fails to uphold important principles and represent political communities (Bloemraad et al. 2008; Bellamy 2008). Although nation-states pursue a range of naturalization processes and practices to bring migrants under the umbrella of national citizenship, a growing number of migrants remain without formal citizenship and consequently lack the rights citizens take for granted. Furthermore, international agencies that advocate on behalf of these migrants possess neither the right nor the means to interfere in the "internal" affairs of nation-states (Yuval-Davis 1999).

Trends of globalization and transnationalism, in particular, have challenged understandings of citizenship centred on the nation-state (Tambini 2001; Spiro 2008; Joppke 2010). Some scholars have recently suggested that citizenship should be refocused, away from the scale of the nation-state and oriented towards personhood, universality, and human rights (e.g., Basok 2004; Kofman 2005). Others have argued for reconfiguring citizenship. We will briefly discuss the notions of nested, transnational, postnational, and stakeholder citizenships, which offer new geographies of citizenship and suggest that multiple forms and geographical scales of citizenship can coexist.

Nested citizenship follows Rogers Brubaker's (1992) idea that political membership involves an inner circle of citizenship (based on nationality), and an outer circle of denizenship (based on residency). Similarly, nested citizenship refers to membership at multiple scales of governance, ranging from an inner circle of a particular locality to regional and transnational scales. Nested scales of citizenship are not independent of each other, but are interconnected. Moreover, they are organized hierarchically, with the inner circle being of greater significance than outer circles (Kivisto 2007; Kivisto and Faist 2007).

Transnational citizenship is characterized by an expansion of citizenship beyond the national framework. Rainer Bauböck (1994) observes in the context of transnational citizenship, first, a clash between principles of liberal democracy and current forms of exclusion from citizenship at the scale of nation-states; second, the emergence of interstate citizenship in certain regions of the world; and third, the evolution of universal human rights as an element of international law. As rights, and claims to rights, are no longer confined to national boundaries, migrants respond fluidly and opportunistically to varying political-economic conditions. For example, in the context of transnational mobile elites, Aihwa Ong (1993, 1999, 2006) speaks of "flexible citizenship" as a mechanism to mobilize a range of resources, entitlements, and protections.

Postnational citizenship is based on claims and entitlements associated with human and universal rights. It awards the right and duty of participation to every person within the authority structure and public life of a polity, regardless of their historical or cultural ties to that community (Soysal 1994). Yasemin Nuhoğlu Soysal (1994) anchors postnational citizenship in international human rights law, but stresses the extension of rights and entitlements based on length of residency and the accumulation of social and economic contributions to a community. Although postnationalism may weaken the boundaries of the state, the state is nonetheless responsible for upholding postnational citizenship entitlements of persons residing within its territory, independent of these persons' formal national membership (Spiro 2007).

The idea of *stakeholder citizenship* proposes that rights and entitlements should be grounded in place of residence; everyone who resides in a territory and is subject to its laws should be represented in the making of the laws as stakeholders. Stakeholders in this sense have a moral claim to be recognized as citizens and to be represented in democratic self-government. Bauböck (2008) posits that citizenship status and rights should be extended to all persons whose circumstances of life tie their personal fate to the long-term prospects of a political community. Similarly, the concept of "denizen" refers to foreign citizens who enjoy domestic rights derived from residency (Bauböck 2008; Hammar 1990).

As this review of citizenship concepts shows, scholarship has acknowledged that citizenship entitlements and the material practices of citizenship are becoming decoupled from the nation-state. Yet, nation-states continue to hold substantial power over the formal rules and rights associated with citizenship (Bloemraad et al. 2008). In the next section, we discuss the principles of citizenship employed by the nation-state.

CITIZENSHIP PRINCIPLES

Citizenship principles define the way through which a person becomes a citizen of a nation-state. Two citizenship principles apply in most countries today. The first, *jus sanguinis*, refers to citizenship based on blood lineage. For example, until Germany recently changed its citizenship law, the children of German emigrants carried German citizenship, even though they had not set foot in the country for generations, while foreigners born on German soil were not given citizenship. The second is *jus soli*, referring to citizenship based on the land. Traditional immigration countries, including

Canada, follow this citizenship principle, whereby individuals born in the territory of a nation-state are awarded citizenship regardless of their parents' citizenship (Castles and Davidson 2000). Typically, nation-states award citizenship through a combination of these two principles.

A rarely used third citizenship principle is *jus domicile*: citizenship based on location of residency. At the core of *jus domicile* is the notion of home and the bonds of association that persons have with the political community in which they reside (Kostakopoulou 2008). *Jus domicile* has been discussed in the United Kingdom, where the Committee of Ministers of the Council of Europe defined it in 1972 as:

> The concept of domicile imports a legal relationship between a person and a country governed by a particular system of law or a place within such a country. This relationship is inferred from the fact that a person voluntarily establishes or retains his [sic] sole or principal residence within that country or at that place with the intention of making and retaining in that country or place the centre of his personal, social and economic interests. This intention may be inferred, *inter alia*, from the period of his residence, past and prospective, as well as from the existence of other ties of a personal or business nature between that person and that country or place. (cited in Hammar 1990, 193)

Jus domicile can been considered a complementary citizenship principle for situations in which a permanent inconsistency exists between place of birth or blood lineage and country of residence. Dora Kostakopoulou (2008) further differentiates between domicile of choice and domicile of birth, arguing that citizenship and entitlements based on choice of residence and place of birth can coexist. The discussion below focuses on *jus domicile* of choice. In a way, *jus domicile* can be regarded as a more legitimate principle than *jus sanguinis* or *jus soli*, because citizenship does not depend on the accident of birth in a territory or to particular parents (Bauböck 1994).

According to Kostakopoulou (2008), the principle of *jus domicile* entails two requirements: factum, the taking up of residence in a particular country as an inhabitant, and animus, a freely formed intention to reside there permanently or indefinitely. In other words, the citizenship principle based on *jus domicile* is possible only when the state gives inhabitants the option to remain at a place of residence and does not force them to leave.

The incorporation of the *jus domicile* principle into citizenship law and practice responds to contemporary material practices of increased human mobility. *Jus domicile* holds the possibility of defining every member of a community as a potential citizen (Bauböck 1994); it promises to treat every contributing resident as belonging to the political community.

It could be argued that Canadian immigration and citizenship policies already implement the *jus domicile* principle in that foreign permanent residents, i.e., "landed immigrants," acquire an entitlement to Canadian citizenship if they have remained in the country for at least three out of five years. The difference between Canada's current naturalization practice and the *jus domicile* principle in the way we discuss it is that permanent residency is granted on a highly selective and inequitable basis. The majority of TFWs have no option of retaining permanent residency in Canada and subsequent citizenship. Yet, they are making similar local connections and contributions to the national and/or local community as permanent residents.

In the next section, we apply the ideas and concepts developed above to the case of Canada's TFWP. Our aim is to explore the possibility of incorporating the *jus domicile* principle into contemporary migration policies and practices. In addition, we investigate the geographical scale at which *jus domicile* would be feasible.

TEMPORARY FOREIGN WORKERS IN CANADA

While throughout Canada's history many foreign-born workers have been permitted to settle permanently in the country (Knowles 2007), others have been denied long-term residence and remain excluded from the national political community (Satzewich 1991). As early as the 1880s, Chinese labourers were not only exploited and abused when they worked on the Canadian Pacific Railway, but at the end of their contracts, Canada's government also denied these workers the right to belong to the nation and rejected any responsibility for these workers' welfare (Avery 1988; Kelley and Trebilcock 1998).

In 1973 the Non-Immigrant Employment Authorization Program (NIEAP) created the official category of TFW. Between 1973 and 2002, the number of TFWs entering Canada increased from just over 14,000 to over 228,000 (Sharma 2006). Under the NIEAP, workers experienced substandard working conditions, work permits were tied to a specific employer, there were restrictions on the workers' labour market entry and mobility, and workers had to leave Canada to apply for subsequent work visas. The NIEAP also established a rotational system of migration whereby migrants repeatedly came and went, thus becoming "permanently temporary" (Fudge and MacPhail 2009; Sharma 2006). The NIEAP established the foundation of today's TFWP, which includes the Seasonal Agricultural Workers Program, the Live-In Caregiver Program, and the Low-Skilled TFW Pilot Project, launched in 2002 (CIC 2009a).

In 2006 the number of non-permanent residents who entered Canada exceeded the number of permanent immigrants for the first time. By 2008 Canada admitted just under 400,000 temporary residents and less than 250,000 permanent residents (Office of the Auditor General of Canada 2009; CIC 2009b). Most non-permanent residents are TFWs. Even during the recession of 2009, the number of TFWs increased (CIC 2010b). The general increase of TFWs has been especially notable in Alberta, where the largest numbers of TFWs have been employed. Along with an increase in numbers, there has been a shift toward lower-skilled occupations and towards low-income and "non-traditional" source countries in South Asia, Southeast Asia, and Latin America (Nakashe and Kinoshita 2010; Thomas 2010).

Restrictions on the amount of time TFWs are able to remain in Canada are easing. Since May 2009 it is easier for employers to renew TFWs' one-year work permits for a second year (CIC 2009b). In addition, new legislation simplifies employers' administrative requirements in rehiring TFWs for the same position, enabling TFWs to remain for longer uninterrupted periods of time in Canada (Nakache 2010).

Although TFWs bear the largest costs of labour migration (Hennebry 2008; Martin 2003), the program is largely employer-driven. To hire TFWs, employers must issue a request for a Labour Market Opinion (LMO), which assesses wages and working conditions, the availability of Canadian workers and trainees, labour shortages, and the transfer of skills and knowledge to Canada (HRSDC 2010b). The quick processing time, however, has raised questions about the accuracy and rigour of the LMOs (Nakache 2010; Office of the Auditor General of Canada 2009). Between 2007 and 2010, a pilot project, called the expedited LMO, was put in place to reduce the processing time to five business days for certain occupations in Alberta and British Columbia (HRSDC 2010a).

In 2007 the government announced further changes to the TFWP to facilitate employers' requests to hire low-skilled workers. Regional lists of "Occupations under Pressure" were compiled to further streamline recruitment, requiring employers to advertise a job to Canadian workers for only seven days (Fudge and MacPhail 2009; Flecker 2010). Furthermore, employers have been exempted from obtaining LMOs to recruit workers in certain occupations covered by the North American Free Trade Agreement and the General Agreement on Trade in Services (Thomas 2010). With these measures, employers receive a flexible and on-call foreign labour force that can be dispensed with at any time.

From a foreign worker's perspective, the TFWP is highly problematic. TFWs cannot freely choose an occupation or employer in Canada. Furthermore, employers are required to write an evaluation of the TFW at the end of each contract period, and many employers invite or "name" workers back for the following year. Given their paternalistic relationship with their employers and workers' fear of expulsion from the program or of deportation with loss of employment, workers reportedly follow an unwritten "behavioural code" of remaining unobtrusive, accepting without question accelerated work schedules, extended workdays, and employers' requests for overtime (Binford 2009). In addition, they tend to refrain from reporting illness and injury, and filing complaints about substandard working conditions, long work hours, or other forms of mistreatment.

The abuse and exploitation of TFWs is well documented, especially within the agricultural sector (e.g., Byl and Foster 2009; Basok 2000; CIC 1994; Binford 2009; Smart 1997). Although some measures have been put in place by the government to protect workers from exploitation, they have been insufficient or unsuccessful (Fudge and MacPhail 2009). Since TFWs are prevented from bargaining collectively,[1] they are unable to exercise the few labour rights they possess (Fudge and MacPhail 2009). Clearly, the vulnerability and exploitability of TFWs results from their precarious status, and the lack of citizenship and the associated rights and entitlements.

Citizenship—and the denial of citizenship—are important mechanisms regulating labour markets (Bauder 2006, 2007). The majority of TFWs cluster in specific occupations in the lower end of the labour market, particularly in the service sector (HRSDC 2010a). Meanwhile, the rights and entitlements associated with citizenship permit Canadian citizens to occupy jobs that offer better pay, benefits, and career advancement opportunities. In fact, the availability of a flexible, dispensable, cyclical, and rotational foreign labour force to fill labour-intensive positions at the bottom of the labour market protects the capital-intensive skilled and higher-waged segment of the economy and stabilizes this segment in light of seasonal and cyclical swings (Piore 1979). As TFWs become a permanent feature of the Canadian labour market, these non-citizens are no longer simply a labour reserve army that can be hired and fired based on seasonal and cyclical economic cycles, they constitute an exploitable underclass (Sharma 2006).

The lack of citizenship rights creates and reproduces inequalities among people who are working and residing in the territory of the same nation-state (Stasiulis and Bakan 1997; Bauder 2008). TFWs are caught in a Catch-22 situation. They lack citizenship so their visa can be temporally restricted, they can be denied permanent residence, and they cannot accumulate social and economic rights and entitlement and claims to citizenship (Soysal 1994). Yet their contributions to the community justify their formal membership in this community. Arguably, their contributions even exceed that of many citizens, due to the sacrifices they make, the abuses they suffer, and the exploitation they experience (Balibar 2000).

To meet the entitlement of TFWs for community membership, an additional principle of citizenship beyond the birthrights of *jus soli* and *jus sanguinis* is needed. Below, we explore the principle of *jus domicile* in the context of TFWs.

JUS DOMICILE AND TEMPORARY FOREIGN WORKERS

The citizenship principle of *jus domicile* responds to contemporary patterns of human mobility and can thus be used as a formal mechanism for TFWs to claim rights and entitlements based on de facto membership in a community. TFWs participate in local and national economies and civic society as workers, consumers, and residents. As long as they make these contributions, they fulfil the requirements for the *jus domicile* principle of citizenship and the associated right to stay permanently and indefinitely. However, if they move away and thereby cease to make such contributions, their citizenship would expire. Multiple *jus domicile* citizenships would not accumulate over time. Yet citizenship acquired through *jus domicile* would complement other layers of citizenship, including citizenship acquired through *jus soli* or *jus sanguinis*.

The *jus domicile* principle of citizenship presents a mechanism to institutionalize normative notions of nested, transnational, postnational, and stakeholder citizenships. It would formalize the particular layer of citizenship linked to place of residence that is "nested" within other forms of citizenship that TFWs possess. *Jus domicile* citizenship would also express forms of transnational citizenship in that it would permit TFWs to claim their rights and entitlements outside the boundaries of the territorial nation-state of their original (*jus soli* and/or *jus sanguinis*) formal citizenship. By the same token, the state would assume the same responsibility of TFWs on its territory as it does of all its citizens.

In terms of postnational citizenship, *jus domicile* would formally recognize the accumulation of rights and entitlements based on residency and the participation and contribution of TFWs in the economic, social, and public life of a community, regardless of the citizenship they acquired at birth. Finally, *jus domicile* would implement stakeholder citizenship grounded in rights and entitlements based on residence. Using *jus domicile*, TFWs could claim formal citizenship based on their stake in the community.

An important practical consideration is at which point a TFW would receive *jus domicile* citizenship. As Bauböck (1994) remarks, host states can easily manipulate residence permits so that some immigrants are not allowed to stay long enough to become citizens. To protect TFWs from abuse and exploitation, citizenship privileges and entitlements should apply as soon as a TFW assumes residency at a particular location. Conversely, a TFW's contribution to and stake in a community is likely to accumulate over time, in which case citizenship should be granted after a certain period of residency. In Canada's Live-In Caregiver Program, TFWs are granted permanent residency after two years with the prospect of formal citizenship after an additional three years. Yet, within the first two years, workers remain extremely vulnerable and often suffer from abuse and maltreatment. The valuable "price" of future citizenship deters these TFWs from claiming the rights and entitlements they already possess.

Jus domicile would be consistent with Canada's history of labour migration and contemporary permanent immigration policy. Canada has historically linked migration with citizenship acquisition, and many generations of immigrants have become citizens through the contributions they have made to Canada and local communities. Today's TFWs deserve the same opportunity (Siemiatycki 2010). If Canadian immigration and migration policy serves the purpose to fill labour shortages, then the workers who migrate to Canada should be able to claim the necessary rights and entitlement to uphold Canada's high wage and labour standards. *Jus domicile* would inhibit the reproduction of a vulnerable and exploitable underclass in the form of TFWs.

A further benefit of *jus domicile* would be to eliminate the need for TFWs to go underground and work in the informal economy if they wish to switch employers or want to remain in Canada after their contract expired. Working conditions in the informal economy are often even more abusive than they are under the TFWP.

The Canadian state has been alerted by the prospect of TFWs joining the informal economy, as Citizenship and Immigration Canada communicates to employers in the *Temporary Foreign Worker Guidelines*:

> While there is a reluctance on the part of CIC and HRSDC to support work permits for lower-skilled workers because their skills profile would not normally qualify them for permanent immigration to Canada, concerns regarding these persons going out of status and remaining in Canada illegally are mitigated when the foreign national has been nominated for permanent residence. (CIC 2010a)

If given *jus domicile* citizenship, TFWs would formally be able to compete for jobs with other immigrants and Canadian citizens. *Jus domicile* is a constraint on employers' access to cheap and docile labour, since improved access to rights and entitlement and the prospect of permanency would prevent wages from spiralling downward, which can be a consequence of the presence of vulnerable and exploitable workers who are denied these rights and entitlements (Bauder 2006; Sweetman and Warman 2010).

Furthermore, *jus domicile* would address the problem of deskilling and lack of "Canadian experience," which current immigrants often face. TFWs who successfully participate in the labour market, gain recognized Canadian work experience and would be well prepared for the Canadian labour market (Sweetman and Warman 2010). Thomas (2010) has found that temporary residents are more likely to speak English than recent immigrants, are younger than permanent residents, are more likely to live in less populated parts of the country, and are more likely to have post-secondary education than permanent immigrants selected by the points system. In addition, the weekly earnings of male TFWs are higher than those of recently landed immigrants (Warman 2009, 2010).

Lastly, *jus domicile* would recognize the links that already exist between TFWs and their Canadian communities. With the recent legislation allowing TFWs to remain in Canada for longer periods of uninterrupted time and the increasing numbers of TFWs who are becoming "permanently temporary" (CIC 2009a; Thomas 2010), their connections within communities will intensify and their contributions to these communities will increase.

Kostakopoulou (2008) outlines three main objections to the idea of *jus domicile* which can be fittingly applied to the TFWP in Canada. First, it can be argued that migrants lack the loyalty required to be full members of a political community after a relatively short period of residence. This reason for denying citizenship to TFWs assumes them to be unable to develop an appreciation of and commitment to Canada. Under the democratic principle of participation in a community, however, citizenship rights should be extended to all contributing members independent of their perceived degree of loyalty.

Second, from a transnational perspective, *jus domicile* holds on to territoriality while migrants' lives are already transnational. Therefore, citizenship should be conceived more radically in a deterritorial manner. A similar point has long been made by Austro-Marxist Otto Bauer (1924) and has theoretical merit. Pragmatically, however, we reach a similar conclusion as Laura Harris in Chapter 1: states have authority over particular territories and territorial citizenship is unlikely to disappear anytime soon.

Third, *jus domicile* is a theoretical concept that is not pragmatically feasible. We do not share this objection. In fact, in this chapter we have applied the *jus domicile* principle to the concrete case of the TFWP in Canada. As we have shown, citizenship through *jus domicile* is feasible for TFWs.

DISCUSSION

The current Canadian government has little interest in pursuing pathways to permanency for TFWs. Permanency would defeat the very purpose of the TFWP, as it is designed to ensure that workers are temporary and can be denied the rights and entitlements of permanency and citizenship. Yet, workers do possess moral claims to rights and entitlements that contradict government intentions.

Furthermore, the TFWP does not stand alone in terms of economic migration to Canada. It functions in connection with permanent immigration through the points system, the Provincial Nominee Programs, and the Canadian Experience Class. These three programs offer permanent residence with the prospect of citizenship. The idea of *jus domicile* does not contradict the spirit of Canada's current immigration programs.

In a way, the Canadian Experience Class already follows the principle of *jus domicile* by offering temporary workers the prospect of permanent residency. This program began in 2008 and was designed as a pathway for highly skilled TFWs and international students with Canadian education to apply for permanent residency. It emphasizes and endorses Canadian work or education experience, something that TFWs possess. In 2009 the federal government expected between 10,000 and 12,000 applicants, but received only about 1,000 applications (CIC 2009b). For low-skilled TFWs (other than Live-in Caregivers), however, the Canadian Experience Class does not provide a pathway to citizenship—which may explain the low numbers of applications (Nakashe and Kinoshita 2010).

To truly live up to the *jus domicile* principle of citizenship, the Canadian Experience Class should not distinguish between persons based on their skills; as in other citizenship principles, citizenship based on *jus domicile* spans ethnic, social, and class divisions. Furthermore, *jus domicile* citizenship must be a right and cannot be conferred selectively on some residents and denied to others. This right must not be subject to the manipulation of residency permits in such a way that some residents are excluded from claiming it. This is precisely the case, for example, when residency time restrictions prevent TFWs from accumulating the necessary time for *jus domicile* citizenship (Bauder 2010).

Similarly, some Provincial Nominee Programs offer pathways to permanency and citizenship to TFWs. Since these programs are provincial, TFWs may be eligible for permanent residency in some provinces and not others, based on the province or territory of their original work permit (House of Commons Canada 2009). In this case, *jus domicile* citizenship is effectively reconfigured to the provincial scale.

More problematically, applications from TFWs for permanent residency through a Provincial Nominee Program are tied to a job with a specific employer. If a worker is laid off before attaining permanent residency, the application is often cancelled (Nakashe and Kinoshita 2010). The *jus domicile* principle of citizenship would rectify this problem.

Manitoba has been the most progressive of all provinces with respect to its Provincial Nominee Program. In this province, employers are able to nominate low-skilled TFWs for permanent residency after only six months of residency. Approximately 70 percent of all TFWs who arrive in Manitoba apply for permanent residency (Bucklaschuck et al. 2009). British Columbia, Alberta, and Saskatchewan have recently expanded their Provincial Nominee Programs to include lower-skilled occupations in specific industries (Nakashe and Kinoshita 2010).

Critics may intervene that awarding citizenship to TFWs through the principle of *jus domicile* would effectively delegate immigration selection and citizenship decisions to employers and exclude persons who are unattractive to Canadian employers or who migrate for other reasons than employment. However, *jus domicile* is by no means a principle restricted to TFWs. It can equally be applied to all migrants, including students, refugees, and to migrants with precarious status and of various socio-economic classes and migration histories. In this paper, we have merely used the case of TFWs to explore the appeal, utility, and feasibility of this principle.

Finally, we suggest exploring the feasibility of revamping Canada's citizenship system and situating *jus domicile* at its centre. Accordingly, citizenship could be granted based on de facto membership in a community and not the "accident of birth." This suggestion also permits thinking seriously about the proper geographical scales of citizenship. Traditionally, citizenship has been tied to rigid notions of the nation-state and the boundaries of national territory. Recently, less rigid notions of citizenship have challenged these territorial demarcations. Although *jus domicile* is still a territorial principle, it can be applied at variable geographical scales. For example, scholars have recommended extending voting rights in municipal elections to permanent-resident non-citizens (Siemiatycki 2006). Such rights would effectively implement *jus domicile* at the local and municipal scale. Furthermore, provinces are already deeply engaged in selecting and extending rights to immigrants, amounting effectively to a form of citizenship at the provincial scale. In a similar way, we believe that *jus domicile* can be used to extend formal citizenships to migrants at urban, provincial, or other geographical scales.

ENDNOTE

1. In *Fraser v. Ontario*, the Supreme Court of Canada (2008) ruled that the constitution does not afford agricultural workers a right to bargain collectively, thereby preventing them from exercising their labour rights.

ACKNOWLEDGEMENTS

We thank Aparna Sundar, Judith Bernhard, and Phillipa Campsey for helpful comments and suggestions. An earlier version of this chapter was presented in the *CERIS Working Paper Series*.

REFERENCES

Avery, D. 1988. "Continental European Immigrant Workers in Canada, 1896–1919: From 'Stalwart Peasants' to 'Radical Proletariat.'" *Canadian Review of Sociology and Anthropology* 12 (1): 53–64.

Balibar, E. 2000. "What We Owe to the Sans-Papiers." In *Social Insecurity*, edited by L. Guenther and H. Heesters, 42–43. Toronto: Anansi.

Basok, T. 2000. "He Came, He Saw, He Stayed. Guest Worker Programs and the Issue of Non-Return." *International Migration* 38 (2): 215–238.

———. 2004. "Post-National Citizenship, Social Exclusion, and Migrants' Rights: Mexican Seasonal Workers in Canada." *Citizenship Studies* 8 (1): 47–64.

Bauböck, R. 1994. *Transnational Citizenship: Membership and Rights in International Migration*. Aldershot: E. Elgar.

———. 2008. "Citizens on the Move: Democratic Standards for Migrants' Membership." *Canadian Diversity* 6 (4): 7–12.

Bauder, H. 2006. *Labor Movement: How Migration Regulates Labor Markets*. New York: Oxford University Press.

———. 2007. "What a Difference Citizenship Makes: Migrant Workers in Rural Ontario." *Our Diverse Cities* 4: 95–98.

———. 2008. "Citizenship as Capital: The Distinction of Migrant Labour." *Alternatives: Global, Local, Political* 33: 315–333.

———. 2010. "Foreign Workers Present a Moral Dilemma: Canada has the Capacity, and Obligation to Integrate Guest Workers." *Edmonton Journal* (November 15): A17.

Bauer, O. 1924. *Die Nationalitätsfrage und die Sozialdemokratie*. 2nd ed. Wien: Wiener Volksbuchhandlung.

Bellamy, R. 2008. *Citizenship: A Very Short Introduction*. Oxford: Oxford University Press.

Bigo, D. 2002. "Security and Immigration: Toward a Critique of the Governmentality of Unease." *Alternatives* 27: 63–92.

Binford, L. 2009. "From Fields of Power to Fields of Sweat: The Dual Process of Constructing Temporary Migrant Labour in Mexico and Canada." *Third World Quarterly* 30 (3): 503–517.

Bloemraad, I. 2000. "Citizenship and Immigration: A Current Review." *Journal of International Migration and Integration* 1 (1): 9–37.

Bloemraad, I., A. Korteweg, and G. Yurdakul. 2008. "Citizenship and Immigration: Multiculturalism, Assimilation, and Challenges to the Nation-State." *Annual Review of Sociology* 34: 153–179.

Brubaker, R. 1992. *Citizenship and Nationhood in France and Germany*. Cambridge: Harvard University Press.

Bucklaschuck, J., A. Moss, and R. Annis. 2009. "Temporary May Not Always Be Temporary. The Impact of 'Transitional' Foreign Workers and Increasing Diversity in Brandon, Manitoba." *Our Diverse Cities* 6 (Spring): 64–70.

Burke, A. 2002. "Aporias of Security." *Alternatives* 27: 1–27.

Byl, Y., and J. Foster. 2009. *Entrenching Exploitation: The Second Report of the Alberta Federation of Labour Temporary Foreign Worker Advocate*. Edmonton: Alberta Federation of Labour.

Castles, S., and A. Davidson. 2000. *Citizenship and Migration: Globalization and the Politics of Belonging*. New York: Routledge.

Citizenship and Immigration Canada (CIC). 1994. *Hiring Foreign Workers: Facts for Canadian Employers*. Ottawa: Minister of Supply and Services.

———. 2009a. "Changes to the Temporary Foreign Worker Program: Pilot Project for Occupations Requiring Lower Levels of Formal Training" (NOC C and D). Accessed August 4, 2011. Ottawa: Citizenship and Immigration Canada. www.cic.gc.ca/english/work/low-skill.asp.

———. 2009b. "Facts and Figures 2008—Immigration Overview: Permanent and Temporary Residents." Accessed August 4, 2011. Ottawa: Citizenship and Immigration Canada.

———. 2010a. *FW 1 Temporary Foreign Worker Guidelines*. Ottawa: Citizenship and Immigration Canada. Accessed August 4, 2011. www.cic.gc.ca/english/resources/manuals/fw/fw01-eng.pdf.

———. 2010b. "Facts and Figures 2009: Preliminary Tables—Permanent and Temporary Residents." Ottawa: Citizenship and Immigration Canada.

Cohen, E. 2009. *Semi-Citizenship in Democratic Politics*. Cambridge: Cambridge University Press.

Flecker, K. 2010. "Building a Disposable Workforce through Temporary Migration Policy." *Canadian Issues* (Spring): 99–103.

Fudge, J., and F. MacPhail. 2009. "The Temporary Foreign Worker Program in Canada: Low-Skilled Workers as an Extreme Form of Flexible Labour." *Comparative Labor Law and Policy Journal* 31: 101–139.

Gustafson, P. 2005. "International Migration and National Belonging in the Swedish Debate on Dual Citizenship." *Acta Sociologica* 48 (1): 5–19.

Hammar, T. 1990. *Democracy and the Nation State: Aliens, Denizens, and Citizens in a World of International Migration*. Hampshire: Ashgate.

Hennebry, J. 2008. "Bienvenidos a Canadá? Globalization and the Migration Industry Surrounding Temporary Agricultural Migration in Canada." *Canadian Studies in Population* 35 (2): 339–356.

House of Commons Canada. 2009. "Standing Committee on Citizenship and Immigration. Temporary Foreign Workers and Non-Status Workers." Ottawa.

Human Resources and Skills Development Canada (HRSDC). 2010a. "Temporary Foreign Worker Program—Labour Market Opinion (LMO) Statistics. Archived Annual Statistics 2006–2009." Accessed August 4, 2011. www.hrsdc.gc.ca/eng/workplaceskills/foreign_workers/stats/archive/annual2006-2009/annual_stats_list.shtml.

———. 2010b. "Steps to Hire TFWs." Ottawa.

Joppke, C. 2010. *Citizenship and Immigration.* Cambridge: Polity.

Kelley, N., and M. Trebilcock. 1998. *The Making of the Mosaic: A History of Canadian Immigration Policy.* Toronto: University of Toronto Press.

Kivisto, P. 2007. "Conclusion: The Boundaries of Citizenship in a Transnational Age." In *Dual Citizenship in Global Perspective: From Unitary to Multiple Citizenship*, edited by T. Faist and P. Kivisto, 272–287. Hampshire: Palgrave MacMillan.

Kivisto, P., and T. Faist. 2007. *Citizenship: Discourse, Theory, and Transnational Prospects.* Malden: Blackwell Publishing.

Knowles, V. 2007. *Strangers at Our Gates: Canadian Immigration and Immigration Policy, 1,540–2,006.* Toronto: Dundurn Press.

Kofman, E. 2005. "Citizenship, Migration and the Reassertion of National Identity." *Citizenship Studies* 9 (5): 453–467.

Kostakopoulou, D. 2008. *The Future Governance of Citizenship.* Cambridge: Cambridge University Press.

Kymlicka, W. 1995. *Multicultural Citizenship: A Liberal Theory of Minority Rights.* Oxford: Clarendon Press.

Lipset, S. 1965. "Introduction." In *Citizenship and Social Class*, edited by T. H. Marshall, v–xxii. New York: Doubleday.

Marshall, T. H. 1965. *Class, Citizenship, and Social Development: Essays.* New York: Doubleday.

Martin, P. 2003. *Managing Labor Migration: Temporary Worker Programs for the 21st Century.* Geneva: International Institute for Labor Studies.

Nakache, D. 2010. "Temporary Workers: Permanent Rights?" *Canadian Issues* (Spring): 45–48.

Nakache, D., and P. Kinoshita. 2010. "The Canadian Temporary Foreign Worker Program. Do Short-Term Economic Needs Prevail over Human Rights Concerns?" *IRPP Study* No. 5.

Office of the Auditor General of Canada. 2009. "Chapter 2—Selecting Foreign Workers under the Immigration Program." Accessed February 6, 2010. www.oag-bvg.gc.ca/internet/English/parl_oag_200911_02_e_33203.html.

Ong, A. 1993. "On the Edge of Empires: Flexible Citizenship among Chinese in Diaspora." *Positions: East Asia Cultures Critique* 3 (1): 745–778.

———. 1999. *Flexible Citizenship: The Cultural Logistics of Transnationality.* Durham: Duke University Press.

———. 2006. "Mutations in Citizenship." *Theory, Culture, and Society* 23 (2–3): 499–531.

Piore, M. 1979. *Birds of Passage: Migrant Labor and Industrial Societies.* Cambridge: Cambridge University Press.

Sassen, S. 1998. *Globalization and Its Discontents: Essays and the New Mobility of People and Money.* New York: New York Press.

Satzewich, V. 1991. *Racism and the Incorporation of Foreign Labour: Farm Labour Migration to Canada since 1945.* New York: Routledge.

Sharma, N. 2006. *Home Economics: Nationalism and the Making of 'Migrant Workers' in Canada.* Toronto: University of Toronto Press.

Siemiatycki, M. 2006. *The Municipal Franchise and Social Inclusion in Toronto: Policy and Practice.* Toronto: Inclusive Cities Canada, Community Social Planning Council of Toronto (CSPC).

———. 2010. "Marginalizing Migrants: Canada's Rising Reliance on Temporary Foreign Workers." *Canadian Issues* (Spring): 60–63.

Smart, J. 1997. "Borrowed Men on Borrowed Time: Globalization, Labour Migration, and Local Economies in Alberta." *Canadian Journal of Regional Science* 20 (1–2): 141–156.

Soysal, Y. 1994. *Limits of Citizenship: Migrants and Postnational Membership in Europe.* Chicago: The University of Chicago Press.

Spiro, P. 2008. *Beyond Citizenship: American Identity After Globalization.* Oxford: Oxford University Press.

Stasiulis, D., and A. Bakan. 1997. "Negotiating Citizenship: The Case of Foreign Domestic Workers in Canada." *Feminist Review* 57: 112–139.

Supreme Court of Canada. 2008. "Fraser v. Ontario, (Attorney General)" 2008 ONCA: 760.

Sweetman, A., and C. Warman. 2010. "Canada's Temporary Foreign Workers Program." *Canadian Issues* (Spring): 19–24.

Tambini, D. 2001. "Post-National Citizenship." *Ethnic and Race Studies* 24 (2): 195–212.

Thomas, D. 2010. "Foreign Nationals Working Temporarily in Canada." *Canadian Social Trends* 90: 34–48.

Wæver, O. 1995. "Securitization and Desecuritization." In *On Security*, edited by R. D. Lipschutz, 46–86. New York: Columbia University Press.

Warman, C. 2009. "The Earnings Outcomes of Temporary Foreign Workers in Canada." *Economics Department Working Paper*, Queen's University. Kingston.

Warman, C. 2010. "The Portability of Human Capital of Male Temporary Foreign Workers: You Can Bring It With You." In *Canadian Immigration: Economic Evidence for a Dynamic Policy Environment*, edited by T. MacDonald, E. Ruddick, A. Sweetman, and C. Worswick, 209–233. Montreal: McGill-Queen's University Press.

Weinstock, D. 2008. "The Theory and Practice of Citizenship in the 21st Century: A Few International Trends." *Canadian Diversity* 6 (4): 3–6.

Young, I. 1989. "Polity and Group Differences: A Critique of the Ideal of Universal Citizenship." *Ethics* 9 (2): 250–274.

Yuval-Davis, N. 1999. "The 'Multi-Layered Citizen': Citizenship in the Age of 'Glocalization.'" *International Feminist Journal of Politics* 1 (1): 119–136.

Chapter 3

RACE IN DEMOCRATIC SPACES: THE POLITICS OF RACIAL EMBODIMENT IN THE CITY OF TORONTO

SHANA ALMEIDA

> Since 9/11, Muslim is a euphemism for walking bomb.
>
> Racism is a growing problem in Toronto. How do I know? I know because the number of attacks on me keeps increasing.
>
> There is no safe place …
>
> (City of Toronto 2003)

INTRODUCTION

The above comments and others from Toronto residents were to frame the direction of the new City of Toronto Plan of Action for the Elimination of Racism and Discrimination. The Plan was sparked by Michael Ornstein's (2000) study *Ethno-Racial Inequality in the City of Toronto: Analysis of the 1996 Census*, which concluded that for ethno-racial minorities with similar education to those of European origin, levels of unemployment and poverty are significantly higher for racial minority groups. To prepare the Plan, the City of Toronto undertook over 50 consultation sessions across the city, asking for input from residents, community groups, and organizations on how to combat racism and discrimination. The official Plan of Action was approved on April 14, 2003, by Toronto's City Council, and included in the final report on the city-wide consultations (titled "Just Do It!") strategic directions on political leadership, advocacy, economic participation, public education and awareness, service delivery, building strong communities, and accountability.

In this chapter I draw on the work of Dorothy E. Smith's (2006b) *Institutional Ethnography* (IE), in particular the notions of intertextual hierarchy and the ideological circle, to support the argument that the ideology of higher-order texts regulates and standardizes other texts, which organizes how work is carried out across local settings. Furthermore, the textual analysis of the Plan of Action will reveal the circulation and recirculation of normative discourse for the reproduction of ruling relations, hegemony, and the continued subjugation and political and economic exclusion of racialized bodies across time and space. These forces of reproduction are supported by nationalist practices in Canada and by extension in the City of Toronto. In the first part of the chapter, I provide an overview of the current readings on race and politics in Canada and in the City of Toronto, including underlying principles and assumptions. I then briefly describe my method of inquiry and use various examples within the Plan of Action to illuminate how the City of Toronto redeploys nationalist and colonial discourses to conceal racist practices and whiteness. In the later part of the chapter, I discuss the pervasiveness of "diversity discourse" in the Plan, and how it perpetuates the marginalization and commodification of racialized bodies in democratic spaces. Finally, I include excerpts from the plan to emphasize how sequences of text organize interpretations, experiences, and activities in the local setting in restricted ways.

CURRENT READINGS OF RACE AND POLITICS

> What does it mean when the tools of a racist patriarchy are used to examine that same patriarchy? It means that only the most narrow perimeters of change are possible. (Audre Lorde [cited in DeVault 1999, 46])

Government bodies and state policies in Canada continue to be shaped by racism in the political and civil spheres. Although interest in the relationship between race and politics in Canada has increased over the past few years, there is relatively little research on this topic (Dhillon 2005; Saloojee and Siemiatycki 2002; Lapp 1999). Racialized bodies have been significantly under-represented or absent in Canadian political systems (Bird 2005). Using ethno-racial profiles of elected politicians as an indicator of who has access to political power, Jerome Black and Aleem Lakhani (1997) suggest that the under-representation of racialized bodies is a symptom of a system that does not respond to the policy interests of racialized groups. For example, a report by Access Alliance Multicultural Community Health Centre (2005) shows that racialized minorities experience racism in such forms as unemployment, poverty, discrimination, and barriers to quality health care, education, and housing. These issues can be addressed through policy changes that are shaped and affected by politicians; yet, they remain largely unaddressed because the racism experienced by racialized communities makes them less likely to acquire the resources necessary to achieve political representation, participation, and/or political influence to shape policy that might change their circumstances (Bird 2005). Thus racism both *reinforces and is reinforced by the political sphere*, which allows for the continued marginalization and exclusion of racialized groups and their policy interests.

Frances Henry and Carol Tator (1994) find that although commitments are made to ensuring equality in Canada's "diverse" nation, in practice individuals, organizations, and institutions work to maintain and protect the status quo and preserve existing power structures. "Democratic racism," in which liberal values of equality, fairness, and democratic participation conflict with negative feelings or perceived unreasonable demands of people of colour, creates conditions for systemic discrimination and differential treatment in institutional settings. The lived experiences of people of colour are inconsistent with the way in which politicians, bureaucrats, journalists, and educators represent their realities in order to accommodate and re-inscribe Canada's sense of multiculturalism and liberal-democracy (Henry and Tator 1994).

Multiculturalism in Canada creates a racial hierarchy in which the dominant group's power is never made explicit (Essed 1991; James 1999). Similarly, Roxanna Ng (1995) argues that multiculturalism has been so embedded as a social fact in Canadian society that the ruling relations that multiculturalism draws on have been completely erased from view. Multiculturalism becomes a liberal approach to "managing" race relations in such a way that is more acceptable to the dominant group (Jeffery 2002). Unless combined with a specific anti-racist policy, multiculturalism does nothing to address racism or white-supremacist thinking (Philip 1992). As such, the concept of difference is handled in two ways: either the existence of Otherness is denied, or it is tolerated (Razack and Jeffery 2002). The principle of tolerance disputes inequality by acknowledging that people are simply "different" (Essed 1991). However, the emphasis on tolerance in Canada suggests that while one should accept that others are different, one group is dominant and superior (Henry et al. 2000). Whiteness, as a symbol of power, prestige, progress, and intelligence, still prevails. Yet another aspect of multiculturalism is the idea of colour-blindness, a significant component of liberal discourse in which white people insist they do not notice skin colour of a person of colour (Henry et al. 2000). Resting on the notion of universalism and the belief that what we have in common is stronger than what separates us, the goal is a "colour-blind" society in which no group receives special care of treatment (Fleras and Elliott 2002). Ruth Frankenberg (1993) further examines colour-blindness or colour-evasion as a way to avoid talking about power held by whites. Multiculturalism, according to Carl James (1999), equates "culture" with people who are not "Canadians," who speak in foreign languages and follow foreign customs with respect to food, dress, worship, and tradition. They are described as non-English- and/or non-French-speaking ethnic and racial minorities; immigrants who identify with their country of origin and who are encouraged to keep the languages and traditions of "their country" while living in Canada (James 1999; Yee and Dumbrill 2003). Augie Fleras and Jean Elliott (2002) argue that for immigrant groups, attaining a level of equality and success depends on the willingness to reject their background and assimilate into society. Conversely, accents and communication differences can lead to social and economic exclusion. These factors create difficulties for achieving full and equal participation in society (Fleras and Elliott 2002). Racialized immigrants continue to be seen as "guests" in Canada who are expected to behave in ways that conform to an implicit Canadian "norm." These immigrant "groups" must in fact live and carry out their day-to-day activities within legal, political, social, and economic boundaries defined by the dominant group if they want to be classified as "members of society."

Members of the dominant group also have more opportunities to collectively organize around their interests, to gain public support for their efforts, and have easier access to key decision-makers, creating a political process that reproduces unequal access to power (Goonewardena, Rankin, and Weinstock 2004). As such, changing social, economic, and political policies aiming to combat racism may lack political support (Altilia 2003; Henry and Tator 1994). As Miu Chung Yan (2003) argues, the state instead creates legislation to reify these socio-political relations of power and processes that sustain racism in Canada. Karen Bird (2005) and Anver Saloojee and Myer Siemiatycki (2002) suggest that this is evident in all levels of government in Canada, including the municipal government of Toronto.

Municipalities provide services and programs that have become increasingly relevant to the welfare and security of the Canadian population. Engin Isin and Myer Siemiatycki (1997) observe that these municipally driven services and programs play an important role in meeting the everyday needs of immigrant and diverse communities, from housing, to recreation services, to public health, to transportation. However, Myer Siemiatycki and Anver Salojee (2002) suggest, as one of the most multicultural and multiracial cities in the world the City of Toronto has yet to meet the challenge of creating a truly inclusive society, where all can participate in the social, cultural, and political life of the city. How does the City of Toronto approach this problem, in light of the fact that the city consists now of over 50 percent of people of colour (Altilia 2003; Saloojee and Siemiatycki 2002)?

Toronto's approach is reflected in the motto, "Diversity our Strength." This motto implies a celebration of ethnic harmony in one of the world's most diverse cities (Antonius et al. 2005; Saloojee and Siemiatycki 2002; Altilia 2003). The City of Toronto has created policies, programs, and services for its residents, business owners, and stakeholder groups; yet, research indicates that it consistently excludes racialized communities that make up the majority of Toronto's population today (Altilia 2003). John Paul Catungal and Deborah Leslie (2009) argue with respect to ethno-racial difference in Toronto that diversity is included in city policies and practices to promote economic capacity and to market the city for trade and investment. In her study of Toronto, Carol Altilia (2003) argues that the concept of diversity is a function of the dominant group's discourse, useful to the maintenance of power because it precludes analyses of inequities, socially constructed racial differences, and the relationships that create them (Altilia 2003). Furthermore, Anna Kirova (2008) defines diversity as a mechanism used by the dominant (white) group to essentialize difference, where the question, different *from what?*, is not interrogated. Politicians thus claim to diminish the racial barriers to full participation by embracing diversity and by establishing committees and task forces that have no legislative power to address the "overt" experiences of racism (Henry and Tator 1994). As such, the exclusion of racialized communities in municipal government is not prioritized, or even addressed.

From these writings it is difficult not to acknowledge the perniciousness of racism at every level in Canadian politics. Furthermore, everyday racist experiences, like the ones noted at the outset of this paper, continue to exist, in spite of the legislative actions and strategic directions offered by the City of Toronto to address and/or to eliminate them. What ought to be further examined is the ideology and ruling relations that coordinate anti-racist legislative efforts in Toronto, "one of the most diverse cities in the world" (City of Toronto 2003, 2).

METHODOLOGY: INSTITUTIONAL ETHNOGRAPHY

Institutional Ethnography (IE) is an approach to research that begins at the everyday experience as the entry point to understanding how ruling relations work (Smith 2006a; Campbell and Gregor 2004; Campbell and Manicom 1995). Relations of ruling are set in various organizational settings, including bureaucracies, administrations, management, and the media; through texts and discourse they coordinate multiple experiences and control the distribution and redistribution of stories (DeVault and McCoy 2006). Roxanna Ng (2000) also defines the state, its policies, programs, and bodies, as an organization that coordinates and administers ruling. According to Marie L. Campbell and Frances M. Gregor (2004), the work of the IE researcher is to make sense of social relations of ruling in the context of capitalism, patriarchy, race, policy, the economy, and so on, following Dorothy Smith's contribution to the field of social research to understand how everyday life, work, and action shapes ideas, discourses, and knowledge (Campbell and Gregor 2004; Griffith 1995). IE research explores how stories are organized across time and space, how they emerge from a specific history, and how they unfold from social relations in the everyday (DeVault 1999). IE research accomplishes a shift from exploring *why* experiences happen to *how* experiences happen (Deveau 2008).

Furthermore, IE research explores the bifurcation between the everyday experience and institutional practice. It begins with the experience, and then locates the practices that construct the experience as something different from how it was experienced (Grahame 1998; Campbell and Manicom 1995). As Campbell and Gregor (2004) suggest, people's experiences, claims, and needs disappear when organized into textual form, because they are made to fit a pre-existing "master plan" that is already created elsewhere. Drawing on Smith's work, identifying and explicating ruling relations, Joan Eveline, Carol Bacchi, and Jennifer Binns (2009) investigate the experiences of Indigenous peoples in political spaces to explain how their lives were coordinated by government bodies and texts, racist language, and laws. Ng (1995) applies textual analysis to explicate what ruling relations and ideological frame(s) shape the prime minister's policy pronouncement on multiculturalism and related texts. Ng concludes that these texts regulate Canadian society's ways of thinking about diverse populations. In IE, texts do not just "pop" into existence, nor are they naturally occurring; rather, they are to be understood as a moment in a sequence, activated by the social relations that continue to be authorized in the making of the text and in activating the text in local settings. Smith (2006b, 78) calls this sequence "inter-textual hierarchy": "the work that is done to produce the appropriate text must ... be readable as a text that fulfills the function ascribed to it in the regulatory text." The circular nature of intertextual hierarchies is integral to the existence of social and ruling relations.

Ng's textual analysis also uncovers how texts facilitate the circulation of discourse in Canadian society through agents who take up the discourse and redistribute it in their everyday activities. As she argues, it is through this redistribution that multiculturalism discourse becomes currency for the Canadian public to think about society and how individuals operate within it (Ng 1995). Miu Chung Yan (2003) also draws on IE to identify a discursive practice that is formed through the creation of various documents, such as acts, policies, and reports, that circulate the ideology of the group in power to other spaces. For example, as Anna Kirova (2008) explains, redistribution through texts is exemplified in the transfer of multicultural discourse from federal multiculturalism policy to provincial multicultural education policy. To entrench the discourse across levels of government Miu Chung Yan (2003) argues that the multicultural/diversity ideology of the state is expressed in a series of policies and legislation, and an interrelation—what Yan calls an "ideological circle"(128)—between these documents, which creates a dialogue or discourse on social relations regarding race. Although the City of Toronto's aim with the Plan of Action for the Elimination of Racism and Discrimination is to challenge the socio-racial and economic disparities experienced by Toronto's residents, my analysis of the text will show that this text reflects the ideology and ruling relations of the nationalist agenda in Canada. In the analysis I also explore the intertextual, ideological circle of colonialism, culture, and civilization that is codified through local policies, activities, and practices in Toronto.

INTERPRETATION OF THE PLAN OF ACTION FOR THE ELIMINATION OF RACISM AND DISCRIMINATION

"We": Invoking a (Canadian) Nationalist Agenda

> Shared Future and Heritage: Our future as a city of people from diverse backgrounds is a shared future. We may come from different countries and speak many languages, but our home and our city

of choice is Toronto. We endorse the principle of Aboriginal self-determination. Together we are one as we build a common future which respects our diverse histories. (City of Toronto 2003, 17)

Kay Anderson (1991) states that unpacking the unified, "one-character nation" concept that sustains multicultural rhetoric in Canada reveals a clear picture of a mainstream (Anglo-European) society to which "others" are expected to contribute. Similarly, Sara Ahmed (2000) deconstructs the "we" in multicultural discourse, identifying an authorized subject who tells the story from a particular vantage point of generously "allowing others in" to mix or be appropriated into a pre-existing culture. This "we" builds a common strategy of living with difference, deciding who should be tolerated, how the "stranger" should behave, and what languages they should speak. The "stranger" or newcomer to the national space needs to perform in certain ways, but it is still "we" who must live with it (or more specifically, live with "them"). Teun Van Dijk (1993, 78) further suggests that the "we" in multicultural rhetoric implies that "we have done our best, we have done everything we could for you, and now it is your turn."

In its Plan of Action for the Elimination of Racism and Discrimination, the City of Toronto draws from the ideology of nationalism and the idea of the "true" Canadian; the liberal/democratic character who is confronted with "minority groups demanding recognition of their identity, and accommodation of their cultural differences" (Kymlicka 1995, 10). The "Shared Future and Heritage" section of the plan suggests that people from diverse backgrounds in Toronto can be excused for coming from different countries and speaking other languages as long as they realize that in "our home" (which "others" choose to inhabit or invade) they are expected to ascribe to a seemingly monocultural way of living and being that is distinctly "Torontonian." This tolerance of "otherness" is exemplified in the following passage: "We may come from different countries and speak many languages, *but* our home and our city of choice is Toronto" (City of Toronto 2003, 17, emphasis added). This statement assumes the existence of a territory or space to be claimed as "ours," a master of this space who is already well-acquainted with it, and a racial "Other" who lands in this space and who needs to identify Toronto, and *only* Toronto, as "home." The concept of "home" used in the Plan of Action is often used in nationalist agendas to describe the comforts of the familiar, the well-known, and the secure, that which is not "strange" (Hage 2000). The plan implies that those who don't feel at home in Toronto don't belong, but more than this, those who don't *make us feel at home* don't belong either. In the section Shared Future and Heritage, the Plan avoids naming race, dominance, and/or whiteness, a tactic inherent in nationalist rhetoric. Further, it exonerates itself as racist because "we" are willing to exist and share a future alongside "others," which racists would never do (Ahmed 2004). Bannerji (2000) argues that the construction of homogeneous "Canadianness" and denial of race that is built into national imagery is an extension of colonial practices that exclude immigrants and the Aboriginal population from fully participating in civil society. The Plan of Action of the Elimination of Racism and Discrimination constructs a homogeneous "Torontonian" through the same denial of race, and through the same construction of the strange "Other" that redefines boundaries of belonging in the nation.

Civil Society and the Native Other

> We recognize and support the unique history and position of the urban Aboriginal population and right to self-determination. (City of Toronto 2003, 18)

In recognizing and supporting the "unique history" of Native others, the City of Toronto escapes naming and taking any responsibility for the systemic inequality and racial domination that fracture and perpetuate violence on Aboriginal communities (St. Denis 2004). Daniel Coleman (2006) shows that in the Enlightenment period, the modern, civil (white, male) subject marked the Aboriginal, savage, wild body as uncivil. He argues that in the creation of the Canadian liberal state, where equality and liberty were to be shared by all, the modern subject excluded the uncivilized, non-human Aboriginal. This exclusion of Aboriginal and racialized others continues to be upheld by the privilege of the civil subject and his legacy of colonial conquest.

The City of Toronto's statement with respect to the history and self-determination of Aboriginal peoples is sufficiently awkward, to say the least. Some Indigenous scholars have argued that encouragement of fundamentalism and cultural revitalization (i.e., preservation of traditions, behaviours, and homogeneity) of Aboriginal peoples maintains a separation between "outsiders" and "insiders" in Canada (St. Denis 2004). The City's claim to support the right to self-determination involves the maintenance of this strict separation between Native communities and the civil, political sphere. For the City and its residents, this separation also eases the "colonial shadow" cast over Canada's national innocence and reifies the psychic underpinnings of the liberal subject's claim to settler status in a nation where Aboriginals were dying or already dead (Bergland 2000). In addition, the City mentions Aboriginal peoples as being part of one future that "we" will build together, alongside those who speak different languages or come from different countries. The above-cited passage obscures Canada's violent colonial history and at the same time maps the colonizer as the real, true owner of "our" space. That the City regards this continued violence towards Aboriginal peoples as a "unique history and position" only reifies the ideological, nationalist agenda embedded within and produced through colonialism.

The Power of Capital and the "Good Sell"

> [I]ntegrate into the City's labour force development plans co-operative strategies to address unique needs of diverse communities to ameliorate labour market and economic disparities, implement mentoring programs to assist employees and immigrant workers … (City of Toronto 2003, 6)

The Plan of Action for the Elimination of Racism and Discrimination begins with the claim that "Toronto is one of the most diverse cities in the world and has gained an international reputation for the successful *management of its diversity*" (emphasis added, City of Toronto 2003, 2). John Paul Catungal and Deborah Leslie (2009) argue that diversity, particularly ethno-racial difference in Toronto, has become a commodity. As alluded to earlier, diversity as a concept and as a discourse is used frequently by the City of Toronto to promote a strong economy and to attract tourism, investment, and capital. The City of Toronto sells its diverse (ethno-racial) population in order to attract capitalist ventures, tourism, and a new place to live, and at the same time make claims to manage its diversity effectively. Sara Ahmed (2000) argues that the "management" of diversity implies a force that needs to be contained by government policy, otherwise there is a risk for diversity to get out of control. The implication is that Toronto has just enough diversity to be attractive to outsiders, yet *not too much diversity* to pose any kind of real threat that would upset or impinge on social (white) order.

David Theo Goldberg (2009) explains that the modern state that is subject to forces of globalization must figure out how to frame and manage its population. As capitalism expands its reach across the globe, neo-liberalism becomes the mechanism by which to encourage the freedom of movement and capital across political and national boundaries, while retaining a national character that expels or excludes racialized bodies. As neo-liberal values become more entrenched with globalization, racism in the forms of exclusion, control, and humiliation become relegated to the private sphere. Sara Ahmed (2000) argues that multiculturalism is a neo-liberal mechanism of the state to manage diversity in the interests of the majority because it prevents any real talk of race or racism in public spaces. Multiculturalism strengthens the state's relationship with the private sphere by reifying a rhetoric of "raceless" difference, within a global context and within a nationalist framework. This "raceless" difference allows for the broader trend of what Yasmin Abu-Laban and Christina Gabriel (2002, 12) call "'selling diversity'—whereby the skills, talents, and ethnic backgrounds of men and women are commodified, marketed, and billed as trade-enhancing." Furthermore, as Himani Bannerji (2000) argues, as an ideological tool, diversity simultaneously repackages unemployment and underemployment of racialized groups into issues of culture rather than as evidence of racism.

The City of Toronto Plan of Action for the Elimination of Racism and Discrimination acknowledges labour market and economic disparities between racialized communities and the European-origin population, and suggests that mentorship opportunities would alleviate these "conditions." The City of Toronto recirculates the ideology of diversity, as identified by Bannerji, suggesting that issues of unemployment could be resolved by mentoring and that racialized bodies should mimic the culture of those who are entrusted with power and civility. What is interesting in this part of the Plan is how the city disseminates strategies to help those who have not succeeded, and then immediately juxtaposes them with those who have: "the Plan will publicize and celebrate the success and achievements of diverse people and communities to counter negative stereotypes and help the public understand their contributions to Toronto" (City of Toronto 2003, 6). The strategic placing of these two passages—"implement mentoring programs to assist employees and immigrant workers" followed by "publicize and celebrate the success and achievements of diverse people and communities to counter negative stereotypes and help the public understand their contributions to Toronto"—indicates the desire to individualize the failures of bodies which just happen to be racialized, further displacing claims of racism. Ghassan Hage (2000) also notes that understanding racism simply as stereotyping implies that anyone can be racist, because anyone can create and reinforce stereotypes about another group. As such, racialized bodies need not make claims of racism in the workforce because there is no racism; those who aren't succeeding simply need to learn from those who are established and those who are white in order to be *racially palatable*. Education and skills become irrelevant when one is culturally inferior or inept. This civilizing practice disguised as a mutually beneficial opportunity afforded by diversity, in fact, is "a mannered racism, even exaggeratedly mannerist, civil to a fault, behaviour by the book" (Goldberg 2009, 342). Through this generous offering of civility, ruling relations based on race are maintained.

The Pleasure of Race

> Diversity is a fundamental characteristic of our city. It gives Toronto strength through an ability to value, celebrate and respect differences. It is this recognition of diversity, which makes Toronto one of the most creative, caring and successful cities in the world. (City of Toronto 2003, 20)

There is a certain irony attached to the statement that diversity makes Toronto one of the most caring cities in the world in a report that seeks to eliminate racism and discrimination. Those who feel that being Muslim is equated with a walking bomb, those who experience increasing racial attacks, and those who never feel safe would hardly call Toronto "caring." What is behind this rhetoric of success, security, and celebration of diversity in Toronto? To address this question, the discussion should include the notion of race as pleasure. According to Anthony Farley (1997), race is a form of pleasure. The white subject experiences this pleasure in the body when he humiliates the Other and then denies that race exists in the first place. "Diversity," as discourse, sets the stage in which racism is denied as an expression or practice in the public and private spheres; it also permits the colonial, liberal subject to perpetuate dominance in the forms of nationalism and civility, and political and economic exclusion. The pleasure of race is derived from the white subject's continual gaze on the racialized Other's inferiority and subordination. Whites are simultaneously "masters and innocents" (Farley 1997). Those who are not subordinated, humiliated, and oppressed are white, powerful, and justified.

Farley (2007) further argues that the state is especially instrumental in creating spaces for race-pleasure to occur. The City of Toronto Plan of Action for the Elimination of Racism and Discrimination is one of the ways in which race-pleasure is brought to life. The white subject has an opportunity to objectify the racialized body in the public encounter. He wants to produce and elicit experiences of racism because of his passion for race-pleasure. And so, the racialized body complies, and says that it experiences being Muslim as being equated to a walking bomb; it experiences increasing racial attacks; it never feels safe. The racialized body is humiliated when these experiences of pain are consumed, stolen, pacified, and made to fit within a pre-existing agenda that reifies domination. Farley (2007) notes that in translating experiences to text, the political descriptions of experiences of the colour line never reflect the actual experiences of the colour line. The racialized body sustains the most injury in the moment when the denial of racism is even more humiliating than the act of racism itself (Farley 2007).

The City of Toronto writes about this pleasurable experience of "diversity" because of what it gains and accomplishes for the white subject as the non-Other on the "right" side of the colour line. This humiliation that the white subject continues to inflict on racialized bodies confirms the pleasure of racial violence that colonialism, dominance, and the national story engender.

"Diversity" Discourse and Democracy

> "Diversity Our Strength" (Toronto's Motto)

Michel Foucault has argued that subjects seldom pay attention to the repetition and recirculation of discourse in the everyday. Instead of asking about what authors reveal in their texts, Foucault (1981a, 52–53) suggests asking instead about what subject-positions are made possible within such texts: "[D]iscourse is not simply that which translates struggles or systems of domination, but is the thing for which and by which there is struggle." In 1970, Foucault also describes discourses as being linked through various textual forms as an ideological force, shaping knowledge of the everyday world and interests in a particular way to reify conformity with socially constructed norms (Griffith 1995). Smith (2006a) further argues that discourse establishes the groundwork for telling stories about people and reconstructs their lived realities into something other than what they are. The "telling of stories" thus moves beyond the individual experience as the stories are already coordinated by circulating texts. Individual experiences, practices, and reasoning are replaced by discourse so that the former appear as isolated or unique occurrences (Grahame 1998).

Eveline, Bacchi, and Binns (2009) explain how "diversity" discourses reference the western business world and the concept of "diversity management," which circulate and recirculate in textual form in sites of ruling such as administrations, bureaucracies, and the state. "Diversity" discourse, akin to multiculturalism, presents itself as value-free and neutral, and signifies pluralism and difference across horizontally arranged social space (Bannerji 2000). This discourse is a form of "ideological trafficking between nationality and ethnicity" (McLaren 1997, 8, cited in Bannerji 2000), as the subjects who create and benefit from the diversity discourse remain hidden.

One of the most powerful aspects of diversity discourse is that it tends to conflate multiculturalism, which celebrates and manages differences, and anti-racism, which seeks to address racism, racialization, and all other forms of related discrimination (Yan 2003). As Himani Bannerji (2000) explains, what makes the concept of diversity so dangerous in this regard is that in discourses of difference, race loses its historical, ontological, political, and economic uses (or gains) and becomes a celebration of cultures disconnected from power. The assumption generated by diversity discourse is that racism simply cannot exist in a democratic society; thus, when racism is exposed it is regarded as an isolated incident or the outcome of a long-time tradition that is no longer an identifiable part of Canada's democratic nature (Henry et al. 2000). In a society that promotes equality, tolerance, racial harmony, and respect for human rights, the existence of racism is hard to acknowledge, let alone challenge (Henry et al. 2000). According to van Dijk (2002), these denials of racism have a socio-political function. They challenge anti-racist analysis, legitimize white dominance, and become part of the management of race relations. As long as racism is denied, critics are delegitimized and scorned, and the need for heavier laws, regulations, or campaigns to fight discrimination and prejudice can be dismissed. In essence, the denial quells anti-racist resistance, and racism is reproduced (van Dijk 2002). Diversity in the City of Toronto hints at a presence of race but erases the histories of colonialism, race, and privilege that (re-)construct white dominance.

CONCLUSION

Far from being part of the natural world, race has been a historically specific way of seeing and practicing, linked in an ideological circle to the global extension of European domination. During the rise of European power in colonization, the classification of race acquired its meaning as non-white, non-human, and uncivilized. It is in this historical context of colonization that categories of race need to be situated. After hundreds of years, the screen through which racialized groups are filtered has been subtly revised and recycled, but not radically transcended (Anderson 1991). The City of Toronto promotes an "anti-racial" strategy, as opposed to an anti-racist strategy; one which forgets histories and begins at a place where colour doesn't matter (Goldberg 2009). This has lasting implications for experiences of racism in the public and private spheres. What exactly is racism without (the history of) race?

In *"Society Must Be Defended": Lectures at the College de France, 1975–1976*, Michel Foucault (2003) examines the ideology governing the construction of capitalism during the French revolution. He argues that the revolution of the bourgeoisie was presented as ahistorical, which eliminated (or reduced, restricted, colonized, as Foucault puts it) the element of the war between races from the discourse and historical analysis of capitalism. One might argue then that laws governing the formation of knowledge of capitalism arose from the re-invocation of the dominant (read: white, European male) ideology, knowledge, and power from the pre-capitalist period. Foucault also notes that the rise of the bourgeoisie is tainted with liberalism. Foucault (2003, 192) espouses that in capitalism one needs to establish and arrive at a "right relationship of force" in which the violence, war, and appropriation in colonial history is displaced by stories of freedom, rights, resistance, and rebellion. Is this not exactly the direction that multiculturalism and diversity discourse is taking us in, if we have not already arrived? Is this not the same ideology that would contain the national, multicultural success story of integration, freedom, and equality for all across time and space and by extension, the City of Toronto's Plan of Action? The story of Canadian society would be completely de-raced and past experiences of racism would be ghosts that haunt us, while continued violence would become something other than racism. Race is enduring; the social implications of race are experienced everywhere and at all times, yet the City of Toronto's Plan of Action for the Elimination of Racism and Discrimination adheres to the ritual, cyclical violence of the denial of race as only its national and colonial past knows and embodies.

A final note regarding IE and the circulation of normative discourses for the reproduction of ruling relations: I have included below excerpts from the Plan of Action which describe texts that the Plan will reinforce, and texts that will be produced as a result of the plan.

> The proposed actions in the Plan of Action relate to and reinforce the implementation of the recommendations of the Final Report of the Task Force on Community Access and Equity. (City of Toronto 2003, 4)

> As noted above, the 97 recommendations in the Final Report of the Task Force include actions for the elimination of racism and discrimination, and are complementary to the actions proposed in "Just Do It!" (City of Toronto 2003, 5)

> The City will build an organization which is responsive to the diversity among City residents by developing an Action Plan Guide on access, equity and diversity to be used by departments and agencies, boards and commissions in developing action plans; developing an Accessibility Plan and report (Ontarians with Disabilities Act); completing the employment equity workforce survey; using the survey results to develop measures and actions to improve the representation of designated groups in the City's workforce; implementing an employment accommodation policy ... (City of Toronto 2003, 5)

> [T]he Inter-departmental staff team on access and equity function as a corporate co-ordinating group for the implementation of the Plan of Action, Accessibility Plan and the recommendations of the Final Report of the Task Force on Community Access and Equity, assisting the Chief Administrative Officer to provide regular reports on progress to Council. (City of Toronto 2003, 7)

> Develop a Management Guide to assist with the development of Access and Equity Action Plans... (City of Toronto 2003, 49)

One might only imagine how forms of racism, violence, and inequality will be taken up next.

ACKNOWLEDGEMENTS

I thank Dr. Sherene Razack for her continued interest, insight, and guidance in my work, which began in the course "Race and Knowledge Production: Issues in Research" in the Department of Sociology and Equity Studies in Education (SESE) at the Ontario Institute for Studies in Education.

REFERENCES

Abu-Laban, Y., and C. Gabriel. 2002. *Selling Diversity: Immigration, Multiculturalism, Employment Equity, and Globalization.* Toronto: Broadview Press.

Access Aliance Multicultural Community Health Centre. 2005. *Racialised Groups and Health Status: A Literature Review Exploring Poverty, Housing, Race-Based Discrimination and Access to Health Care as Determinants of Health for Racialised Groups.* Toronto: Access Alliance.

Ahmed, S. 2000. *Strange Encounters: Embodied Others in Post-Coloniality.* London and New York: Routledge.

———. 2004. "Declarations of Whiteness: The Non-Performativity of Anti-Racism." *Borderlands* 3 (2): 1–26.

Altilia, C. 2003. "Planning For Diversity in the Global City: The Toronto Case." *FES Outstanding Graduate Student Paper Series* 8 (4). Accessed August 4, 2011. www.yorku.ca/fes/research/students/outstanding/docs/CarolAltilia.pdf

Anderson, K. J. 1991. *Vancouver's Chinatown: Racial Discourse in Canada, 1875–1980*. Montreal: McGill-Queen's University Press.

Antonius, R., J. C. Icart, M. Labelle, and the International Observatory of Racism and Discrimination Centre for Research on Immigration, Ethnicity and Citizenship. 2005. "Indicators for Evaluating Municipal Policies Aimed at Fighting Racism and Discrimination." *UNESCO Discussion Paper Series* Number 3. unesdoc.unesco.org/images/0014/001496/149624e.pdf

Bannerji, H. 2000. "The Paradox of Diversity: The Construction of a Multicultural Canada and 'Women of Colour.'" *Women's Studies International Forum* 23 (5): 537–560.

Bergland, R. 2000. *The National Uncanny: Indian Ghosts and American Subjects*. Hanover and London: University Press of New England.

Bird, K. 2005. "Guess Who's Running For Office? Visible Minority Representation in the Canadian Election." *Canadian Issues* (Summer): 80–83.

Black, J. H., and A. S. Lakhani. 1997. "Ethnoracial Diversity in the House of Commons: An Analysis of Numerical Representation in the 35th Parliament." *Canadian Ethnic Studies* (November): 13–33.

Campbell, M., and F. M. Gregor. 2004. *Mapping Social Relations: A Primer in Doing Institutional Ethnography*. Walnut Creek, CA: AltaMira Press.

Campbell, M., and A. Manicom. 1995. "Introduction." In *Knowledge, Experience, and Ruling Relations*, edited by Marie L. Campbell and Ann Manicom, 3–17. Toronto: University of Toronto Press.

Catungal, J. P., and D. Leslie. 2009. "Contesting the Creative City: Race, Nation, Multiculturalism." *Geoforum* 40: 701–704.

City of Toronto. 2003. "City of Toronto Plan of Action for the Elimination of Racism and Discrimination." Accessed November 7, 2008. www.toronto.ca/diversity/reports.htm

Coleman, D. 2006. *White Civility: The Literary Project of English Canada*. Toronto: University of Toronto Press.

DeVault, M. L. 1999. *Liberating Method: Feminism and Social Research*. Philadelphia: Temple University Press.

DeVault, M. L., and L. McCoy. 2006. "Institutional Ethnography: Using Interviews toInvestigate Ruling Relations." In *Institutional Ethnography as Practice*, edited by Dorothy E. Smith, 15–44. Lanham, MD: Rowman & Littlefield Publishers, Inc.

Deveau, J. L. 2008. "Examining the Institutional Ethnographer's Toolkit." *The Journal of the Society for Socialist Studies* 4 (2): 1–20.

Dhillon, S. 2005. "Political Parties and Ethnic Participation: A Question of Access." *Canadian Issues* (Summer): 85–88.

Essed, P. 1991. *Understanding Everyday Racism: An Interdisciplinary Theory*. Newbury Park, CA: Sage Publications, Inc.

Eveline, J., C. L. Bacchi, and J. Binns. 2009. "Gender Mainstreaming Versus Diversity Mainstreaming: Methodology as Emancipatory Politics." *Gender, Work and Organization* 16 (2): 198–216.

Farley, A. 1997. "The Black Body as Fetish Object." *Oregon Law Review* 76: 457–535.

Fleras, A., and J. L. Elliott. 2002. *Unequal Relations: An Introduction to Race and Ethnic Dynamics in Canada*. Toronto: Prentice Hall Publishing.

Foucault, M. 1981. "The Order of Discourse." In *Untying the Text: A Post-Structuralist Reader*, edited by R. Young, 48–78. London: Routledge and Kegan Paul.

———. 2003. *A Society Must Be Defended: Lectures at the College de France, 1975–1976*. New York: Picador.

Frankenberg, R. 1993. *White Women, Race Matters: The Social Construction of Whiteness*. Minneapolis, MN: University of Minnesota Press.

Goldberg, D. T. 2009. *The Threat of Race: Reflections on Racial Neoliberalism*. Malden, MA: Blackwell Publishing.

Goonewardena, K., K. Rankin, and S. Weinstock. 2004. "Diversity and Planning Education: A Canadian Perspective." *Canadian Journal of Urban Research* 13 (1): 1–26.

Grahame, P. R. 1998. "Ethnography, Institutions, and the Problematic of the Everyday World." *Human Studies* 21: 347–360.

Griffith, A. I. 1995. "Mothering, Schooling, and Children's Development." In *Knowledge, Experience, and Ruling Relations*, edited by M. L. Campbell and A. Manicom, 108–121. Toronto: University of Toronto Press.

Hage, G. 2000. *White Nation: Fantasies of White Supremacy in a Multicultural Society*. New York: Routledge.

Henry, F., and C. Tator. 1994. "The Ideology of Racism: Democratic Racism." *Canadian Ethnic Studies* 26 (2): 1–10.

Henry, F., C. Tator, W. Mattis, and T. Rees. 2000. *The Colour of Democracy: Racism in Canadian Society*. Toronto: Harcourt Canada Ltd.

Isin, E., and M. Siemiatycki. 1997. "Immigration, Diversity and Urban Citizenship in Toronto." *Canadian Journal of Regional Science* 21 (2): 73–102.

James, C. E. 1999. *Seeing Ourselves: Exploring Race, Ethnicity and Culture: Second Edition*. Toronto: Thompson Educational Publishing, Inc.

Jeffery, D. 2002. "A Terrain of Struggle: Reading Race in Social Work Education." PhD Diss., University of Toronto.

Kirova, A. 2008. "Critical and Emerging Discourses in Multicultural Education Literature: A Review." *Canadian Ethnic Studies* 40 (1-2): 101–124.

Kymlicka, W. 1995. *Multicultural Citizenship: A Liberal Theory of Minority Rights*. Oxford: Clarendon Press.

Lapp, M. 1999. "Ethnic Group Leaders and the Mobilization of Voter Turnout: Evidence from Five Montreal Communities." *Canadian Ethnic Studies* 31 (2): 17–32.

Ng, R. 1995. "Multiculturalism as Ideology: A Textual Analysis." In *Knowledge, Experience, and Ruling Relations*, edited by M. L. Campbell and A. Manicom, 3–17. Toronto: University of Toronto Press.

———. 2000. "Restructuring Gender, Race, and Class Relations: The Case of Garment Workers and Labour Adjustment." In *Restructuring Caring Labour: Discourse, State Practice, and Everyday Life*, edited by S. M. Neysmith, 226–245. New York: Oxford University Press.

Ornstein, M. 2000. "Ethno-Racial Inequality in the City of Toronto: An Analysis of the 1996 Census." Accessed November 7, 2008. tobiashouse.ca/passport/profiles/pdf/Ethno-Racial_Inequality.pdf

Philip, M. N. 1992. *Frontiers: Essays and Writings on Racism and Culture*. Toronto: Mercury Press.

Razack, N., and D. Jeffery. 2002. "Critical Race Discourse and Tenets for SocialWork." *Canadian Social Work Review* 19 (2): 257–271.

Siemiatycki, M., and A. Saloojee. 2002. "Ethno-Racial Political Representation inToronto: Patterns and Problems."*Journal of International Migration and Integration* 3 (2): 241–273.

———. 2006a. "Introduction." In *Institutional Ethnography as Practice*, edited by D. E. Smith, 1–11. Lanham, MD: Rowman & Littlefield Publishers, Inc.

———. 2006b. "Incorporating Texts into Ethnographic Practice." In *Institutional Ethnography as Practice*, edited by D. Smith, 65–99. Lanham, MD: Rowman & Littlefield Publishers, Inc.

St. Denis, V. 2004. "Real Indians: Cultural Revitalization and Fundamentalism in Aboriginal Education." In *Contesting Fundamentalism*, edited by C. Schick, J. Jaffe, and A. Watkinson, 35–47. Halifax: Fernwood Press.

van Dijk, T. A. 1993. *Elite Discourse and Racism*. California: Sage Publications, Inc.

———. 2002. "Denying Racism: Elite Discourse and Racism". In *Race Critical Theories*, edited by P. Essed and D. Goldberg, 307–324. Malden, MA: Blackwell Publishers Ltd.

Yan, M. C. 2003. "Antiracism Discourse: The Ideological Circle in a Child World." *Journal of Sociology and Social Welfare* 1:127–144.

Yee, J., and G. C. Dumbrill. 2003. "Whiteout: Looking for Race in Canadian Social Work Practice." In *Multicultural Social Work in Canada: Working With Diverse Ethno-Racial Communities*, edited by A. Al-Krenawi and J. R. Graham. Toronto: Oxford University Press.

Part Two

MIGRANTS AS LABOUR

Many immigrants have decided to migrate to a new place in search of economic opportunities. By the same token, government immigration policies are often designed to select the most suitable workers, with the aim of attracting the human capital—i.e., education, job skills, and employment experience—and labour power that would boost the national economy. An important aspect of immigration, therefore, is that immigrants are labour/human capital.

However, the experiences that immigrants have in the labour market often do not reflect their expectations. For example, the human capital that many highly skilled immigrants bring with them often does not translate into commensurate employment. Rather, immigrants are frequently experiencing deskilling and the devaluation of their labour. Other migrants, such as temporary foreign workers, find themselves in employment circumstances that are highly constraining and sometimes oppressive and exploitative. The so-called invisible hand of the market that is supposed to match workers with corresponding jobs in an impartial way seems to fail when it comes to immigration.

The chapters in Part Two leave behind the idea that the market mechanism is a perfect method of matching immigrant labour with jobs. Rather, the authors of these chapters apply a political economy approach to migration and show how political structures, social practices, and cultural processes regulate the labour market for immigrants and shape the role migrants play in local and national economies. The authors thus contribute important perspectives to the relationship between immigration and neo-liberal economic policies, instigating labour competition, flexibilizing labour markets, and lowering labour standards.

In the context of this political economy approach, the chapters explore interrelated themes, such as neo-liberal regulation and governance, labour organizing, resistance, and workers' agency. Cities, urban regimes, and municipal policies have emerged as critical contexts at which the interrelations between these themes can be observed. Three of the four chapters in this part therefore focus explicitly on the "global" city, where global flows of migrant labour, capital, and information converge.

In the opening chapter, Martina Benz examines in which way the global city provides a "political opportunity structure" for labour struggles of migrants. In particular, Benz develops Saskia Sassen's idea that global cities offer strategic sites that enable marginalized immigrant workers to develop new forms of transnational politics. She applies this idea to the case of immigrant domestic workers in New York City and their organizing and campaigning efforts, which culminated in the adoption of the Domestic Workers Bill of Rights by the Senate of the State of New York in June 2010. The chapter identifies factors that led to the success of the immigrant domestic workers' campaign and discusses the limits and ambivalences of the workers' victory.

Temporary foreign workers are another group of migrants that often experience marginalization and exploitation in the labour market. In Chapter 5, Ethel Tungohan investigates the Canadian government's effort to promote temporary migration through programs like the Seasonal Agricultural Workers Program, the Live-In Caregiver Program, and the Temporary Foreign Worker Program. While this chapter connects to the discussion of Chapter 2 (Part One), it focuses more specifically on the regulation of temporary labour migration and the resulting vulnerabilities and exploitation of labour. Tungohan argues that the lack of standardization in migration policy across Canada, coupled with the absence of adequate labour protection, have exacerbated migrant workers' vulnerabilities. While temporary labour migrants are formally protected by the labour and work safety guidelines established by federal and provincial governments, in practice these guidelines are inconsistently applied. Echoing Martina Benz's discussion in Chapter 4, Tungohan concludes that municipal governments in major cities may emerge as crucial context for advocacy for vulnerable migrant workers.

Labour markets are not only regulated by governments but also by social, economic, and cultural practices. Hongxia Shan, in Chapter 6, examines the role of immigrants as strategic actors who respond to the particular constraints and opportunities they confront in the labour market. Her empirical work brings out the psychological and emotional aspects of immigrant labour—a point that has been neglected in the literature. Using a case study of Chinese immigrant engineers in Canada and applying a critical transformative learning perspective, Shan shows how immigrant workers optimize their job opportunities. Her interviews reveal that Chinese immigrant engineers, on the one hand, learned to market themselves aggressively and adopt an entrepreneurial approach that suits the cultural and economic conventions that exist in the Canadian labour market. On the other hand, they are internalizing their secondary status in the labour market. Such a contradictory learning phenomenon, Shan argues, is embedded in an interlocking set of social relations such as race and class.

The concluding chapter of Part Two presents a Toronto-based case study of the taxi industry. Similar to Benz (Chapter 4), Aparna Sundar explores how the global city provides a particular set of contexts and relations in which immigrant labour is disadvantaged, marginalized, gendered, and racialized, but also presents an arena for organizing and resistance. The City of Toronto carried out reforms to its taxi industry on the grounds that the industry projects a negative image of the city that could harm its identity as a world-class city for business and tourism. Sundar examines the manner in which the emphasis on customer service, professionalization, and self-management has led to increased policing and regulation at the expense of improved working conditions for the industry's largely racialized workers. Her chapter points to the contradictions in the strategies cities use to project themselves as "world-class," while relying on highly stratified and racialized labour. In addition, the chapter explores the complex ways in which taxi drivers are organizing and resisting their working conditions.

Chapter 4

THE GLOBAL CITY AS POLITICAL OPPORTUNITY STRUCTURE FOR IMMIGRANT WORKERS' STRUGGLE: THE CASE OF DOMESTIC WORKER ORGANIZING IN NEW YORK CITY

MARTINA BENZ

INTRODUCTION

Domestic workers[1] in the United States are largely excluded from labour laws and face multiple discriminations as immigrants, women of colour, and low-wage workers. With the growing importance of paid domestic labour, however, immigrant domestic workers have started to organize and demand equal rights and recognition as workers. Most of this organizing has taken place in urban areas. In this chapter, I explore the role of global cities in offering strategic sites that enable marginalized immigrant workers to develop new forms of transnational politics. Saskia Sassen (2000, 88) characterized the global city as "a strategic site … for new kinds of political operations." Because global conflicts localize in urban space, it is here, where new subjectivities, organizations, alliances, and mobilizations emerge (Sassen 2004, 2006).

The City of New York exemplifies this urban space. In 2010 the New York-based migrant domestic workers' organization Domestic Workers United (DWU) achieved through its Bill of Rights Campaign (2003–2010) the historic inclusion of household workers into United States labour law in New York State. This represents an important victory for the domestic workers' movement in the United States and beyond as it challenges the traditional negligence of household work as labour and grants domestic workers recognition and equal rights as workers.

The global city provided the context in which DWU organized and campaigned for these domestic workers' labour rights. In this chapter, I will discuss DWU's

Domestic Workers' Bill of Rights Campaign and pursue the following research questions: how was the context of the global city supportive to mobilize support and build alliances? Is the achievement of the Domestic Workers' Bill of Rights an example for a newly emerging transnational politics? How does this achievement enable immigrant workers to demand legal and material improvements? To address these questions, I analyze interviews I conducted with members and organizers of DWU between 2006 and 2009.

In the first section, I will introduce Sassen's global city hypothesis and interpret it as a form of political opportunity structure with a variety of dimensions. The second section will outline the situation of domestic workers, the character and specific contradictions of paid household labour, and the associated challenges of organizing in the domestic service industry. Third, I will analyze the DWU's Bill of Rights Campaign, asking what enabled the group to achieve the historic labour law inclusion for domestic workers. Finally, I will recapitulate Sassen's thesis and draw conclusions about the limits and possibilities of domestic workers' organizing.

THE GLOBAL CITY AS STRATEGIC SITE

According to Saskia Sassen, the global city is a necessary base of international business *and* a "strategic site" to contest the new global order (Sassen 2000, 2002, 2004, 2006). To administer their global operations, transnational companies need a workforce of highly specialized service professionals and a certain technical, political, and social infrastructure. The global city thus has emerged as the "commanding heights" of globalization—with a number of consequences for these cities' local urban social and economic structure. While a large part of manufacturing has been shifted to locations outside of these urban spaces, either to overseas or rural areas, the global city developed a post-industrial socio-economic structure, characterized by a polarized service economy: a class of well-paid professionals finds its counterpart in the massive growth of an informalized low-wage sector, mostly constituted by immigrant workers, many of whom are undocumented (Aguiar and Herod 2006; Bernhardt, McGrath, and DeFilippis 2007).

With this polarized structure, global cities reproduce global conflicts within local urban space. Considering this new geography of polarization, Sassen (2000, 90) conceptualizes the global city as "a site for new claims: by global capital, which uses the city as an 'organizational commodity,' but also by disadvantaged sectors of the urban population, frequently as internationalized ... in large cities as capital." Indeed, global cities have in the last decade been arenas for the development of new forms of labour and social justice organizing in which immigrants take a leading role (Jayaraman and Ness 2003; Ness 2005; Tait 2005; Milkman 2006; Fine 2006). DWU is an example of such new migrant labour activism.

In the study of social movements, the term *political opportunity structures* refers to a conjuncture that encourages, supports, or alleviates the formation of social movements. Protest movements and organizing efforts are not primarily explained by "internal" factors, such as resources, but the structural context is regarded as crucial for the emergence and development of social movements (Neidhardt and Rucht 1991). Following Sassen, I suggest that the global city provides a particular political opportunity structure for immigrant organizing.

First, the global city is a strategic site for social struggles because it inhabits both the leading sectors of global capital and the growing share of impoverished workers: immigrants, people of colour, poor women. Thus, global cities become strategic sites for conflicts and contestations that refer to global relations of power. The city emerges as a strategic site where new claims and new ways of politics start to take form (Sassen 2006, 314–315). Second, global cities are places where "new types of citizenship practices" can emerge (Sassen 2006, 315). As historically citizenship evolved in cities, citizenship practices today are based on the "'presence' of those without power and a politics that claims rights to the city" (Sassen 2006, 315). Even though migrant workers lack power, because they are crucial for the global city's economy they are able to gain presence and emerge as political actors. Sassen's idea of citizenship practices differs from the nation-state related principles of citizenship discussed by Laura Harris in Chapter 1 and resembles more an idea of transnational citizenship (Bauböck 1994) "characterized by an expansion of citizenship beyond the national framework" (Austin and Bauder, Chapter 2).

Third, for these new political actors, the city offers new "operational and rhetorical openings" (Sassen 2006, 316), as it provides a terrain for new alliances between different marginalized groups: "The growing numbers and diversity of the disadvantaged in these cities under these conditions become heuristic in that they become present to each other. It is the fact of such 'presence,' rather than power per se, that generates operational and rhetorical openings" (Sassen 2006, 317).

The Character and Contradictions of Commodified Domestic Labour

Domestic work is a fundamental yet neglected part of the global economy. Insufficient public childcare and elderly care systems, demographic changes, and the growth in women's labour market participation resulted in a rising demand for paid domestic services (ILO 2010). This development is related to a change in gender regimes. While in the Fordist accumulation regime, the norm was that men worked as wage labourers outside the home while women provided unpaid care work in the home, the post-Fordist gender regime allows middle-class women to participate in the professional labour market while delegating household and care work to other women of a lower-class status, particularly immigrant women (Young 1998; Anderson 2001, 2006; 2007). In the global city, domestic workers provide the "work that makes all other work possible," as a DWU slogan says.[2] Over the last decades, well-educated women entered the labour market and constitute today a large share of the workforce in the post-industrial high-end service industry. Meanwhile, they remained responsible for the maintenance of the home and child- or elderly care. Hence, parallel to the growth in income polarization increased the demand for domestic workers in global cities (Hondagneu-Sotelo 2001).

> More people are working and they are working longer hours. Even individuals without children feel overwhelmed by the much-bemoaned "time-squeeze," which makes it more difficult to find time for both daily domestic duties and leisure.... As free time shrinks, people who can afford it seek relief by paying a housecleaner to attend to domestic grit and grime once every week or two. Increasing numbers of Americans thus purchase from nanny/housekeepers and housecleaners the work once performed by wives and mothers. (Hondagneu-Sotelo 2001, 5)

Today as in the past, "domestic work perpetuates hierarchies based on race, ethnicity, indigenous status, caste, and nationality" (ILO 2010, 5). Commodified household labour is, as the British sociologist Bridget Anderson (2001) explains, not "just another job." Housework is associated with inferior status and socially devalued. Often, domestic work is not even regarded as real "work": as a consequence, labour law and court cases deny domestic workers labour rights (Ontiveros 2007; Boris and Klein 2010). The demand for domestic services is gendered and racialized. Employing women who are classified as "other" helps employers to manage the intimate labour relation in their home as it allows them to "imagine private work as an opportunity rather than a drudgery, and themselves as benefactors as well as employers" (Anderson 2007, 262). Furthermore, due to their marginalized position on the labour market, immigrant women workers provide the flexibility and reliability employers require (Anderson 2007).

In the United States, domestic work was historically slave labour and, after Abolition, continued to be performed predominantly by black and/or immigrant women. Today, paid housework is predominantly provided by migrant women, many of whom are undocumented (Nadasen and Williams 2010). The post-Fordist commodification of care work thus takes place in the context of unequal North-South relations where "global care chains" (Hochschild 2000) transfer reproductive labour from the South to the North (Parrenas 2000). In the global city, this phenomenon is localized as new racialized class difference between women.

Labour Conditions of Domestic Workers in New York City

There are about 200,000 household workers in the New York metropolitan area. The overarching majority of these workers (99 percent) are immigrants, 76 percent are non-United States citizens, 93 percent are female, and 95 percent are people of color (DWU/Datacenter 2006, 10). Working conditions of household workers in New

York are marked by a general lack of industry standards. Most domestic workers are employed without a contract. The working hours are expansive while half of the workforce makes less than US $10 per hour (DWU/Datacenter 2006, 16). Nevertheless, 72 percent of New York's domestic workers regularly send remittances to support family members back home (DWU/Datacenter 2006, 26). Employers often expect workers to be available 10–12 hours per day, while overtime pay or other additional job benefits are rare (DWU/Datacenter 2006, 17). When they are sick or need to take care of one of their own family members, domestic workers risk losing their job as they have no right for sick leave, not to speak of paid vacation or health insurance (DWU/Datacenter 2006, 22, 23). At the same time, domestic work is demanding and often includes many different responsibilities—from child care to cleaning, running errands, cooking, and more (DWU/Datacenter 2006, 20; Anderson 2001, 26).

Being employed informally in private homes puts domestic workers in a vulnerable position towards their employers. Many domestic workers experience verbal and physical abuse on the job (DWU/Datacenter 2006, 21). This is exacerbated when migrant domestic workers' status depends on their job, as it is the case when their B1-, A3-, or G5-visa is sponsored by their employer (DWU/Datacenter 2006, 29; Parrenas 2010, 134–135). Live-in domestic workers, who are twice as likely to hold an employer-sponsored visa, tend to work longer hours and to be paid less than their live-out counterparts (DWU/Datacenter 2006, 27).

Domestic Workers United

Domestic Workers United was founded in 2000. The organization emerged from a network of Southeast Asian, Malay, Filipino, Indian, Bangladeshi, Sri Lankan, and Pakistani domestic workers. In 1998 the members in this network started the Women Workers Project of the Committee Against Anti-Asian Violence (CAAAV), as they realized the growing importance of domestic work as employment for migrant women workers. With a socio-economic transformation to a post-industrial city, the employment of domestic workers had grown by 24 percent in New York City (DWU/Datacenter 2006, 9). As a founding member of DWU explained: "[B]ecause of global restructuring ... Asian women [in New York City] were moving out of factory work into service work. And a lot of the women in the community were taking up domestic work. And, so we saw it as one of the industries where the presence of Asian women is going to grow" (personal interview).

Missing in this development was a unifying organization that was able to organize domestic workers across divisions of nationality, race, and ethnicity. As one of the founders of DWU recalls:

> Domestic Workers United ... started because the specific ethnic community organizing of [sic] domestic workers was limited in its ability to have an impact for the entire sector. And so, there needed to

> be a union, an independent union that was just focused on building the power of the workforce as a sector, particularly because the largest populations of workers in the industry, which were Caribbean and Latina, were actually not being directly organized by any of the existing organizations. (personal interview)

In this context, DWU was founded to serve both as an independent union for all domestic workers in New York, as well as an organization for those women who were not represented by the existing associations. Today, DWU organizes mainly Latina, Caribbean, and African migrant domestic workers. In 2010, it counted about 2,300 members and employed 4 full-time staff (Hobden 2010, 3). Together with the other New York-based migrant women organizations—Adhikaar for Human Rights, UNITY Housecleaners, DAMAYAN Migrant Workers Association, Haitian Women for Haitian Refugees, and Andolan Organizing South Asian Workers—DWU forms the New York Domestic Workers Justice Coalition (DWU et al. 2010).

Organizing Domestic Workers

Although organizing migrant domestic workers is complicated by the character of the industry, domestic workers have a long history of labour struggles (Boris and Nadasen 2008). Today, migrant domestic workers are on the forefront of transnational labour organizing (IDWN/IUF 2010), even though their organizing is only supported by unions in some countries (Ally 2005; Ford 2004) and often restricted by government measures and migration policies (Yeoh, Huang, and Devasahayam 2004; Piper 2006). In the United States, union organizing has been limited to publicly employed home-care workers (Delph and Quan 2006; Boris and Klein 2007), while domestic workers organized associations and worker centres outside of unions (Fine 2007).

Whereas from the perspective of unions, organizing a powerless and marginal workforce such as domestic workers is often seen as too difficult, DWU believes that migrant women workers are of strategic importance for the social justice movement. As a DWU organizer explains:

> [T]his [is] the workforce that we believe, this is the population that we believe [needs] to be at the forefront of any social justice movement in this country. I mean, if this social justice movement is going to be the kind of movement that creates the kind of change that we need in this country, it's going to have to be the voices of working-class women of colour [that] are going to have to lead. And so, part of it is about making sure that our members see their role in that movement-building process and are able to step into that role with grace. (personal interview)

Grassroots organizing and campaigning have provided the foundation for DWU's organizational development. Nanny training and justice for exploited workers campaigns attract domestic workers to the organization, create credibility for DWU, and produce a shared identity as "domestic workers."

DWU's first large-scale political campaign for a standard contract in New York found widespread sympathies and support. In 2003 DWU won a legal challenge, the so-called "Nanny Bill," that required domestic workers' agencies to inform both workers and employers about their rights and obligations (Hobden 2010). This victory created decisive momentum: in contrast to the daily experience of powerlessness and marginalization, it suddenly seemed possible to achieve change. Encouraged by this victory, DWU's general membership convention decided in 2003 to take the next step: to start a campaign for a Domestic Workers' Bill of Rights in New York State.

The Domestic Workers' Bill of Rights Campaign

DWU's call for a Domestic Workers' Bill of Rights was a reaction to the exclusion of household workers from most United States labour laws. In the United States, domestic workers are not covered by the National Labor Relations Act (NLRA) that guarantees workers' organizing and collective bargaining rights. Furthermore, many domestic workers are not covered by the federal Fair Labor Standards Act (FLSA), granting employees minimum wage, maximum limits for working hours, and overtime pay. Not even anti-discrimination laws used to cover domestic workers. Therefore, the workforce consisting mostly of black and immigrant women was not protected against discrimination based on race, colour, religion, gender, national origin, or age (Ontiveros 2007).

The demands of the Domestic Workers' Bill of Rights have been based on domestic workers' grievances and needs. The first draft of 2003 included a living wage of US $14 per hour, overtime pay, paid holidays, vacation, health benefits, paid sick days, termination notice, and severance pay. In addition, it demanded the end of exclusionary language in New York labour law and the inclusion of domestic workers in the definition of "employee." Finally, the domestic workers' bill called for the prohibition on trafficking in domestic workers (Hobden 2010). While the campaign aimed for legislative reform, it had been clear that the fundamental disrespect and devaluation of domestic work needed to be challenged in order to gain support for the Domestic Workers' Bill of Rights.

DWU's strategy and organizing model reflects this close relation between value change and policy change with a strong emphasis on worker leadership, broad alliances, movement coalitions, and strategic framings. Below, I review important aspects of this model.

Workers' Leadership: DWU strived to enable domestic workers themselves to take a leading role in the development of the campaign. Educated through DWU's leadership development training, household workers were encouraged to speak up at public hearings, in schools, universities, and religious congregations. "It was ... the voices of domestic workers, their stories and direct experience in the workplace that first caused legislators to take a pause and consider the issue. When a domestic worker imparts her personal experience of exploitation, it can be very moving. When hundreds of domestic workers echo her story, it becomes virtually impossible to deny the reality of the situation" (Hobden 2010, 17). At press conferences and in interviews, DWU members reported about their daily experiences as domestic workers. With this strategy, DWU also succeeded in gaining attention and coverage in the local and regional press. The *New York Times* even dedicated editorials to the Bill of Rights Campaign in 2009 and 2010.

Beyond the impact on the media and the public, DWU members had the experience of stepping outside their invisibility. Although this alone can certainly not alter living and working conditions, domestic workers gained self-esteem and felt less isolated through speaking out about their situation and experiencing public attention, which positively impacted their capacity to negotiate and defend themselves.

Broad Alliances: DWU established alliances with other civil society representatives, organizations, associations, institutions, and groups in order to win support for domestic workers' demands. The group invited representatives from community organizations and workers' centres, academic institutions, student groups and university faculty, trade unions and religious congregations to join the campaign committee, and established multiple avenues to inform about the situation of domestic workers and the Bill of Rights Campaign. As part of this strategy, domestic workers even used church services as campaigning arenas:

> We reached out to the churches, and we had a month dedicated to the domestic workers, called "Domestic Workers in the Pulpit".... This is where domestic workers got into the pulpit and spoke to the congregations around the state. We told them about the industry, the exploitations and the abuses that were happening in the industry. People sitting in the congregations were able to identify themselves with these issues.... So they came forward and helped to build our strength by spreading the word to different churches that we were unable to get into.(Gill-Campbell 2011, 4)

This not only widened the support base for the DWU's campaign demands, but the Bill of Rights Campaign itself became a collective endeavour advanced and developed by many different actors. "[E]ventually, campaign meetings became open to any and all who wanted to help. By 2008, the campaign enjoyed the support of over 100 organizations in New York City" (Hobden 2010, 17). Each of these individuals and groups supported the campaign with their available resources. Students may volunteer or intern, institutions such as trade unions, other non-profits or universities may provide access to infrastructure for meetings and training, and again others support the organization with financial means or media contacts.

A particular alliance that developed through these partnerships is Employers for Justice, a group of progressive employers, organized through the community organization Jews for Racial and Economic Justice (JFREJ). Employers for Justice is informed about household workers' rights and the need for the regulation of the industry from the perspective of employers. Many supported DWU's demands based on their own experiences of discomfort as employers in an informal environment. Employers for Justice supported the Bill of Rights Campaign by speaking in solidarity with domestic workers at press conferences and public hearings, providing an important supportive perspective and an important positive example that demonstrated that it is in fact possible to employ a domestic worker and respect her rights.

Other important supporters of the Domestic Workers' Bill of Rights Campaign were unions and other labour movement representatives. DWU built alliances both at the rank and file level, supporting other organizing and worker justice campaigns, as well as with the leadership of organized labour. John Sweeney, then president of the American Federation of Labor and Congress of Industrial Organizations (AFL-CIO)—the largest United States trade union federation—even accompanied DWU to the state capital Albany to lobby for the Bill of Rights. This support of organized labour was decisive in lending DWU legitimacy as part of the labour movement. Alliances like these allowed DWU to broaden their support in progressive middle-class milieus in New York City and were critical to winning the support of crucial political actors who supported the Bill in the Senate and Assembly (Hobden 2010).

Movement Coalitions: An important aspect of the Domestic Workers' Bill of Rights Campaign was to frame the demands of domestic workers in a way that allowed many different actors to identify with them. DWU was successful in uniting many movements whose different perspectives and issues intersected with the situation and demands of domestic workers. As a DWU organizer explains:

> [T]hrough strengthening … the voice of domestic workers we feel that we can actually have an impact on a number of movements—whether it is the labour movement, the women's movement, the immigrant rights movement. Because of the positioning of domestic workers as a historically excluded workforce of women of colour, that on some level can actually speak to a number of movements, and actually compel to democratize and politicise … or actually challenge some of the ways that different movements have replicated forms of oppression.… I think … it's also … the racial justice movement, to the extent that it doesn't take up questions of patriarchy. It's all the movements because domestic workers are so at the intersection of all different forms of oppression. So we feel that we have a really

> important position, an important role to challenge all these different movements, to take on the intersections of oppressions. (personal interview)

Over the last years, DWU knit a close network with other domestic workers' organizations from all corners of the United States. At the United States Social Forum in Atlanta 2007, they formed the National Domestic Workers Alliance (NDWA), extending the struggle of domestic workers to the national scale. By 2010 the association had grown from 15 to 19 member organizations in 11 United States cities. Internationally, the NDWA is organized in a network of household workers' associations that strives for a strong International Labour Organization (ILO) Convention to set standards and raise protections for domestic workers worldwide (Obias 2009). DWU, furthermore, considers itself as part of a broader movement and partners with other grassroots alliances such as the Right to the City Alliance, the Pushback Network, the National Day Labor Organizing Network, the Grassroots Global Justice Alliance, and Jobs with Justice (Goldberg 2010).

Strategic Framing: Finally, the combination of a characterization of domestic labour as "work that makes all other work possible" and the articulation of the campaign as a rights issue provided a combination of framings[3] that triggered public interest, organized awareness, and motivated support for the Domestic Workers' Bill of Rights Campaign among a broad base of possible supporters and sympathizers. The presentation of domestic work as "work that makes all other work possible" helped to argue for the fundamental centrality of domestic workers' services to the functioning of the global city. This frame touched the biographical experience of many people depending on caregivers at some point in their life. Furthermore, there is a dimension of historical continuity of domestic work as immigrant labour in a city with a large population of people with immigrant backgrounds. The broad support for the Domestic Workers' Bill of Rights Campaign therefore can in part be explained by the resonance with the plight of domestic workers and their demand for justice found among different groups of people in New York City. This is supported by the following quote by a DWU organizer:

> The president of the AFL-CIO comes to Albany to lobby with us, you know, I mean, that is unheard of. But his mother was a domestic worker for 40 years, and so, he gets it. I mean a lot of the labour leaders today are Irish or of Irish descent and their mothers and their aunts came over and were domestic workers, so, a lot of them get it. I mean the sector really touches a lot of different people. So we have found a lot of support. I mean, every—when we have a sector that is 200,000 women, right, either you are going to be raised by a domestic worker or your mother is a domestic worker, your aunt is a domestic worker—somebody has a relationship to a domestic worker around

you, if you don't yourself, and so, if we are able to talk about that and really make people think about that, which we are, through our campaigns, then I think it's very easy for people to support. (personal interview)

With the framing of domestic workers' demands as Bill of Rights, DWU calls for the immediate inclusion of domestic workers as an act of reinstalling justice and overcoming a legacy of race- and gender-based exploitation in the domestic work industry. Translating domestic workers' demands into the logic of legal entitlements, DWU integrated them into a familiar political language of liberal values that many people understand. These aspects allowed the Domestic Workers' Bill of Rights Campaign to mobilize broad public attention and sympathy. In the absence of any organized opposition—an advantage of the non-existence of an employer association (Hobden 2010)—this support finally impelled New York State legislators to vote for the Domestic Workers' Bill of Rights that went into effect on November 30, 2010, (DWU et al. 2010).

After more than six years of organizing and campaigning, DWU finally won labour law inclusion for domestic workers in New York State. In order to allow the labour reform to pass, however, DWU had to make significant concessions. In its final version, the Bill of Rights includes overtime pay, a weekly day off, three days paid leave per year, and the same labour rights and anti-discrimination protection as all other workers in New York State. DWU's demands for termination notice, severance pay, health benefits, and a guaranteed living wage of US $14 per hour, however, were rejected.

Without doubt, DWU's success is remarkable: not only did the organization achieve legal change in New York State law, but also it created awareness of the situation of domestic workers. Thus, the Domestic Workers' Bill of Rights Campaign was not only about labour law reform but also called for the moral duty of state and society to acknowledge the centrality of care work. With the inclusion into labour law, domestic workers are now entitled to take their employers to court if they do not respect the law. This is a great and important change—a change that will eventually help individual domestic workers in New York to defend and protect themselves and improve their working and living conditions.

THE GLOBAL CITY THESIS RECONSIDERED

The campaign for the Domestic Workers' Bill of Rights provides an example for how immigrants appear as new political actors and achieve recognition in the global city. With respect to the localization of global conflict, the organization of domestic workers in New York is a result of a global conflict over care work arising from global care chains that supply care work through female labour migration, allowing industrial countries to resolve a crisis around reproduction that would otherwise necessitate a change of labour relations and require a new valorisation of reproductive labour (Hochschild 2000). By demanding rights and respect, domestic workers call for a new global political economy of care work.

The Domestic Workers' Bill of Rights Campaign exemplifies how immigrant workers' struggles can overcome the limitations that older structures of solidarity have faced in the light of a restructured political-economy context. The political opportunity structure of the global city has encouraged and enabled the emergence of such new forms of claims making and organizing.

Considering the strong demand for care work, it is not surprising that domestic workers are an important part of this new movement. The inclusion into standard labour laws constitutes a victory for a workforce that is still highly invisible. It shows that domestic workers are not only able to organize, but also that they are capable of constituting themselves as new political actors. Against the background of the social devaluation of their labour, the creation of a shared identity as domestic workers proved powerful to unify migrant women of diverse national backgrounds.

While at first glance the Domestic Workers' Bill of Rights Campaign appears mostly oriented towards the local and regional scales, transnational networks and contacts were important for the campaign's success. Furthermore, DWU has been involved in transnational networks of domestic workers' organizations that share contacts and organizing experiences. As the organizing of domestic workers in New York City was inspired by domestic workers' struggles in Hong Kong, so will household workers in other cities in the United States, Canada, and elsewhere learn from DWU's campaign (Obias 2009). The success of the Domestic Workers' Bill of Rights in New York will help domestic workers' organizations elsewhere in the United States to make similar advances: currently, there are campaigns for labour law inclusion in California where it will be more difficult for lawmakers to reject the reform now that it has been adopted in New York. Parallel to the Bill of Rights Campaign, domestic workers' organizations worldwide have fought for the adoption of an ILO Convention on "Decent Work for Domestic Workers" (Schwenken 2010).

The Domestic Workers' Bill of Rights Campaign demonstrated the critical importance of broad alliances. The diversity of groups and political organizations endorsing the Domestic Workers' Bill of Rights shows how the situation of household workers became a unifying symbol for social justice in the global city. Finally, the informational infrastructure of the global city with large universities, the presence of international media, NGOs, and international organizations facilitated the efforts of raising awareness of household workers' rights and knitting a diverse network of supporters.

NEW RIGHTS, OLD CONDITIONS?

With the Domestic Workers' Bill of Rights, household workers in New York gained anti-discrimination protection, minimum wage guarantee, overtime pay, one mandatory day off per week, and three paid days off per year. Together with the adoption of the Bill of Rights, the New York Legislator commissioned a feasibility study for the inclusion of domestic workers in collective bargaining structures. The study concludes that, while there are a number of challenges to the application of collective bargaining, "[i]n sum, there are feasible options for organizing domestic workers" (NYS Department of Labor 2010, 29).

There is reason for scepticism, however, regarding how far the Domestic Workers' Bill of Rights alone is able to alter the everyday working and living conditions of household workers, given that they are structured by far-reaching power inequalities. As rights remain dependent on someone claiming them and the state guaranteeing them, legislative change alone does not automatically translate into improvements. While acknowledgements and awareness emerged in response to the devaluation of household work, such acknowledgement can easily become a substitute for material improvement for domestic workers. Furthermore, the Domestic Workers' Bill of Rights in its current form covers only the most basic demands of household workers. A living wage, sick leave, termination notice, and severance pay are excluded from the bill. Thus, to significantly improve domestic workers' living and working conditions will require further organizing.

Regardless of the adoption of the Domestic Workers' Bill of Rights, most household workers continue to be employed without a written contract. Many have neither immigration papers nor work permits in the United States and many more are too afraid of losing theirs. These factors limit the capacity of the bill, and call for a strong union and support network to safeguard these rights for all domestic workers.

ACKNOWLEDGEMENTS

I want to thank the reviewers of this volume for their feedback and comments on an earlier version of this chapter.

ENDNOTES

1. In this chapter, I use the term *domestic worker* or *household worker* to refer to people who perform paid care work in private homes. Defining domestic work is complicated: despite its name, domestic work does not only take place inside the house. It also entails picking up children from school and running errands. In the United States, the legal definition of domestic workers includes, "anyone employed to work in a private home by the head(s) of household, including nannies, housekeepers, elderly companions, cleaners, babysitters, baby nurses and cooks" (Hobden 2010, 7).
2. The close connection between the functioning of New York's economy and domestic workers' labour power became clear during the financial crises in 2008: with big banks and insurance

companies filing for bankruptcy, about 20,000 domestic workers lost their jobs overnight (Scelfo 2008).

3. See for example Benford and Snow (2000) for a discussion of their framing approach.

REFERENCES

Aguiar, L., and A. Herod. 2006. "Introduction: Geographies of Neoliberalism." In *The Dirty Work of Neoliberalism: Cleaners in the Global Economy*, edited by L. Aguiar and A. Herod, 11–15. Oxford: Wiley-Blackwell.

Ally, S. 2005. "Caring about Care Workers: Organizing in the Female Shadow of Globalization." *Labour, Capital and Society* 1–2: 185–207.

Anderson, B. 2001."Just Another Job? Paying for Domestic Work." *Gender and Development* 9 (1): 25–33.

———. 2006. *Doing the Dirty Work? Migrantinnen in der bezahlten Hausarbeit*. German Edition: Berlin: Assoziation A.

———. 2007. "A Very Private Business: Exploring the Demand for Migrant Domestic Workers." *European Journal for Women's Studies* 3: 247–264.

Bauböck, R. 1994. *Transnational Citizenship: Membership and Rights in International Migration*. Aldershot: E.Elgar.

Benford, R. D., and D. Snow. 2000. "Framing Processes and Social Movements: An Overview and Assessment." *Annual Review of Sociology* 26: 611–639.

Bernhardt, A., S. McGrath, and J. DeFilippis. 2007. "Unregulated Work in the Global City: Employment and Labor Law Violations in New York City." Accessed February 6, 2011. nelp.3cdn.net/cc4d61e5942f9cfdc5_d6m6bgaq4.pdf.

Boris, E., and P. Nadasen. 2008. "Domestic Workers Organize!" *WorkingUSA: The Journal of Labor and Society* (December): 413–437.

Boris, E., and J. Klein. 2010. "'Not Really a Worker': Home-Based Unions Challenged in Court." *Labor Notes*, October 19. Accessed August 4, 2011. labornotes.org/2010/10/%E2%80%98not-really-worker%E2%80%99-home-based-unions-challenged-court.

———. 2007. "'We Were the Invisible Workforce': Unionizing Home Care." In *The Sex of Class: Women Transforming American Labor*, edited by D. S. Cobble, 177–193. Ithaca, London: Cornell University Press.

Delp, L., and K. Quan. 2002. "Homecare Worker Organizing in California: An Analysis of a Successful Strategy." *Labor Studies Journal* 1: 1–23.

Domestic Workers United (DWU) & Datacenter. 2006. "Home Is Where the Work Is: Inside New York's Domestic Work Industry." New York: Datacenter. Accessed November 5, 2010. www.datacenter.org/wp-content/uploads/homeiswheretheworkis.pdf.

Domestic Workers United (DWU), National Domestic Workers Alliance, the Community Development Project, and the Urban Justice Center. 2010. "Domestic Workers and Collective Bargaining. A Proposal for the Immediate Inclusion of Domestic Workers in the New York State Labor Relations Act." Accessed August 4, 2011. www.urbanjustice.org/pdf/publications/Domestic_Workers_and_Collective_Bargaining.pdf.

Fine, J. 2007. "Worker Centers and Immigrant Women." In *The Sex of Class: Women Transforming American Labor*, edited by D. S. Cobble, 211–230. Ithaca: ILR Press.

———. 2006. *Worker Centers: Organizing Communities at the Edge of the Dream*. Ithaca: Cornell University Press.

Ford, M. 2004. "Organizing the Unorganizable: Unions, NGOs, and Indonesian Migrant Labour." *International Migration* 42 (5): 99–119.

Gill-Campbell, J. 2011. "Organizing Upgrade." Accessed June 8, 2011. www.organizingupgrade.com/2011/01/lessons-from-domestic-workers-victory.

Goldberg, H. 2010. "Ai-Jen Poo: Organizing with Love." *Organizing Upgrade: Left Organizers Respond to the Changing Times*. Accessed May 30, 2011. www.organizingupgrade.com/2010/02/organizing-with-love/.

Hobden, C. 2010. "Winning Fair Labour Standards for Domestic Workers: Lessons from the Campaign for a Domestic Worker Bill of Rights in New York State." GURN discussion paper (14). Geneva: International Labour Organization.

Hochschild, A. R. 2000. "The Nanny Chain." *The American Prospect* 11 (3): 1–4.

Hondagneu-Sotelo, P. 2001. *Doméstica: ImmigrantWorkers Cleaning and Caring in the Shadows of Affluence*. Berkeley, Los Angeles, London: University of California Press.

International Labour Organization (ILO). 2010. *Decent Work for Domestic Workers*. Report 4 (1). Geneva: International Labour Office.

International Domestic Workers Network (IDWN) and International Union of Food, Agricultural, Hotel, Restaurant, Catering, Tobacco, and Allied Workers' Associations (IUF). 2010. "Platform of Demands: International Domestic Workers Network." 99th Session. Geneva: International Labour Conference.

Jayaraman, S., and I. Ness, eds. 2005. *The New Urban Immigrant Workforce: Innovative Models for Labor Organizing*. Armonk: M. E. Sharpe, Inc.

Milkman, R. 2006. *L. A. Story: Immigrant Workers and the Future of the U.S. Labor Movement*. New York: Russell Sage Foundation.

Nadasen, P., and T. Williams. 2010. "Valuing Domestic Work." *New Feminist Solution Series* Vol. 5. New York City: The Barnard Center for Research on Women. Accessed May 30, 2011. www.barnard.edu/bcrw/newfeministsolutions/reports/NFS5-Valuing-Domestic-Work.pdf.

Neidhardt, F., and D. Rucht. 1991. "The Analysis of Social Movements: The State of the Art and Some Perspectives for Further Research." In *Research on Social Movements: The State of the Art in Western Europe and the USA*, edited by D. Rucht, 421–464. Boulder: Campus Verlag.

Ness, I. 2005. *Immigrants, Unions, and the New U.S. Labor Market*. Philadelphia: Temple University Press.

New York State Department of Labor. 2010. "Feasibility of Domestic Worker Collective Bargaining." Accessed June 6, 2011. www.labor.ny.gov/sites/legal/laws/pdf_word_docs/domestic-workers/domestic-workers-feasibility-study.pdf.

Obias, L. 2009. "Organizing Domestic Workers: The National Domestic Workers Alliance." *S&F Online* 8.1 (Fall). Barnard Center for Research on Women.

Ontiveros, M. L. 2007."Female Immigrant Workers and the Law: Limits and Opportunities." In *The Sex of Class: Women Transforming American Labor*, edited by D. Cobble, 235–252. Ithaca, London: Cornell University Press.

Parrenas, R. S. 2000. "Migrant Filipina Domestic Workers and the International Division of Reproductive Labor." *Gender and Society* 14 (4): 560–580.

———. 2010. "'Partial Citizenship' and the Ideology of Women's Domesticity in State Policies on Foreign Domestic Workers." In *Care and Migration: Die Ent-Sorgung menschlicher Reproduktionsarbeit entlang von Geschlechter-und Armutgrenzen*, edited by U. Apitzsch and M. Schmidbaur, 127–140. Opladen & Farmington Hills, MI: Verlag Barbara Budrich.

Piper, N. 2006. "Migrant Worker Activism in Singapore and Malaysia: Freedom of Association and the Role of the State." *Asian & Pacific Migration Journal* 15 (3):359–380.

Sassen, S. 2000. "The Global City: Stratgic Site/New Frontier." *American Studies* (2–3): 79–95.

———. 2002. "Analytic Borderlands: Economy and Culture in the Global City." In *Crossing Borders and Shifting Boundaries*, edited by I. Lenz, H. Lutz, M. Morokvasic-Müller, C. Schöning-Kalender, and H. Schwenken, 131–143. Opladen: Leske+Budrich Verlag.

———. 2004. "Going Beyond the National State in the USA: The Politics of Minoritized Groups in Global Cities." *Diogenes* 203: 59–65.

———. 2006. *Territory, Authority, Rights*. Princeton: Princeton University Press.

Scelfo, J. 2008. "Trickledown Downsizing." *New York Times*, November 11.

Schwenken, H. 2010. Transnationale und lokale Organisierungsprozesse für eine ILO-Konvention "Decent Work for Domestic Workers." In *Care und Migration: Die Ent-Sorgung menschlicher Reproduktionsarbeit entlang von Geschlechter- und Armutgrenzen*, edited by U. Apitzsch and M. Schmidbaur, 191–206. Opladen & Farmington Hills, MI: Verlag Barbara Budrich.

Tait, V. 2005. *Poor Workers' Unions: Rebuilding Labor from Below*. Cambridge, MA: South End Press.

Yeoh, B., S. Huang, and T.W. Devasahayam. 2004. "Diasporic Subjects in the Nation: Foreign Domestic Workers, the Reach of the Law and Civil Society in Singapore." *Asian Studies Review* 28 (1): 7–23.

Young, B. 1998. "Genderregime und Staat in der globalen Netzwerkökonomie." *PROKLA: Zeitschrift für kritische Sozialwissenschaft* 111: 175–198.

Chapter 5

PROTECTING TEMPORARY LABOUR MIGRANTS: AN EMERGING ROLE FOR GLOBAL CITIES?

ETHEL TUNGOHAN

INTRODUCTION

The belief that temporary labour migration benefits all parties involved is pervasive among Canadian policy-makers. For instance, Jason Kenney, the current Minister of Citizenship, Immigration, and Multiculturalism, sees temporary labour migration as the solution to employers' problems of labour shortages and migrant workers' economic difficulties (Kenney 2009). Canada's temporary labour migration programs, which include the Live-In Caregiver Program (LCP), the Seasonal Agricultural Workers Program (SAWP), and the Temporary Foreign Worker Program (TFWP), have expanded considerably in recent years. In 2007 there were 199,580 temporary foreign workers working in Canada, a number that increased to 250,492 in 2008 and 282,771 in 2009 (CIC 2009a). In contrast, permanent immigration to Canada has only faced moderate increases during the same period; there were 236,754 permanent immigrants who arrived in Canada in 2007; 247,246 in 2008; and 252,124 in 2009 (CIC 2009b).

These trends have led policy analysts to conclude that "[m]igrant workers can no longer be considered a minor part of the work force ... in fact, if present trends continue, non-Canadian workers will account for a larger share of total hours worked compared to Canadian workers" (Weston and Scarpa de Masellis 2003, 4). That the numbers of temporary foreign workers have surpassed the numbers of permanent migrants is indicative of a growing preference for temporary labour migration over permanent migration. This has led some commentators to speculate that the Canadian government is endorsing a "quiet shift" away from permanent migration, which has been the basis for Canadian immigration policy from Confederation onwards (Valiani 2009). The LCP, the SAWP, and the TFWP have resulted in the creation of a "two-tiered" society whereby workers are segmented on the basis of "skill" and migration status (Canadian Council for Refugees 2010; Alboim 2009).

Preventing migrant workers' exploitation becomes challenging when temporary labour migration programs are not centrally supervised. Issues of political accountability abound, especially in terms of determining which government bodies are responsible for ensuring the well-being of migrant workers. The governance of temporary labour migration programs is described as a case of "jurisdictional football" (Hennebry 2010), whereby competing bureaucratic agencies and government offices are simultaneously responsible for the LCP, the SAWP, and the TFWP. Theoretically, the responsibilities of various bodies are clearly delineated. In practice, however, bureaucrats and policy-makers are unclear on what their respective roles constitute. While the federal government through Citizenship and Immigration Canada (CIC), Human Resources and Skills Development Canada (HRSDC), Service Canada, and the Canadian Border Services Agency works with provincial governments in setting migration policy and in determining the numbers and types of migrant workers to accept, competing agendas make cooperation difficult. The situation is rendered even more complicated as the involvement of municipal governments in immigration policy is increasing and municipalities are beginning to realize that high numbers of temporary labour migrants necessitate the development of clear guidelines.

This chapter complements Chapter 2, in which Carly Austin and Harald Bauder suggest that temporary foreign workers in Canada require pathways to permanency and citizenship. My perspective, however, differs in that I argue that Canada's temporary labour migration programs present a conundrum for federalism. While maintaining joint federal-provincial supervision over immigration policy is crucial, there is also an accompanying need to ensure that Canada's long-term interests are taken into account. The lack of standardization in temporary labour migration policy creates a discrepancy between meeting economic needs and maintaining political divisions of power. I will develop this argument in two sections. The next section explains the shift towards temporary migration in Canada and provides a comparison of the LCP, the SAWP, and the TFWP. This section also addresses the creation of a "two-tiered" system, which segments migrants on the basis of "skill." The section thereafter discusses the difficulties in coordinating across federal, provincial, and municipal bodies in the management of temporary labour migration programs. I end with a conclusion, arguing in favour of an enhanced role for municipalities in migration management.

CANADIAN IMMIGRATION POLICY: A COMPARATIVE ASSESSMENT OF TEMPORARY LABOUR MIGRATION PROGRAMS

Historically, Canadian immigration policy was based on excluding "undesirable" groups of people from entering the country. Immigration policy sought to ensure the maintenance of "Canadian identity" by making it harder for groups deemed racially inferior to enter the country. As such, immigration officials used a racial hierarchy that placed "white" British and Americans on top, Northern and Western Europeans at the middle, and "Jews, Blacks, and Orientals [sic] as a last resort at the bottom" (Jakubowski 2003, 105). The establishment of the points system in 1967 began assessing potential immigrants on the basis of "education and training, personal suitability, occupational demand, occupational skill, age, arranged employment, knowledge of French or English, relatives in Canada, and employment opportunities in area of destination" (Jakubowski 2003, 109); it eliminated racial criteria and put into place a process whereby "everyone seeking admission to Canada is assessed under the same set of standards regardless of race, religion or country of origin" (Jakubowski 2003, 109). Quebec, under the Cullen-Couture agreement of 1976, was able to establish its own immigration criteria through an independent points system that enabled the recruitment of immigrants who met Quebec's linguistic and cultural requirements (Kelley and Trebilcock 1998, 392).

The points system allowed high numbers of non-European immigrants to enter Canada; although, high influxes of new immigrants soon led to a belief among policy-makers that the immigration system needed to be reformed. Nandita Sharma's (2006) examination of Canadian parliamentary debates from 1969 to 1973 shows that it was in the immediate period after the points system was first established when the discourse on immigration became fixated on the "problems" caused by immigration: immigrants—especially non-white immigrants—were blamed for a variety of social ills, ranging from high unemployment to growing state spending, concerns that abound even today. The belief that immigrants from non-traditional source countries were taking advantage of Canada because of their "inability to adapt" to a country deemed more "sophisticated, industrialized, and urban" (Sharma 2006, 87) led MPs to consider ways to limit the purported dangers caused by immigration. Immigration policy then shifted to exclude economically "undesirable" immigrants[1] through the passage of Bill C-197 in 1972, which made it illegal for people to apply for permanent residency once inside the country. This meant that people who had been working as migrant labourers in Canada were unable to apply for permanent residency; the duration of time migrants spent in Canada, their community involvement, and the presence of family—which arguably establish one's membership in Canadian society—became inconsequential.[2]

The introduction of the Non-Immigrant Employment Authorization Program (NIEAP) in 1973 was a logical successor of Bill C-197, reflecting Canadian policy-makers' desire for immigration reform (Sharma 2006, 104). The NIEAP marked the beginning of Canada's reliance on temporary labour migration to solve the problem of labour shortages. Prior to the NIEAP, temporary labour migration into Canada was restricted to labour exchange arrangements with Caribbean countries in agricultural and care work sectors, whereby small numbers of individuals from Barbados, Jamaica, and Trinidad entered Canada as "supplementary labour" and worked in farms and households. While there were myriad restrictions facing migrant workers, such as close monitoring and regular health checkups (Henry 1998), they nevertheless still had the right to apply for permanent residency after a year's labour (Daenzar 1997).

By encompassing multiple "low-skilled" job sectors—including care and agricultural work—and by removing migrant workers' ability to become permanent residents, the NIEAP institutionalized temporary labour migration into Canada and created a separation between "temporary" (i.e., unskilled) and "permanent" (i.e., skilled) migrants. The NIEAP enables the recruitment of migrant workers for a set period of time, allowing employers to benefit from the constant supply of cheap and flexible workers. Although the law specifies that "location of employment, type of employment, condition of employment, and length of employment must be prearranged beforehand" (Sharma 2006, 104), migrant workers have minimal control over their work conditions after entering Canada. Given that there is a lack of supervision over workplaces employing migrant workers, abusive work conditions prevail, with multiple cases of migrant workers complaining that the terms of their employment contracts are not being met. Most migrant workers, however, endured deleterious labour conditions rather than risk being terminated, especially since migrant workers were immediately repatriated if they were unable to find jobs after leaving their previous workplaces. Restrictions on migrant mobility, in conjunction with experiences of social isolation and discrimination and laws outlawing union and civil society membership, make it difficult for migrant workers to ask for fair treatment under the NIEAP. This situation led some commentators to lament that the conditions built into the NIEAP are akin to bonded labour, especially since migrant workers' bargaining power is significantly reduced (e.g., Basok 2002; Sharma 2006). The problem that temporary labour migration programs create an "underclass" of workers still exists. The distinction between "skilled" and "unskilled," and "permanent" and "temporary work" continues to form the basis for Canadian migration policy. Below I review Canada's three temporary labour migration programs.

Migrant Domestic Worker Programs

Changes to Canada's migrant domestic worker policies were first implemented after migrant domestic workers from the Caribbean and from the Philippines brought the Canadian public's attention to their experiences of abuse under the existing program (Ramirez 1982; Domingo 2006). In response to these demands, the federal government through the leadership of Employment and Immigration Minister Lloyd Axworthy convened a Task Force on Immigration Practices, which led to the establishment of the Foreign Domestic Movement (FDM) in 1981 (Daenzar 1997). Axworthy deemed the FDM a suitable compromise to the federal government's interests in maintaining control over the entry of "suitable" groups and its recognition that migrant workers were rendered vulnerable by existing arrangements. Thus, the FDM stipulated that migrant workers could apply for permanent residency after 24 months of continuous live-in employment in the same household following a "post-entry" evaluation of the migrants' "suitability" to Canada. This evaluation permitted immigration authorities to act as gatekeepers and to use arbitrary criteria judging migrants' suitability, judging migrants on their assimilation into Canadian culture, on their economic performance, or other criteria (Daenzar 1997).

More significantly, immigration authorities were able to judge migrants on these criteria on the basis of information given by migrants' employers. This stipulation magnifies the power held by migrants' employers, making migrants depend on their employers for access to good labour and living conditions and, crucially, also for access to permanent settlement. Clearly, the Canadian government instituted a policy that admitted migrants partially on the basis of the length of time they had stayed in Canada but mostly on the basis of their assimilability. The FDM showed that the Canadian government was interested not in the "question of how policies should change to affect greater fairness and justice for immigrant non-citizen servants" but was rather invested in "how Canada can continue to serve the interests of influential Canadians while purporting to redress domestic exploitation" (Daenzar 1997, 91).

The LCP, founded in 1992, attempted to redress some of the shortcomings of the FDM, again as a result of the activism of civil society groups consisting of domestic workers (Khan 2009). The biggest change pertains to terminology; whereas the FDM recruited foreign domestic workers, the LCP recruited caregivers in an attempt to "professionalize" the program. Such a change in terminology was supposed to ensure that live-in caregivers are employed specifically to provide unsupervised "care work," a category that encompasses a broad range of activities like child care, elderly care, and care for people with disabilities. As such, more systematic checks were implemented to allow for the entry of "qualified" migrants: migrants were now required to be high school graduates and to be fluent in either English or French. They were also supposed to show that they had received sufficient training as caregivers, either through a six-month intensive education course or through prior work experience (Macklin 1992).

Nonetheless, efforts to professionalize the program failed. Though caregivers are "professionals" and are not supposed to perform menial household tasks, they are oftentimes asked to do so by their employers (England and Stiell 2008), drawing into question the effectiveness of the shift from "domestic worker" to "caregiver." Moreover, while the LCP promised more thorough governmental interventions in the event of migrant abuse and eliminated the requirement that caregivers needed to upgrade their educational credentials and do volunteer work in order to be eligible for permanent residency (England and Stiell 2008), the live-in requirement and 24-month "temporary" status remained mandatory. In fact, interviews that I have held with migrant domestic worker activists whose campaigns led to the creation of the LCP show their ambivalence towards these changes, which they see as being unsuccessful in creating substantive improvements. Ongoing civil society activism contesting the deleterious impacts of the LCP in the lives of live-in caregivers and their families show continued opposition to the conditions of migrant domestic work (Pratt 2007). The LCP, therefore, continues to be controversial, especially among live-in caregivers themselves, who see the benefits of maintaining a program that allows migrants eventual access to permanent residency but who are also cognizant of the harms live-in caregivers face.

Seasonal Agricultural Workers Program (SAWP)

Not much has changed since the SAWP was first established. Continuous labour shortages in agricultural work led to an expansion of the program; while there were 265 Jamaican men who were initially admitted into Canada as farm workers in 1965, there were close to 20,000 workers from the Caribbean and from Mexico in 2001, though this figure dropped to 17,000 workers in 2009. Mexican men have dominated the SAWP since the late 1980s as a result of NAFTA (Preibisch and Binford 2007) and perhaps also as a consequence of endemic racial bias against Jamaican men (Satzewich 1991) and employers' perception that Mexican men are more "docile" workers (Basok 2002). Currently, the Canadian government is seeking to expand the SAWP by signing bilateral agreements with more sending countries (Basok 2002), by broadening the range of jobs farm owners can ask migrants to do (Basok 2002), and by expanding the program to include more women farmers (Preibisch and Hermoso Santamaria 2006). Nine out of 12 provinces now employ migrant farm workers.[3] Although the majority of them go to Quebec and Ontario, a sizable number of migrants are heading to British Columbia and Alberta (HRSDC 2010a).

On face value, the conditions under the SAWP appear straightforward for potential migrant workers and farm owners. For migrant workers to qualify for entry through SAWP, their home countries need to have signed a bilateral agreement with Canada.[4] Potential migrant workers also need to show evidence to their home country's Ministry of Labour that they are impoverished and lack assets such as land and education, which are not coincidentally "the inverse of the qualities needed to apply for landed immigrant status" in Canada (Preibisch and Hermoso Santamaria 2006, 112). Farm owners make a formal request to HRSDC showing that they have the financial means to support migrant workers and that they have tried—and failed—to recruit Canadian workers (Basok 2002; Preibisch and Hermoso Santamaria 2006). HRSDC then makes a "labour market opinion" (LMO) judging the legitimacy of this request, and accordingly approves/rejects the farm owner's request. Once a request is approved, the farm owner is required to pay for the migrant workers' airfare and visa costs, and to provide food and housing and register the migrant worker with the applicable workers' compensation and health board (HRSDC 2009a). The farm owner can deduct these costs from migrant workers' salaries (Basok 2002). After the migrant workers are "matched" to the farm and receive help to complete paperwork from their countries' Ministry of Labour, CIC issues a temporary workers' visa for up to eight months (HRSDC 2009b). Before working, both employers and employee need to agree on an employment contract. The contract determines labour conditions, including the wage the migrant worker will receive, which is required to conform to the provincial minimum wage, the wage determined by HRSDC, or the rate Canadian workers are paid for the same work, depending on which is highest (HRSDC 2009a). While working, migrant workers are not allowed to work for more than eight hours a day, and are supposed to be given one day off every week. Migrant workers are forbidden from switching employers after arriving to Canada without getting permission from HRSDC and their sending country's ministry. Employers who illegally hire a migrant worker are fined $5,000 and/or face imprisonment; migrant workers who are caught are immediately repatriated (Basok 2002).

A considerable disjunction exists between the formal terms of SAWP and the realities of agricultural work. Some scholars have argued that the SAWP contravenes the Canadian Charter of Rights, the United Nations Convention of Migrant Workers, and "best practices" guidelines set by the International Organization for Migration (IOM) and the International Labour Organization (ILO) (e.g., Suen 2000; Hennebry and Preibisch 2010). By using deportation as a threat and by telling migrant workers that they may receive an unfavourable report, farm owners are able to keep workers in line (Binford 2006). HRSDC's "unwritten rule" that migrant workers would have to be employed on the same farm for three consecutive seasons before being allowed to transfer also coerces migrants into accepting oppressive working conditions (Binford 2006).

Temporary Foreign Worker Program (TFWP)

Changes to Canada's temporary labour migration program were established in 2002 after yet another attempt at immigration reform by the federal government (Valiani 2009). Since its inception, the Temporary Foreign Worker Program (TFWP) began to distinguish between migrants' skill sets through the creation of a "National Occupation Classification System," which specifies the types of jobs and education levels that fall into each category (Alberta Federation of Labour 2009). "High-skilled" jobs, which are included in categories 0 (managerial), A (professional), and B (skilled and technical), are "professional jobs" that require "some post-secondary training"; whereas the "low-skilled" jobs in categories C (intermediate and clerical) and D (elemental and labourer) are described as "occupations requiring little to no job training or education level" and usually encompass jobs in "cleaning, hospitality, manufacturing, oil and gas and construction" (Elgersma 2007, 4). The process for entering Canada is the same for migrants in all categories; their prospective employers are required to submit an application for an LMO to HRSDC and Service Canada, which jointly administer these applications. In order to get approval, prospective employers need to prove that there are no Canadians who are qualified to work in the jobs in question and that the presence of migrant workers does not "negatively" impact the Canadian labour market (HRSDC 2010b). Once a positive LMO is issued, the employer sends a copy of the letter to the migrant worker, who applies at CIC for a work permit. Migrant workers intending to work in Quebec need to forward a "Quebec Acceptance Certificate for Temporary Work," which authorizes the employer to represent the migrant worker. Once this certificate is issued and after a positive evaluation from the Canadian Border Services Agency at the migrant's port of entry, the migrant can enter Canada.

Despite the fact that migrants in all categories have to undergo similar application processes, migrants coming into Canada under the "skilled" category are treated markedly better and given significantly more freedom than migrants in the low-skilled category. High-skilled migrants, for instance, have more mobility rights and can bring their families into Canada; since 2001, their spouses are also permitted to work in Canada (Elgersma 2007). More importantly, "skilled" migrants are encouraged to stay in Canada through the Canadian Experience Class (CEC) program or through the Provincial Nominee Program (PNP), which is valid in all provinces except Quebec, where a separate system facilitates the entry of migrants. The CEC was established in 2008 and expedites the permanent residency applications of "skilled" migrants who are either employed in any of 38 listed professions, which employers have told the Canadian government require more professionals, or who are international students who graduated from a Canadian post-secondary institution and have one year of "skilled" work experience (CIC 2010a). Qualifying for the CEC program puts migrants ahead of the queue of other permanent resident applicants (Valiani 2009).[5]

The Provincial Nominee Program (PNP) is another route through which skilled migrants can apply for permanent residency. Similar to the CEC, the PNP prioritizes the permanent residency applications of migrants who work in any of the target "strategic occupations" identified by each province, although, unlike the CEC, qualifying for permanent residency under the PNP requires that potential migrants have a permanent job offer from their employers (CIC 2010b). Because the CEC and the PNP are reliant on employer recommendations for permanent residency and are in fact explicitly described by some provincial governments as being "employer-driven," private stakeholders play a large role in determining which migrants are able to settle permanently. This situation leads to an explicit preference for "skilled" workers at the expense of "unskilled" workers, including many women from developing countries (Canadian Council for Refugees 2010). Interestingly, the PNP was only supposed to complement the points system but may eventually replace the points system and become Canada's primary route to permanent migration (Alboim 2009, 35).

In contrast to "high-skilled" workers, "low-skilled" migrants face more restrictions. They are denied the option of bringing their families to Canada. They frequently have substandard medical care and housing because numerous employers violate rules of mandatory payments for migrants' health insurance and providing adequate housing. In the absence of government-sponsored protection, they lack resources to combat employer abuse. Thus, they have reported feeling socially stigmatized. Unsurprisingly, the terms of their employment contract are skewed towards the employer (Alberta Federation of Labour 2009). Unlike high-skilled migrants, they are denied the option of applying for permanent residency and are only permitted to work in Canada for a maximum of four years, which has led some migrants to stay in Canada "illegally" or to find ways to stay due to humanitarian reasons (Elgersma 2007; Valiani 2010). Employers are likely to be reluctant to nominate their employees because of financial costs. Sponsoring their employees' PNP applications require that they finance programs that will enhance their employees' cultural adaptation (e.g., through funding English as a Second Language classes). They are also asked to provide wage increases over the duration of the work permit. Since employers are permitted to recruit and to hire new migrant workers to replace those whose work permits have expired or whose wages have risen too much, low-skilled migrants' chances of getting sponsorship from their employers remain dismal.

The majority of migrants entering Canada through the TFWP do so as low-skilled workers, which is a result of the federal government's promotion of the "Low Skill Pilot Project." This project attempts to increase the number of migrant workers in categories C and D. The aforementioned policy changes that were implemented in 2002 were intended to increase low-skilled migration into Canada (CIC 2009c). The rise in the numbers of low-skilled workers is evident when comparing the numbers of migrants working in Canada through the TFWP in each category (Table 5.1). Although the number of migrants working in Canada increased in each category, a relative shift towards low-skilled occupations occurred. While high-skilled migrants consisted of 40.9 percent of all temporary labour migrants in 2006 and 39 percent in 2007, they comprised only 35.7 percent in 2008 (CIC 2009d). Conversely, low-skilled migrants consisted of 33.6 percent in 2006 and 37.3 percent in 2007 but comprised 38.5 percent of all temporary labour migrants in 2008 (CIC 2009d). These numbers are indicative of the movement towards low-skilled temporary labour migration.

Table 5.1: Temporary Labour Migrants in Canada by Occupational Skill Level (2006–2008)

Occupational Skill Level	2006	2007	2008
Level 0 (Managerial)	11,969 (7.4%)	13,385 (6.7%)	14,698 (5.9%)
Level A (Professional)	35,247 (21.9%)	37,867 (18.9%)	39,709 (15.8%)
Level B (Skilled and Technical)	18,761 (11.6%)	26,732 (13.4%)	35,071 (14%)
Level C (Intermediate and Clerical)	51,196 (31.7%)	65,691 (32.9%)	77,566 (30.9%)
Level D (Elemental and Labourer)	3,042 (1.9%)	8,786 (4.4%)	19,078 (7.6%)
Level not stated	41,080 (25.5%)	47,480 (23.7%)	65,107 (25.9%)

Source: CIC 2009d.

Permanent Versus Temporary and High-Skilled Versus Low-Skilled

Aside from the types of jobs associated with each program, the most significant difference between the LCP, the SAWP, and the TFWP concerns the length of time migrants are allowed to stay in Canada. Live-in caregivers are required to live and work with the same employer for 24 months before being allowed to apply for permanent residency, whereas seasonal agricultural workers may stay for a maximum of only eight months and may not apply for permanent resident status. Migrants entering Canada through the TFWP, in contrast, are allowed to work in Canada for up to four years and may be allowed to apply for permanent residency depending on their perceived skill level. Low-skilled migrants are unlikely to apply for permanent residency under the CEC or the PNP.

The demographics of these programs also differ. The LCP is dominated by women, primarily from the Philippines, most of whom have post-secondary education degrees (Diocson 2003). In contrast, the SAWP consists primarily of men from Caribbean countries and Mexico who have to prove that they lack education and live in near poverty (Basok 2002). Interestingly, data on the gender composition of each occupational level under the TFWP shows that there are more men entering Canada as "high-skilled" migrants and more women are entering Canada as "low-skilled" migrants (CIC 2009e). There is no published information on the levels of education migrants have in each category,[6] or on source countries for each migrant group.

Beyond these differences, the LCP, the SAWP, and the TFWP are similar in that migrants in all programs are placed in precarious work conditions. Their temporary work status makes them vulnerable to abuse. Temporary labour migration programs effectively distinguish between "skilled" labour (i.e., immigrants) that are deemed acceptable for permanent settlement and "unskilled" labour (i.e., non-immigrants/migrant workers) that need to be governed through multiple rights restrictions. In sum, high-skilled immigrants face substantial advantages over "low skilled" migrants. The irony, of course, is that there is a constant need for workers in industries such as care work, construction, agriculture, customer service, etc.; so-called "low-skilled" migrant workers are part of industries that have a continuous, even "permanent" need for labour. Thus, the shift away from permanent towards temporary migration may have negative long-term consequences, which federal, provincial, and municipal bodies may not be able to foresee because of the lack of coordination in the management of temporary labour migration programs.

WHO IS IN CHARGE OF WHAT? JURISDICTIONAL COMPLICATIONS AND TEMPORARY LABOUR MIGRATION

Civil society activists have long argued that the desire to make Canada economically competitive by segmenting workers into migrants and non-migrants, and skilled and unskilled workers, is not only a short-sighted economic policy (Alboim 2009) but also comes at the expense of meeting political obligations of fair and just treatment for everyone (Suen 2000; Khan 2009). What Jeffery Reitz (2004, 107) described as a "cautious" approach to temporary labour migration in the 1990s has been abandoned in favour of an unrestrained policy of economic expansion that has complicated federal, provincial, and municipal roles.

The Problem of Competing Stakeholders

The lack of political accountability over the management of three different temporary labour migration programs—each of which are subjected to different rules—can partially be explained when considering that each of these programs is supervised by CIC, HRSDC, Service Canada, and the Canadian Border Services Agency and operates under the regulations established by 12 different provinces and territories and countless municipalities. Officially, each federal and provincial body has designated responsibilities. CIC's official mandate is to "manage access to Canada to protect the security and health of Canadians and the integrity of Canadian laws" (CIC 2010c). It oversees all of Canada's migration programs and sets short- and long-term targets to meet Canada's economic and political needs and obligations through immigration.[7] The decision to prioritize temporary migration through the recruitment of low-skilled temporary labour migrants, for instance, was a CIC initiative. HRSDC and Service Canada assess the Canadian labour market's needs to ensure that migrant workers who enter Canada are not going to negatively impact Canadians' employment prospects. A secondary responsibility entrusted to the two agencies is to ensure that migrant workers' wages and working conditions remain similar to other (non-migrant) workers in the same occupation (HRSDC 2010a). The Canadian Border Services Agency enforces border protection by regulating the entry of migrant workers and determining the authenticity of their work permits (HRSDC 2010a). Provincial governments, on the other hand, work closely with CIC, HRSDC, and Service Canada to ensure that job sectors lacking workers are filled by migrant workers although they have also been given permission by the federal government to set their own economic and immigration agendas through PNPs.

In practice, these roles are not clearly delineated. Critics have pointed to the difficulties in coordinating federal and provincial bodies on the issue of migration management. In some cases, there is a complete absence in coordination. This is exemplified by the existence of separate and distinct permanent immigration programs at the national and provincial levels. Admittedly, the federal government has previously entered immigration policy agreements with provinces, aptly illustrating the "flexibility" of federal arrangements with regard to immigration (Kelley and Trebilcock 1998, 392). Nevertheless, the emergence of PNPs recruiting migrant workers entering through the TFWP is the first time that immigration decisions are being devolved to provinces to meet their economic needs. This economic motivation is striking considering how previous immigration arrangements like the Cullen-Couture agreement were based on the need for provinces to meet cultural priorities. Since PNPs are managed solely by provincial governments, they exist outside the supervision of federal agencies, making it difficult to regulate PNPs. Different PNPs are governed by different rules on application fees and eligibility and have conflicting requirements regarding temporary labour migration experience, leading to a rise in unethical practices, such as fraud, charges of illegal fees, etc. (Alboim 2009). Moreover, while maintaining provincial autonomy in immigration arguably helps provinces meet their distinct labour needs, the lack of federal-provincial coordination hampers these goals because nominees are not beholden to the provinces that have nominated them and may move away, resulting in continued labour shortages for the provinces (Alboim 2009). Consequently, some provinces have resorted to the temporary solution of expanding their PNPs and the recruitment of temporary labour migrants through the LCP, the SAWP, and TFWP. While the federal government through CIC and HRSDC are currently trying to work closely with "interested" provinces and territories to ensure that temporary labour migration programs promote regional (as opposed to provincial) economic stability and growth, these negotiations are in their initial stages and are not compulsory (CIC 2010d). The absence of coordination between federal agencies and provinces remains a problem, leading provinces to abandon long-term solutions in favour of short-term fixes that negatively affect other provinces.

There are other cases of insufficient coordination between federal and provincial bodies. For example, the issue of migrant protection is a joint responsibility, with each government delegated with certain tasks. The federal government is in charge of enforcing federal labour and employment laws, whereas provincial governments are entrusted with ensuring migrants' well-being and safety by enforcing employment contracts, guaranteeing migrants' health and safety, monitoring migrants' housing, and protecting migrants' rights. In practice, however, it is unclear which bodies should be held accountable for migrant safety. The lack of standardization in provincial policy regarding the safety and well-being of migrant workers exacerbates problems of accountability. Whereas Alberta, Manitoba, Ontario, and Saskatchewan have made an effort to protect migrant workers through the creation of special advisory offices and telephone hotlines for migrant workers and through the passage of special laws,[8] the other provinces have made no such efforts and have instead delegated the responsibility to protect temporary migrants to provincial offices such as provincial work and safety boards. As a result, temporary labour migrants in provinces without immediately obvious mechanisms for migrant protection are disadvantaged. In fact, activists report that many migrants who have sought advice for labour problems were rebuffed by both the provincial offices and by HRSDC and CIC, with representatives from each body insisting that their organization was not in charge of migrant well-being (Alberta Federation of Labour 2009). HRSDC (2011, "Enforcing the terms and conditions of the employment contract") even issued a statement disavowing its responsibilities in enforcing the employment contract between employers and migrant workers, claiming that:

> The Government of Canada is not a party to the contract. Human Resources and Skills Development Canada (HRSDC)/Service Canada has no authority to intervene in the employer-employee relationship or to enforce the terms and conditions of employment. It is the responsibility of the employer and worker to familiarize themselves with laws that apply to them and to look after their own interests.

Indeed, although the federal government through HRSDC has made recent attempts to get involved in migrant safety, as exemplified by its recent establishment of a "monitoring initiative" of employers to "show their compliance" (HRSDC 2010b), these attempts are skewed towards the employer and offer very minimal protections to the workers. The discrepancy between the "over-regulation" of migrant workers and the "under-regulation" of temporary labour migration programs (Arat-Koc 2003) gives credence to the charges made by activists that Canada's temporary labour migration programs are mismanaged to the point where ascertaining political accountability for migrant vulnerability is almost impossible (Preibisch 2010; Canadian Council for Refugees 2010; Alboim 2009; Alberta Federation of Labour 2009).

Other Actors

The entrance of "other" actors complicates the management of temporary labour migration programs. In particular, the role of municipalities in temporary labour migration has yet to be determined. They may not have an official role to play in immigration policy yet they are fast becoming an emerging partner in the management of labour migration programs, particularly municipalities in urban areas with high concentrations of migrants. Although municipalities pursue varying approaches to deal with migration issues (Good 2005), they are becoming increasingly involved in the protection of temporary labour migrants. The municipality of Vancouver, for example, surveyed Filipina women who were part of the LCP in order to determine the special services they would require to combat labour abuse and social isolation. This project established a list of best practices which included the creation of "welcome services" and a "buddy system" to help live-in caregivers adjust to Canada (Spigelman 2000). To use another example, the cities of Toronto and Edmonton have special offices on immigration and settlement that offer assistance for newcomers, including temporary labour migrants. They provide recreational opportunities, health services, and adaptation programs, among many initiatives. John C. Reilly from the Office of Diversity and Inclusion in Edmonton admitted that Edmonton's "Settlement and Immigration" policy was similar to Toronto's programs in that both municipalities recognized the need for municipalities to be more involved in integrating migrants as a result of the "limitations" of existing federal and provincial policies (Parliament of Canada 2011). In short, because municipalities are the closest point of contact for migrant workers seeking governmental assistance for housing, health care, protection, etc., municipalities' roles are expanding.

The implications of an expanded role for municipalities in migration policy merits further examination since municipalities—unlike the federal and provincial governments—are forbidden by the constitution from playing a principal role in intergovernmental relations (Turgeon 2009). Put differently, the federal and provincial governments have equal powers but municipal governments remain subordinate to provincial governments (Turgeon 2009). However, the involvement of municipalities in migrants' lives belies this division of power. Since municipalities are more involved in the day-to-day needs of migrant workers than federal and provincial governments, they factually play an important role in migration management. Indeed, municipalities are arguably subverting the power distinctions between the three levels of government that have formally been put into place. As Martina Benz demonstrated in Chapter 4, the global city provides an important context for worker's struggles. In the context of temporary labour migration, it is not entirely unfeasible to imagine that these "global cities" (Sassen 2006), with their own governance structure, more ably caters to migrants' needs. Hence, new power-sharing arrangements that are reflective of these new arrangements need to be conceived.

Employers and businesses are other emerging actors that influence migration policy, including policies over temporary labour migration. Since the LCP, the SAWP, and the TFWP are employer-driven, employers play an integral role in meeting the recruitment goals set by federal and provincial governments. The sponsorship of employers is also necessary for migrant workers seeking permanent residency through the PNP. Furthermore, federal and provincial governments consult businesses when they set migration quotas and establish the list of recommended professions for the recruitment of migrants under the points system. Thus, migration decisions are being devolved onto private employers and private businesses.

The implications of the presence of the private sector as a "fourth" partner in making migration decisions require further scrutiny. Off-loading migration decisions puts a greater amount of power onto the private sector and heightens the potential for employer abuse. Furthermore, employers and businesses may not have Canada's long-term settlement needs in mind when making recommendations. Since applications from temporary and permanent economic migrants are already being processed faster than other applications, enhancements of employers' and businesses' influence over migration decisions would lead economic needs to be prioritized over human considerations. The absence of concrete policies protecting temporary labour migrants resulting from "jurisdictional football" between different levels of governments makes it difficult to protect temporary labour migrants from the actions and decisions of employers and businesses.

CONCLUSION

The Canadian migration system is currently transitioning from prioritizing permanent settlement to endorsing temporary migration. Although the NIEAP was initially established to minimize the purported social harms caused by undesirable low-skilled migrants who have entered the country en masse through the points system, it was never intended to replace permanent migration. Indeed, until the late 1990s, temporary labour migration was a specialized program that enabled the recruitment of live-in caregivers, migrant farm workers, and skilled professionals. The decision to promote the recruitment of low-skilled workers through the TFWP led to an explosion of the number of low-skilled migrant workers entering Canada. Unlike their high-skilled counterparts, these low-skilled migrant workers are subjected to multiple rights restrictions such as prohibitions on mobility and employer transfer. More significantly, low-skilled migrant workers are highly unlikely to be able to apply for permanent residency. Unsurprisingly, the rise in the numbers of low-skilled workers has led to a concurrent rise in reported instances of labour abuse. The lack of accountability in the management of these programs, as exemplified by the difficulties that migrant workers face when trying to seek protection, increases migrants' vulnerability. The absence of standardization in migrant protection results in uneven policies on migrant protection across the country.

Furthermore, the roles of federal, provincial, and municipal governments are undergoing a transition. Whereas the responsibility for immigration has historically rested on the federal government, changes in migration policy have led to a diminution of the federal government's role, as exemplified by the growing prominence of the PNP. This has also led to the concurrent increase in the role of provincial and municipal governments and businesses.

While ensuring greater federal-provincial cooperation in the management of temporary labour migration programs is crucial, allowing municipalities to be a "third" partner in decision-making is also important. Municipalities are increasingly assuming an enhanced role in integration and settlement issues. Not only are municipalities more accessible to temporary labour migrants, they are also more responsive when addressing temporary labour migrants' specific needs. Indeed, activists working on behalf of temporary labour migrants work closely with municipalities to promote specific campaigns; activists I have interviewed, for example, have liaised closely with municipal health bodies to promote heath awareness among temporary labour migrants. Forming formal relationships between all three levels of government should therefore be encouraged. Specifically, collaborative arrangements between federal, provincial, and municipal governments such as the City-Wide Local Immigration Partnership between the federal and Ontario governments and the City of Toronto enable greater responsiveness for migrants' specific needs and should be widely implemented. Municipalities are already a principal actor in promoting migrants' settlement and integration needs. They should now be considered alongside federal and provincial governments when setting immigration policy. When it comes to establishing clear and concrete programs that effectively respond to the needs of temporary labour migrants and that address the policy gaps created by overlapping federal and provincial jurisdictions, municipalities are at the forefront.

ENDNOTES

1. It should be noted that there are clear linkages between economic and racial "undesirability." Immigration officials assessed potential immigrants' "job qualifications" on the basis of racial and national stereotypes. Thus, Sedef Arat-Koç (2003) documents how British and Irish women working as caregivers were seen by immigration officials as "nursemaids," and were therefore deemed eligible to enter the country as permanent residents, whereas women from developing countries working in the same field were seen as "nannies," and were rendered ineligible for permanent entry.
2. Joseph Carens (2003, 2008) provides sound criteria for determining the legitimacy of migrants' claims for inclusion.
3. British Columbia, Alberta, Saskatchewan, Manitoba, Ontario, Quebec, New Brunswick, Nova Scotia, and Prince Edward Island are part of the SAWP (HRSDC 2009a).
4. To be specific, migrants would have to be from Mexico, Anguilla, Antigua and Barbuda, Barbados, Dominica, Grenada, Jamaica, Montserrat, St. Kitts and Nevis, St. Lucia, St. Vincent, and Trinidad and Tobago (HRSDC 2009a).
5. Prioritizing people entering through the CEC leads to delays for applicants under other migration streams, such as "family" class migrants.
6. Even though migrant workers' designation as "low-skilled" is in no way indicative of their actual education or income levels in their home countries.
7. CIC also sets targets for the numbers of migrants who are allowed to enter Canada for humanitarian reasons.
8. Examples of these include Manitoba's New Worker Recruitment and Protection Act and Ontario's Employment Protection for Foreign Nationals Act.

REFERENCES

Alberta Federation of Labour. 2009. *Entrenching Exploitation: The Second Report of the Alberta Federation of Labour Temporary Foreign Worker Advocate*. Edmonton, AB: Alberta Federation of Labour

Alboim, N. 2009. *Adjusting the Balance: Fixing Canada's Economic Immigration Policies*. Toronto: Maytree Foundation.

Arat-Koç, S. 2003. "Good Enough to Work but not Good Enough to Stay: Foreign Domestic Workers and the Law." In *Locating Law: Race, Class, Gender Connections*, edited by E. Comack, 125–152. Halifax: Fernwood Publishing.

Basok, T. 2002. *Tortillas and Tomatoes: Transmigrant Mexican Harvesters in Canada*. Montreal and Kingston: McGill-Queens University Press.

Binford, L. 2006. "Seasonal Agricultural Workers Program and Mexian Development." *Focal Policy Paper*. Accessed August 4, 2011. www.focal.ca/pdf/migration_Binford_seasonal%20agricultural%20workers%20program%20Mexican%20development_August%202006_FPP-06-07.pdf.

Canadian Council for Refugees (CCR). 2010. "From Permanent to Temporary Migration: Canada's Dramatic Shift." Montreal and Quebec: Canadian Council for Refugees.

Carens, J. 2003. "Who Should Get In: the Ethics of Immigration Admissions." *Ethics and International Affairs* 33 (4): 1082–1097.

———. 2008. "Live-in Domestics, Seasonal Agricultural Workers, and Others Hard to Locate on the Map of Democracy." *Journal of Political Philosophy* 16 (4): 414–445.

Citizenship and Immigration Canada (CIC). 2009a. "Facts and Figures 2009 – Immigration Overview: Permanent and Temporary Residents." Accessed August 4, 2011. www.cic.gc.ca/english/resources/statistics/facts2009/temporary/02.asp.

———. 2009b. "Facts and Figures 2009 – Immigration Overview: Permanent and Temporary Residents." Accessed August 4, 2011. www.cic.gc.ca/english/resources/statistics/facts2009/permanent/02.asp.

———. 2009c. "Low Skill Pilot Project." Accessed August 4, 2011. www.cic.gc.ca/english/work/low-skill.asp.

———. 2009d. "Facts and Figures 2008: Immigration Overview, Permanent and Temporary Residents." Accessed August 4, 2011. www.cic.gc.ca/english/resources/statistics/facts2008/temporary/08.asp.

———. 2009e. "Total Entries of Foreign Workers by Gender and Occupational Skill Level." Accessed August 4, 2011. www.cic.gc.ca/english/resources/statistics/facts2008/temporary/07.asp.

———. 2010a. "Canadian Experience Class." Accessed August 4, 2011. www.cic.gc.ca/english/immigrate/cec/index.asp.

———. 2010b. "Provincial Nominee Program." Accessed August 4, 2011. www.cic.gc.ca/english/immigrate/provincial/apply-who.asp.

———. 2010c. "Citizenship and Immigration Canada: What We Do." Accessed August 4, 2011. www.cic.gc.ca/english/department/what.asp.

———. 2010d. "Strategic Outcomes and Program Activity Architecture: Temporary Resident Program." Accessed August 4, 2011. www.cic.gc.ca/english/department/paa/activity-02.asp.

Daenzar, P. 1997. "An Affair between Nations: International Relations and the Movement of Household Service Workers." In *Not One of the Family: Foreign Domestic Workers in Canada*, edited by A. Bakan and D. Stasiulis. Toronto, ON: University of Toronto Press.

Diocson, C. 2003. "Organizing and Mobilizing Filipino Migrant Women in Canada." Asian Pacific Research Network. Accessed August 4, 2011. www.aprnet.org/conferences-a-workshop/97-impact-of-globalization-on-women-labor/163-organizing-and-mobilizing-filipino-migrant-women-in-canada.

Domingo, A. (Producer). 2006. *Foreign Domestics: The Right to Stay.* [DVD] Toronto, ON: Omni TV Films.

Elgersma, S. 2007. *Temporary Foreign Workers.* Ottawa: Canada Library of Parliament – Social and Political Affairs Division.

England, K., and B. Stiell. 2008. "They Think You're as Stupid as Your English Is: Constructing Domestic Workers in Toronto." In *Feminisms in Geography: Rethinking Space, Places, and Knowledges*, edited by P. Moss and K. Lanham Falconer Al-Hindi. MD: Rowman & Littlefield Publishers, Inc.

Good, K. 2005. "Patterns of Politics in Canada's Immigrant-Receiving Cities and Suburbs: How Immigrant Settlement Patterns Shape the Municipal Role in Multiculturalism Policy." *Policy Studies* 26 (3–4): 262–289.

Hennebry, J. 2010. "Who Has their Eye on the Ball? Jurisdictional Football and Canada's Temporary Foreign Worker Program." *Policy Options* 63: 62–68.

Hennebry, J., and K. Preibisch. 2010. "A Model for Managed Migration? Re-examining Best Practices in Canada's Seasonal Agricultural Worker Program." *International Migration* 49. doi:10.1111/j.1468-2435.2009.00598.x.

Henry, A. 1998. *Taking Back Control: African Canadian Women Teachers' Lives and Practices*. Albany, New York: State University of New York Press.

Human Resources and Skills Development Canada (HRSDC). 2009a. "Temporary Foreign Worker Program Agreement for the Employment in Canada of Seasonal Agricultural Workers." Temporary Foreign Workers in Canada. No longer available online.

———. 2009b. "Temporary Foreign Worker Program." Temporary Foreign Workers in Canada. Accessed August 4, 2011. www.hrsdc.gc.ca/eng/workplaceskills/foreign_workers/sawp.shtml.

———. 2010a. "Temporary Foreign Worker Program Labour Market Opinions and Statistics." Temporary Foreign Worker Program. Accessed March 31, 2010. www.hrsdc.gc.ca/eng/workplaceskills/foreign_workers/stats/annual/table10a.shtml

———. 2010b. "Temporary Foreign Program: Monitoring Initiative Fact Sheet." No longer available online.

———.2011. "Instruction Sheet to Accompany Employment Contract." Temporary Foreign Worker Program. Accessed February 28, 2011. www.hrsdc.gc.ca/eng/workplaceskills/foreign_workers/contracts-forms/annex2.shtml.

Jacubowski, L. M. 2003. "Managing Canadian Immigration: Racism, Ethnicity Selectivity, and the Law." In *Locating Law: Race, Class, Gender Connections*, edited by E. Comack, 98–123. Halifax: Fernwood Publishing.

Kelley, N., and M. Trebilcock. 1998. *The Making of the Mosaic: A History of Canadian Immigration Policy*. Toronto: University of Toronto Press.

Kenney, J. 2009. "Speaking Notes for the Honourable Jason Kenney, PC MP, Minister of Citizenship, Immigration, and Multiculturalism." Immigration to Canada. No longer available online.

Khan, S. 2009. "From Labour of Love to Decent Work: Protecting the Human Rights of Caregivers in Canada." *Canadian Journal of Law and Society* 24 (1): 23–44.

Macklin, A. 1992. "Foreign Domestic Workers: Surrogate Wives or Mail Order Servant?" *McGill Law Journal* 37: 681–760.

Parliament of Canada. 2011. "Proceedings of the Standard Senate Committee on Social Affairs, Science, and Technology." Accessed February 9, 2011. www.parl.gc.ca/Content/SEN/Committee/403/soci/19eva-e.htm?comm_id=47&Language=E&Parl=40&Ses=3.

Pratt, G. 2007. "Seeing Beyond the State: Towards Transnational Feminist Organizing." In *Critical Transnational Feminist Praxis*, edited by A. Swarr and R. Nagar. Albany, NY: SUNY Press.

Preibisch K., and L. Binford. 2007. "Interrogating Racialized Global Labour Supply: An Exploration of the Racial/National Replaceme of Foreign Agricultural Workers in Canada." *Canadian Review of Sociology* 44(1): 5–36.

Preibisch, K., and L. M. Hermoso Santamaria. 2006. "Engendering Labour Migration: The Case of Foreign Workers in Canadian Agriculture." In *Women, Migration and Citizenship: Making Local, National, and Transnational Connections*, edited by E. Tastsoglou and A. Dobrowolsky. Burlington, VT: Ashgate.

Ramirez, J. 1982. "Domestic Workers Organize!" *Canadian Women's Studies* 4 (2): 89–91.

Reitz, J. 2004. "Canada: Immigration and Nation-Building in a Transition Economy." In *Controlling Immigration: A Global Perspective*, edited by W. Cornelius, J. F. Hollifield, and P. L. Martin. 97–133. Stanford: Stanford University Press.

Sassen, S. 2006. *Territory, Authority, Rights: From Medieval to Global Assemblages*. Princeton: Princeton University Press.

Satzewich, V. 1991. *Racism and the Incorporation of Foreign Migrant Labour: Farm Labour Migration to Canada since 1945*. New York, NY: Routledge.

Sharma, N. 2006. *Home Economics: Nationalism and the Making of Migrant Workers in Canada*. Toronto: University of Toronto Press.

Spigelman, M. 2000. "Building Community: A Framework of Services for the Filipino Community in the Lower Mainland Region of British Columbia." Martin Spigelman Research Associates. Accessed August 4, 2011. vancouver.ca/commsvcs/socialplanning/initiatives/multicult/PDF/ReportFilipino.pdf.

Suen, R. 2000. "You Sure Know How to Pick 'Em: Human Rights and Migrant Farm Workers in Canada." *Georgetown Immigration Law Journal* 15: 199–227.

Turgeon, L. 2009. "Cities within the Canadian System." In *Contemporary Canadian Federalism: Foundations, Traditions, Institutions*, edited by A. G. Gagnon. Toronto: University of Toronto Press.

Valiani, S. 2009. "The Shift in Canadian Immigration Policy and Unheeded Lessons of the Live-in Caregiver Program." *MRZine*. Accessed July 10, 2010. mrzine.monthlyreview.org/2009/valiani030309.html.

Weston, A., and L. Scarpa de Masellis. 2003. *Hemispheric Integration and Trade Relations: Implications for Canada's Seasonal Agricultural Workers Program – Executive Summary*. Ottawa: North-South Institute.

Chapter 6

ARTICULATING THE SELF TO THE ENGINEERING MARKET: CHINESE IMMIGRANTS' EXPERIENCES FROM A CRITICAL TRANSFORMATIVE LEARNING PERSPECTIVE

HONGXIA SHAN

INTRODUCTION

To sustain economic and population growth, Canada has adopted the point system to attract internationally trained professionals and skilled workers. Currently, skilled immigrants, most of whom come from non-European immigrant source countries such as China and India, constitute more than 50 percent of all immigration to Canada (CIC 2007). Despite their educational and professional backgrounds that enabled them to immigrate to Canada, many of the skilled immigrants have encountered problems locating jobs in their trained professions.

The disjuncture between the promises and perils of immigration has prompted researchers to explore the barriers immigrants face in the labour market. Some studies have suggested that immigrants are prevented from succeeding economically in Canada because they lack in English proficiency (Boyd 1990), "Canadian economy usable" literacy (Ferrer, Green, and Riddell 2004), and cultural and social capitals (Bauder 2005; Fagnan 1995). Other studies have also directed critiques towards structural issues such as devaluation of immigrants' credentials (e.g., Ferrer and Riddell 2004; Galarneau and Morissette 2008), demand for Canadian work experience (e.g., Slade 2003), arcane and exclusive licensure practices (Girard and Bauder 2007), and institutionalized racism and sexism entrenched in the host society (e.g., Ng 1988; Man 2004).

Compared with the attention researchers paid to the barriers immigrants face in Canada, relatively few studies have addressed how immigrants make their entrance to the labour market despite these barriers. The existent studies that look at immigrants' labour market navigation experiences often focus on immigrants' general job search strategies. For instance, some immigrants are found to be using ethnic ties and holding different job preferences within and outside ethnic economies (Sanders, Nee, and Sernau 2002; Frijters, Shields, and Price 2005). Skilled immigrants may do more volunteer work than Canadian born persons, although volunteer work does not always lead to paid jobs (Slade and Schugurensky 2005; Slade, Luo, and Schugurensky 2005). Compared with the Canadian-born and earlier immigrant cohorts, recent immigrants are more likely to "attend schools," and pursue re-certification, retraining, and further education to improve their employment prospects (Ng et al. 2006; Shan 2009). Indeed, post-secondary education obtained in Canada is particularly effective in enhancing adult immigrants' labour market position (e.g., Adamuti-Trache and Sweet 2010; Li 2001). While there is sufficient understanding of the general routes through which immigrants may optimize their employment opportunities, there is still a lack of understanding of how immigrants, with their particular personal and professional history and cultural backgrounds, make personal changes while establishing themselves in specific professional fields.

In this chapter, I fill in this void of the literature by examining the experiences of 14 Chinese immigrant engineers from an integrative transformative learning perspective. In the following section, I introduce the integrative transformative perspective. Then I discuss the research methods. Thereafter, I present the results demonstrating how immigrant research respondents managed their job search processes and discuss the gender, race, and class relations that constitute immigrants' learning experiences. To conclude the paper, I recap the research findings and propose future research directions.

THE INTEGRATIVE PERSPECTIVE OF TRANSFORMATIVE LEARNING

Transformative learning, first proposed by Jack Mezirow (1978), deals with learning that takes place when people make transitions in life. According to Mezirow, transformative learning is "the social process of construing and appropriating a new or revised interpretation of the meaning of one's experiences as a guide to action" (Mezirow 1994, 222–223). People are meaning-seeking beings (Jarvis 1986). Mezirow states that a person's meaning perspective is acquired often uncritically in the course of childhood through socialization and acculturation. However, people are capable of reflection and developing an enhanced level of awareness of beliefs and feelings. Acquired perspective or meaning schemes may undergo transformation when a person encounters a disorienting dilemma or a radically different and incongruent experience that cannot be assimilated into the existing meaning structure. As part of transformative learning, a person may engage in critical reflection, explore different roles and options, plan a new course of action, assume new roles, and negotiate and renegotiate relationships (Mezirow 1991).

The understanding of transformative learning has come a long way since the publication in 1978 of Mezirow's pioneering study of women returning to community colleges (e.g., Mezirow 2006, 2000; Taylor 1997). Most notably, Daniel Schugurensky (2002) has posited that transformative learning should incorporate more systematically the influence of context. In the same vein, Edmund O'Sullivan (2003) has proposed an integrative perspective of transformative learning where learning is perceived to be a holistic process involving the self and the world. He says:

> Transformative learning involves experiencing a deep, structural shift in the basic premises of thought, feeling and actions. It is a shift of consciousness that dramatically and permanently alters our way of being in the world. Such a shift involves our understanding of ourselves and our self-locations; our relationships with other humans and with the natural world, our understanding of relations of power in interlocking structures of class, race and gender. (O'Sullivan 2003, 326)

In this chapter, I focus on immigrants' transformative learning experiences which involve perspective and perception changes, while giving special attention to the social and power relations of gender, race, and class that shape these experiences.

RESEARCH DESIGN, METHODS, AND RESPONDENTS

The data of the chapter come from the first phase of a two-phase study that examined Chinese immigrants' learning experiences in the engineering profession. Engineering is a major field of training for immigrants who have come to Canada in the recent years (Lemay 2007). While foreign-born engineers are less likely than their Canadian counterparts to be hired in this profession (Boyd 1990; Boyd and Thomas 2001; 2002), foreign-born Chinese are still more than twice as likely as the local Canadians to work in sciences and engineering fields (Chui, Tran, and Flanders 2005). Given this particular picture and trend, Chinese immigrants' experiences in negotiating occupational niches will provide insights into the mutually constitutive property of individual practices and the organizational complexity of the Canadian labour market.

The field research was conducted in Edmonton, Alberta, and Toronto, Ontario. Toronto ranks first and Edmonton fifth as popular destinations for Chinese immigrants (Chui, Tran, and Flanders 2005). Both cities have high concentrations of registered engineers in the disciplines of civil, electrical, mechanical, and chemical engineering (Ekos Research Associates Inc. 2003). In the first phase of the study, I conducted 14 life history style interviews (Cole and Knowles 2001; Plummer 2001) with Chinese immigrant engineers who had worked in the traditional engineering fields of civil, mechanical, chemical, and electrical engineering in both China and

Canada. These respondents were reached through word of mouth, and through posting on popular Chinese websites in Canada. Seven respondents were in Edmonton (two women, four men), and seven in Toronto (three women, four men). At the time of the interviews, the respondents had stayed in Canada less than 10 years. Ten respondents were between 30 and 40 years of age, and 4 between 41 and 50. Thirteen respondents were married and 12 of them had at least 1 child. Eight respondents had a spouse who also had engineering backgrounds. Before immigrating to Canada, one respondent held a doctoral degree; seven had at least one master's degree; the remaining six had a bachelor degree.

Interviews with immigrants averaged three hours. They focused on respondents' life and work experiences after they graduated in China, with particular emphasis on their transitional moments and struggles, as well as their shifting perceptions when they tried to integrate into the engineering workforce in Canada. During the interviews, I tried to understand how immigrants "experience[d] their present in light of their past personal biography and their subjectively projected future" (Olssen 2006, 44). All interviews were transcribed verbatim in the language in which they were taken, Chinese and/or English, and sent back to respondents for "validity check" (Plummer 2001, 157), unless the respondents indicated that they did not wish to read the transcripts. To analyze immigrants' stories, I looked for common themes, focusing not only on respondents' conscious self-presentation, but also the larger social relations shaping and transforming their subjectivities and changing practices (Olssen 2006; Cole and Knowles 2001).

IMMIGRANTS' PERSPECTIVE AND PRACTICE CHANGES IN PROFESSIONAL PURSUIT

It took the participants between 1 and 24 months to get their first engineering jobs in Canada. To optimize their job opportunities in the engineering field, they undertook a range of strategies, such as going through training programs, returning to schools, applying for professional engineer licences, using immigrant training services, and making friends mostly within, and sometimes outside of, the Chinese immigrant community. In this chapter, I focus only on their strategies related to perspective and practice changes. These are: marketing the self, professional repositioning, and becoming mobile workers.

Learning to Market the Self

One of the strategies that all immigrant respondents found important is self-marketing. Coming from a socialist market economy, few of the immigrants had experience looking for jobs in a "free" capitalist market economy. China used to practice state posting for university graduate students, and workers' labour market mobility was restricted by the residential registration system (Knight and Song,1995; Li and Zax 2007). It was not until the end of the 1980s that China adopted a new policy: "Job Assignments for Graduate Students from Higher Education." This policy encouraged employers to make merit-based recruitment decisions and enabled students in many disciplines to freely look for jobs. Despite this policy, at the time when most of the respondents graduated, state planning was yet to completely give way to market regulation (Knight and Song 1995). Thirteen of the respondents were posted to their first engineering job with state-owned workplaces. Most of them stayed with their first workplace until emigration; only two respondents moved on to work in foreign ventures, and one resigned from his job to open his own business prior to immigration.

A disorienting dilemma (Mezirow 1991) for almost all respondents was that as much as they believed in themselves as competent engineering practitioners, they were having a hard time bringing the message across to employers. There was a clear process for them to learn the ropes of job search in Canada. For example, a colleague from the United States sensitized Dong,[1] an HVAC engineer in Toronto, to the idea that labour in Canada is a commodity. He said:

> I have an [American colleague] in China [from an international program]. He [gave me some advice about life in Canada]: "When you are looking for a job, you are a commodity. You need to sell this commodity. Everyone is a commodity. When you look for jobs, you are selling yourself. You should see how much money you are worth. If you are worth much, you do not have to sell yourself short." (personal interview)

In his examination of the labour market strategies of immigrants from South Asia and Yugoslavia, Harald Bauder (2005) finds that immigrants' cultural habitus, or long-lasting dispositions formed in a particular social context, may contradict Canadian labour market conventions. My study further points out that in the face of conflicting practice and beliefs, immigrants' meaning schemes may undergo transformation so that they fit into new ways to conduct themselves. For instance, immigrants in the study started to learn that the labour market is regulated by the logic of market exchange when they had to translate their work experiences into a marketable resumé. Some of the interviewees initially assumed that a resumé meant a brief written account of their educational and professional qualifications and experiences. Over time, they came to see a resumé as a document produced for the consumption of employers and started using resumés to speak to the skill expectations of employers. For example, Fan, a mechanical engineer by training, explained how he changed his job search practices in Toronto:

> Initially, I put in my resumé what I was good at. I did not try to match myself with what was written in job ads. They did not even give me an

interview opportunity. Later, I tried to align myself with what is required in the job ads. I put exactly the kind of skills that they required [in the job ads]. But of course, you should not lie. What you should do is to put down what you have that can match the job. Actually if you do not study their job descriptions, and you present who you are, experts could still tell that both resumés are the same although the presentations are different. However, if they do not pay close attention, they would dismiss those experiences as irrelevant. (personal interview)

While initially Fan presented who he was, and how he could be useful, he later learned to bracket certain aspects of the self and shape himself into a "product" demanded by employers.

One barrier that almost all immigrants reported that obstructs their smooth transition into the Canadian labour market was language and communication. Only one respondent expressed that he had no problem with English communication; one other believed that his English was "perfectly functional" at work. All others indicated that their English was "not great," "not really good," "less than satisfactory," "poor," or "extremely poor." Meanwhile, they also suggested that communication is not solely about English facility, but more about getting across their technological strengths and potential for productivity. Fu, a civil engineer in the oil industry, for instance, had 10 failed interviews in Alberta before he finally "sold" his offshore structural backgrounds to the first structural engineer who interviewed him (all other interviewers were human resources recruiters). Gu, a female HVAC engineer in Toronto, had a unique experience in an interview; instead of a person-to-person conversation, she was asked to perform an AutoCAD test. Eddy, a civil engineer said that when he went for an interview, he did not even know how to respond to, "How are you." However, he was able to communicate with the interviewer over the design of a project in "broken English" and "with the assistance of a pen." For the respondents, it was not because they had good English skills that they were offered an engineering job; it was because they could "do the job." In other words, they were hired because they were able to convince the employers that they would perform.

Professional Repositioning

To speak to employers' labour and productive needs may involve changing to a different field in which labour demand exists. For instance, some respondents changed from offshore structure design to onshore structure design, some from industrial automation to chemical engineering, and some from wastewater treatment to cosmetic lab work. Professional repositioning may also involve immigrants downplaying their employment goals. In this study, 13 participants started their engineering careers in Canada at a lower level than their last positions prior to immigration. The majority of them got their first engineering jobs as draftspersons, technicians, or designers.

Immigrants' professional repositioning practices were based on their perception of labour needs in specific fields. Through the introduction of a Chinese friend, Fan found his first job, for which he deduced engineering formulas for computer programmers. However, he could not stand the owner of the company and tried to change jobs. Interestingly, he did not intend to change back to mechanical engineering, his field of training in China. Instead, he started to switch to structural design through attending a training program at a private school in Toronto.

> Actually I am not very interested in structural work, not in residential structural work. I am always interested in heavy mechanical engineering, as I studied mechanical engineering at school. I studied things about cranes. So when I chose to do my postgraduate program [in China], I chose hydro-power.... The major reason for me to study structural [in Toronto] was that I did not want to stay with the previous company anymore. As long as I could find a place and leave that company, I would be fine. I could not find any other channels.... [R]esidential structure had a bigger market. There are a lot of job ads for structural engineers. (personal interview)

Respondents learned about their job prospects in ad hoc ways: from a training program, through reading newspapers (in both English and Chinese) and studying job advertisements, and from acquaintances and friends. Eddy in Toronto remarked that he studied job advertisements to identify what technical backgrounds he needed to get into his field of practice.

> When I decided to look for an engineering job, I looked at the job section [of the *Toronto Star*] more carefully. I also went on some job search engines ... in the job ads, I found that [many engineering companies] needed AutoCAD 2000, and Microstation for example.... I made a few Chinese friends [here], who have engineering backgrounds as well. I invited them over to my house for beer. One of them gave me a few tips about AutoCAD. (personal interview)

Gu looked at job advertisements to identify job niches in which she might have a better chance.

> At that time, I was applying for CAD drafter. At that time, they were looking for CAD drafters.... In China, [we do not have distinction between engineers and drafters].... We have only engineers [doing all jobs]....Here, [my husband and I] sometimes went online to look at other people's resumés. We also looked at job advertisement and information. We saw that they had designers and drafters. We

thought that drafter positions are lower. As we were new, we thought those would be easier for us. (personal interview)

In this case, Gu tried to align herself with the skill and labour demand of employers through downplaying her job expectation. A drafter is not expected to design or conduct calculation work. The job of a drafter is to computerize the blueprint and the design work of engineers. In China, there was no corresponding position. Yet, just because this position required little of her expertise, Gu decided that she had a better chance with it.

Becoming Mobile Workers at the Beck and Call of Capital

Some of the respondents, particularly those in Edmonton, pointed out that being at the right "place" and "time" was a crucial condition for people to get jobs. Five of the Toronto respondents chose Toronto as their landing city; only one of the Edmonton respondents chose to land in Edmonton. One respondent relocated to Edmonton for postgraduate studies; five relocated for job-related reasons.

Dong was a senior mechanical engineer in a big oil field in China. He initially landed in Vancouver in 2001. A year later, he moved to Alberta in search of a job. This relocation decision came about after carefully processing a mix of information. When he first landed in Vancouver, he was constantly told by his fellow Chinese that it was impossible for newcomers to find professional jobs. However, Dong did not give up his search and began looking for a job in Alberta after a few encounters with employers.

> When I first landed in Vancouver, I did not know much really. After a year, I found out that it was very hard for *people like us* to find jobs in Vancouver.... I went to see a few managers in engineering companies. I thought that if it was possible, I should go back to designing work. I talked with these managers ... and got to know that there had been people leaving Vancouver and that a lot of people had been laid off [in Vancouver] and gone to Alberta. I was not familiar with Alberta at that time either ... [but] I thought to myself that I was not going to work at [a] labour job all my life. (personal interview; author's emphasis)

Dong believed that as one of the "others," he needed to avoid competing in a market where local engineers were having problems getting jobs. He subsequently moved to Alberta.

To compete in the labour market, many of the respondents were compelled to be mobile at the beck and call of capital. In an email communication, which I conducted after the interview, George offered some updated information of himself:

> [Y]ou must [have heard] about the [additional] 20 percent oil royalty [proposal]. [My company] had a few projects suspended, but [it already] hired additional hands for those project[s]. I heard that they would lay off people. As a contract worker, I will be among the first [to leave]. I am looking for jobs again and I might take up a job in Saskatoon. (personal communication)

George and other interviewees in Edmonton were concerned about the possibility that the oil economy in Alberta might sharply decline. At the time when we communicated over email, some oil companies slashed or threatened to cut back their investment in Alberta because of proposed royalty hikes by the provincial government. Respondents conveyed a sense of insecurity they felt in a volatile capitalist market where they occupied a secondary status.

CONSTITUTING IMMIGRANTS' LEARNING AND CHANGE: GENDER, RACE, AND CLASS RELATIONS

While the immigrant respondents became market-driven and entrepreneurial in their career pursuits, they also internalized a secondary labour status and downplayed their professional aspirations, at least in the initial period after immigration. This contradictory learning phenomenon is, the study further shows, embedded in what Bauder (2006) would call processes of social distinction, cultural judgement, and a wider neo-liberal project to render migrants a subordinate labour pool in the host society. The processes shaping immigrants' learning experiences, I argue, are not solely a cultural and economic phenomenon. They are also gendered and racializing processes.

Clearly, immigrants' perspective changes took place as they moved from one social, cultural, and economic context to another. When they refashioned their job search practices, they were experimenting with re-articulating themselves, and "feeling" their ways to fit in with the exchange relations of a post-industrial capitalist society. In this process, they learned to change from presenting what they can do and who they are, or in Marxist language, what their use value is, to communicating what employers look for, or what their exchange value is.

At the core of immigrants' changing practices is what some respondents called a "cultural shift." Eddy, for example, described a typical cultural shift that the immigrant respondents made.

> My experience [working in Canada] is that if you want to move up and get your hands on more responsibilities, as an immigrant, you need to *zi wo biao xian* [volunteer or promote yourself, and demonstrate or showcase your value]. [Employers] would not automatically trust you. You could

> be a big name in China. Here you are nothing but an immigrant. [Your employers] do not know you. You have to make it possible for them to know what you can do. *Zi wo biao xian*. That is absolutely a taboo in China. In China, people would consider you *zi wo peng zhang* [conceited]. You need to be all humble in front of all your people [in China], be they your higher-ups or subordinates. Here, without *zi wo biao xian*, you never expect people to even spot you. (personal interview)

What Eddy related here was a shift from a collective Chinese culture to an individualistic Western culture, and specifically to a macho and competitive engineering culture in North America. As part of the shift, the immigrants were made to see the differential social and market values attributed to different "cultural" practices. For instance, many of them indicated that they were not appreciated as who they were especially at the beginning of their jobs because they were too "humble" and not good at "claiming credits." Some of them were compelled to manage their cultural beliefs or cultural habitus, and to take on local mannerisms, by becoming more assertive or "aggressive" in marketing and presenting the self.

While they managed their ways of presentation and interactions, I argue, they also participated in a racializing process where a hierarchical order is attributed to different cultures. For instance, George explained the difficulty he had while trying to fit in this way:

> The biggest barrier is language. The second biggest barrier is culture. Certain things are ... difficult ... to change. The Chineseness is in your blood.... We are not brought up to be belligerent. We do not criticize easily ... [S]ome of us do not take criticism well as a result. Because of all that, you do not see many Chinese ... in leadership positions. We do not appear as assertive as the local white.... The Eastern Europeans are more than assertive; they are aggressive. They do much better than the Chinese [in terms of making it to the management positions].... I have also known some Indians and South Asians. They speak better English than the Chinese. Many of them do on-site inspection. Some ... also made it to management positions.... [Presumably] they knew how to deal with the English-speaking people. But I also witnessed some rubbing the boss the wrong way. (personal interview)

Of note, while immigrants negotiated their positions in the engineering profession, they also positioned themselves culturally in relation to other ethnic groups. While doing so, they are also implicated in a racialization process through which culture and cultural habitus of different ethnic groups are classified, essentialized, and accorded with differential values, with highest value attributed to the kind of "assertiveness" practiced by the local "white" people. Most interestingly, cultural proximity to the local "white" people is used to naturalize the hierarchical locations of different ethnic groups in the engineering profession.

Immigrants' marketing endeavours should not be considered solely an individual practice. Often, it is a familial strategy. Eight respondents had a spouse with engineering background. Typically, it is often the husband who went out to learn, for example, English and job search strategies, while the wives took up service jobs to sustain the family. In one case where the husband did a factory job to support his wife's re-schooling, he said that it was because he "[was] a man" and he had the "responsibility to protect the woman" from labour-intensive work.

When asked why the husband was the first person to focus on obtaining a professional job, a few respondents reported that the husbands' English was better than the wives'. That the women were not confident with their English communication may reflect the differential professional exposure and training men and women engineers had prior to immigration. Among the five women respondents, only one participated in company-sponsored English training in China. In contrast, four male interviewees were sent by their companies to work and study in the United States and in Canada for at least one month and up to a year. Dong remarked that he had a training opportunity abroad but "gave" it to his wife, because he had "way more opportunities."

The uneven gendered dynamic that comes with men and women engineers' career opportunities in China is further reinforced during the immigration process. Further, my study suggests that women engineers may also be double-burdened with both career pursuit and household responsibilities. When asked how the couples managed their household work, no female respondent complained about their other half. In fact, all remarked that the spouses "helped out". Presumably, women still play a greater role within the household, which may have put them at a further disadvantage in their job search process.

CONCLUSION AND FUTURE RESEARCH

In Chapter 7, Aparna Sundar will discuss how the taxi industry was restructured to manage immigrant workers in the metropolitan city of Toronto. In this chapter, I focused on how immigrants governed themselves in their job search process from an integrative transformative learning perspective. The results show that to optimize their job opportunities in the engineering profession, the immigrants refashioned their personal perspectives and practices. The experiences of the 14 Chinese immigrant engineers should not be generalized to the entire Chinese immigrant population in Canada. Nor should they be considered practices particular to the Chinese. These immigrants' reflective and deliberate job search efforts, however, point to a host of social and power relations, which converge to produce secondary labour out of people who speak and conduct themselves differently from the "mainstream" society.

The uneven relations of power help us understand the structural vulnerability of immigrant labour, as well as the susceptibility of their cultural practices to dismissal, or as something to be "managed."

The study suggests that to succeed in the labour market, immigrants need to take on Canadian mannerisms and to cast off their cultural differences as much as possible. In other words, their job search process serves as a hegemonic procedure to homogenize the conduct of the immigrant labour force. While transformative learning theorists such as O'Sullivin (2003) suggest that perspective shifts are transformative and lasting, this may not be the case for the immigrants. As cultural habitus are long-lasting dispositions formed in a particular social and historical context, adult immigrants may as well be drawing on different repertoires of cultural knowledge in different circumstances. The study does not offer conclusions on whether immigrants' perspective changes during their job search are permanent or performative, and how that would affect their long-term workplace and social integration process. Given that my qualitative study captures only a few immigrants' experiences during the first few years in Canada, I cannot offer an answer to this question. More qualitative studies are needed to understand the roles that "culture shift" and "cultural negotiation" play in shaping immigrants' work and life world in the long term.

ENDNOTES

1. All names used are pseudonyms to protect the identity of the research participants. Both English and Chinese names are used as pseudonyms to reflect the mixed name preferences of the research participants.

ACKNOWLEDGEMENTS

I acknowledge the intellectual guidance that Roxana Ng, Kiran Mirchandani, and Nancy Jackson provided for my dissertation work, on which this chapter is based. I also want to thank Harald Bauder and other reviewers for their critical feedbacks on this chapter.

REFERENCES

Adamuti-Trache, M., and R. Sweet. 2010. "Adult Immigrants' Participation in Canadian Education and Training." *Canadian Journal for the Study of Adult Education* 22 (2): 1–26.

Bauder, H. 2005. "Habitus, Rules of the Labour Market and Employment Strategies of Immigrants in Vancouver, Canada." *Social and Cultural Geography* 6 (1): 81–97.

———. 2006. *Labor Movement: How Migration Regulates Labor Markets.* New York: Oxford University Press.

Boyd, M. 1990. "Immigrant Women: Language, Socioeconomic Inequalities, and Policy Issues." In *Ethnic Demography: Canadian Immigrant, Racial, and Cultural Variations* edited by S. S. Halli, F. Trovato, and L. Driedger, 275–296. Ottawa: Carleton University Press.

Boyd, M., and D. Thomas. 2001. "Match or Mismatch? The Labour Market Performances of Foreign-born Engineers." *Population Research and Policy Review* 20: 107–133.

——. 2002. "Skilled Immigrant Labour: Country of Origin and the Occupational Locations of Male Engineers." *Canadian Studies in Population* 29 (1): 71–99.

Chui, T., K. Tran, and J. Flanders. 2005. "Chinese Canadians: Enriching the Cultural Mosaic." *Canadian Social Trends* (Spring): 24–32.

Citizenship and Immigration Canada (CIC). 2007. "Facts and Figures 2007 – Immigration Overview: Permanent and Temporary Residents." No longer available online.

Cole, A. L., and G. J. Knowles. 2001. *Lives in Context: The Art of Life History Research.* Walnut Creek, CA: AltaMira Press.

Ekos Research Associates Inc. 2003. "2002 National Survey of Professional Engineers: Final Report." Submitted to Canadian Council of Professional Engineers. Accessed August 4, 2011. www.engineerscanada.ca/e/files/surveysummary2002.pdf.

Fagnan, S. 1995. "Canadian Immigrant Earnings, 1971–86." In *Diminishing Returns in the Economics of Canada's Recent Immigration Policy*, edited by D. G. DeVoretz, 166–208. Ottawa: Howe Institute.

Ferrer, A., D. A. Green, and W. C. Riddell. 2004. "The Effect of Literacy on Immigrant Earnings." Ottawa: Statistics Canada. Accessed February 10, 2006. dsp-psd.pwgsc.gc.ca/Collection/CS89-552-12E.pdf.

Ferrer, A., and C. Riddell. 2004. "Education, Credentials and Immigrant Earnings." Department of Economics, University of British Columbia. Accessed January 21, 2008. econ.ucalgary.ca/fac-files/af/anapaper.pdf.

Frijters, P., M. A. Shields, and S. W. Price. 2005. "Job Search Methods and Their Success: A Comparison of Immigrants and Natives in the UK." *The Economic Journal* 115 (November): F359–376.

Galarneau, D., and R. Morissette. 2008. *Immigrants' Education and Required Job Skills.* Ottawa: Statistics Canada. Accessed December 12, 2008. www.statcan.gc.ca/pub/75-001-x/2008112/pdf/10766-eng.pdf.

Girard, E., and H. Bauder. 2007. "The Making of an 'Arcane' Infrastructure: Professional Engineering Regulation in Canada, 1867–1937." *The Canadian Geographer* 51 (2): 233–246.

Jarvis, P. 1986. *Sociological Perspectives on Lifelong Education and Lifelong Learning.* Athens: University of Georgia.

Knight, J., and L. Song. 1995. "Towards a Labour Market in China." *Oxford Review of Economic Policy* 11 (4): 97–117.

Lemay, M. 2007. "From Consideration to Integration: Canadian Engineering and International Engineering Graduates." *Canadian Issues* (Spring): 81–84.

Li, P. S. 2001. "The Market Worth of Immigrants' Educational Credentials." *Canadian Public Policy* 27 (1): 23–38.

Li, H., and J. Zax. 2000. "Economic Transition and Labor Supply in China." In *China's Labor Market and Problems of Employment*, edited by Y. Wang and A. Chen, 217–233. Southwest: University of Economics and Finance Press.

Man, G. 2004. "Gender, Work and Migration: Deskilling Chinese Immigrant Women in Canada." *Women's Studies International Forum* 27 (2):135–148.

Mezirow, J. 1978. "Perspective Transformation." *Adult Education* 28 (2): 100–110.

———. 1991. *Transformative Dimensions of Adult Learning.* Oxford: Jossey-Bass.

———. 1994. "Response to Mark Tennant and Michael Newman." *Adult Education Quarterly* 44: 222–232.

———. 2000. "Learning to Think Like an Adult: Core Concepts of Transformation Theory." In *Learning as Transformation: Critical Perspectives on a Theory in Progress*, edited by J. Mezirow and Associates, 3–34. San Francisco, CA: Jossey-Bass.

Mezirow, J. 2006. "An Overview on Transformative Learning." In *Lifelong Learning: Concepts and Contexts*, edited by J. Crowther and P. Sutherland, 24–38. New York: Routledge Taylor and Francis Group.

O'Sullivan, E. 2003. "Bringing a Perspective of Transformative Learning to Globalized Consumption." *International Journal of Consumer Studies* 27 (4): 326–330.

Olssen, M. 2006. "Understanding the Mechanisms of Neoliberal Control: Lifelong Learning, Flexibility and Knowledge Capitalism." *International Journal of Lifelong Education* 25 (3): 213–230.

Ng, R. 1988. "Immigrant Women and Institutionalized Racism." In *Changing Patterns, Women in Canada*, edited by S. Burt, L. Code, and L. Dorney, 184–203. Toronto: MandS.

Ng, R., G. Man, H. Shan, and L. Liu. 2006. "Learning to be Good Citizens: Informal Learning and the Labour Market Experiences of Professional Chinese Immigrant Women." Final report for the Centre of Excellence on Research on Immigration and Settlement. Accessed January 12, 2008. ceris.metropolis.net/Virtual%20Library/RFPReports/Ng2005.pdf.

Plummer, K. 2001. *Documents of Life 2: An Invitation to a Critical Humanism.* London: Sage Publications.

Sanders, J., V. Nee, and S. Sernau. 2002. "Asian Immigrants' Reliance on Social Ties in Multiethnic Labor Market." *Social Forces* 81 (1): 281–314.

Shan, H. 2009. "Shaping the Re-training and Re-education Experiences of Immigrant Women: The Credential and Certificate Regime in Canada." *The International Journal of Lifelong Education* 28 (3): 353–369.

Schugurensky, D. 2002. "Transformative Learning and Transformative Politics: The Pedagogical Dimension of Participatory Democracy and Social Action." In *Expanding the Boundaries of Transformative Learning*, edited by E. O'Sullivan, A. Morrell, and M. O'Connor, 59–76. New York: Palgrave.

Slade, B. 2003. "A Critical Feminist Analysis of the Marginalization of Immigrant Women Engineers: Subtle Semantics, Redundant Assessments and Conflicting Jurisdictions." Master of Arts Thesis, OISE, University of Toronto.

Slade, B., Y. Luo, and D. Schugurensky. 2005. "Seeking 'Canadian Experience':The Informal Learning of New Immigrants as Volunteer Workers." Presented at the Canadian Association for the Study of Adult Education (CASAE) 24 Conference, London, Ontario, University of Western Ontario.

Taylor, E. W. 1997. "Building Upon the Theoretical Debated: A Critical Review of the Empirical Studies of Mezirow's Transformative Learning Theory." *Adult Education Quarterly* 48: 32–57.

Chapter 7

MAKING A "GLOBAL" CITY: RACIALIZATION, PRECARIOUSNESS, AND REGULATION IN THE TORONTO TAXI INDUSTRY

APARNA SUNDAR

INTRODUCTION

The ubiquity of the immigrant worker in the service sector has come to symbolize the global city, with the taxi industry as a prime example. As participants in a growing number of international conferences, festivals, and business meetings fly into Toronto, they are met and taken to their destination by a taxi driver who himself has journeyed here from some part of the Global South. The trajectories of the taxi drivers greeting visitors in any other "global city," at least in North America, such as New York or San Francisco or Vancouver, are similar (Schaller Consulting 2004), so that the first sign of the "sleepiness" or smaller-town nature of a city is how "white" its cabbies are. For residents of the global city as well, a ride in a taxi has come to be a quick and easy way of discussing life or politics in some distant part of the world, a conversation that in its recounting often becomes as much about the passenger's own cosmopolitanism as it is about the cosmopolitanism of the city; rarely, however, is it about the cosmopolitanism of the driver, who is quoted instead as an authentic representative of some essentially "other," less global, place.

Transnational circuits of migration, and the cosmopolitanism represented by the consequent social diversity of labour, mark two aspects of the global city, more broadly defined as a node in the global flows of capital, information, and entrepreneurial or creative classes (Brenner and Keil 2006; Kipfer and Keil 2002). Stefan Kipfer and Roger Keil (2002) have argued that global cities are necessarily "competitive cities," competing to attract capital, investment, and personnel from each other. To be competitive, global cities must be able to offer a diverse workforce, but must be able to limit demands for redistribution (wages) and for recognition (accommodation, anti-racism) and representation. The need to manage these tensions and conflicts means that global cities do not simply come into being; they need to be made.

The taxi industry is symbolically and materially implicated in both these senses of the global: the fact that the majority of its drivers are racialized immigrants is taken as evidence of the global and multicultural nature of the city; and the industry itself is in the front line of the city's effort to be attractive to tourist and investor alike. Despite this situation, the industry has been largely absent from studies of the making of the competitive global city (Boudreau, Keil, and Young 2009; Tufts 2004). In this chapter I seek to rectify this absence, arguing that a focus on the industry can deepen our understanding of the strategies through which global cities seek to be competitive.

The taxi industry is also important in the context of thinking about issues of immigration and settlement. A common sense and almost apocryphal claim made about Toronto's taxi drivers is that many of them are unemployed doctors and highly qualified professionals whose foreign credentials were not recognized by Canadian employers. The discussion then inevitably turns to issues of credentialization, structural racism, and the racialization of employment and poverty. It has been well documented that the Canadian labour market is structured by immigration and racialization, so that racialized immigrants find themselves in jobs well below their level of qualification, and end up forming the majority of workers in the low-paid, precarious sectors of the service economy (Galabuzi 2004, 2006; Goldring and Landolt 2009; Teelucksingh and Galabuzi 2005). From a different but related position, Harald Bauder (2006) has argued that immigration structures labour markets, citing Manuel Castell's early insight that immigrants do not come to do low-end jobs others will not do, but that jobs remain or become low-income because an army of immigrants can be drawn on to fill them. Research by Sara Abraham, Aparna Sundar, and Dale Whitmore (2008) and Abdulhamid Hathiyani (2007) did show a fair number of bachelor's degrees and higher among taxi drivers; a study of New York taxi drivers also found that the immigrant drivers were better educated than their American-born peers (Schaller Consulting 2004).

However, as several drivers interviewed by Abraham, Sundar, and Whitmore (2008) asked in the course of their interviews, is the only reason we care about taxi work the possibility that some highly qualified individuals end up doing it? What about the conditions within the industry for those who work in it? Just by the conservative estimate that over 70 percent of Toronto's 10,000 taxicab drivers are racialized men and first-generation immigrants, albeit that many have been here for several decades, conditions in the industry are important for thinking about the possibility of income security, capital formation, and social mobility among immigrant families in terms other than the deskilling and downward mobility of professional immigrants. As Boudreau, Keil, and Young (2009, 95) have noted, the increased focus of much anti-racism/equity work on the credentialization of higher-skilled workers has resulted in drawing attention away from the persistence of racism and exploitation among lower-skilled workers who make up the bulk of a neo-liberal capitalist economy.

Multiple forms of labour relationships exist in the taxi industry, making attention to conditions of work in the Toronto taxi industry valuable to thinking about labour more broadly. The taxi industry is anomalous in many respects. Capital in this industry is largely local rather than transnational, as in retail or hospitality. The structure of the industry is tied to the municipal regime, and yet drivers, even though they perform a relatively essential service, are not city employees and do not figure in discussions on the public sector. Although there are obvious points of capital formation within the industry, namely among those who own and lease out standard licence plates and those who own and run brokerages, the low income accruing to the drivers cannot be understood simply in terms of its direct relationship to capital. Rather, it must also be understood in terms of the benefits to the competitive city, as well as to the urban public at large, of people performing an important city service for less than minimum wage. Part of the problem lies in the fact that drivers, despite a diversity of relationships to ownership and capital in the industry, are all designated "self-employed" and are not subject to provisions protecting employees. Further, despite the fact that all other aspects of the industry are regulated by the municipality, classification of labour and conditions of work are under provincial jurisdiction, creating, as will be seen below, room for the municipal government to plead inability to act on these matters.

The very specificity and anomalousness of the taxi industry makes it interesting (similar to the domestic workers industry, see Chapter 4) as a mirror into larger trends in neo-liberal municipal restructuring for competitiveness and into various forms of precarious labour, created by the vagaries and inconsistencies of labour law as well as by processes of immigration and racialization. Yet there is very little written about the taxi industry or work within it. In this chapter I seek to address this gap, both by providing an overview of the structure and nature of ownership and work within the Toronto taxi industry as a large employer of immigrant men, and by beginning to explore ways of thinking about this work in relation to discussions of the competitive city, and of racialization and precarious work.

The empirical core of the chapter consists of an analysis of the Report of the 1998 Toronto Task Force to Review the Toronto Taxi Industry, which put in place the reforms and regulations that structure the industry today. The paper also draws on the published and unpublished findings of a pilot study carried out by two colleagues and myself (see Abraham, Sundar, and Whitmore 2008), supplemented by follow-up personal interviews by myself. The following sections examine the theorization of the competitive city, the history of Toronto's taxi industry, the report by the task force and its outcomes, the racialization and precariousness of taxi work, and taxi drivers' resistance as a way of re-imagining the global.

THE COMPETITIVE CITY

Global city theorists argue that global cities are not simply cities with numerous headquarters of transnational capital, but also of social and political contradictions and of the struggle of actors on several scales of the globalization process. For them, global cities are the products of "glocalization" processes, key to which is the process by which transnational migrants become forces in urban politics and the municipal arena (Sassen 1998 cited in Kipfer and Keil 2002). But, as critics have argued, global cities are as much of an aspiration as an empirical category (Brenner and Keil 2006). It is this aspiration to global city status that is captured in the concept of the "competitive city," developed by Kipfer and Keil (2002, 235) to describe a "new modality of regulating and managing the process of global-city formation":

> The competitive city has three major dimensions: the entrepreneurial city (Harvey 1989), the city of difference (Jacobs and Fincher 1998), and the revanchist city (Smith 1996). These dimensions each comprise a set of policies, ideological forms, and state orientations that articulate strategies of accumulation (the entrepreneurial city), patterns of class formation (the city of difference), and forms of social control (the revanchist city). These different aspects of the competitive city ... are tied to an overarching (imputed or material) imperative of intercity competition that treats cities as homogenous units that compete with each for investment and mobile segments of new urban middle classes through strategies of municipal state restructuring and policies of economic development, finance, taxation, land-use planning, urban design, "culture," diversity management, policing, and workfare. Competitive city governance is thus not reducible to the economic and social policies of neoliberalism. It represents a broader project of cementing and reordering the social and moral landscape of the contemporary urban order. (Kipfer and Keil 2002, 235)

Toronto's governance was aimed at moulding it into a "competitive city" following the establishment of the amalgamated City of Toronto in 1998 out of six existing municipalities. The amalgamation was legislated by the Progressive Conservative government in power in Ontario, and was part of a larger package of downloading to the city, deregulation of urban planning and development controls, erosion of employment standards, deregulation of rent controls, facilitation of privatization of municipal utilities, halt to social housing construction, enactment of workfare, and undermining of civilian oversight of policing (Kipfer and Keil 2002; Allahwala, Boudreau, Keil 2010). The "competitive city" strategy was reflected in the visioning and planning processes involved in developing the city's new official plan, its waterfront redevelopment strategy, and its bid for the 2008 Olympic Games. I outline the three dimensions of the competitive city strategy in Toronto below.

The entrepreneurial city was to be achieved by economic development aimed at promoting Toronto as an investment platform, attracting large development projects such as the Olympics, and reinforcing the dominant global city industries, such as finance, media, IT, tourism, and entertainment (City of Toronto 2000 cited in Keil and Kipfer 2002). This development was coupled with a move toward new public management techniques.

The city of difference was evidenced in municipal policies and discourses that supported the integration of "culture" and an aesthetic of diversity into urban development and strategies of economic competitiveness. Diversity was to be used to attract tourism and market the city's bid for the 2008 Summer Olympics. In this bid process, Toronto's diversity, ethnic harmony, and multiculturalism were advanced as its most important asset in its competition with other cities. Yet very few real city resources were devoted to equity issues (Kipfer and Keil 2002).

The revanchist city became visible through a wide range of policies around policing, workfare, social housing administration, parks management, urban planning, and immigration control, that subordinated social policy to "coercive and segregative forms of social control" (Kipfer and Keil 2002, 250). These policies were aimed at making urban space safe, clean, and secure for investors, real-estate capital, and the new urban middle classes. The arguments for taxi reform outlined below echo this revanchist vision, whereby "traditional reform vocabulary—quality of life, public space—now tends to refer to the degree to which commuters, tourists, and the inner-city gentry can enjoy urbane lifestyles without being disturbed by signs of destitution and the presence of unworthy publics" (Kipfer and Keil 2002, 250).

While the strategies for a competitive city provide the context from which to understand the particular nature of the reforms in the taxi industry, the initial, and explicit, impetus for the reforms came from conditions within the industry itself. I turn now, therefore, to the history of the industry.

THE TORONTO TAXI INDUSTRY: A BRIEF HISTORY

The first taxicab company in Toronto was established by Thornton Blackburn, an African-American who came to Canada via the Underground Railroad in 1834; by 1885 there were 285 registered taxicabs in Toronto. City documents from this period show a degree of regulation of the industry, in the form of licences to operate a taxicab and other rules to guide its operation. By 1931 concerns about the disorganization, lack of safety, and corruption within the industry, as well as the falling revenues for cab owners in the context of the Great Depression, led to the establishment of an inquiry, which resulted in the 1932 *Report of the Advisory Committee on Taxicabs to the Commissioners of Police of the City of Toronto*. Chief among the reforms that followed from this report included the standardization of fares, the installation of meters, and the limitation of the number of licences issued each year (Morley 2009).

The Report of the 1998 Task Force to Review the Taxi Industry (Task Force Report) identifies two key moments that shaped the character of the industry in the second half of the twentieth century. The first was in 1963, when the Metro Licensing Commission (MLC) allowed licences to be sold on the open market. This transformed the licence, from a permit to operate a taxi for a living into a capital asset. The second change occurred in 1974, when the Commission legalized the long-term leasing of taxicab licences. According to the Task Force Report, this change was implemented in part because the Commission felt it was unable to enforce the then current bylaw prohibiting leasing, due to collusion between the driver and owner. It was also felt to be cheaper for drivers to lease than to rent on a daily basis. In addition, the changes appear to have been a response to a perception by many drivers that leasing would allow them to achieve the status of entrepreneur rather than driver/employee.

These two features of the taxicab licences led to dramatic changes in the structure of the industry in the following two decades. First, there was a shift to leasing rather than owner-operated taxis. Plate leasing went from 32.1 percent of available plates in 1982 to 78.0 percent in 1997. Second, there was a sharp rise in the market value of the licences. The average value of the plate went up from $45,024 in 1982 to $80,000 in 1997. The rate of return on the lease rates remained relatively stable at about 12.6 percent per annum.

Lease fees received by the owner are net income, as there are minimal or no operating costs attached to leasing a plate. The value of the plate thus increased dramatically with the increase in leasing, and the plate began to be seen primarily as an investment opportunity. The increased price put the ownership of a plate beyond the reach of an average driver and led to an increase in the number of speculative or absentee owners.

The effect of the increase in leasing had a strong adverse impact on the industry. Since the owners' financial benefits came from plate lease revenues, they had no incentive to provide a higher quality of service. At tribunal hearings, plate owners invariably denied any knowledge or responsibility for dangerous or unsafe taxicabs. Lessees bore the brunt of risk in the industry: they provided the car, paid for all equipment, brokerage and other fees, insurance, gas, and all repairs and maintenance costs. The high cost of leasing, combined with other operating costs, led drivers to compromise on maintenance or vehicle replacement in order to cut expenses. The lease offered the lessee no protection, since it could be cancelled without cause on seven days' notice. The owners' agents would cancel the leases if they could strike a more lucrative deal with someone else.

Increased complaints from members of the industry and of the public, captured in a series of articles in the *Toronto Star* in 1997–1998 (Cheney 1998a, 1998b, 1998c, 1998d; Slaughter 1998; Toronto Star Editorial 1998), led to recognition of the need for reform of the industry. In 1996 the Thomas Subcommittee Report was released by the municipal By-Law Sub-Committee on Taxicab Leasing and Related Matters. In 1998 the City of Toronto undertook a comprehensive review of the taxi industry. The Report of the Task Force to Review the Taxi Industry was published later that year, and has structured conditions in the industry since.

RESTRUCTURING THE TAXI INDUSTRY: THE TASK FORCE TO REVIEW THE TAXI INDUSTRY

A Task Force to Review the Taxi Industry, consisting of seven city councillors, was established in April 1998 by Toronto City Council. It gave its report in October 1998. The report notes that the Task Force was established to look into concerns emerging from the deterioration of the taxi industry as a result of leasing. These included: the deterioration of the quality, safety, and reliability of taxis; the deterioration of customer service; the significant growth of middlemen in the industry; the growth of absentee owners and passive investors; and the impact of these last two factors on the ability of drivers to earn a fair wage.

The Task Force gathered information through a number of means. Public deputations were held where stakeholders, including drivers, owners, designated agents, tourism industry representatives, the Toronto Board of Trade, and a few members of the taxi-riding public, presented their individual perspectives on the problems facing the industry and proposed solutions for reform. Taxi industry stakeholders were also invited to submit written materials or provide comments to the Task Force hotline. Best practices from five other municipal jurisdictions—London, England, New York City, Halifax, Vancouver, and Montreal—that had attempted recent reform of their taxi industries were studied. Following these steps, five workshops were held with stakeholders to discuss various recommendations and options. The report notes the diversity of positions expressed and the fact that even the drivers themselves did not always speak with one voice. Given this diversity of voices, it is revealing which ones were paid special attention and addressed through the recommendations.

Almost at the outset, the report frames the imperatives for taxi reform as tied to the needs of the global or "world-class city." The immediate concern with the industry that led to the establishment of the Task Force was that existing conditions cast "an unacceptable, negative reflection on the image of the City of Toronto as a world class city." The submission from the Board of Trade was adduced to make this point:

> The Toronto Board of Trade advises that "tourism is the largest and fastest growing industry in the world and contributes almost $5 billion annually to the Toronto economy." ... There is little debate that the conditions and quality of service of the taxicab industry is [sic] of substantial importance to Toronto's promotion as a world class city. The taxicab industry's influence on the Toronto image can

affect tourism and are [sic] important considerations in initiatives such as the 2008 Olympic Games. (Toronto Task Force to Review the Taxi Industry 1998)

This wider framework within which to consider taxicab reform was reinforced by citing letters from the public:

> The City has received many complaints from the public and visitors who are dissatisfied with the service provided by Toronto taxicabs. Some speak of rudeness and refusal to accept passengers who are traveling a short distance. Other letters address the physical condition of taxicabs that feel unsafe and leave a poor impression on [sic] the City of Toronto. Some link the state of Toronto taxicabs as a negative in the bid to host the Olympics in 2008. One such letter from a concerned citizen referred to the deplorable state of taxis in Toronto and compared them to service "reminiscent of the third world with beaten up cars and interiors, non-existent suspensions and questionable safety standards. Add to this surly drivers with few language skills and little or no city knowledge and we've got a major problem." The content of this letter reflects a common public perception of the taxicab industry as the message is repeated in many letters received by the Task Force. (Toronto Task Force to Review the Taxi Industry 1998)

Thus, it was not only the cars but the drivers themselves, with their limited (English) language skills and poor manners, who created entirely the wrong "third world" image for a world-class city like Toronto. From this situation it followed naturally that what needed reform was not only the licensing structure of the industry, but also the drivers themselves.

This orientation is reflected in the shift to customer service as the overarching goal of the recommendations, and in the details of the Ambassador program which sought simultaneously to do away with leasing and to create a new breed of professional, well-trained drivers. The final recommendations were organized around five points "to focus on customer service." These recommendations were:

1. Create a Taxicab Passenger Bill of Rights: to focus the industry on customer service;
2. Improve the cabs: retire dilapidated cabs and replace with newer, quality vehicles;
3. Improve training: so that all people in the industry, owners and drivers, know what the public expects and have the skill to do the job;

4. Create Ambassador class cabs: to put greater pride of ownership behind the wheel,. and
5. Strengthen [e]nforcement: to make sure it all happens. (Toronto Task Force to Review the Taxi Industry 1998)

The Taxicab Passenger Bill contains 18 "rights," drawn almost verbatim from a similar Bill of Rights adopted by New York City as part of the radical neo-liberal restructuring of the taxi industry in favour of capital (Mathew 2005). Although there was little agreement on other reforms in the workshops, all five of them seemed to have agreed that a Taxicab Passenger Bill of Rights, visibly posted in each taxicab, would prove an effective measure to communicate a positive vision for the taxi industry to customers. As noted in the Task Force Report, "[m]any suggested that it would set expectations for customers and performance requirements for drivers" (Toronto Task Force to Review the Taxi Industry 1998.)

The Ambassador class program represented an uneasy compromise between a variety of competing demands and recommendations around industry quality and the rights of drivers. For instance, Plan 2001, a reform package submitted by the Toronto Taxi Drivers Association, set out conditions for a transformed taxi industry to be implemented by the year 2001. While this plan, too, made reference to the importance of the 2008 Olympic Games and the contribution that a vibrant taxi industry would make to tourism and business, it also proposed a Taxi Driver's Bill of Rights that provided for:

1. A clean, well-maintained, modern vehicle that is capable of safe and economic operation and providing optimum comfort to the passenger.
2. Healthy and reasonably safe working conditions for the benefit of both driver and the customer.
3. An economic return on investment that will permit the earning of the minimum statutory hourly wage in addition to all operating expenses including fringe benefits.
4. Fringe benefits to provide domestic security and enhance driver morale:
   - An accident and sickness plan for drivers and their families
   - A disability plan for drivers
   - Life insurance and a savings and pension plan
   - An annual physical and dental examination
5. A set maximum number of hours of driving per week to ensure the safety of the public.
6. A straightforward set of rules and regulations for the industry that are easily understood and that are enforced consistently and fairly and evenhandedly so that a driver always can know where he stands and the public has prompt redress of complaints.

7. A voice by way of elected representation in the regulation and management of the industry. (Toronto Task Force to Review the Taxi Industry 1998)

Likewise, Councillor Howard Moscoe, who was on the Task Force and headed the Planning and Transportation Committee, put forward a proposal for the city to buy back the standard licences at current market value and then lease them out to drivers. The report notes that this proposal, and Plan 2001 described above, could not be adopted in full because matters such as economic return, fringe benefits, and the establishment of a Taxi Driver's Bill of Rights, were business-related and "deny intervention by the City." Further, the possibility of the city buying back licences from owners and then serving as the sole leasing authority was deemed legally impossible by Toronto legal services. On this matter, the report concludes: "With respect to municipal licensing [sic] purposes, in simple terms, the courts have limited the licensing [sic] authority of municipalities to regulating for municipal purposes and not participating in the business arrangements between industry participants" (Toronto Task Force to Review the Taxi Industry 1998). In short, all matters related to labour standards were a matter for provincial legislation, and not within the jurisdiction of the city.

Instead of these proposed reforms, the city recommended the creation of a new class of licences or plates—the Ambassador licences—named to express the "quality image that is so critical for the industry and the City," given that taxis and their drivers were "ambassadors to the city." Taxis carrying the Ambassador plate could be driven only by the plate holder and neither leased nor transferred (bequeathed or sold). Ambassador vehicles were to be subject to more strict quality standards and drivers were to undergo a training program.

Explicit within the Ambassador program, as with the broader emphasis on customer service, was the importance of training, and of increased regulation. A car driven under an Ambassador plate had to be replaced every seven years. Frequent inspections were required to ensure safety standards were met, as well as standards laid out in the Taxicab Passenger Bill of Rights (such as around cleanliness). The list of bylaws regulating taxi work—failure of which to meet could be penalized—became longer following these reforms.

A final recommendation by the Task Force was that of "industry self-management." This was described as "an initiative introduced by the Province of Ontario that by partnership assists businesses to manage themselves" (Toronto Task Force to Review the Taxi Industry 1998). The report notes that because there were a number of issues that the city was not mandated to address by regulatory means, it was important for the city to work in partnership with representatives of the industry to address them. A Taxicab Advisory Committee, which had existed periodically in previous periods, was identified as the ideal vehicle for this self-management. This measure seemed to go some way to addressing the proposal made in the recommendations of the Toronto

Taxi Drivers Association for elected representation in the management of the industry. It failed, however, to distinguish between the diverse positions within the industry, such as lease drivers, Ambassador drivers, absentee owners, and brokers, thus creating a false impression of a harmony of interests between industry participants and overlooking the possibility that the more powerful among them might dominate.

THE OUTCOME OF THE REFORMS: THE PRESENT STRUCTURE OF THE INDUSTRY

The Task Force did not propose any cap on the number of Ambassador plates to be issued over time, following the London, England, model of deregulation that removed a fixed quota on new entrants but ensured self-selection and regulation through the high standards required of them. On the other hand, unlike the pro-capital reforms in New York, the Task Force aimed to shift the bulk of the industry into the hands of owner-operators by ensuring that all new licences could only be held by them (Mathew 2005; Schaller 2007; Toronto Task Force to Review the Taxi Industry 1998). It did so, however, without eliminating the old "standard" licences, which can still be sold or leased, and thus serve as capital. In terms of regulating the operation of taxis, likewise, there has been both an enormous growth in the regulation of licenced taxis for compliance with a long list of bylaws (many of them generated by the Taxicab Passenger Bill of Rights), and a continuing failure to control unlicenced operators, and in particular, the "poaching" of customers by airport cabs and limousine companies. Thus, the reforms have had both a re-regulating and a deregulating effect.

Although the city has not issued as many Ambassador plates as originally envisaged, the outcome of the Ambassador program has been to increase the number of plates in the industry and create an even more fragmented industry structure (Abraham, Sundar, and Whitmore 2008). With the introduction of the Ambassador plates and the continuation of the standard plates, there now exists a two-tier system of ownership in the industry as well as multiple categories of operators. As of October 2006 there were 3,480 Standard Taxicab Owner Licences, 1,403 Ambassador Taxicab Owner Licences, and 85 Accessible Taxicab Owner Licences. While Ambassador licence owners are required to operate their own vehicles and are not allowed to lease or rent them out, of the 3,480 standard licence owners, only 809 or 23 percent operate their own vehicles. The others either lease them out directly or through an agent.

Non-owning drivers fall into two categories. The first are lease drivers who lease the plate on a long-term basis either directly from the plate owner, or, more frequently, from an agent who is often a brokerage. At present, the lease rate is about $1,350 per month. In addition to the lease rent, drivers are responsible for owning and maintaining their own vehicles, and for paying fees to a brokerage for dispatch services. Drivers holding a lease on a car may also rent it to another driver for a daily shift. The second category of non-owning drivers are shift drivers who rent the taxicab (car and plate) for a daily or weekly rental fee from the lessee or brokerage, which bears the maintenance costs of the vehicle. The driver must pay for operating costs, such as gas and traffic tickets.

The capital-labour relationship within the taxi industry cannot be fully understood without reference to a third actor, and one which remained largely untouched by the 1998 reforms: the brokerage. A brokerage is a company that plays two roles: it operates a dispatch service, and it controls a number of plates, each attached to a vehicle. The brokerage or its owners may own some of the plates themselves. However, other investors own the bulk of the plates the brokerage controls. These owners appoint the brokerage or its officers as their "designated agent," meaning the brokerage is responsible for managing the plate and is authorized to lease it out. In return the brokerage pays the owner a regular fee. This system allows control of a large number of plates to be concentrated in a single brokerage. The brokerage leases each plate and vehicle to drivers either on a per-shift basis to shift drivers (as described above), or on a long-term basis to a single driver who maintains control of the vehicle and is responsible for maintenance and repairs. Often in this case, the driver actually buys the vehicle, but signs ownership over to the plate owner to comply with bylaw requirements that the plate and car be leased together. Each brokerage also operates a dispatch service for the benefit of drivers to whom it leases taxis, as well as for owner-operators, both of whom pay a flat fee of roughly $450 for the use of the dispatch service. Owners or lessees using a brokerage are required to paint their cars the colours of the brokerage. While the approximately 2,000 drivers who are owner-operators, either as standard or Ambassador licence plate holders, pay the brokerage only for dispatch, over 7,000 of Toronto's taxi drivers who operate as shift or lease drivers depend on the brokerages for their work. Brokerages thus serve as the public face of the industry, and as sites for the concentration of both capital and labour control in the industry. For this reason, they have had a significant presence at City Hall, including on the Taxicab Advisory Committee.

Aside from adding a layer of complexity and competition to the industry, the reforms do not seem to have addressed the precariousness of work in the taxi industry. Gerry Rodgers (cited in Vosko 2006, 15–16) identifies four dimensions central to establishing whether a job is precarious. These are: the degree of certainty of continuing employment; control over the labour process, working conditions, wages, and work intensity linked to the presence or absence of a trade union; the degree of regulatory protection provided through union representation or the law; and income level sufficient to maintain the workers and their dependents. On almost all these dimensions, as I demonstrate below, employment in the taxi industry continues to be highly precarious. It is not clear that the reforms have addressed the problems they were intended to address.

The introduction of Ambassador plates did not lead to a drop in the lease rates. Nor have incomes in the industry significantly improved; to the contrary, industry members argue that the increase in the number of taxis has led to an overcrowded market. Abraham, Sundar, and Whitmore's 2008 study provides a good sense of the differential incomes in the industry. Ambassador drivers (who are not allowed to rent or lease out their vehicle) made an average of $6.49 per hour, and worked an average of 70 hours a week. Lease drivers who did not rent their cars out to other drivers for the second shift made $3.44 per hour on average and worked 72 hours a week. Shift drivers who rented a taxi on a daily basis from an owner, lessee, or brokerage made an average of $2.83 an hour and worked 77 hours a week. Lease drivers who rented their cars out to other drivers for a second shift did best, making $8.81 an hour and working only 62 hours a week on average. These figures, even if they do represent the lower end of the possible spectrum of earnings, make it clear that even the best earning category in the industry, (aside from the standard plate owner-operator, about whom there is more below) earns less than the hourly minimum wage, and is forced to work inordinately long hours just to make a living wage.

Taxi drivers, even those who rent or lease their vehicles, are deemed "independent contractors" under labour law, which means that they are not covered by laws that regulate the working conditions of employees, such as maximum working hours, minimum wages, sick leave, employment insurance, or pensions (Coiquaud 2009; Fudge, Tucker, Vosko 2003; Langille and Davidov 1999). Despite recent city legislation extending the period of notice the plate owner must provide a lessee before terminating the lease, from 7 to 60 days (Canadian News Wire 2010), non-owners in the industry remain vulnerable to contingencies arising from sickness, or disputes with the owner or brokerage. All drivers, even shift drivers, have a degree of flexibility over their own work once they are on the road, but the need to work over 70-hour weeks to make a living wage serves a sufficiently disciplining function. As noted in the Task Force Report, regulating for work conditions is outside the city's jurisdiction.

Conditions are different for the standard plate owner. Although Abraham, Sundar, and Whitmore's (2008) study does not provide figures for owner-operators of standard plate cabs, the incomes of owner-operators would be similar to that of the lease driver who rented out the car to a second driver. But their costs would be lower, since they would not have to pay the $1,500 a month for the lease, thus increasing their net earnings significantly. Further, they can choose to lease out the plate entirely and work elsewhere. The plate itself constitutes an investment which can be used to provide earnings after retirement, and can be left to dependants upon the owner's death. In comparison to the standard plate, the problems with the Ambassador program become starkly apparent, for the Ambassador plates earns money for their owners only to the extent that they use it. Upon retirement or death, it reverts to the city. Thus the Ambassador plate owners occupy an anomalous position, and one which means they are only marginally better off than the lessees. Like all taxi drivers, they do not derive the benefits of employee status, but unlike the standard plate owners, the Ambassador plate cannot be considered an investment and they cannot be considered small businesspersons either. Thus, despite the relative security of owning a licence, the Ambassador plate owner-operators' status may still be classified as precarious: their earnings are low, they are forced to self-exploit to ensure a living wage, and they have little security against unexpected contingencies such as ill health.

In her analysis of precarious work, Leah Vosko is concerned not to separate work performed for the market from social reproduction, i.e. "the daily and intergenerational maintenance of the working population" (Vosko 2006: 17). In this context, work in the taxi industry must be examined not only for its failure to provide a living wage, or long-term earnings, but also for the daily toll it takes on health and family life. Drivers interviewed by Abraham, Sundar, and Whitmore (2008) noted again and again the negative health effects of long hours spent driving, and the inability to take time off when sick. One driver said: "Very few of us expect to live beyond 55," (Abraham, Sundar, and Whitmore 2008, 23; see also Facey 2003; Lewchuk, de Wolff, and King 2006; Mathew 2005). Even more they spoke of the costs to family life.

RACIALIZATION AND PRECARIOUSNESS IN TAXI WORK

The taxi industry has a long history of attracting new immigrants because of its relative ease of entry. The growth of immigration from non-European source countries over the last three decades is reflected in the taxi industry: industry members estimate that over 70 percent of Toronto's 10,000 drivers (including owners-operators) are racialized men. Of Abraham, Sundar, and Whitmore's (2008) sample of 100 drivers, all but two had been born outside of Canada and almost all of these in Asia, Africa, or the Caribbean. All of them except two were Canadian citizens, and most had been working in the industry for at least a decade. As noted at the beginning of the chapter, it has become the common sense of the city that the racialized composition of its taxi drivers is the outcome of the ways in which structural racism in Canada enforces the downward mobility of skilled immigrants. Drivers themselves seem less exercised by this deskilling than by the ways in which they believe this structural racism reinforces the precariousness of their work in the industry.

In interviews and focus groups by Abraham, Sundar, and Whitmore (2008), and currently in an individual Ambassador owner's case before the Ontario Human Rights Commission (Javed 2010), Ambassador drivers have argued that the Ambassador program was racially discriminatory in intent. They argue that its timing coincided with the influx of larger numbers of immigrants from non-European countries, and that it functioned as a way of preventing them from acquiring capital in the industry. Although it is difficult to assess whether the program had this economic intent, it is clear from the Task Force Report that many of its recommendations were addressed specifically to the "problem" of the non-English speaking, immigrant driver. Regardless of the intent of the program, its critics are right about its effects: while the majority of new entrants to the industry still work as lease or shift drivers, even those who manage to obtain an Ambassador plate are unable, because of the limitations built into the program, to convert this into a long-term investment in the industry.

If the Taxicab Passenger Bill of Rights and the new bylaws affecting vehicle and behaviour standards were written with the non-English speaking, immigrant driver in mind, they have, predictably, created openings for an "everyday racism" to work in tandem with, and underwrite, both precariousness and regulation. Jessica Walters's (2008) interviews reveal how racist prejudices sit just under the surface and erupt almost immediately in the context of disputes between passengers and drivers over fares and and other issues. With the adoption of such a Passenger's Bill of Rights in New York City, drivers facing an increase of verbal abuse, physical threats and attacks, and even cheating, following the events of September 2001, felt unable to speak back because under the Passenger's Bill of Rights such resistance might be construed as "discourteous" (Mathew 2005; Das Gupta 2004).

For the drivers, the increased number of bylaws has provided the police with more ways to harass them. While police insist that they are merely enforcing the bylaws, drivers complain of multiple ticketing when pulled over for a single offence, ticketing for "insubordination," of assumptions about their ignorance of the laws because of their immigrant status, and racial profiling. A common sentiment expressed by drivers was that "they treat us like garbage" (Abraham, Sundar, and Whitmore 2008; Walters 2008). Drivers also argue that the police are slow to respond to calls from them, a belief that has consequences for the drivers' own safety: most are reluctant to call the police except in the most egregious of assaults, and rarely report routine fare-jumping and related disputes, which along with verbal abuse, they accept as the psychological costs of the job.

Drivers also attribute their lack of voice and representation at the city to the structure of dominant interests in the industry and to racialization. The Taxicab Advisory Committee established following the Task Force Report broke down shortly thereafter because of concerns over the lack of transparency and accountability in the relationship between some of its members and the relevant city councillors. Broker and standard plate owner representatives on the committee continued to be consulted as the best representatives of "industry interests" even after it broke down, while drivers lost access to city council. As *Globe and Mail* columnist John Barber (2007) observed, part of the reason why city council was always able to confuse drivers and dismiss their demands (such as around the regulation of airport limousines) was that they were seen as "immigrants" and unfamiliar with the mores and practices of Canadian political life.

Even more problematic than the treatment by the city, perhaps, is the manner in which these prejudices have shaped organizing efforts among drivers. I have heard a leading member of the Toronto Taxi Industry Alliance, an organization that represents all interests in the industry including brokers, stating more than once (at public meetings and in private conversations) that drivers are suspicious of authority, including that of the police, because of their treatment by such authorities in their "homelands." As drivers have retorted: even if this were true, it doesn't say much for the authorities in Canada that nothing in the drivers' decades-long experience of Canadian authorities has softened that suspicion! Established non-racialized members of the industry also ascribe the failure of past efforts at unionizing to the influence of "tribal" leaders pushing the politics of "back home" within the communities of racialized drivers.

Comments from customers ("Hey cabbie, where are you from?") and from the police ("Where did you get your licence?" "We don't do things like that around here.") (Walters 2008) along with those from city authorities and industry leaders described above, suggest that the racialized taxicab driver, despite Canadian citizenship and years on the job, remains an outsider to the global city. The rigorous training and licencing requirements envisaged by the Task Force in its efforts to remake a "third world" workforce into one fit for a world-class city have failed to keep the drivers' bodies from continuing to be read as permanently immigrant, newcomer, and in need of regulation.

RESISTANCE AS RE-IMAGINING THE GLOBAL

Resistance by taxi drivers in North American cities has been based on understanding the politics of taxi work as inextricable from the larger politics of the city. For them, changing conditions in the industry requires challenging the competitive, neo-liberal cosmopolitan vision of the global city by inserting themselves into it as globalized and racialized actors. In New York the Taxi Workers Alliance has been massively successful in organizing a significant proportion of the city's drivers around issues of licencing, fares, and regulation. Even as they have organized strikes and demonstrations around these issues, a key part of their efforts has been aimed at public education campaigns that challenge racism and connect the processes of the global economy that caused them to migrate to the USA with the forces seeking to control their labour within the industry. They have sought through these efforts to expand the vision of the global city as encompassing their stories of displacement and continuing transnational engagement (Mathew 2005).

Toronto has had a long but not very successful history of taxi driver organizing. Those involved in organizing efforts over the years ascribe the failure of such efforts to: the fragmented nature of the industry, with different groups of drivers occupying quite different structural positions within it; the fact that drivers have very little time or money to spare for such efforts; destructive interventions by the brokerages; and the inability of the traditional unions who initiated the organizing to grasp and work with aspects of the drivers' working lives such as the constant racism and fear they live with, and the complexity of their frequently transnational engagements and concerns (personal interviews). Two new initiatives, both no more than a couple of years old, may finally begin to change this history.

The first of the new initiatives in Toronto is the Toronto United Taxi Drivers Association. The association has its origins in the efforts of a group of Ethiopian-Eritrean drivers to organize along ethnic lines before moving on to federate into a larger drivers' association, and now has over 500 members spanning ethnic communities. Its vision rests on the importance of community and identity as a crucial resource in mobilizing, rather than a barrier to some greater universalism. In organizing along ethnic lines, members are creating the space to explore their own strategies of resistance to the multiculturalism of the Canadian state which had, in effect, "co-opted political space available to minority groups for mobilization or resistance along ethnic or racial lines" (Croucher 1997 cited in Boudreau, Keil, and Young 2009, 87; see also Goonewardena and Kipfer 2005). The second initiative is the outcome of some drivers reaching out to an established union, the United Steelworkers, who were already in the process of establishing an independent workers' unit for live-in caregivers. This led to the formation of another association, the Taxiworkers Association, which has about 700 members.

The majority of the drivers in both associations are Ambassador plate owners, and campaigning for reforms to the Ambassador licence and the two-tier licencing structure of the industry has been foremost on both their agendas. This has limitations, as it does not address the conditions of lease and shift workers; in fact, by calling for Ambassador plates to be converted into standard plates, they are opening the door for several hundred more lease and shift drivers to enter the industry without improving the conditions within which they would be working. It is nevertheless important that their claims are framed in terms of the structural exclusion of more recent, largely racialized immigrants through the Ambassador licence, and in terms of the right to a living wage, health, social security, and leisure as "self-employed" workers. This suggests that for them a global city is also one where its inhabitants can live a full life, as family members and members of their communities, whether local or geographically distant. Like in New York, these new initiatives in Toronto are attempts by the drivers to work from and integrate their position as immigrant, transnational, and racialized into new ways of thinking about what it means to be truly global and to live in a global city.

CONCLUSION

Strategies of competitiveness in making the global city have rested on economic development, diversity management, and revanchist social regulation. In this chapter, I have demonstrated the application of these strategies in the reforms to the Toronto taxi industry, which is seen as being in the front line of the new global economy of tourism and transnational business, and whose multicultural workforce embodies the diversity and multiculturalism of the global city. While framed in the tropes of entrepreneurship, self-management, and partnership, the reforms have increased the precariousness of labour in the industry, as well as forms of disciplinary regulation, embedded in assumptions about "race" and processes of racialization. In resisting their precarious and regulated position in the industry, drivers have also begun to resist the managed diversity of the global city and to insert their own lived experience as globalized actors into its public life.

ACKNOWLEDGEMENTS

I would like to thank my fellow taxi researchers, Sara Abraham, Dale Whitmore, and Sanjay Talreja, for many fruitful discussions; members of the taxi industry, especially

Mohammed Omar and Owen Leach, for sharing their enormous knowledge of the industry; and Harald Bauder and the other reviewers for helping make this a better chapter.

REFERENCES

Abraham, S., A. Sundar, and D. Whitmore. 2008. *Toronto Taxi Drivers: Ambassadors of the City— A Report on Working Conditions.* Accessed August 4, 2011. www.taxi-cab-dispatch-software.com/taxi-cab-dispatch-software-toronto.pdf.

Allahwala, A., J. A. Boudreau, and R. Keil. 2010. "Neo-Liberal Governance: Entrepreneurial Municipal Regimes in Canada." In *Canadian Cities in Transition: New Directions in the Twenty-First Century, Fourth Edition*, edited by T. Bunting, P. Filion, and R. Walker, 210–224. Toronto: Oxford University Press.

Barber, J. 2007. "Victory for Cabbies Vanishes like Morning Mist." *The Globe and Mail*, September 27.

Bauder, H. 2006. *Labor Movement: How Migration Regulates Labor Markets.* New York: Oxford University Press.

Boudreau, J. A., R. Keil, and D. Young. 2009. *Changing Toronto: Governing Urban Neoliberalism.* Toronto: University of Toronto Press.

Brenner, N., and R. Keil. 2006. *The Global Cities Reader.* New York: Routledge.

By-Law Sub Committee. 1996. "Taxicab Leasing and Related Matters." (The Thomas Subcommittee Report). Accessed September 10, 2010. Toronto. www.taxi-library.org/thomas.htm.

Canadian News Wire. 2010. "Victory for Taxi Workers at Toronto City Hall." June 16. Accessed August 4, 2011. www.newswire.ca/en/releases/archive/June2010/16/c5468.html.

Cheney, P. 1998a. "A License to Print Money." *Toronto Star*, March 14.

———. 1998b. "King of the Cabs." *Toronto Star*, March 14.

———. 1998c. "Cabby's Life is Long Days, Low Pay, No Hope." *Toronto Star*, March 15.

———. 1998d. "Insults Fly at Taxi Talks." *Toronto Star*, March 25.

City of Toronto. 2000. "Toronto at the Crossroads: Shaping our Future." *Toronto Plan Directions Report.* Toronto: Urban Planning and Development Services.

Coiquaud, U. 2009. "Le difficile encadrement juridique des travailleurs autonomes en situation précaire: le cas des chauffeurs locataires de taxi." *Relations Industrielles* 64 (1): 95–111.

Cranford, C., J. Fudge, E. Tucker, and L. F. Vosko. 2005. *Self-Employed Workers Organize: Law, Policy and Unions.* Montreal and Kingston: McGill-Queen's University Press.

Das Gupta, M. 2004. "A View of Post-9/11 Justice from Below." *Peace Review* 16 (2): 141–148.

Facey, M. 2003. "The Health Effects of Taxi Driving." *Canadian Journal of Public Health* 94 (4): 254–257.

Fudge, J., E. Tucker, and L. F. Vosko. 2003. "Employee or Independent Contractor? Charting the Significance of the Distinction in Canada." *Canadian Labour and Employment Law Journal* 10: 193.

Galabuzi, G. E. 2004. "Racializing the Division of Labour: Neoliberal Restructuring and the Economic Segregation of Canada's Racialized Groups." In *Challenging the Market: The Struggle to Regulate Work and Income*, edited by J. Standford and L. Vosko, 175–204. Montreal: McGill-Queen's University Press.

———. 2006. *Canada's Economic Apartheid: The Social Exclusion of Racialized Groups in the New Century*. Toronto: Canadian Scholars' Press.

Goldring, L., and P. Landolt. 2009. "Immigrants and Precarious Employment in the New Economy. Introduction to Research Briefs." Toronto: Immigrants and Precarious Employment Project.

Goonewardena, K., and S. Kipfer. 2005. "Spaces of Difference: Reflections from Toronto on Multiculturalism, Bourgeois Urbanism and the Possibility of Radical Urban Politics." *International Journal of Urban and Regional Research* 29 (3): 670–678.

Harvey, D. 1989. "From Managerialism to Entrepreneurialism: The Transformation of Urban Governance in Late Capitalism." *Geografiska Annaler Series B* 71B (1): 3–18.

Hathiyani, A. 2007. "Professional Immigrants on a Road to Driving Taxis in Toronto." *Our Diverse Cities* 4 (Fall): 128–133.

Jacobs, J. M., and R. Fincher. 1998. "Introduction." In *Cities of Difference*, edited by R. Fincher and J. M. Jacobs, 1–16. New York: Guidlford.

Javed, N. 2010. "Not All Cab Licenses Equal, Driver Says." *Toronto Star*, January 25.

Kipfer, S., and R. Keil. 2002. "Toronto Inc? Planning the Competitive City in the New Toronto." *Antipode* 34 (2): 227–264.

Langille, B., and G. Davidov. 1999. "Beyond Employees and Independent Contractors: A View from Canada." *Comparative Labour Law and Policy Journal* 21: 7–45.

Lewchuk, W., A. de Wolff, and A. King. 2006. "The Hidden Costs of Precarious Employment: Health and the Employment Relationship." In *Precarious Employment: Understanding Labour Market Insecurity in Canada*, edited by L. Vosko, 141–162. Montreal: McGill-Queen's University Press.

Mathew, B. 2005. *Taxi! Cabs and Capitalism in New York City*. New York: The New Press.

Morley, K. 2009. "The Toronto Taxicab Industry: Past, Present and Future." Accessed July 29, 2010. www.wheelchairtransit.com/spage-blog/detail-100.html.

Sassen, S. 1998. "Whose City Is It? Globalization and the Formation of New Claims." In *Globalization and its Discontents: Essays on the New Mobility of People and Money*, edited by S. Sassen, xix–xxxvi. New York: The New Press.

Schaller, B. 2007. "Entry Controls in Taxi Regulation: Implications of US and Canadian Experience for Taxi Regulation and Deregulation." *Transport Policy* 14: 490–506.

Schaller Consulting. 2004. *The Changing Face of Taxi and Limousine Drivers: U.S., Large States and Metro Areas, and New York City*. Accessed June 7, 2010. New York. www.schallerconsult.com/taxi/taxidriver.pdf.

Slaughter, M. "Surprising Collection of People Hold Plates." *Toronto Star*, March 14.

Smith, N. 1996. *The New Urban Frontier: Gentrification and the Revanchist City*. London: Routledge.

Teelucksingh, C., and G. E. Galabuzi. 2005. "Impact of Race and Immigrant Status on Employment Opportunities and Outcomes in the Canadian Labour Market." *CERIS Policy Matters* 22 (November).

Toronto Star Editorial. 1998. "Time to Overhaul Toronto's Taxi Business." *Toronto Star*, March 18.

Toronto Task Force to Review the Taxi Industry. 1998. "Report to Review the Toronto Taxi Industry." Toronto. Acccessed August 4, 2011. www.taxi-library.org/tor98-01.htm.

Tufts, S. 2004. "Building the 'Competitive City': Labour and Toronto's Bid to Host the Olympic Games." *Geoforum* 35: 47–58.

Vosko, L. F., ed. 2006. *Precarious Employment: Understanding Labour Market Insecurity in Canada.* Montreal and Kingston: McGill-Queen's University Press.

Walters, J. 2008. "Hey Cabbie! Where are you from? An Examination of Everyday Racism in Toronto's Taxi Industry." Toronto: Ryerson University. Accessed August 4, 2011. http://digitalcommons.ryerson.ca/dissertations/88/.

Workers' Action Centre. 2007. *Working on the Edge.* Toronto: Workers' Action Centre.

Part Three

IDENTITIES AND COMMUNITIES

Immigration and settlement is a deeply social and cultural experience. This experience complements the economic dimension of immigration and settlement—the need to put food on the table, the struggle against exploitation, and the importance of migration labour to industrialized economies—which was the theme of Part Two. The central topics weaving through Part Three and tying the four chapters together relate to the notions of identity and community.

Identity is a complex idea. Identities can be self-ascribed and imposed by others; they can be expressed through multiple dimensions, including origin, ethnicity, religion, race, and gender; they exist at the individual and collective scales; they are materially referenced but also discursively produced; and they are continuously shifting and transforming. In the context of migration and settlement, an added dimension is that people change the geographical contexts that frame their identities.

The notion of identity relates to the concept of community: identities are typically expressed in the context of communities. For example, a residential community may carry an identity such as Little Italy or Chinatown, reflecting a particular settlement history; or a community of immigrants may embrace collective identities as, say, German-Canadians. By the same token, wider communities frame the identities of subpopulations. For example, immigrants from the Indian subcontinent only acquire their "South Asian" identity once they have arrived in North America.

Rather than attempting to summarize the various dimensions of identity and community—which would be an impossible task given the complexity of the matter—the chapters below present empirical studies limited in scope, dealing with the construction of identity and community in particular migration and settlement context. In this way, the chapters illustrate various approaches to this topic.

In the opening chapter, Varvara Mukhina investigates cross-national marriage of Russian-speaking women in Japan. This chapter builds on existing research on cross-national marriages that has neglected aspects of culture and identity. Mukhina's empirical fieldwork and in-depth interviews with Russian and Ukrainian women reveal the importance of three interrelated dimensions in framing the marital satisfaction of migrating wives: the relations with their husband, relations with the local community, and relations with the state. The findings of the study point toward the need to conceptually distinguish between cross-national, intercultural, and other types of marriages. Although situated in Japan, the empirical research and its theoretical implications are relevant to other national contexts.

In Chapter 9, Tara Gilkinson and Geneviève Sauvé focus the discussion on Canada. Their quantitative research draws on data from the fifth wave (2005–2006) of the World Values Survey to analyze associations with various collective identities: citizen of the world, North America, Canada, province/region, and local community. The analysis compares the responses of recent immigrants, earlier immigrant cohorts, and Canadian-born individuals. Gilkinson and Sauvé are especially interested in the questions of how immigrants and non-immigrants associate with various collective identities; whether Canadian-born respondents are more likely to identify as Canadian citizens than immigrants; what variables help explain an individual's identity as a citizen of Canada; and whether the strong identification with one particular identity excludes the association with another identity.

Tahira Gonsalves maintains a focus on Canada but explores identity from a qualitative perspective. In Chapter 10, she investigates religious and secular identities in a plural Canada. Although religious identity is an important dimension of immigrant life it has arguably been neglected in the literature. Gonsalves applies a method that differs from the empirical chapters in this part, instead drawing on examples of second-generation Muslim youth identities and on debates around the proposed usage of Sharia law for civil dispute resolution in Ontario. Through these examples, Gonsalves explores the relationships between secularism, multiculturalism, and citizenship in Canada. To adequately address the daily needs of a plural population, she argues, requires the incorporation of religious discourse in policy making. Indeed, religiously based claims in the public sphere come not only from immigrants, but also from native-born Canadians.

Chapter 11 zooms in on Toronto while widening the discussion to the transnational contexts of Israel and the former Soviet Union. Lea Soibelman explores the transnational migration of Jews who left the former Soviet Union for Israel in the late 1980s and early 1990s and arrived in Toronto as "secondary migrants" in the late 1990s and early 2000s. In this chapter, Soibelman investigates the unique character of this group of migrants, their transnational practices, and their identity shifts and fluctuations through multiple migrations. This chapter illustrates, in particular, how identities are negotiated in the process of migration by migrants as well as the communities they encounter.

Chapter 8

INVESTIGATING DIMENSIONS OF CROSS-NATIONAL MARRIAGES: A CASE OF RUSSIAN-SPEAKING WIVES IN JAPAN

VARVARA MUKHINA

INTRODUCTION

Cross-national marriages have become a widespread phenomenon in the modern internationalizing world, and they have received significant public and academic attention. Despite the complexity of this phenomenon, a narrow focus on the cultural differences between the spouses has become a "hot topic" in the media. Similarly, most of the academic literature on cross-national marriages is devoted to problems of cultural differences and intercultural communication (Romano 2008; Breger and Hill 1998). Conversely, social dimensions related to immigration and settlement in a new place are underestimated or ignored. This overestimation of the significance of cultural factors is a major limitation of current research on cross-national marriages.

Most studies do not distinguish cross-national marriages involving two citizens of different countries from interfaith, interracial, and inter-ethnic marriages between members of different communities in the same country. For example, the editors of the well-known (albeit somewhat dated) volume *Cross-Cultural Marriage: Identity and Choice* (Breger and Hill 1998) do not make clear theoretical distinctions between cases when one marries the member of another cultural community of the same country that is not related to migration and the cases when one marries the citizen of another country and faces the necessity of migration. On the other hand, I argue that these are distinct situations, as in the case of cross-national marriage (marriage with a citizen of another country) in which case cultural differences are coupled with structural difficulties of incorporating in the new nation. Only one chapter makes an explicit remark about the interaction between cross-national and cross-cultural aspects of marriage and recognizes that research on "marriage, and intermarriage—interracial, interethnic or interfaith—within one country may have relevance for international mixed marriages." Yet, researchers, like the authors of this chapter, tend to refrain from engaging in the complexities of cross-national/cross-cultural marriage; marrying a foreigner seems "rather a different matter from marrying a member of another ethnic group in one's own country" (Khatib-Chahidi, Hill, and Paton 1998, 49–50). The sparse research that considers the meaning of immigration for marital relations focuses on migrant couples, where both partners are nationals of the same country and move to the new country together (Hyman, Guruge, and Mason 2008; Youakim 2004). In other words, cross-national marriage is ascribed to the cross-cultural field and not the field of migration research.

In this chapter I present the results of a study of a community of Russian-speaking women married to Japanese men living in Japan. I define "cross-national marriage" as the marriage between the citizens of different countries, which necessarily leads to the migration of one of the spouses. This type of marriage differs from "cross-cultural marriage," defined as the marriage between members of different ethnic, religious, or racial communities of the same country but that does not always entail migration. The objectives of this study are 1) to reveal important dimensions of cross-national marriages; and 2) to investigate how the factors of culture and immigration are related to women's attitudes towards their marriages. The findings from this case study are relevant to understanding the situation of cross-national marriages in other industrialized countries.

Below I first review the context of cross-national marriages in Japan, followed by a description of the method of the empirical study and the presentation of the results. Finally, I present my conclusions.

CROSS-NATIONAL MARRIAGES IN JAPAN

Despite Japan's great economic success between 1960 and 1973 and the resulting intensification of international economic and social exchanges, Japanese society has remained highly ethnically homogeneous. According to a report of the Ministry of Justice (2010), the number of foreigners registered in Japan in 2009 was about 2 million, which represents less than 2 percent of Japan's overall population of 126 million. The distribution of foreigners varies greatly by geography: the numbers tend to be larger in big cities, and one-fifth of all foreigners (more than 400,000) lives in the capital district of Tokyo.

It is not surprising that the rate of cross-national marriages is also very low and comprised less than 5 (4.85) percent or 34,393 of the overall 707,734 marriages registered in 2009. Almost 78 percent of foreign spouses are women and only 22 percent are men. The majority of foreign wives are from China (47.6 percent), the Philippines (21.5 percent), South Korea (15.4 percent), and Thailand (4.6 percent); most foreign husbands are from South Korea (24.6 percent), the United States (19 percent), China (12.9 percent), and Great Britain (4.8 percent).

Marriages between Japanese and Russian-speaking spouses (Russian-speaking wife in most cases) constitute a minor share of cross-national marriages in Japan. According to the Ministry of Justice, there are 1,965 Russian, 527 Ukrainian, 93 Belarusian, and 64 Uzbek citizens with the resident status of "Spouse of a Japanese National." Most foreign spouses apply for permanent resident status after the minimum resident requirement of five years. Likely, most of the 2,096 Russian, 403 Ukrainian, 56 Belarusian and 22 Uzbek registered permanent residents are also in the cross-national marriages with Japanese citizens (Ministry of Justice 2010). Therefore, the number of Russian-speaking spouses in Japan can be estimated between 3,000 and 5,000.

Similar to other developed countries, Japan has faced population migration from agricultural districts to large cities. This migration has been gender-coloured. As the elder sons of rural families still often accept the responsibility as the sole inheritor of the family estate, they do not leave their parents' home and stay in rural areas. This condition resulted in a "bride deficit" in the rural parts of Japan. Cross-national marriages appeared to be the solution to this problem. This situation frames the context of the empirical study.

METHOD

The case of Russian-speaking wives married to Japanese men and living in Japan reveals the roles of culture and migration in cross-national marriage. In this case, women of an individual-oriented tradition have moved to an ethnically and racially homogeneous country emphasizing "group-oriented" culture. In addition, this case represents a common tendency in cross-national marriages, in that women from developing countries move to economically more developed countries.

Qualitative methods were used to reveal previously untheorized dimensions of cross-national marriage. Precise attention was given to how migrant wives evaluate their experiences of cross-national marriage and what factors they mention as important dimensions influencing their marital satisfaction. In the first year, the study focused on the capital district around Tokyo. The second year was devoted to extensive fieldwork at several distant communities on the island Kyushu in the southwest region of Japan. I attended women's and children's birthday parties, holiday parties and get-togethers; I also tried to provide some support in the women's everyday lives such as baby-sitting, translating important documentation, interpreting consultations on divorce processes, etc. Furthermore, I conducted extensive participant observation of the Russian-Speaking Women Internet Community in Japan over the two-year study period.

In addition, I interviewed 20 women (18 Russian and 2 Ukrainian). The participants were referred through personal contacts and the Internet community; some I met during fieldwork activities. I intentionally tried to access women who live close and far from the capital and in large cities and small towns, anticipating that the different contexts would provide different perspectives.

In general, the participants were young (average age of 30), in marriages lasting from 1 to 21 years (with an average of 4.5 years), and had relatively high levels of education (10 women with undergraduate degrees, 4 with graduate degrees). Most women had either no children or young children; two women had children from a previous marriage. Typical for Russian-Japanese marriages, many women met their husbands-to-be in Japanese nightclubs where they initially worked as dancers. A few couples in my sample became acquainted during the husband's or wife's work or study abroad, through the Internet, or through marital matching agencies. Except for Marina who was introduced to her husband through the marital matching agency, the sample does not include any cases of arranged marriages.

Most women were part-time workers or professional homemakers at the time of the study. It is typical in Japan with its traditional gender roles that women take care of the family and work part-time (usually in the service sector) when the husband's income is insufficient to meet the family's needs. In addition, the unique and complex Japanese script makes it difficult for foreigners to obtain jobs that match their aspirations.

All interview participants were given a brief explanation of the study and then asked to participate in an interview. Interviews were conducted between May 2008 and June 2010. All interviews were conducted in Russian, and lasted from 45 minutes to 2.5 hours. An open-ended questionnaire was developed on the basis of the literature (e.g., Lewis and Spanier 1979). The initial questionnaire was revised to include new and previously untheorized issues mentioned by the participants or found during the fieldwork. After the interview, all women were asked to complete a fact sheet on demographics and a small questionnaire. The interviews were recorded, transcribed, and analyzed using an open coding technique. Inductive method was used to define the categories, while continual reference to the previous research (deductive method) helped to investigate new themes for interviews and interpret the data. Not all categories were mentioned in every interview; some were mentioned frequently, others more seldom; however, all of them were given equal value in the analysis. In the sections below, I changed the names of the women to ensure confidentiality.

FINDINGS

Three dimensions of cross-national marriages were mentioned by participants in the study: 1) relations with the spouse, 2) relations with the local community, and 3) relations with the state. Figure 8.1 summarizes the three dimensions of cross-national marriage.

Figure 8.1: Dimensions of Cross-National Marriage

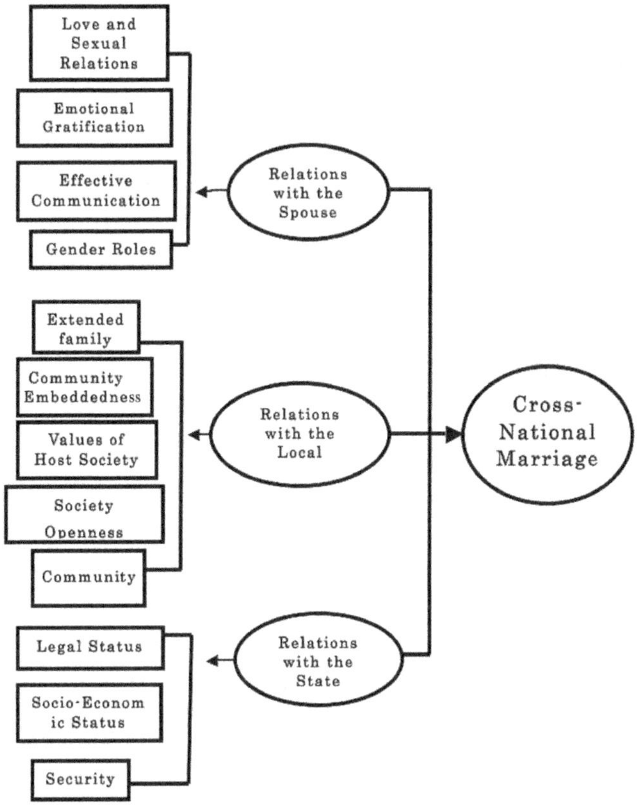

```
         Love and
         Sexual
         Relations
           │
         Emotional
         Gratification
           │                    Relations
         Effective      ←──     with the
         Communication          Spouse
           │
         Gender Roles

         Extended
         family
           │
         Community
         Embeddedness                              Cross-
           │                    Relations         National
         Values of      ←──     with the    ──→   Marriage
         Host Society           Local
           │
         Society
         Openness
           │
         Community

         Legal Status
           │                    Relations
         Socio-Econom   ←──     with the
         ic Status              State
           │
         Security
```

Source: Created by author.

Relations with the Spouse

The first dimension focuses on the micro-context of daily relations. This dimension includes aspects of love and sexual relations, emotional gratification, effective communication, and gender role consensus.

Love and Sexual Relations

According to Abraham Maslow's (1977) hierarchy of needs, love (belonging) and sexual relations (physical needs) are basic needs of human beings. In most societies they are traditionally prescribed to be satisfied in the marriage union. Most of the respondents reported "love" as their main reason for marriage and an important aspect of the evaluation of their marriage. Conversely, three women (Nadia, Larisa, and Polina) who reported strong dissatisfaction with the sexual relations with their husbands also mentioned that they had been considering divorce. Two respondents, who were contacted during the field study but refused the formal interview, admitted that they married their husbands to have an opportunity to live in Japan. They mentioned having no "sexual relations" with their husbands. At the same time, they noted that such relations were highly desirable for a "true" marriage. They also expressed their hope for a second marriage that would be a "true" one.

Expressions of love may differ between countries and cultures. For Russian and Ukrainian women expressions of love mean, first of all, the affirmation of their femininity and beauty, whereas for Japanese wives it may also mean the husband's provision of economic stability of the family. In a non-Japanese context, Mai Yamani (1998) finds in her study of cross-national marriage between Saudi Arabian women and Pakistani men that in the world of Islam marriage for love is constructed as opposite of arranged marriage; love is a shameful concept that "implies putting one's own individual interests above those of the well-being of the extended family" (Yamani 1998, 163). Correspondingly, the importance of this factor may differ for different partners in the cross-national marriage.

Emotional Gratification

The aspect of emotional gratification involves support, trust, and mutual understanding. As Vasilisa, a 32-year-old wife from Kyushu in her ninth year of marriage, explained: "The problems in cross-national marriages may be the same [as like-national ones], but we feel them more acutely. Because it hurts a lot, when you did it all for him, I mean, when you moved to a foreign country and changed everything, but he is not willing to support or understand you" (personal interview). Migrant spouses in cross-national marriages often cannot fully enjoy their previous social network, and all social ties are frequently narrowed to spousal relations. Therefore, it becomes crucially important how their emotional needs are met in spousal relations. Galina and Nadia also used the argument that their respective husbands were "the only intimate person they had" in Japan. The part of Nadia's interview below shows how she relates her migration and the importance of emotional gratification in spousal relations.

> Interviewer: Do you remember the situations, when you felt support of your spouse? (Pause) Or maybe the lack of support?
>
> Nadia: Yes, we had it at the beginning. Saying, I started crying, but he didn't try to set me at rest. That time, to tell the truth, yes. I was shocked. This is my husband! I had nobody here, who would support me! That hurt me very much. To tell the truth, we had such an episode. But then I thought: "Maybe this [is] not the reason to … quarrel. I will try to explain it, and if he does not understand … maybe we have no future. Because it is very important! The support of your intimate people is very important!" "But I tried to explain: "You know, I can't live without it! Moreover, I am alone here. I am Russian. If you fail to support me … I will, probably … How can I trust you then. This is the most important."

Effective Communication
Communication should be understood in a broad sense as the process of encoding and decoding different cultural patterns. Communication problems were reported to arise from an incomplete understanding of the partner's language and cultural background. Such problems were mentioned by 5 of the 20 women in the sample (Galina, Nadia, Margarita, Maria, and Polina). Four of them were recently married, between one month and two years ago. Only Maria was in the fifth year of her marriage and the kind of problems she mentioned were different. All women explained that they cannot communicate their ideas as effectively as they wish. Maria further explained that her husband used to misinterpret her words every time he was drunk. Neither of the five women took professional training in Japanese before marriage and all had lived for only a relatively short period in Japan. Selena's words, however, exemplify the idea that communication problems can be overcome and a better understanding of a partner's motivation and local settings can be achieved with time:

> Interviewer: When you have some conflicts, what is the most frequent reason for them? And how often do you quarrel?
>
> Selena: We did have quarrels at the beginning. Because of the misunderstandings, right? But then we knew each other better. We understood that it was not just my love for quarrels. We realized that I just didn't understand something. Or he didn't understand something. But it lessened gradually. We make fun of it now. I don't know ... I think it is not so related to different cultures. You just have to get used to each other, to know each other better. I think it would be the same if I had been married to the Russian. You have to understand each other, to know each other better first.

Gender Roles
In *Russian Gender Order*, Zdravomyslova and Temkina (2007) describe three gender models for women in post-Soviet Russia: 1) working mother; 2) professional homemaker; and 3) sexualized femininity. These gender models differ from the Soviet gender order, in which professional employment was the duty of every man *and* woman. The gender model "'working mother" means that women combine work and home based on their preference or economic need. The model "professional homemaker" regenerates the traditional labour division where the husband is the only breadwinner of the family. While this model resonates in religious discourse, where maternity and care are considered the natural attributes of femininity, it lacks legitimacy among the followers of Russia's long tradition of dual-earner families. The third model, "sexualized femininity," relates lifestyle with sexual attractiveness. According to this model,

the maintenance of sexual attractiveness becomes the priority of the woman and she can expect or even demand that a man satisfies her needs (Zdravomyslova and Temkina 2007, 187–200). Although these ideal types can be very seldom observed in actuality, they serve as a tool to analyze gender roles of the women in the sample.

In contemporary Japan, with its history of rapid economic growth, when men were mobilized to work long hours, earned sufficient salaries to provide for the entire family, and women took care of the family, professional homemaker had been an attractive role for women. According to the Ministry of Health, Labour, and Welfare of Japan (2010), 41.3 percent of women in the period 2000–2004 left paid employment after giving birth to their first child and 25.2 percent of women were not employed before their first pregnancy. However, the economic recession of the past years put pressure on many families and forced many women to work part-time. There is also a distinct minority of career-oriented women, who suffer however from low-status positions and lower earning potential, poor support systems for working mothers, and lacking pregnancy and maternity support (Refsing 1998, 199). In addition, expectations of very long working hours prevent many women from becoming the sole provider of the family, or combining working with motherhood. As a result, most women leave their full-time jobs when they get married and play the role of a "good wife and wise mother." Furthermore, sexual attractiveness is not valued as a woman's primary quality in Japanese society. Instead, as Refsing (1998, 199) expresses, women "are encouraged to strive for the ideals of mildness (*yasashisa*), stoicism (*gaman*), consideration of others (*omoiyari*) and other traditional female virtues."

Ten of the 20 women in my sample were "professional homemakers"; 7 women were working mothers or working wives (as some of them had no children); only 3 women were "career-oriented professionals." Seven women reported that their gender identities were in conflict with their actual gender roles in the family. Galina and Nadia, who were professional homemakers and were encouraged to play the role of "good wife and wise mother," reported that, in fact, they desired to be a "sexually attractive woman for her husband." Vasilisa, Margarita, and Polina, who were professional homemakers, spoke about their identity crises as professionals. Professional homemaker Tamara expressed her desire to work part-time, but she did not receive the necessary permission from her in-laws. Finally, working mother Albina was dreaming of staying at home and becoming a professional homemaker, but could not quit her job as her husband refused to be the sole provider for the family.

These conflicts between the women's gender identities and the gender roles they actually perform are not specific to cross-national marriages. Rather, modern Russian and Japanese societies present a diversity of gender models that inevitably leads to identity conflicts. However, in the case of cross-national marriages these conflicts are caused not only by personal preferences and economic need but also by structural limitations imposed by migration.

Relations with the Local Community

The second dimension includes the aspects of extended family, community embeddedness, the values of the host society, community openness, and community support.

Extended Family

In many cases, when a migrant wife moves to the new country alone, without relatives, she finds herself as the only foreigner in the family. The situation when a foreign spouse enters a large family and lives with in-laws puts additional strain on spousal relations. It is more difficult to negotiate family relations when the wife is in an unequal position of "one versus many." Four women in the sample lived with their in-laws, one woman lived right next door to her husband's family, two women lived separately but the husband's family had strong ties with them. All of these women mentioned the great authority and influence of their husband's family over their private life. The lack of private space and time (Marina); the double burden of household chores (Albina and Tamara); the constant interference and lecturing on how they should rear children and keep the household (Lena, Polina); and dependence in decision-making processes (like Tamara who was supposed to get the in-laws' permission to acquire paid part-time employment) were mentioned as the reasons for conflicts and dissatisfaction.

The very situation of migration put the wives in positions in which they could not use the ties with their own family as a power resource in negotiating everyday practices and/or decision-making. Most social and cultural practices common among their families in Russia and Ukraine were discredited as useless in the new country with its different climate and economic, political, and social systems. Conversely, practices enacted by the husbands' families were presented as useful and necessary. Those wives who lived in nuclear rather than extended families enjoyed more egalitarian negotiations of everyday practices with their husbands. For example, Albina addressed the issue of romper suits for their baby. Although winter in Japan is milder than in Russia, Albina considered it rather cold for a baby and did not approve the Japanese way of clothing babies in romper suits that leave heels bare. She asked her friend to send romper suits from Russia, but her mother- and sisters-in-law cut that part of the suits to open the heels, as they considered that those romper suits were suitable only for severe Russian winters.

Community Embeddedness

Community embeddedness was also mentioned as an important aspect of cross-national marriage. Although there were wives who had Japanese friends and those who had only Russian-speaking friends, both groups reported that the presence of acquaintances was very important for their psychological well-being. On the one hand, acquaintances fulfil the human need to belong to any group, including a professional community, a group based on leisure activities, a parents' committee at school, or an ethnic community. On the other hand, migrant wives who move to a new place often lose the ties to their established communities at the place of origin and have to create new ties with the community where they now live. Not belonging to any group for an extended period can result in the feeling of exclusion from social life. Vasilisa recalled:

> You have to start everything again. From the zero point. I mean, you go outside, you are walking down the street—you are 20 years old—and you meet NOBODY. That scared me. That scared me so much. Because I was very sociable person, I had a lot of friends, acquaintances [in Ukraine]. But here, you walk, and walk, and walk, and you see nobody. I mean, of course, you meet people outside, but no familiar faces. (personal interview)

Interestingly, most of the employed women mentioned that the main reason for employment was to find friends and to broaden contacts. All three professionally oriented women and three of seven working mothers had both Japanese and Russian friends. Conversely, most of the professional homemakers joined ethnic Russian-Ukrainian communities where they maintained social contacts. Two of the professional homemakers had no friends at all. These findings indicate that participation in social life is an important dimension of cross-national marriage, but also that employment can facilitate community embeddedness.

Values of Host Society

Another aspect of the relations with the local community dimension relates to the understanding of the values of the host society. Some women reported feeling marginalized, as they could not understand the values of the people around them and felt that other people did not understand them. This psychological isolation resulted in physical isolation. Even when the local (or ethnic) community was open to the individual, the individual was not always open to a community that did not share the same values. For example, the two women who had no friends mentioned a sense of discomfort produced by their lives in isolation, but neither of them wanted to join either native or foreign local ethnic communities.

Nevertheless, my sample included participants who strongly appreciated the values of Japanese society, those who did not, and those who felt ambiguous about these values. For example, 31-year-old Selena explained that, on the one hand, she admires how the Japanese take care of disabled people and are eager to help others. On the other hand, she also called Japan "the materialistic society" practicing a cult of food. She noted the particular stress on practical things but felt a neglect of the spiritual sphere. She reported beginning to visit the Orthodox Church in Japan, although she never did so when she lived in Russia. Vasilisa sees the numerous constraints of

Japanese society as the obstacles for self-expression and realization of individuality. In her interview Vasilisa said that she did not want her children to adopt the values of this society. Other women expressed similar feelings.

Community Openness

The case of Selena, who was learning Japanese at the university, shows that community openness to diversity is an important aspect of cross-national marriage. Soon after marriage her husband was transferred from the head office in the capital to a branch office in a city where she was almost the only foreigner. Although Selena could speak Japanese well, she did not manage to find a job, even one that did not require special training. During the job interview she was told that the firm had never employed a foreigner and that the employer was afraid a foreign employee would confuse clients. In addition, she did not make any friends in this city and was thinking about returning to Russia. When the husband was transferred back to the head office in Tokyo, she found employment in a bakery shop. In Tokyo she met her university friends, who also had married Japanese men and lived in the capital. She said:

> The society is more diverse in Tokyo, they have Japanese and they have foreigners. When the society is homogeneous, it is more difficult for the European … the Russian … the "other." Because you feel, "You are different!" Such alienation, right? To take the situation with the job. The first reason why they could not employ me, as they said, was "that I was different … that it was the first time in their practice." I mean, in the province you feel your "difference" more distinctly. You feel this alienation. While in Tokyo you feel much better, not because of communication, because they don't reject you, because you can take some place in society.

Selena's case illustrates the importance of society openness for well-being and life satisfaction.

Community Support

Community support was mentioned as another important aspect of cross-national marriage. As all women in the sample moved to live abroad for their marriage, they found themselves in a situation in which they could not count on the understanding or support of their community back home. Thus, it became very important to receive support from the local community. As Vasilisa realized, cool relations with in-laws were not such a rare thing, even in Ukraine. However, in the situation of her cross-cultural marriage, she could not depend on the help from her relatives or friends back home with such things as babysitting; she could rely only on herself. Later, however,

Vasilisa found that support from the Russian-speaking ethnic community. Members of this community watched her babies when she had a part-time job.

Although relations with the local community are not something that is specific to cross-national marriages, it has greater importance in this kind of marriage in which one spouse is migrating to an unfamiliar place distant from this same person's existing community and support network. The spouse who moves abroad cannot keep the former ties and often has to reconstruct a social network from scratch. This problem, however, may be less severe for those women who had lived for a long period in the country (working or studying) before their marriage.

Relations with the State

In this final part I consider how foreign spouses are being incorporated in the new nation and how they are making meaning from their experience of transition to another state.

Legal Status

Although it is often thought that marriage will automatically grant a valid reason for legal residence in the country, this is not always the case. In Japan, the registration of marriage and the acquisition of a visa or residency status are two different procedures. Two members of the Internet community that I examined had overstayed the period of their visas. Even after marrying a Japanese man and giving birth to a child in that marriage, they still could not obtain a spousal visa. One of them was waiting for years in Ukraine; the other one was living in Japan without a legal residency permit.

Galina, a 29-year-old wife living in Tokyo who had been married for three years at the time of the interview, had entered Japan with the entertainer visa but overstayed it. She met a man who agreed to marry her, but he did not trust her feelings for him; therefore, he refused to sponsor her spousal visa. She was subsequently arrested on the street for staying in Japan "illegally" and spent a month in prison. After a month, her husband helped her to get out of jail and she finally got a spousal visa. When she recounted her experience of staying in Japan without legal permission, she acknowledged the constant anxiety and that she did not feel safe for a moment. Furthermore, she also could not get health insurance, a bank account, or a legal job.

Since the spousal visa needs to be extended periodically, even women who possess spousal visas may continue to feel anxiety. In the case of Japan, a spousal visa is usually issued for one year. After a second one-year extension, spouses can then obtain a three-year visa. After five years in Japan they can apply for a permanent residence permit. Whether the visa would be prolonged or not depended on the women's relations with their husbands. This resulted in a power inequality in the family, in which some women were afraid to negotiate their rights and lifestyles or to quarrel at least until they could obtain permanent residency.

Socio-Economic Status

Moving to a foreign country was also associated with the necessity to reconstruct one's socio-economic status. Although 13 of the wives in the sample had undergraduate or graduate qualifications, which they obtained in their countries of origin, they had to content themselves with the role of homemaker or could only obtain a part-time job in the service sector. This deskilling is consistent with the findings of other studies. Rosemary Breger's (1998, 145) study of foreign wives in Germany shows that the tendency to discount foreign qualifications "creates a potentially conflict-laden power imbalance" between spouses. In their study of the impact of migration on marital relations of Ethiopian immigrants in Toronto, Ilene Hyman, Sepali Guruge, and Robin Mason (2008) also mentioned the loss of income and status as important changes caused by migration. Especially the male participants in their study suffered from downward status mobility and a loss of authority in the family, which raised the relative significance of women's income and their authority in the family. For the women in my study, the devaluation of their professional qualifications resulted in the feeling that they lack "a proper place in the new country," increased their dependence on the spouse, and, in some cases, reinforced the gender identity crisis discussed above.

All participants were asked to explain whether there were negotiations around which country the couple would choose to settle in and why it was decided that the women would move to Japan rather than the men moving to Russia or Ukraine. Five women replied that there were no negotiations and that it was a "natural mutual decision." Four women said that their husbands refused to move abroad as they could not speak Russian, even as their wives did not speak Japanese fluently at the time of the decision. Seven wives replied that they decided to live in Japan because that was the place of their husbands' work. The remaining four wives explicitly stated that, as they understood, in the case of their husbands' migration he would not be able to provide for the family, and they were not ready to become the main breadwinner. Maintaining the family's socio-economic status and gender roles within the family thus contributed to the decision in which country to locate.

Security

The final aspect mentioned by the participants relates to the security of the destination country. Although there were cases such as Galina who reported that she "couldn't feel safe for a moment" because she didn't have a valid visa, most women explained that Japan was a much more secure country than Russia or Ukraine. Russian women especially mentioned the problems of drug and alcohol addiction and high crime rates in contemporary Russia. They valued the fact that they could bring up their children in a more stable and safe environment, and with good medical care provisions. One woman, Larisa, also confessed that she had considered divorce but decided to remain in that marriage because there would be better life chances for her six-year-old son if she were to stay in Japan.

CONCLUSION

This study investigated basic dimensions of cross-national marriage reported by Russian-speaking migrant wives living in Japan. Based on extensive fieldwork and in-depth interviews, the study found three dimensions that migrant women considered important for evaluating their marriages: relations with the husband, relations with the local community, and relations with the state. These three dimensions are likely not unique to the specific case of Russian-speaking women married to Japanese men and living in Japan. Rather, they illustrate the complexity of the situation for couples who marry across other national borders. In particular, when wives follow their husbands to more industrialized countries, I would expect similarities to the case study I presented above.

Some women reported communication problems with their spouses; some exercised social practices and embraced gender roles that conflicted with the expectations of their in-laws. Some women did not appreciate the values of Japanese society, which, in certain cases, resulted in their social marginalization. Yet, many women referred to cultural differences as the most important benefit of cross-national marriage, and they were able to overcome their initial cultural differences with their husbands. Some women also evaluated positively the fact that they and their children could enjoy two cultural traditions.

The process of immigration, however, was a burden to most women and was often associated with disempowerment. The women's previous values and everyday practices were often disregarded in the context of the new society. They could not draw on their ties with the family, friends, and colleagues at the place of origin to help in difficult situations or to negotiate their roles in the new family. The fact that all participants of the study were foreign citizens and suffered from the devaluation of their job qualifications resulted in their dependency on the native spouse, and in the case of some women, contributed to their identity crisis. Yet, many women reported that they enjoyed living in a country with low crime rates, good medical coverage, and social and economic stability.

Both cultural factors and factors related to immigration are important in the context of cross-national marriage. Cultural factors seemed to have greater importance for intimate relations with the spouse and relatives; factors related to immigration were of greater significance for interactions with the state. However, the two factors were interrelated and could not always be neatly separated one from another, as the case of gender roles or relations with the extended family exemplified.

The results of this study reaffirm my initial thesis that immigration is an important variable of marriage. Conflating cross-national marriage with other forms of intermarriages, including as cross-cultural marriage, leads to overstating the importance of culture in respect to the spousal relationship. The present study shows that although the cultural component is no doubt an important variable of cross-national marriage, the debate of cross-national marriage cannot be reduced to cultural differences alone.

REFERENCES

Breger, R. 1998. "Love and the State: Women, Mixed Marriages and the Law in Germany." In *Cross-Cultural Marriage: Identity and Choice*, edited by R. Breger and R. Hill, 129–152. Oxford, UK: Berg.

Breger, R., and R. Hill. 1998. "Introducing Mixed Marriages." In *Cross-Cultural Marriage: Identity and Choice*, edited by R. Breger and R. Hill, 1–32. Oxford, UK: Berg.

Goble, F. G. 2004. *The Third Force: The Psychology of Abraham Maslow*. NC: Maurice Bassett Publishing.

Hyman, I., S. Guruge, and R. Mason. 2008. "Impact of Migration on Marital Relationships: A Study of Ethiopian Immigrants in Toronto." *Comparative Family Studies* (2): 149–170.

Khatib-Chahidi, J., R. Hill, and R. Paton. 1998. "Chance, Choice and Circumstance: A Study of Women in Cross-Cultural Marriage." In *Cross-Cultural Marriage: Identity and Choice*, edited by R. Berger and R. Hill, 49–66. Oxford, UK: Berg.

Lewis, R. A., and G. B. Spanier. 1979. "Theorizing About Quality and Stability of Marriage." In *Contemporary Theories about the Family*, edited by W. R. Burr, R. Hill, F. I. Nye, and R. L. Reiss. New York: Free Press.

Maslow, A. H. 1977. *Motivation und Persönlichkeit*. Olten: Walter-Verlag: 74–105.

Ministry of Justice, Japan. 2010. Statistics on Registered Foreigners. Accessed October 16, 2010. www.moj.go.jp/housei/toukei/toukei_ichiran_touroku.html.

Ministry of Health, Labour, and Welfare, Japan. 2010. Statistics on Population Dynamics, Marriage. Accessed October 16, 2010. www.e-stat.go.jp/SG1/estat/List.do?lid=000001066477.

Refsing, K. 1998. "Gender Identity and Gender Role Patterns in Cross-Cultural Marriages: the Japanese-Danish Case." In *Cross-Cultural Marriage: Identity and Choice*, edited by R. Breger and R. Hill, 193–208. Oxford, UK: Berg.

Romano, D. 2008, 1988. *Intercultural Marriages: Promises and Pitfalls*. Boston: Intercultural Press.

Yamani, M. 1998. "Cross-Cultural Marriage Within Islam: Ideals and Reality." In *Cross-Cultural Marriage: Identity and Choice*, edited by R. Breger and R. Hill, 153–169. Oxford, UK: Berg.

Youakim, J. M. 2004. "Marriage in the Context of Immigration." *The American Journal of Psychoanalysis* 64: 155–165.

Zdravomyslova, E., and A. Temkina, eds. 2007. *Российскийгендерныйпорядок: социологическийподход* [*Russian Gender Order: Sociologic Perspective*]. Saint-Petersburg: European University in Saint-Petersburg Press.

Chapter 9

RECENT IMMIGRANTS, EARLIER IMMIGRANTS, AND THE CANADIAN-BORN: ASSOCIATION WITH COLLECTIVE IDENTITIES

TARA GILKINSON AND GENEVIÈVE SAUVÉ

INTRODUCTION

The degree to which immigrants associate with their community, province, or country may be a useful indicator of the effectiveness of Canada's integration policies and programs. Due to the increase in the ethnocultural and linguistic diversity of immigrants to Canada over the past 15 years,[1] the degree to which immigrants identify as a citizen of Canada and as a member of their local community may prove to be particularly significant.

Collective identities are statements about categorical membership, which can be understood to be, on the one hand, socially constructed, yet, on the other, real and meaningful. Levels of identification provide insight into feelings of belonging, perceptions of settlement, and overall life satisfaction, and therefore, can be used as important indicators of social integration. High levels of identification have "widespread instrumental value in virtue of satisfying desire or needs to belong (or to identify with others, or be recognized by others) and thereby secure goods such as psychological security, self-esteem and feelings of being at home in the world" (Mason 2000, 54).

According to an analysis of Statistics Canada's General Social Survey (GSS) on social engagement, levels of life satisfaction were the highest among individuals who reported a very strong level of belonging to their community (Schellenberg 2004a). Moreover, results from the Canadian Community Health Survey indicate that "close to two-thirds of those who felt a very strong or somewhat strong sense of community belonging reported excellent or very good general health. By contrast, about half (51 percent) of those with weak sense of belonging viewed their general health favourably" (Shields 2008, 5).

This study draws on data from the fifth wave (2006) of the World Values Survey (WVS) and builds on the work of Neil Nevitte (2008) to analyze respondents' association with various collective identities (citizen of the world, North America, Canada, province/region, and local community). The analysis compares the responses of the Canadian-born with recent immigrants and established immigrants. In this chapter, we undertake to answer the following questions: How do recent immigrants, earlier immigrants, and the Canadian-born compare in the degree to which they identify/associate with various collective identities? Are the Canadian-born more likely to identify as Canadian citizens than earlier and recent immigrants? Are there variables that are associated with an individual's likelihood of identifying as a citizen of Canada? Do individuals who strongly identify with other collective identities (e.g., world citizen and local community) demonstrate a greater likelihood of identifying as a citizen of Canada?

The chapter proceeds as follows. After a literature review on identity, identification, and migration, the next sections present a descriptive analysis, followed by regression results and discussion. The conclusion summarizes the main findings and discusses some policy implications of the research.

LITERATURE REVIEW

The Concept of Identity

Identity is about definition; it is what makes us who we are. "There is a very deep ontological longing in people to feel complete, which manifests itself in a desire to belong to something that is greater than oneself and to participate actively in the life of this supra-individual entity" (Létourneau 2001, 5). Some researchers argue that collective identities matter primarily on the premise that they are related to social cohesion (Jenson 1998; Muir 2007). According to Rick Muir (2007), shared values, shared action, and shared identity lead to social cohesion. In this context, identity brings two important attributes to the table: "affective attachment and easy-to-generalise, imagined solidarities between large numbers of people" (Muir 2007, 8). Collective identity "involves the imaginative leap of bringing people together with large numbers of others under one symbolic roof and ... allows us to generalise from individual encounters to a sense of solidarity with the broader community" (Muir 2007, 9). Furthermore, "shared identity has the potential to make a distinct and valuable contribution to social cohesion through its ability to foster affective ties between potentially quite large numbers of people" (Muir 2007, 17).

What makes individuals who they are is not only their personal traits and characteristics but also their membership—attributed by oneself or ascribed by others—in (real or imagined) social categories and social groups. In its social context, identity can be defined as "the distinctive character belonging to any given individual, or shared by all members of a particular social category or group.... 'Identity' may be distinguished from 'identification'; the former is a label whereas the latter refers to the classifying act itself" (Rummens 2001, 3).

The sociological literature suggests that identity and the related concept of identification are about situating an individual actor in society, about classification or categorization (Tajfel 1974; Rummens 2001; Ashmore, Deaux, and McLaughlin-Volpe 2004), and about the labelling of individuals and groups who share a *sameness* (Tastsoglou 2001; Bokser-Liwerant 2002). As Henri Tajfel (1974, 69), developer of social identity theory in the 1970s, indicates, identity in a social context involves "the individual's self-concept which derives from his [sic] knowledge of his [sic] membership of a social group (or groups) together with the emotional significance attached to that membership."

David Snow (2001, 2) distinguishes between personal, social, and collective identity: "personal identities are the attributes and meaning attributed to oneself by the actor; they are self-designations and self-attributions regarded as personally distinctive." Meanwhile, social identities are "the identities attributed or imputed to others in an attempt to situate them in social space. They are grounded in established social roles" (Snow 2001, 2). Snow (2001) believes that collective identities have embedded within them a corresponding sense of collective agency facilitating collective action. He states:

> Although there is no consensual definition of collective identity, discussions of the concept invariably suggest that its essence resides in a shared sense of "one-ness" or "we-ness" anchored in real or imagined shared attributes and experiences among those who comprise the collectivity and in relation or contrast to one or more actual or imagined sets of "others." (Snow 2001, 2)

In the literature the concept of identity is also associated with the idea of boundaries. More specifically, identities are bounded in that they confer not only a sense of sameness, but also of difference or distinctiveness from outsiders (Tajfel 1974; Tastsoglou 2001; Bokser-Liwerant 2002; Muir 2007).

The Characteristics of Identity

Identities are generally understood to be constructed, multiple, dynamic, relational, and negotiated, and to vary in their salience. Current research suggests that identities are constructed, meaning that they are created, shaped, and formulated by individuals as social actors, by groups and their social environments, as opposed to being essential or predetermined (e.g., Rummens 2001; Létourneau 2001; Frideres 2002; Ashmore, Deaux, and McLaughlin-Volpe 2004). According to Jocelyn Létourneau (2001, 5), "there is general agreement that collective identity ... is 'constructed,' that is to say, manufactured from elements drawn from historical materials and reified (or petrified) as identity references." James Frideres (2002, 4) explains that identities "change as a consequence of both internal and external pressures."

In addition, identities are understood to be multiple, in that they can be numerous and varied. A given individual can have a variety of identities, which can intersect, overlap, conflict, and collide (e.g., Peressini 1993; Rummens 2001; Létourneau 2001; Tastsoglou 2001; Snow 2001). According to Joanna Anneke Rummens (2001, 4), "there are almost an unlimited number of 'identities' that are ascribed to and/or assumed by individuals and groups as social actors." Identities are also thought of as being dynamic in that they are understood to be fluid and malleable rather than fixed or static, and they may change over time and from place to place (e.g., Létourneau 2001; Bokser-Liwerant 2002; Croucher 2004; Rashid 2007). Létourneau (2001, 2), for example, understands identity as a "continual re-interpretation of the self. This is why it is said that identity is not fixed but changing and alive."

Identities are generally put forward as being relational (e.g., Tajfel 1974; Létourneau 2001; Frideres 2002). What is meant by the relational nature of identity is two-fold. Firstly, identity is relational in that it is socially embedded, inter-subjective, and not constructed in isolation from its social context. In short, individual identity is the product of a self-definition (or self-narration) process and of "external definition" (or "external narration") by others, whether individually or collectively. It can therefore be said that identity is a social, inter-subjective activity because it is the product of a relationship with the other in which the reference to others is internalized by the subject (Létourneau 2001, 4). Secondly, identity is relational in that it is generally understood to be other-referenced. It says something about same-ness but also about difference and about others. Identity thus implies comparison, contrast, and boundaries. "The definition of a group (national, racial or any other) makes no sense unless there are other groups around. A group becomes a group in the sense of being perceived as having common characteristics or a common fate only because other groups are present in the environment" (Tajfel 1974, 71–72).

Finally, identities are negotiated, contested, and may or may not be taken up by the individual actor or group (e.g., Rummens 2001; Hoerder, Hébert, and Schmitt 2006; Rashid 2007; Muir 2007). Muir (2007, 11), for example, states that identity "is a process in which meaning is constantly being asserted, contested and negotiated." Rummens (2001, 15) asserts that identities "are not just ascribed or achieved as part of the individual's socialization and developmental process, they are also socially constructed and negotiated by social actors. These identifications of self and/or others may be accepted or they may be contested."

What Happens to National Identities in the Process of Migration?
Frideres (2002, 1–2) explains that immigrants "find the process of physically relocating presents a new definition of who they are." Peter Grant (2007, 89) further remarks

that immigrants "often internalize a new national identity when they move to another country (psychological acculturation), although doing so means identifying with a culture that has values and traditions different from those of their culture of origin." This process of internalization—this change in the self-concept—if well realized, results in the development of a new national identity for the individual.

Some authors associate the development of a new national identity with successful integration. David Walters and his associates (2007, 60) argue that "identification with the host society is important for national unity." While the successful integration process involves acculturation and thus a shift in national identification, it does not imply that immigrants do, or should, put aside previous national identities.

The concept of transnationalism relates to the transcendence of national boundaries and the involvement of several nations or nationalities (e.g., Gardiner Barber 2003; Croucher 2004; Ehrkampand Leitner 2006; Grant 2007). Pauline Gardiner Barber (2003) argues that as "a global process migration produces citizens who have multiple connections and attachments. Immigrants view the world comparatively through a lens we now describe as transnational.... Thus it may be said that all migrants, potentially at least, hold transnational identities" (Gardiner Barber 2003, 45).

> The concept of transnationalism ... suggests that immigrants forge and sustain familial, economic, cultural, and political ties and identities across national borders, in both home and host societies.... In short, contemporary migrants are embedded in, identify with, and participate in multiple communities, and are not just, nor even primarily, anchored in one national collectivity. (Ehrkamp and Leitner 2006, 1593)

The literature reviewed above suggests that different factors may impact upon the development of a new national identity by immigrants. These include, but are not limited to: the time spent in the country of destination (Grant 2007; Walters, Phythian, and Anisef 2007); the acquisition of formal citizenship (Krzyzanowsli and Wodak 2007; Walters, Phythian, and Anisef 2007); the degree of correspondence or incompatibility between the cultures of origin and of destination (Grant 2007); and the experiences in the host society (Grant 2007; Krzyzanowsli and Wodak 2007).

Collective Identities and Belonging amongst Canadians

Identity is a concept that can be operationalised in different ways for empirical study. As previously noted, collective identity is related to belonging. This is the measure used in the studies of Grant Schellenberg (2003; 2004) and Ipsos Reid (2007). A similar measure is also used in the cross-country comparison by Leslie Laczko (2005).

Ipsos Reid conducted a national survey in 2007 that "explores the levels of social engagement and attachment to Canada among English-speaking first and second generation Canadian immigrants, and compares findings to a nationally representative sample of Canadians" (Ipsos Reid 2007, 1). Respondents were asked how strong their sense of belonging was to Canada. Their findings reveal that 88 percent of second-generation Canadians reported their sense of belonging as *strong*, compared to 81 percent of first-generation immigrants and 79 percent of the general population; while 71 percent of second-generation Canadians indicated that their sense of belonging was *very strong*, compared to 58 percent of first-generation Canadians and 62 percent of the general population[2] (Ipsos Reid 2007, 4).

Cycle 17 of Statistics Canada's GSS (GSS 17), conducted in 2003, focused on social engagement and included questions on the sense of belonging to Canada, to the province, and to the community. According to the results, immigrants reported a stronger sense of belonging to Canada than the Canadian-born population (Schellenberg 2004). Results also showed that the sense of belonging to one's community did not vary considerably between the Canadian-born and immigrant populations (Schellenberg 2004).

Finally, the analysis by Laczko (2005), using data from the 1995 International Social Survey Program (ISSP), examined data from 24 countries (including Canada), first as a whole, and then in a cross-country comparison. While the study did not explore "sense of belonging," the 1995 ISSP used a similar measure, asking survey respondents about how "close" they feel to various levels of community (neighbourhood or village, town or city, province, country, and continent), and about their willingness to geographically relocate. Laczko found considerable cross-national similarities, and notes that "people [including Canadians] feel closest to their country or national society, and least to their continent" (Laczko 2005, 522–523). With regard to Canadian results, the author also found that Canadians express "relatively low levels of attachment to local communities" (Laczko 2005, 527).

METHODOLOGY

The World Values Survey (WVS) is a "worldwide investigation of sociocultural and political change. The longitudinal survey has been conducted by a network of social scientists at leading universities all around world" (WVS 2008). Five waves of the survey have been carried out in 1981, 1990–1991, 1995–1997, 1999–2001 and most recently 2005–2006.

The WVS presents a national representative sample of Canadian residents 18 years of age and older. The core survey sample (total population N=1,765) was expanded in 2000 and 2006 to include a larger sample of recent immigrants, which allows for comparisons between the responses of recent immigrants (persons not born in Canada who have lived in the country for a period of less than 10 years); earlier immigrants (persons not born in Canada who have lived in the country 10 years or more); and Canadian-born respondents. The new immigrant sample targeted new immigrants in Vancouver (N=151), Toronto (N=157), and Montreal (N=192) and supplemented the core survey.[3] The core WVS sample was combined with the new immigrant sample, and then the population was sorted into three groups: Canadian-born (N=1,766), recent immigrants (N=570), and earlier immigrants (N=298).

Survey participants were asked whether they strongly agree, agree, disagree, or strongly disagree with the statement: "I see myself as ... a citizen of the world/a citizen of North America/a citizen of Canada as a whole/a citizen of my province or region/a member of my local community." The percentages of the three population groups were contrasted in order to examine how the patterns of identification compare across the population groups (see Appendix for data tables).

To gain further insight into the variables that are associated with an individual's likelihood of identifying themselves with Canada as a whole (dependent variable), ordered logistic regression analyses were completed along with a pseudo r-squared test for goodness-of-fit. Ordered logistic regression is a useful technique for making predictions about the strength of the relationship between dependent and independent variables when the dependent variable is ordered. Ordered logistic regression is most suitable when dealing with an ordered dependent variable with a limited range of categories because it avoids biased estimates which often come from the assumption that there is equal distance between the dependent variable categories. The regression analyses were conducted using the new immigrant sample which enabled the separation of Canadian-born, earlier immigrant, and recent immigrant populations.

Odds ratios and p-values were also calculated. Odds ratios greater than one indicate that the association of the independent variable with identification as a citizen of Canada is positive, while those less than one indicate that the association of the independent variable with identification as a citizen of Canada is negative. Odds ratios close to one indicate that changes in the independent variable are not associated with the dependent variable. To deal with missing data, "don't know" and refused responses were excluded from the calculations.

RESULTS AND DISCUSSION

Descriptive Analysis

According to Will Kymlicka (1998, 173), the basis for social unity "is not shared values but a shared identity.... People decide whom they want to share a country with by asking whom they identify with, whom they feel solidarity with." As John Harles (1997, 717) explains, "[P]erhaps the most profound mark of a well-integrated polity is the strong sense of belonging felt by its members. A fundamental integrative question about immigrants, then, is whether the newcomers' understanding of themselves—their idea of 'us'—includes Canada. Do immigrants in any way 'feel' Canadian?" The 2006 WVS data suggests that the answer to this question is a resounding "yes."

The WVS data indicates that recent immigrants, earlier immigrants, and the Canadian-born collectively express high levels of positive identification as a citizen of Canada, as a citizen of their province/region, and as a citizen of their community (see Figures 9.1 and 9.2). The findings show that 96.6 percent of the Canadian-born population, 96.2 percent of earlier immigrants, and 95.4 percent of recent immigrants either "agree" or "strongly agree" that they view themselves as a citizen of Canada as a whole. Levels of identification with one's province or region are also high: 98.1 percent of the Canadian-born respondents, 92.9 percent of earlier immigrants, and 90.4 percent of recent immigrants either "agree" or "strongly agree" that they view themselves as a citizen of their province or region. Furthermore, the results indicate that respondents in all three categories express positive identification with their communities: 91.5 percent of Canadians, 87.7 percent of earlier immigrants, and 86.9 percent of recent immigrants "agree" or "strongly agree" that they perceive themselves to be a member of their local community.

Figure 9.1: "Strongly Agree" with Collective Identities

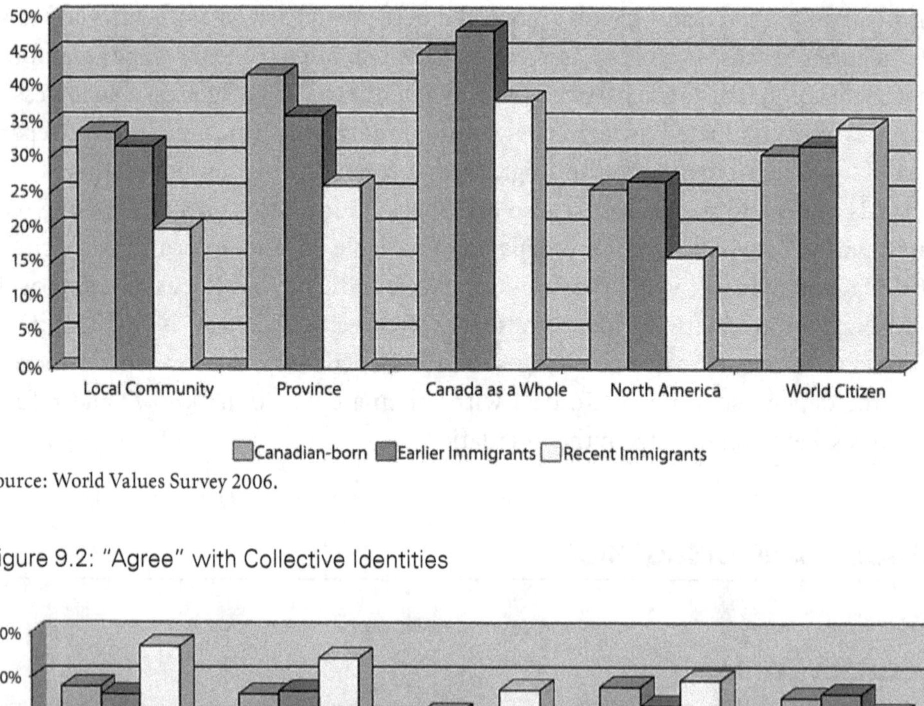

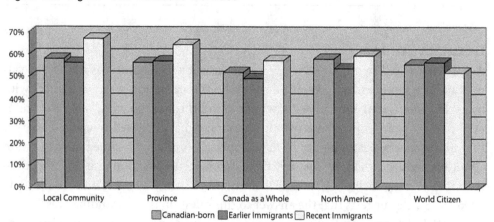

Source: World Values Survey 2006.

Figure 9.2: "Agree" with Collective Identities

Source: World Values Survey 2006.

Overall, it appears that all three groups feel the strongest identification with Canada as a whole, and the weakest identification with North America (Figure 9.1). This finding is consistent with Laczko's (2005, 522–525) multinational survey results, which concluded that the national society "remains the strongest focus of feelings of closeness, and the larger continent is the weakest focus." The findings from the 2006 WVS also indicate that recent immigrants have the highest likelihood of strongly identifying as a world citizen.

When looking at differences between the three groups (Canadian-born, earlier immigrant, and recent immigrant population), with the exception of identification as a world citizen, the results show a decreased tendency for recent immigrants to "strongly agree" with any collective identity. One potential explanation for this finding is that the lower levels of community identification amongst recent immigrants points to the existence of barriers to full integration. As we noted in the review of the literature, identity is an important indicator of both integration and social cohesion. Therefore, lower levels of identification with one's country, province, or community may have negative effects upon civic engagement and sense of belonging.

However, it may not be reasonable to expect recent immigrants to display (in a relatively short period of time) the same levels of identification as do earlier immigrants and the Canadian-born population. The lower levels of identification showcase the reality that it takes time to develop a substantial bond with one's community, province, or country. Therefore, individuals who have had less time to establish a relationship with their community, province, and with Canada, may feel less connected.

According to Ulf Hedetoft (2002, 3), the degree to which one displays a sense of belonging is "processed through and coloured by memory and by experiences, sensations and ideas encountered in other spheres and in different contexts." Hedetoft (2002, 3) argues that these feelings of belonging are conditioned by "social and psychological concreteness—persons, landscapes, sensory experiences and 'mental mappings' of an immediate and familiar kind" and must always pass "through mental processing, personal and collective experiences, and the … psychological filter of 'memory'—all of which shape each individual's images and perceptions of belonging, giving them depth and value, and engendering the meaning they have for different persons. "Therefore, the degree to which recent immigrants identify with various Canadian identities may likely be rooted in a sense of familiarity and history, which may take time to develop.

Furthermore, identity is always in the process of evolving (Létourneau 2001; Bokser-Liwerant 2002; Croucher 2004; Rashid 2007). The extent to which an individual identifies with their community is not fixed but fluid and changing, and involves continuous reinterpretation. Therefore, it can be argued that as recent immigrants invest more into their communities, the degree to which they identify with their local community will also increase. This identification is dynamic, and occurs as a consequence of both internal and external pressures. This argument is supported by very similar expressed levels of identification among the Canadian-born and earlier immigrants to various collective identities.

In fact, the WVS results show that earlier immigrants express the highest levels of identification with Canada as a whole: 48.1 percent of earlier immigrants "strongly agree" that they view themselves as a citizen of Canada, compared to 44.8 percent of Canadian-born, and 38.2 percent of recent immigrants. This finding is supported by results from the 2003 GSS, which concluded that recent immigrants were "somewhat less likely than earlier arrivals to describe their sense of belonging as 'very strong'" (Schellenberg, 2003, 6). Schellenberg (2003, 6) argues that "this may be due to the fact that they had resided in Canada for less time than others and had had less opportunity to cultivate a strong sense of attachment.... [F]eelings of belonging were also associated with the length of time that individuals had resided in a province or city."

A final consideration is necessary when exploring the possible reasons behind the lower observed levels of identification as a Canadian citizen amongst recent immigrants. As is addressed later in the chapter, there are limitations inherent to the dataset used. Amongst these limitations is the manner in which the series of questions on identity have been posed in the WVS, namely their inclusion of the concept of "citizenship." Given that recent immigrants are less likely than earlier immigrants (and of course the Canadian-born) to hold legal Canadian citizenship (Statistics Canada 2007b), lower reported levels of identification as a "citizen" of Canada could partially reflect new immigrant participants' interpretation of the survey question.

Although recent immigrants are less likely to "strongly agree" with most collective identities (Figure 9.1), they are more likely to "agree" that they view themselves as a member of their local community, province, of Canada as a whole, and as a citizen of North America (Figure 9.2).

In terms of negative responses (disagree/strongly disagree), there are variations between the three groups (Canadian-born, earlier immigrants, and recent immigrants) (Figure 9.3). Earlier immigrants have the highest rate of disagreeing or strongly disagreeing that they view themselves as a member of their community. This finding raises some concerns that warrant further investigation. Recent immigrants have the highest rate of negatively responding that they view themselves as a citizen of their province or region, of Canada as a whole, and as a citizen of North America, while the Canadian-born population has the lowest levels of responding that they "disagree" or "strongly disagree."

In terms of national pride, recent immigrants, earlier immigrants, and the Canadian-born population collectively express high levels (see Figure 9.4). Nevitte (2008, 8) explains these findings in the following way:

> Immigrants exhibit marginally higher levels of national pride than Canadian born respondents. According to the data summarized ... recent and earlier immigrant respondents are most likely to report

that they are "quite proud" or "very proud" to be Canadian. Native born Canadians, however, are more likely to say that they are "very proud" to be Canadian (71.1 percent) than recent (52.2 percent) or earlier immigrants (69.6 percent).

There is also a positive and statistically significant relationship (r=0.243; p<0.01) between national pride and identification with Canada as a whole (Nevitte 2008).

Figure 9.3: "Disagree/Strongly Disagree" with Collective Identities

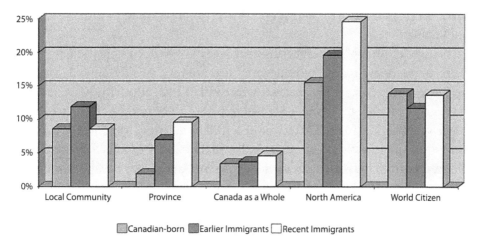

Source: World Values Survey 2006.

Figure 9.4: "Proud" to be Canadian

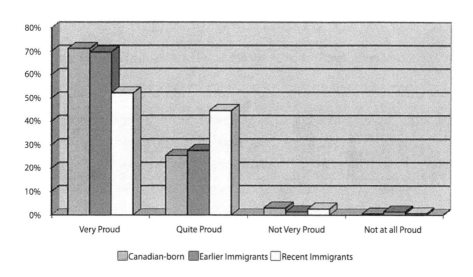

Source: World Values Survey 2006.

Cross-Tabulations

In order to gain further insight into these preliminary findings, cross-tabulations were run for each of the population groups (recent immigrants, earlier immigrants, and the Canadian-born) as well as for the total population.[4] Layers were added using a number of socio-economic and demographic variables including sex, age, education, household income, occupation, employment status, race, and size of town. One trend emerged: although race is not related to substantial differences in response patterns for earlier immigrants and the Canadian-born populations, for recent immigrants racial category influences the degree to which one identifies as a member of their local community, citizen of their province/region, citizen of Canada, and as a world citizen.[5] In this section we conduct an in-depth analysis of race for the recent immigrant population.

Although "ethnicity" is the measured variable in WVS documentation, this variable consists of interviewer-observed categories that are very broadly defined (e.g., Caucasian, Black) and reflects more accurately race rather than ethnicity. Also, because the racial category is an interviewer-observed response, there may be differences between interviewer observations and interviewee self-identification. Moreover, it may be difficult for the interviewer to categorize individuals who are of mixed backgrounds.

For recent immigrants, Caucasians, East Asians, and Arabs have the lowest rate of "strongly" identifying as a member of their local community (Figure 9.5). Only 15.7 percent of Caucasians, 17.7 percent of Arabs, and 19.5 percent of East Asians "strongly agree" that they view themselves as a member of their community. Furthermore, 20.4 percent of Caucasians, 11.3 percent of Arabs, and 10.2 percent of East Asians stated that they "disagree" and do not view themselves as a member of their local community. The Black population has the highest rate of responding that they either "strongly agree" or "agree" with identifying as a member of their local community (97.3 percent), compared to 93.4 percent of South Asians, 89.3 percent of East Asians, 85.4 percent of Arabs, and 77.6 percent of Caucasians.

Figure 9.5: Recent Immigrant Population: Identification as a Member of their Local Community

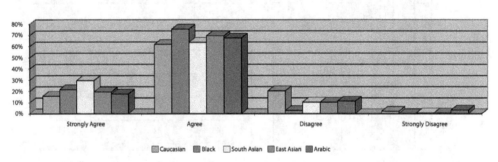

Source: World Values Survey 2006.

Figure 9.6 shows that the Black population has the lowest rate of responding that they either "strongly agree" or "agree" that they view themselves as a citizen of their province or region (75.7 percent) compared to 89.9 percent of Caucasians, 91.2 percent of East Asians, 93.9 percent of South Asians, and 90.5 percent of the Arab population. Figure 9.7 shows that within the recent immigrant population, East Asians have the lowest levels of strongly identifying as a citizen of Canada; only 27.9 percent of East Asian respondents report that they "strongly agree" that they identify as a citizen of Canada.[6] The Black population has the lowest rate of responding that they either "strongly agree" or "agree" that they view themselves as a citizen of Canada (89.5 percent) compared to 93.9 percent of Caucasians, 100 percent of South Asians, 95.1 percent of East Asians, and 96.8 percent of the Arab population.

Figure 9.6: Recent Immigrant Population: Identification as a Citizen of their Province/Region

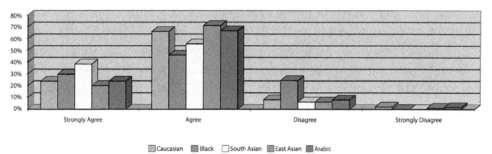

Source: World Values Survey 2006.

Figure 9.7: Recent Immigrant Population: Identification as a Citizen of Canada

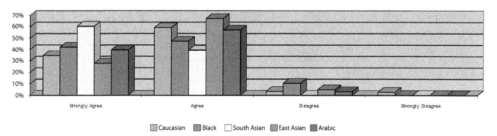

Source: World Values Survey 2006.

The lower rates of positive identification with Canada and with one's province/region among Canada's Black recent immigrant population may be due to experiences such as discrimination and racism that undermine trust and attachment to Canadian society. Results from the 2002 Ethnic Diversity Survey (EDS) show that the Black population is the most likely of all visible minority groups to report experiences of discrimination or unfair treatment; 32 percent of Blacks compared to 21 percent of South Asians and 15 percent of Chinese reported having these types of experiences "sometimes" or "often" in the previous five years (Statistics Canada 2003, 18).

However, the results may also be shaped by the fact that there are a variety of reasons why individuals immigrate to Canada. For refugees, the reasons for coming to Canada are likely very different from other immigrant subgroups (e.g., economic and family class immigrants). As a result of the circumstances under which they arrived, refugees may have a different sense of attachment to Canada. In the last decade, Canada has been accepting more refugees from African countries. For example, in 2006 Ethiopia, Sudan, Democratic Republic of the Congo, and Somalia were among the top 10 source countries for refugees selected under the Resettlement Program (CIC 2007). This may provide insight into the lower levels of attachment to Canada as a whole expressed by the Black recent immigrant population. The WVS data also indicates that the Black population exhibits the highest rate of all racial groups of identifying as a member of their local community. These results require further in-depth analysis.

The findings show that amongst recent immigrants, the South Asian population expresses the highest levels of positive identification as a world citizen, whereas the East Asian population showcases the lowest levels (Figure 9.8): 97.5 percent of the South Asian population either "strongly agree" or "agree" that they view themselves as a world citizen, compared to 88.5 percent of Caucasians, 86.9 percent of the Black population, 85.7 percent of the Arab population, and 80.4 percent of East Asians.

Figure 9.8: Recent Immigrant Population: Identification as a World Citizen

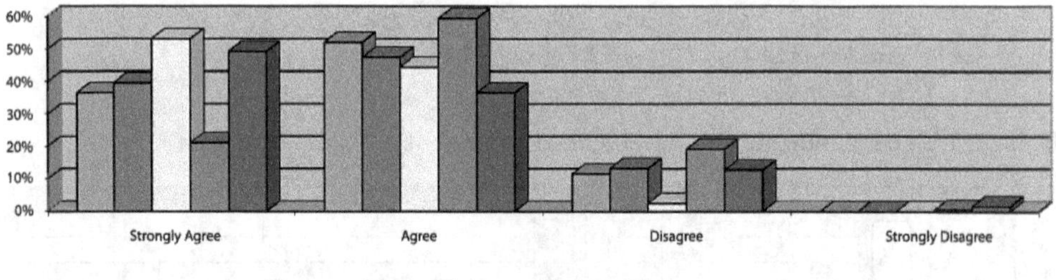

Source: World Values Survey 2006.

Ordered Logistic Regression Analysis

In order to gain insight into variables associated with an individual's likelihood of identifying as a citizen of Canada, an ordered logistic regression analysis was completed. Please see Appendix for variable definitions for the regression models. Table 9.1 displays the findings of the ordered logistic regression, which include coefficients, standard errors, odds ratios (OR), and significance levels.

The pseudo r-squared in the Canadian-born population is 0.310, 0.319 for earlier immigrants, and 0.202 for recent immigrants. This indicates that the selected predictors account for approximately 31 percent, 32 percent, and 20 percent, respectively, of the variance in the outcome variable "identification as a citizen of Canada as a whole." Due to space limitations we are unable to present the findings for the ordered logistic regression for the total sample (including the boosted new immigrant sample).

Table 9.1: Predictors of Identification as a Citizen of Canada—Ordered Logistic Regression

Dependent Variable	Identification as a Citizen of Canada Canadian-Born			Immigrant status Earlier Immigrants			Recent Immigrants		
	Coef	S.E.	Odds Ratio	Coef	S.E.	Odds Ratio	Coef	S.E.	Odds Ratio
Age	0.006	0.004	1.006	0.010	0.012	1.011	0.039	0.015	1.040
Female	-0.179	0.142	0.836	-0.441	0.376	0.643	-0.139	0.233	0.870
Post-Secondary	0.257	0.156	1.293	0.633	0.436	1.884	0.548	0.430	1.729
Low Income	-0.144	0.177	0.866	-0.320	0.476	0.726	0.206	0.275	1.229
High Income	-0.025	0.177	0.975	0.057	0.481	1.059	0.271	0.345	1.312
Quebec	-1.831	0.278	0.160	-1.134	0.780	0.322	-0.126	0.284	0.882
Very Proud to be Canadian	0.996	0.209	2.707	1.658	0.472	5.250	0.828	0.332	2.289
Not a Canadian Citizen							-0.202	0.273	0.817
Interaction:									
Very Proud to be Canadian × Quebec	0.910	0.341	2.483	0.604	0.961	1.829	0.801	0.582	2.227
"Strongly" Identify As:									
World Citizen	1.557	0.200	4.746	0.442	0.514	1.556	1.272	0.266	3.568
Member of Local Community	2.473	0.192	11.856	2.670	0.543	14.434	1.596	0.329	4.933
Citizen of Other Country	-0.304	0.506	0.738	1.531	0.803	4.621	0.622	0.416	1.863
Autonomous Individual	0.674	0.199	1.961	0.977	0.557	2.658	0.750	0.331	2.118
Cut 1	-4.751	0.516		-1.659	0.917		-3.566	1.225	
Cut 2	-2.507	0.342		2.746	0.929		-0.730	0.750	
Cut 3	2.124	0.321					3.489	0.764	
Pseudo R2	0.310			0.319			0.202		
N	1,238			185			403		

* = Significant at p < .05

** = Significant at p < .01

Source: World Values Survey 2006.

The findings from the ordered logistic regression analyses indicate that income status is not related to an individual's likelihood of identifying as a citizen of Canada. This finding is consistent with the results of Walters, Phythian, and Anisef (2007, 60) derived from the EDS, which concluded that "identification with the host society is important for national unity, which appears to be independent of one's level of economic integration." The authors suggest that there is an important distinction between identity integration and economic integration. Their results based on cross-sectional data "provide preliminary evidence that economic integration does not play an integral role in the acculturation of immigrant identities" (Walters, Phythian, and Anisef 2007, 60).

Our results also indicate that, when looking at Canadian-born, recent immigrant, and earlier immigrant respondents separately, the attainment of post-secondary education is not associated with identification as a citizen of Canada. Among recent immigrants, older respondents are slightly more likely to positively identify as a citizen of Canada. Furthermore, the Canadian-born, earlier immigrants, and recent immigrants who are "very proud" to be Canadian, are significantly more likely to positively identify as a citizen of Canada.

Regression results also indicate that Canadian-born individuals who reside in Quebec are less likely to identify as a Canadian citizen. This finding is consistent with Stuart Soroka, Richard Johnson, and Keith Banting's (2007) results based on wave two of the Equality, Security and Community Survey. They found that "Quebec francophones are significantly less attached to Canada (in terms of both the pride and belonging measures) than others" (Soroka, Johnson, and Banting 2007, 584). There is no statistically significant result to suggest that this is also the case for earlier and recent immigrants residing in Quebec.

The results of the ordered regression analysis also suggest that identification as a world citizen is not related to a decreased likelihood to identify as a Canadian citizen, and provides preliminary evidence to dismiss claims that globalization has led to the deterritorialization of identities. According to Jack Jedwab (2007, 67), "some fear that globalization will continue to blur territorial and national boundaries, further directing identities away from a strict focus on national affiliation." The findings indicate that the opposite may, in fact, be the case. It appears that for recent immigrant respondents, the tendency to strongly identify as a world citizen is positively connected to identifying as a citizen of Canada. Our analysis of the total WVS sample (not included in this chapter) confirms this relationship.

These findings support the idea that an individual can have multiple identities and belongings without having them necessarily conflict or collide with each other; they are also consistent with Patricia Ehrkamp and Helga Leitner's (2006, 1,630) argument that although "transnational migrants' practices and identities are multiple and cross territorial [communal boundaries] do[es] not imply that identifications with territorially defined national polities and locales are disappearing." Therefore, they explain that ideas of "deterritorialization and denationalization of citizenship are simplistic and premature" (Ehrkamp and Leitner 2006, 1,630).

Frank Rusciano (2003) conducted an analysis of survey data on 23 nations that examined the construction of national identity. He found support for the theory that "the construction of national identity derives, in part, from a negotiation between a nation's *Selbstbild* (nation's national consciousness, or the image its citizens have of their country) and a nation's *Fremdbild* (or the nation's perceived or actual international image in world opinion)" (Rusciano 2003, 361). Following this theory, one preliminary explanation for our finding is that if identification as a world citizen implies a concern or investment in events that occur at a global scale, it may be the case that individuals who identify as a world citizen may also display a heightened support for Canada and its role in influencing these events. In other words, individuals who identify as a world citizen may place more emphasis on a nation's *Fremdbild*.

Regression results also show that earlier and recent immigrants who strongly identify as a member of their local community are significantly more likely to identify as a citizen of Canada. The robustness of this relationship is confirmed by running the model on data from the total WVS sample (not included here). These findings provide preliminary evidence to suggest that micro-community identification is associated with macro-community identification.

Patrick Pearce (2008) obtained similar results from his analysis of the EDS data. He found that there is a positive relationship between community trust and a sense of belonging at a national level. Pearce (2008, 26) proposes that "one possible explanation for this may be that immigrants see their neighbours as a sample of the entire Canadian population and link their feelings toward their immediate community to their feelings for the wider society." As our literature review suggests, identification carries with it connotations of belonging and has implications for social cohesion. It appears that the degree to which individuals, regardless of whether or not they are immigrants, identify with their local community has significant implications for the cohesiveness of the larger Canadian society.

Ordered logistic regression results further indicate that a strong identification as a citizen of another country is not associated with the degree to which an individual identifies as a citizen of Canada. This finding suggests that dual citizenship may not undermine belonging to Canadian society.

Finally, Canadian-born respondents and recent immigrants who strongly agree that they view themselves as an autonomous individual are significantly more likely to identify as a Canadian citizen than those who did not strongly agree. This result is again confirmed with an analysis of the total WVS sample (not included here). This finding could indicate that values such as self-sufficiency and the freedom to choose and make informed decisions do not contradict the rights and freedoms associated with Canadian citizenship.

CONCLUSION

In this chapter, we provided an overview of literature on identity and findings from an analysis of the Canadian WVS (2006), focusing on three population groups: recent immigrants, earlier immigrants, and the Canadian-born. All three groups collectively express high levels of positive identification as citizens of Canada, citizens of their province/region, and members of their community. Similarly, all three groups expressed very high levels of pride in Canada. These findings are consistent with Pearce's (2008, 20) results, derived from the 2002 EDS, which suggest that "the strong sense of belonging to Canada is perhaps a credit to the Canadian multicultural framework and the federal government's keen interest in developing policies and programs based on research on Canadian social cohesion."

Findings from our descriptive analysis also suggest an overall tendency amongst all three groups to report the strongest identification with Canada, and the weakest identification with North America. Furthermore, recent immigrants are more likely than earlier immigrants and the Canadian-born to strongly identify as a world citizen, and recent immigrants are less likely than earlier immigrants and the Canadian-born to strongly identify with the other collective identities (including Canada, province/region, and community).

Findings from the cross-tabular analysis suggest that for recent immigrants race is a marker of differences in the degree to which one identifies as a member of their community, their province or region, as a citizen of Canada, and citizen of the world. The Black population reports the lowest levels of identification as citizens of Canada and as citizens of their province/region. The role of discriminatory forces within society should be taken into consideration when attempting to gain further insight into these findings. However, the Black population also reports the highest levels of identification with their local community. These results require additional in-depth qualitative and quantitative analysis.

Results from the ordered logistic regression analysis suggest that for recent and earlier immigrants the tendency to "strongly identify" as a member of one's local community is associated with an increased likelihood of identifying as a citizen of Canada. This finding is consistent with Pearce's (2008) conclusion that "there may be an intricate relationship between neighbourhood strength and general community attachment." It is also consistent with John Hipp and Andrew Perrin's (2006) conclusion that proposes feelings towards one's neighbourhood are positively associated with national-level attachment. It may be the case that community-level experiences, interactions, attitudes, and norms are generalized by the individual and projected onto the larger national community.

These results suggest that the experience of integration is very much community-based. Government of Canada programs such as the Welcoming Community Initiative may have a direct and positive impact on the degree to which immigrants associate with various Canadian collective identities by fostering more welcoming communities and by promoting participation. For recent immigrants, the Host Program may also play a significant role in expanding social networks and increasing access to community resources, which in turn, play a role in positively impacting community attachment. Furthermore, these findings allow for the preliminary development of a theory that proposes identity is rooted in a complex web of social relations wherein the strength and security of one collective identity may provide the foundation for the strengthening of other forms of collective identification. As authors of other chapters in this volume have pointed out, relations between local, national, and other geographical scales are critical to understanding issues of immigration and settlement.

The degree to which one feels a sense of attachment and identifies with one's community, province, or country has significant emotional and behavioural connotations, which in turn have an impact on the cohesiveness of communities as well as Canadian society at large. Therefore, one of the various ways in which the Government of Canada can promote Canadian identity is by supporting citizenship uptake among immigrants. Citizenship promotes loyalty and attachment to Canada, nurtures a shared national identity, and in turn, fosters a sense of belonging for newcomers. Therefore, the Government of Canada's continued recognition of citizenship as the ultimate goal of immigration plays a critical role in strengthening a shared national identity and a sense of belonging for immigrants.

Finally, further research is needed to provide insight into these findings. For example, it would be interesting to analyze the responses to the same questions from previous and upcoming waves of the WVS to reveal changes in collective identification over time. Furthermore, the Longitudinal Survey of Immigrants to Canada can provide additional information on levels of belonging among recent immigrants and deliver insight into the role of immigrant category (e.g., refugee, economic and family class immigrants). Qualitative research could also be used to fill gaps in our understanding of the complex and subjective nature of identification and belonging.

LIMITATIONS OF THE RESEARCH

There are several limitations of this study that should be noted. Firstly, due to the subjective nature of the questions, respondents may have a variety of different interpretations about what "seeing themselves as a citizen of Canada as a whole" means. For instance, some individuals may be responding to a factual question about their status as a Canadian citizen whereas others may be assessing the degree to which they associate as Canadians, or feel that they "belong" in Canada. Further muddying the waters, while a question pertaining to legal status as a Canadian citizen was posed to participants in the boosted new immigrant sample of the WVS, a similar question was not posed to core sample participants. Furthermore, respondents may have a variety of different interpretations of what "local community" means because a definition was not provided.

A key limitation of this dataset is that it does not permit analysis by immigration class (e.g., family class, economic class, and refugees); this may have provided valuable insight into differences in responses amongst earlier and recent immigrant subgroups. Moreover, the data does not allow for the separation of the second generation from third-plus generations, all of which are categorized as "Canadian-born." Furthermore, the data does not take into account any subsequent moves within Canada that may have a significant impact upon the degree to which respondents identify with their community and province/region.

ENDNOTES

1. According to the 2006 Census, 19.8 percent of the population of Canada is foreign-born, and there has been a considerable shift in the source countries of immigration (Statistics Canada 2007a). As a result, 70.2 percent of the foreign-born population report a mother tongue other than English or French and 54.3 percent of the foreign-born population indicate that they are visible minorities (Statistics Canada 2008).
2. The data from this study was weighted to ensure each of the three subpopulation groups were reflective of the actual population.
3. Within Montreal, Toronto, and Vancouver, the survey data was weighted to ensure that it accurately reflects the profile of new immigrants within that city by age and gender. The weights were calculated using the data from the 2006 Canadian Census for the Montreal, Toronto, and Vancouver census metropolitan areas.
4. "Total population" figures use data from the core sample only (excludes the boosted new immigrant sample) in order to maintain the representativeness of the data. Adding in the new immigrant sample data would bias the sample towards recent immigrants.
5. Due to insufficient cell counts the category "other" was not included in this analysis.
6. Compared to 34.7 percent of Caucasians, 39.7 percent of Arabs, 42.1 percent of Blacks, and 60.5 percent of South Asians.

ACKNOWLEDGEMENTS

CIC has provided ongoing funding to WVS (including funding for the boosted immigrant sample) and has an agreement to receive some of the Canadian data prior to its public release. Since the microdata was not accessible at the time, the statistical analyses for this chapter are drawn from the work of Neil Nevitte, University of Toronto—Canada's principal investigator for the WVS.

We wish to thank Martha Justus and Chona Iturralde from Citizenship and Immigration Canada for their support in this project. We would also like to thank Anne-Marie Robert and Jessie-Lynn MacDonald for their extensive comments and suggestions, and Neil Nevitte and Wayne Chu for making this chapter possible.

The views expressed in this chapter are those of the authors and do not necessarily represent those of the Government of Canada. All errors are entirely the responsibility of the authors.

REFERENCES

Ashmore, R. D., K. Deaux, and T. McLaughlin-Volpe. 2004. "An Organizing Framework for Collective Identity: Articulation and Significance of Multidimensionality." *Psychological Bulletin* 130: 80–114.

Bokser-Liwerant, J. 2002. "Globalization and Collective Identities." *Social Compass* 49: 253–271.

Citizenship and Immigration Canada (CIC). 2007. "Backgrounder: Refugees and Canada's Refugee System." Accessed December 18, 2009. www.cic.gc.ca/english/department/media/backgrounders/2007/2007-06-20.asp.

Croucher, S. 2004. *Globalization and Belonging: The Politics of Identity in a Changing World*. Lanham, Maryland: Rowman & Littlefield.

Ehrkamp, P., and H. Leitner. 2006. "Rethinking Immigration and Citizenship: New Spaces of Migrant Transnationalism and Belonging." *Environment and Planning* 38: 1,591–1,597.

Frideres, J. S. 2002. "Immigrants, Integration and the Intersection of Identities." Commissioned by Canadian Heritage, 2002. Accessed December 17, 2009. canada.metropolis.net/events/diversity/immigration.pdf.

Gardiner Barber, P. 2003. "Citizenship and Attachment Across Borders? Transnational and Anthropological Research Agenda." *Canadian Diversity* 2: 45–46.

Grant, P. R. 2007. "Sustaining a Strong Cultural and National Identity: The Acculturation of Immigrants and Second-Generation Canadians of Asian and African Descent." *Journal of International Migration and Integration* 8: 89–116.

Harles, J. 1997. "Integration Before Assimilation: Immigration, Multiculturalism and the Canadian Polity." *Canadian Journal of Political Science* 30: 711–737.

Hedetoft, U. 2002. "Discourses and Images of Belonging: Migrants between 'New Racism,' Liberal Nationalism and Globalization." Academy of Migration Studies in Denmark, Working Paper Series 5/2002. Accessed December 5, 2009. www.amid.dk/pub/papers/AMID_5-2002_Hedetoft.pdf.

Hipp, J., and A. Perrin. 2006. "Nested Loyalties: Local Networks' Effects on Neighbourhood and Community Cohesion." *Urban Studies* 43: 2503–,2,523.

Hoerder, D., Y. Hébert, and I. Schmitt. 2006. *Negotiating Transcultural Lives: Belongings and Social Capital among Youth in Comparative Perspectives*. Toronto: University of Toronto Press.

Ipsos Reid. 2007. "Becoming Canadian: Social Engagement and Attachment to Canada among First and Second Generation Canadians." Commissioned by the Dominion Institute. Accessed December 16, 2009. www.dominion.ca/Intergeneration_Immigrant-DI_IR.pdf.

Jedwab, J. 2007. "Dually Divided? The Risks of Linking Debates over Citizenship to Attachment to Canada." *International Journal* 63: 65–78.

Jenson, J. 1998. "Mapping Social Cohesion: The State of Canadian Research." Canadian Policy Research Network. Accessed December 15, 2009. www.cprn.org/documents/15723_en.pdf.

Krzyzanowsli, M., and R. Wodak. 2007. "Multiple Identities, Migration and Belonging:'Voices of Migrants." In *Identity Trouble: Critical Discourse and Contested Identities*, edited by C. R. Caldas-Coulthard and R. Iedema, 95–119. Basignstoke: Palgrave MacMillan.

Kymlicka, W. 1998. *Finding Our Way: Rethinking Ethnocultural Relations in Canada*. Oxford: OxfordUniversity Press.

Laczko, L. 2005. "National and Local Attachments in a Changing World System: Evidence from an International Survey." *International Review of Sociology* 15: 517–528.

Létourneau, J. 2001. "The Question of Identity: Past Findings and Future Outlooks." Commissioned by Canadian Heritage. Accessed December 9, 2009. canada.metropolis.net/events/ethnocultural/publications/Letourneau_e.pdf.

Mason, A. 2000. *Community, Solidarity and Belonging: Levels of Community and the Normative Significance*. Cambridge: Cambridge University Press.

Muir, R. 2007. "The New Identity Politics." Institute for Public Policy Research. Accessed December 5, 2009. http://www.ippr.org/images/media/files/publication/2011/05/New%20identity%20politics_1562.pdf.

Nevitte, N. 2008. "World Values Surveys (Canada): Immigrant and Native Born Respondent Comparisons." Commissioned by Citizenship and Immigration Canada.

Pearce, P. 2008. "Bridging, Bonding, and Trusting: The Influence of Social Capital and Trust on Immigrants' Sense of Belonging to Canada." Atlantic Metropolis Centre, Working Paper Series 18.

Peressini, M. 1993. "Référents et bricolages identitaires: Histoires de vie d'Italo Montréalais." *Revue européenne des migrations internationales* 9: 35–62.

Rashid, T. 2007. "Configuration of National Identity and Citizenship in Australia: Migration, Ethnicity and Religious Minorities." *Alternatives: Turkish Journal of International Relations* 6 (3/4): 1–27. Rummens, J. A. 2001. "An Interdisciplinary Overview of Canadian Research On Identity." Commissioned by the Department of Canadian Heritage. Accessed December 9, 2009. canada.metropolis.net/events/ethnocultural/publications/identity_e.pdf.

Rusciano, F. 2003. "The Construction of National Identity – A 23-Nation Study." *Political Research Quarterly* 56: 361–366.

Schellenberg, G. 2003. General Social Survey on Social Engagement, Cycle 17: An Overview of Findings. Accessed August 5, 2011. www.statcan.gc.ca/bsolc/olc-cel/olc-cel?catno=89-598-X&CHROPG=1&lang=eng.

———. 2004. "Perceptions of Canadians: A Sense of Belonging, Confidence and Trust." *Canadian Social Trends*: 16–21.

Shields, M. 2008. "Community Belonging and Self-Perceived Health." Statistics Canada. Accessed December 9, 2009. www.statcan.gc.ca/pub/82-003-x/2008002/article/10552-eng.pdf.

Snow, D. 2001. "Collective Identity and Expressive Forms" Centre for the Study of Democracy, 01-07. Accessed December 1, 2009. repositories.cdlib.org/csd/01-07.

Soroka, S., R. Johnson, and K. Banting. 2007. "The Ties that Bind? Social Cohesion and Diversity in Canada." In *Belonging? Diversity, Recognition and Shared Citizenship in Canada*, edited by K. Banting, T. J. Dourchene, and F. L. Seidle, 561–600.

Montreal: Institute for Research on Public Policy.

Statistics Canada. 2003. "Ethnic Diversity Survey: Portrait of a Multicultural Society." Accessed December 16, 2009. dsppsd.tpsgc.gc.ca/Collection/Statcan/89-593-X/89-593-XIE2003001.pdf.

———. 2007a. "Immigration in Canada: A Portrait of the Foreign-Born Population, 2006 Census." Ottawa: Statistics Canada. Accessed August 5, 2011. http://www12.statcan.ca/census-recensement/2006/as-sa/97-557/pdf/97-557-XIE2006001.pdf.

———. 2007b. "Immigration and Citizenship, 2006 Census." Catalogue no. 97-562-XCB2006004.

———. 2008. "Census Snapshot – Immigration in Canada: A Portrait of the Foreign-Born Population, 2006 Census" *Canadian Social Trends*: 11–008.

Tajfel, H. 1974. "Social Identity and Intergroup Behaviour." *Social Science Information* 13: 65–93.

Tastsoglou, E. 2001. "Re-Appraising Immigration and Identities: A Synthesis and Directions for Future Research." Commissioned by the Department of Canadian Heritage. Accessed December 16, 2009. canada.metropolis.net/events/ethnocultural/publications/tastsoglou_e.pdf.

Walters, D., D. K. Phythian, and P. Anisef. 2007. "The Acculturation of Canadian Immigrants: Determinants of Ethnic Identification with the Host Society." *Canadian Review of Sociology and Anthropology* 44: 37–64.

World Values Survey (WVS).2009. "Introduction to the World Values Survey." Accessed December 16, 2009. www.worldvaluessurvey.org/.

APPENDIX

Table 9.2: I see myself as a ... member of my Local Community

	Canadian-Born	Earlier Immigrants	Recent Immigrants
Strongly Agree	33.6%	31.6%	19.9%
Agree	57.9%	56.1%	67.0%
Disagree	7.9%	11.9%	12.1%
Strongly Disagree	0.7%	0.3%	1.1%
N	1,756	294	564

Source: Nevitte 2008.

Table 9.3: I see myself as a ... citizen of my Province

	Canadian-Born	Earlier Immigrants	Recent Immigrants
Strongly Agree	41.9%	36.0%	26.1%
Agree	56.2%	56.9%	64.3%
Disagree	1.8%	6.7%	8.5%
Strongly Disagree	0.1%	0.3%	1.1%
N	1,754	297	566

Source: Nevitte 2008.

Table 9.4: I see myself as a citizen of ... Canada as a whole

	Canadian-Born	Earlier Immigrants	Recent Immigrants
Strongly Agree	44.8%	48.1%	38.2%
Agree	51.8%	49.1%	57.2%
Disagree	3.0%	3.4%	3.9%
Strongly Disagree	0.4%	0.3%	0.7%
N	1,758	295	565

Source: Nevitte 2008.

Table 9.5: I see myself as a citizen of ... North America

	Canadian-Born	Earlier Immigrants	Recent Immigrants
Strongly Agree	25.6%	26.8%	16.0%
Agree	57.9%	53.6%	59.4%
Disagree	13.5%	16.5%	21.7%
Strongly Disagree	2.0%	3.1%	2.9%
N	1,744	291	557

Source: Nevitte 2008.

Table 9.6: I see myself as a ... World Citizen

	Canadian-born	Earlier immigrants	Recent immigrants
Strongly Agree	30.6%	31.8%	34.5%
Agree	55.5%	56.4%	51.9%
Disagree	12.1%	9.3%	13.3%
Strongly Disagree	1.8%	2.4%	0.4%
N	1,729	289	565

Source: Nevitte 2008.

Table 9.7: National Pride

	Canadian-Born	Earlier Immigrants	Recent Immigrants
Very Proud	71.1%	69.6%	52.2%
Quite Proud	25.4%	27.6%	44.6%
Not Very Proud	3.0%	1.4%	2.6%
Not at all Proud	0.5%	1.4%	0.6%
N	1,753	283	312

Source: Nevitte 2008.

Chapter 10

RELIGIOUS AND SECULAR IDENTITIES IN A PLURAL CANADA

TAHIRA GONSALVES

Canada is a secular country; religion is generally considered to be a matter of private rather than public life. Within this secularism, however, are embedded various assumptions about religion, culture, and citizenship. These assumptions come to the fore when certain groups—who stand outside the core[1]—push the limits of these concepts.

In this chapter I examine the ways in which second-generation Muslim youth and first- and second-generation Muslim women have pushed the boundaries of secularism, multiculturalism, and citizenship in Canada. I argue that we need to rearticulate these concepts beyond post-Enlightenment thinking, to reflect the changing nature of Canada's plurality.

Secularism has garnered significant media attention of late, given the ways in which "religious" identity claims have been made in the public sphere of many western countries, including Canada. Most notably, the claims by Muslims[2] have confronted the limits of the precarious consensus around "tolerance" in western liberal democratic regimes.

In the sections that follow, I will provide some context around the development of secularism in the West and in Canada. I will then discuss studies that have examined the religious identities of Muslim second-generation youth in North America. Thereafter, I will move to an analysis of the debate around the proposed Sharia tribunal in Canada some years ago. The chapter ends with a discussion of the main ideas.

ORIGINS OF SECULARISM

Charles Taylor has arguably been one of the most influential theorists on secularism, along with his scholarship on multiculturalism and the "politics of recognition." Taylor's account of the origins of secularism, though somewhat different from that of Talal Asad (amongst others), remains an important contribution to the sociology of religion and secularism. Secularism in the West originated in the Wars of Religion in Europe during the sixteenth century. Formed during this period, secularism was further refined during the Enlightenment era. Taylor argues that the notion of secularism always contains some sense of a separation between church and state, but neither this nor its origins in Christendom should render it inappropriate to other places whose histories have progressed differently (Taylor 2009, xvii).

Initially, secularism was one part of a dyad of secular or profane time and eternal or sacred time. Some priests were even considered "secular" as they operated outside of monastic institutions (Taylor 2009, xvii–xviii). Certain functions and institutions came to be transferred to laypersons outside the church, the *process* of secularization began, in the sixteenth century(Taylor 2009, xviii). In time, and through the values embodied within the Enlightenment,[3] the church became formally separated from the state, and religion from politics (Seljak 2008). Eventually, important political functions and institutions became independent from religious control, and their non-religious orientation became dominant (Seljak 2008).

Asad also analyzes secularism and religion as deeply connected rather than as oppositional categories. He highlights the fact that state-legitimized violence has accompanied secularist regimes throughout the world; the struggles and conflicts that took place (and, indeed, continue to take place) show that secularism has always been fraught with tension (Asad 2003). Asad further distinguishes between the "secular" as a concept and "secularism" as a political doctrine, where the former, he argues, preceded the latter (Asad 2003, 16). Thus an examination of the secular must involve an ontological and epistemological understanding of how, "over time a variety of concepts, practices, and sensibilities have come together to form 'the secular'" (Asad 2003, 16). Asad's rendering of the secular and secularism through Western history is more complex than that seen in Taylor's work.[4] However, the broader strokes of both scholars' historical accounts align with the argument that what comes to be known as secular exists in opposition to the religious. Taylor argues that the initial separation of the secular-religious dyad mutates, where the

> "secular" refers to what pertains to a self-sufficient immanent sphere, and its contrast term (often identified as "religious") relates to the transcendent realm. This can then undergo a second mutation, via a denial of the transcendent level, into a dyad in which one term refers to the real (the secular), and the other to what is merely invented (the religious); or where "secular" refers to the institutions we really require to live in "this world," and "religious" or "ecclesial" to optional extras that often disturb the course of this-worldly life. (Taylor 2009, xx)

The first instance of the dominance of the secular, contends Taylor, was established during the French Revolution with the principle of *laïcité* (which translates loosely as secularism) (Taylor 2009, xix). Through *laïcité*, three complex "goods" were sought: liberty, equality, and fraternity (Taylor 2009, xi–xii). Liberty refers to the freedom of people to believe or not to believe. Equality ensures that those who believe and those who do not (or who assume any position in between) are treated in a fair manner. Fraternity refers to the opportunity to be heard, which includes, "the ongoing process of determining what the society is about (its political identity), and how it is going to realize these goals (the exact regime of rights and privileges)" (Taylor 2009, xii). While the first two points of liberty and equality may be more "easily" achievable in a given society, the third—fraternity—seems to be causing the most political turmoil. As Taylor outlines, the notion of fraternity gets at the heart of the value(s) a society decides to privilege as the principle(s) for the formation of laws.

Some address the secularism issue by invoking the sphere of "pure secularism" which is to be governed by reason, free of religion entirely. Taylor critiques this approach by arguing that it is virtually impossible to work out a set of a priori principles that can determine all decisions. The principles must be worked out through a process of mutual negotiation. Forcing a set of pre-decided principles upon those of different persuasions would be a violation of the very principle of fraternity (Taylor 2009, xii–xiii), in particular, in a society in which the population is very diverse.

Other scholars make a distinction between political and social secularism on on the one hand, and a more micro-level approach to understanding the experience of belief at the individual level (Ferrara 2009). Political secularism enacts the French principle of *laïcité*, and equivalent concepts in Italy (*laicità*) and Spain (*laicidad*) (Ferrara 2009, 78). It refers to the separation of church from state, at least in principle. The state has the sole authority and legitimate power.[5]

Social secularism is based on the idea that religion has decreasing influence on institutions of law, politics, and education, that people makes less use of religion to mark rites of passage, and that religion has less influence on people's social networks, values, and motivations (Ferrara 2009). At the micro or individual level, secularism "consists, among other things, of a move from a society where belief in God is unchallenged and indeed unproblematic to one in which it is understood to be one option among others, and frequently not the easiest to embrace" (Taylor cited in Ferrara 2009, 80). However, the idea of increasing social secularization in the modern age, where religion retreats further and further into the private sphere, has also been discounted by sociologists (Casanova 1994; Taylor 2007). David Seljak (2008) argues that the connection between modernization and secularization has not been linear and that religion in fact continues to play a significant part in people's lives all over the world.

In addition, there is a discrepancy between the letter of the law and political practice. In Canada, for instance, there is a presumption that citizens enjoy the complete separation of religion and state. Yet, Canada has an ambiguous articulation of religion's role in public life, beginning with the preamble of the constitution, which states, "Canada is founded upon principles that recognize the Supremacy of God and the rule of law" (Department of Justice 2011). In fact, on paper, Canadians enjoy less separation between the two spheres than their counterparts in the United States. Indeed, a "residual Christianity" still functions within the public sphere in Canada (Seljak 2008, 6). Lack of acknowledgement of this residual Christianity in political and public spheres has created the illusion of neutrality and equality, making it harder for minority groups to express their voice.

Moreover, the neutrality and equality of the public sphere, as initially conceived by Jürgen Habermas, has more recently been called into question (Ismail 2008; Asad 2003). Critics have pointed out that the public sphere in western liberal contexts is in fact based on the exclusion of those who do not fit the mould of the taken-for-granted, autonomous political subject of modernity (Asad 2003; Ismail 2008; Razack 2007). Since his initial conceptualization, Habermas has acknowledged the extra burden that is placed on those who are religious, to translate their claims into a secular language (Ferrara 2009). That is, Habermas argues that forcing religious groups to reconstruct their arguments in a way that makes sense in the secular public sphere is an encumbrance on the religious and violates principles of equity. The extra labour that religious groups must perform is part of what John Rawls has called the "overlapping consensus." Rawls argues that society needs to commit to "public reason" whereby arguments should be made in the public sphere in such a way that those who do not share a moral worldview might still be able to accept the arguments. This process results in the overlapping consensus (Narbey 2005, 124–125).

For Habermas, this "additional burden of translation should be shared among believers and non-believers in order to fully realize the principle of equality across the religious divide, by way of ensuring that also those citizens who find it impossible to 'translate' reasons linked to their faith into religiously neutral reasons, not be deprived of political influence" (Ferrara 2009, 83). Indeed, this is a key point, which resonates with Taylor's conception of fraternity described earlier. Whether one refers to it as a shared burden, fraternity, or as rights and responsibilities towards achieving equity, the practice of secularism involves negotiation. Canada has a long history of this practice, though not without power imbalances, as I will describe in the next section.

SECULARISM IN CANADA

Secularism did not suddenly emerge and take root in Canada. Seljak (2008) describes three periods of church-state relations in Canada. The first period ranged from the early 1600s to the mid-1800s, during which there was an attempt to fully establish the same close connections and workings between aristocratic government and the church, as existed in Europe. The second period, from the mid-1800s to the mid-1900s, saw the creation of a "pluralist establishment" where the main Christian churches acted as a "shadow establishment" to the government. The third period, after World War II, saw the increased separation of church and state and the secularization of Canadian society.

The adoption of secularism in Canada was not uniform across the country; differences existed between Quebec and the rest of Canada. The particular practice of secularism was influenced by notions of identity and nationalism in English and French Canada. In English Canada, "British culture and politics, Protestantism, and a belief in modern political, economic and scientific 'progress' formed the three pillars of Canadian nationalism" (Seljak 2008, 9). For French Canadians, by contrast, "the French language and culture, the Roman Catholic faith, and the traditional agricultural lifestyle (anchored by the patriarchal family) formed the core of ... national identity" (Seljak 2008, 9).

Until the mid-1960s, Canada was seen as a strongly Christian nation. In the period after the 1960s, following the Quiet Revolution in Quebec, a new set of values, based on rights and social justice, was adopted. The church also took up this new rights-based discourse, eschewing to some extent the earlier hierarchies of Christendom. Seljak argues, however, that Canada while no longer "God's Dominion" is still not a post-Christian society, and continues, in fact, to be "residually Christian" (Seljak 2008, 11).

Seljak contends that mere separation between church and state does not address the residually Christian nature of Canadian public life, or the disadvantage to non-Christian religions (Seljak 2008). In fact, the notion of complete separation tends to hide the existent Christian privilege in the public culture and the alienation of some, such as Aboriginal groups who make land claims for spiritual (and material) reasons (Seljak 2008). Seljak further argues that stricter separation between religion and state is frequently associated with discrimination and intolerance against minority religious groups.

Increasingly, second-generation racialized groups are countering this intolerance by framing their concerns within what Taylor calls "the politics of universalism" (Seljak 2008, 10). The politics of universalism differs significantly from the politics of "social hierarchy," which was traditionally practised by the church. The turn from the politics of social hierarchy to universalism coincided with the creation of documents such as the Universal Declaration of Human Rights (1948), the Canadian Charter of Rights and Freedoms (1982), and the Canadian Multiculturalism Act (1988) (Seljak 2008). While such documents, covenants, and declarations were perceived to enforce equity, they also pursued other important motives. A benign reading of these motives includes the recognition of attempts to integrate and assimilate diverse populations to maintain harmony within society in an era of migration and nascent globalization. A more critical reading reveals the ways in which difference is managed through processes of governmentality and surveillance. Such a critical reading can be illustrated by the examples of Muslim second-generation youth in Canada.

MUSLIM SECOND-GENERATION YOUTH

The research conducted on Muslim immigrants in North America and Europe reveals great diversity in attitudes, religiosity, race/ethnicity, class, language, political involvement, educational attainment, the practice of Islam, etc. (Ramji 2008; Beyer 2005; Zine 2007; Levitt 2007). However, a certain homogenization of Islam continues to be perpetuated by some elements of the mainstream media. This categorization (which glosses over the complexity of identities) is necessary for a politics related to nation-building, multiculturalism, and citizenship. And herein resides the tension between the heterogeneous reality and the homogenizing imperatives of policy.

The Muslim community began to grow rapidly in Canada after the 1970s. Since 1981 the number of Muslim immigrants has doubled each decade. Many of the Muslim immigrants are from Pakistan, India, and Iran (Ramji 2008). Studies that consider the integration of immigrants do so often in terms of economic indicators (Boyd 2002) such as employment, accreditation, and income and to a lesser degree in terms of civic and political participation. Many of these indicators are not salient issues for the second-generation though (Ramji 2008). Having grown up in the new homeland, the second-generation is usually fluent in English and/or French and able to find good employment based on their qualifications. Religious identity, on the other hand, has become important for many members of the second-generation. Religious identity is not only manifest in terms of attendance at churches, mosques, temples, or synagogues, but also in terms of diet, consumption and spending practices, education, and judicial, political, and civic participation (Khanlou, Shakya, and Muntaner 2007–2009; Beyer 2005; Zine 2007). The ways in which Muslims practice Islam is then mediated by their beliefs and values, and the relationship between these beliefs and values and various institutions in society.

Sander (1997) develops the four-fold groupings of ethnic, cultural, religious, or political Muslims (Ramji 2008). Ethnic Muslims belong to a group in which the widely held beliefs are Islamic. Cultural Muslims are socialized in an Islamic culture, while religious Muslims perform the Islamic commands. Finally, political Muslims believe in the importance of Islamic conceptions of the social and political spheres (Ramji 2008).

Based on empirical research involving interviews, Rubina Ramji (2008) makes a further classification: Salafists,[7] highly involved Muslims, moderately involved Muslims, and non-believers (Ramji 2008). Many second-generation Muslims are at least highly involved in their religion, unlike their non-Muslim Canadian counterparts among whom secularism is on the rise (Ramji 2008). Ramji points out, however, that men and youth are more likely to be highly involved than women and older youth and adults; for some young men, their religious involvement may be a form of youthful rebellion (Ramji 2008,106).

Importantly, Ramji's research shows that even those who self-identify as Salafists, still feel a sense of belonging in Canada. They see no necessarily irreconcilable differences between themselves as strong believers in Islam and as Canadians. While they may be very critical of certain aspects of Canadian culture, such as (at the time of the research) the federal legislation on same-sex marriage (Ramji 2008), they do not feel alienated from Canada. The highly involved and more liberal in their views and practices, also feel quite at home in Canada. Ramji states: "The vast majority are very comfortable as Muslims and as Canadians. While they are engaging in unique and sometimes unanticipated reconstructions, they are not drawing sharp distinctions between Islam and Canada, between Islam and the West, between homeland and diaspora" (Ramji 2008, 107).

Despite individual variations, Ramji also found distinct patterns among second-generation Muslims in Canada. The majority of them are highly involved, and their Islam is individual rather than community oriented—though many feel a part of a global identity as Muslims. This global identity is fostered especially through their engagement in the Internet. The role of the media also impacts their identity as Muslims. Further, while their Islam is internally highly variable, many associate with politically conservative beliefs. Finally, most Muslims in Ramji's research commend Canadian multicultural policy and feel a kinship between Canadian values and Islamic values such as peace, kindness, and humility (Ramji 2008).

Thus, while second-generation Muslim youth tend to place importance on religious belief in their lives, their belief is individually based, highly variable, and aligned with the Canadian multicultural context. Second-generation Muslim identity claims[7] can thus be conceived as modern claims within the secular Canadian nation-state. This challenges the assumption of these claims for accommodation as being purely "religious." While religion may be the framework in which the claim is articulated, the basis of the claims is founded upon principles of personal belief and the right to practice these beliefs in a public context.

Based on research in the USA, Peggy Levitt argues that religious affiliations are part of immigrants' citizenship identity: "Religious global citizenship has a lot in common with its political equivalent. In exchange for 'obeying the law' and following the denominational rules, 'paying taxes' by contributing dues, and participating in religious and social activities, members gain representation, protection, and access to resources and power" (Levitt 2007, 68). Levitt contends that citizenship is an important lens through which to understand the religious affiliation of people, precisely because the way in which people describe their religious citizenship (rights and responsibilities of belonging to a particular religion) is similar to political citizenship (Levitt 2007). Whether or not religiously based belongings coincide with geographical boundaries, she argues that Islam has a global community identity that transcends national boundaries, with "[t]he Muslim *umma* [as] an imagined religious community governed by Sharia" (Levitt 2007, 84). For these religious global citizens, as she labels them, imagined lands are composed of religious buildings and shrines; they think of themselves as living within this alternative religious world, "with residents, rules, and landmarks that matter ... more to them than their secular equivalents" (Levitt 2007, 83).

As Ramji's research described earlier, Levitt's work shows that the Muslims interviewed also had difficulties with many of the mainstream North American values, which they consider permissive. At the same time, one of the respondents described America as the most Muslim country in the world because people's basic needs are met, which this respondent saw as a very Muslim idea (Levitt 2007). Given Canada's strong welfare state origins, it could be argued that devout Muslims in Canada would also respect the various social programs and view them as being in line with Muslim values.

Both Ramji's and Levitt's research shows that espousing Muslim values is often aligned with what are considered "Canadian values," such as tolerance, thereby dissolving some of the divisions embodied in the eastern versus western values binary. However, these divisions were enacted by the Sharia debate some years ago.

THE "SHARIA DEBATE"

In 2003 Syed Mumtaz Ali, a retired lawyer, announced the founding of the Islamic Institute of Civil Justice (IICJ). He was interested, through this institute, in applying Islamic principles to resolve family disputes within the Muslim community in Canada (Razack 2007, 8; Boyd 2005). While the province of Quebec had rejected faith-based arbitration, in the province of Ontario a choice for arbitration had long existed through the Arbitration Act. Thus in Ontario, individuals may hire third parties "to privately adjudicate their conflicts using any agreed upon rules or laws" (Razack 2007, 5). This law has been used in the context of commercial disputes and by Jews for divorce settlements. Toronto lawyer Amina Sherazee, however, contends that the Arbitration Act does not explicitly mention its use in religious arbitration (Braganza 2005).

When Ontario's Premier Dalton McGuinty and the Attorney General Michael Bryant commissioned a report from Marion Boyd to review the Arbitration Act, many Muslim and other groups began speaking up against the Sharia proposal. Boyd, after reviewing the Act, proposed that it could be extended to Islamic principles, but that various safeguards should be put in place. Boyd further highlighted that any faith-based system must conform to Charter principles (the Canadian Charter of Rights and Freedoms) and must ensure that women are educated about their full rights if they pursue this option (CBC 2005). Nevertheless, many organizations spoke out in opposition to permitting Sharia law, including the National Association of Women and the Law (NAWL), the Canadian Council of Muslim Women, the National Organization of Immigrant and Visible Minority Women of Canada, and Women Living Under Muslim Laws. They argued that Sharia law does not regard women and men as equals and worried, therefore, that women would be coerced to opt for Sharia arbitration without proper consent or choice on their part. Opponents also raised the issue that there are various schools of Islamic jurisprudence, and there was no indication as to which one or which version of Sharia would prevail. These opponents feared that more conservative and patriarchal versions would dominate (Razack 2007; CBC 2005).

A moral and media panic also fostered public opinion that strongly opposed the Sharia tribunal. While the law had not changed and in principle there was nothing stopping Muslims from using the Arbitration Act to settle civil or commercial disputes, the impression created by this controversy was that somehow the law had been changed (Boyd 2005). Various images of Muslim women being stoned for "transgressions" around the world were invoked, stoking the already negative impression of Islamic law (Razack 2007). The provincial government had to clarify that nothing had been changed in law to suddenly make it easier to apply Sharia principles. Sherene Razack also argues that the way in which this debate was monopolized in the name of fighting patriarchy had the effect of quashing any reasoned argument on the part of those who feel strongly about their faith. Essentially, the debate became polarized, representing supporters of Sharia as patriarchal and critics as secular, with no compromising position allowed for those who wanted a non-patriarchal Sharia choice (Razack 2007). In this way, Razack contends, all Muslim women were represented as a group needing protection from Muslim men.

After the Boyd report, the Ontario government initially found no compelling reasons to deny the use of Sharia principles under the Arbitration Act. However, after the public outcry, the government reversed its position and announced that all faith-based arbitration would be stopped (Razack 2007).

DISCUSSION

Canadian secularism contains elements of a "residual Christianity" and embeds the following two notions: firstly, religion is implicitly understood to be Christian and as something to be celebrated in private, with some accepted public manifestations taking, for example, the form of Christian statutory holidays such as Christmas and Easter and the corresponding public displays that are historically entrenched in Canadian society. Secondly, while multiculturalism is the official policy, culture and citizenship are premised on an acceptance of this secularism-with-residual-Christianity. Christianity is the norm, with all other religions standing outside this norm and needing to be accommodated. The growing diversity in Canada makes these notions increasingly untenable. Theologically, Islam may be conceived of in myriad ways and does not fit Western representations of Islam as a homogeneous religion. A more micro-level analysis may indeed reveal an incompatibility between the ontological perceptions of Christians and Muslims, their very worldviews being quite different. What is interesting and important in the studies of Muslim second-generation youth and the voices around the Sharia debate, is that the religious claims of diverse Muslims are founded on rights-based discourses and in constructions of "culture" which are decidedly hybrid, global, and arguably Western. The claims push the boundaries of a "Western" conceptualization of secularism. Given the increasing diversity of the population in recent decades, state secularism must expand once more to incorporate freedom *to* believe in religion, variably defined, rather than freedom *from* religious belief.

At the same time, space must also be reserved for those who continue to want freedom from religion in the public sphere. Taylor's discussion of fraternity is relevant here. The values that Canadian society decides to privilege must reflect changes on the "ground." Today, these changes (claims) challenge the traditional understanding of secularism here, using the language of multiculturalism and citizenship. Muslim second-generation youth may want to claim "religious" identities in a secular context, and, equally, Muslim women may want a Sharia option within the context of the "secular" Canadian state. The principles of secularism are not opposed to the claims of equity-seeking groups simply because they happen to be couched in a "religious" framework. While the ultimate decision by the provincial government was to abolish any religious-based arbitration, the Sharia debate allowed an important dialogue to take place—a dialogue of de-centring the normative construct of "residual Christianity." At broader conceptual and policy levels, Rahnema (2008) argues, Canada needs a "balanced and secular multiculturalism that respects the rights of different ethnic and religious groups, combats racism," and fosters a sense of citizenship for minority groups (Rahnema 2008). At the micro- and individual levels, Asad argues, it is important to understand the ways in which people establish or subvert the conceptual binaries entailed in western notions of secularism (Asad 2003). The recent sociological and cross-disciplinary interest in studying religion moves us closer to unpacking taken-for-granted concepts of secularism, multiculturalism, and citizenship in Canada and indeed around the world.

ENDNOTES

1. The core or mainstream in Canadian society is generally understood to be 'white', middle class and Christian. This generalized group functions as a referent against which all else is measured and compared. On the periphery, at various distances from the core, lie racialized and religious minority groups.
2. Other groups have also made claims for accommodation, but my main interest is in the claims of Muslims in Canada.
3. This particularly benign conception of the Enlightenment does not focus on any of its "darker" sides, that is, its connection with slavery and later colonialism, both of which are imbricated in the racism of the modern world. Asad (2003) attends to these connections in his work, as do various other thinkers, such as Paul Gilroy (2000).
4. This reading is only based on the particular texts that I have cited here by each of these thinkers, and does not cover the entire body of their work.

5. Various versions of secularism also exist in other non-Western countries. In India, for instance, there are two main conceptions of secularism. One is where there is a veneer of state neutrality towards religion, and the other is where there is recognition of the multiplicity of religion in the public sphere (Taylor 2009, xxi).
6. Salafists are "those who espouse forms of Islamic Sunni ideology and practice what they consider to be 'pure' or 'original' forms of Islam" (Ramji 2005, 105).
7. These claims might refer to wearing the hijab or deliberately limiting interactions with members of the opposite sex.

REFERENCES

Asad, T. 2003. *Formations of the Secular: Christianity, Islam, Modernity*. California: Stanford University Press.

Beyer, P. 2005. "Religious Identity and Educational Attainment among Recent Immigrants to Canada: Gender, Age, and 2nd Generation." *International Journal of Migration and Integration* 6 (2): 177–199.

Boyd, Marion. 2005. "Religiously-Based Alternate Dispute Resolution: A Challenge to Multiculturalism." *Canadian Diversity/Diversite canadienne: Negotiating Religious Pluralism* 4 (3): 71–74.

Boyd, Monica. 2002. "Educational Attainment of Immigrant Offspring: Success or Segmented Assimilation." *International Migration Review* 36 (4): 1,037–1,060.

Braganza, Neil. 2005. "Sharia Law: Religious arbitration and the privatization of law." An interview with Amina Sherazee. *New Socialist*. Accessed August 5, 2011. mostlywater.org/node/2651.

Canadian Broadcasting Corporation (CBC). 2005. "Indepth: Islam. Shariah law: FAQs." CBC News Online. May 26, 2005. Accessed February 23, 2010. www.cbc.ca/news/background/islam/shariah-law.html.

Casanova, J. 1994. *Public Religions in the Modern World*. Chicago: University of Chicago Press.

Department of Justice, Canada. 2011. "Consitution Act 1982". Accessed August 5, 2011. laws.justice.gc.ca/eng/Const/Const_index.html.

Ferrara, A. 2009. "The Separation of Religion and Politics in a Post-Secular Society." *Philosophy and Social Criticism* 35 (1–2): 77–91.

Gilroy, P. 2000. *Against Race: Imagining Political Culture Beyond the Color Line*. Cambridge: The Belknap Press of Harvard University Press.

Ismail, S. 2008. "Muslim Public Self-Presentation: Interrogating the Liberal Public Sphere." PSOnline. Accessed August 19, 2009. www.apsanet.org.

Jedwab, J. 2008. "The Rise of the Unmeltable Canadians? Ethnic and National Belonging in Canada's Second Generation." *Canadian Diversity/Diversite canadienne: The Experiences of Second Generation Canadians* 6 (2): 25–34.

Khanlou, N., Y. Shakya, and C. Muntaner. 2007–2009. "Mental Health Services for Newcomer Youth: Exploring Needs and Enhancing Access." Funded by Provincial Centre of Excellence for Child and Youth Mental Health at CHEO.

Narbey, G. 2005. "Can We All Just Get Along?" In *The Human Project: Readings on the Individual, Society, and Culture*, edited by C. Cockerton and M. Chaparian, Chapter 7. Toronto: Pearson Education Canada Inc.

Levitt, P. 2007. *God Needs No Passport: Immigrants and the Changing American Religious Landscape*. New York:The New Press.

Rahnema, S. 2008. "Commentary: Contradictions of 'Dissolving the Diasporas.'" *Journal of Community and Applied Social Psychology* 18: 395–398.

Ramji, R. 2008. "Creating a Genuine Islam." *Canadian Diversity/Diversite canadienne: The Experiences of Second Generation Canadians* 6 (2): 104–109.

Razack, S. H. 2007. "The 'Sharia Law Debate' in Ontario: The Modernity/Premodernity Distinction in Legal Efforts to Protect Women from Culture." *Feminist Legal Studies* 15: 3–32.

Sander, Å. 1997. "To What Extent is the Swedish Muslim Religious?" In *Islam in Europe: The Politics of Religion and Community*, edited by S. Vertovec and C. Peach, 269–289. Warwick: Centre for Research in Ethnic Relations, Universityof Warwick.

Seljak, D. 2008. "Secularization and the Separation of Church and State in Canada." *Canadian Diversity/Diversite Canadienne: Religious Diversity and Canada's Future* 6 (1): 6–24.

Taylor, C. 2009. "What is Secularism?" In *Secularism, Religion and Multiculturalism Citizenship*, edited by G. B. Levey and T. Modood, xi–xxii. Cambridge: Cambridge University Press.

———.2007. *A Secular Age*. Cambridge: Harvard University Press.

Zine, J. 2007. "Safe Havens or Religious 'Ghettos'? Narratives of Islamic Schooling in Canada." *Race, Ethnicity, and Education* 10 (1): 71–92.

Chapter 11

MOVING AROUND THE WORLD: RUSSIAN JEWS FROM ISRAEL IN TORONTO

LEA SOIBELMAN

INTRODUCTION

This chapter explores the "secondary migration of Russian Jews," in particular, the immigration experience of Russian Jews who left the Former Soviet Union (FSU) for Israel in the late 1980s and early 1990s and arrived in the Greater Toronto Area (herein referred to as Toronto), in the late 1990s and early 2000s. Unlike Russian Jews who arrived in Canada directly from the FSU, this group of immigrants had a different journey: they left a hostile FSU for their historical homeland, Israel, and then arrived in Toronto joining another diaspora community, which has been rather welcoming, and in a way, embracing. Thus, they had the experience of living in the diaspora and their homeland, though for some Israel remained a homeland only in the mythical sense.

The study presented in this chapter explores the unique character of this group of migrants, their settlement in Toronto, and their identities and transnational practices. The purpose of the study is to explore the Russian Jewish immigrants' perceptions, ways of thinking, feelings, beliefs, values, views, and arguments related to their settlement experiences in Toronto. This study analyzes qualitative data, collected using a qualitative strategy known as narrative inquiry. I will show that this group of Russian Jews who settled in Toronto after migrating to Israel has particular features that have affected their adjustment and integration. Furthermore, my research reveals how their identities fluctuated as they came to settle in new places.

In the following section I disscuss the history of migration of Russian Jews, a working definition of Russian Jews and theoretical concepts of diaspora, identity, and transnationalism. Next, I discuss Russian Jewish immigration to Israel and Toronto followed by the study methodology and findings analysis. Finally, I present my conclusion.

LITERATURE REVIEW

Historical and Conceptional Context

The migration of Jews from Russia to Canada started at the end of the nineteenth century when thousands of Jews fled economic hardships and massacres in Russian towns and villages. The turmoil of World War I and the 1917 communist revolution induced further migration during the 1920s. Russian and other Eastern European Jews settled in the Prairies, especially in Winnipeg. Between 1914 and 1930, Russian Jewish immigrants kept gradually moving from farms in Western Canada and mines in the north of the country to the "ghettos" of Montreal and Toronto where they established Jewish cultural, charity, and fundraising organizations.

From the onset of the Great Depression until the end of World War II, Canada practically shut its doors to Jewish immigration. Not until 1948 did thousands of Jews, predominantly Holocaust survivors, find refuge in Canada. Between 1950 and 1953, several thousand Jewish refugees from Eastern Europe, including Russian Jews, managed to enter Canada before the Cold War again prevented entry (Cohen 2001, 215). In 1972, after years of pressure from the Western World, the Soviet government announced that Jews could leave for Israel. Russian Jews were motivated to leave the communist Soviet Union for several reasons: anti-Semitism, discrimination, lack of freedom and human rights, family reunification, and economic hardships.

In the post-communist FSU many of the "push" factors for Russian Jews were similar to those of previous immigrant cohorts. In addition, worsening of the economic decline, political disintegration, and ethnic strife in the country motivated many people to leave. The large wave of Russian Jews from Israel to Canada started in the middle of 1990s. The secondary migration of Russian Jews from Israel to Canada was typically prompted by fear of war and terrorism, mandatory military service, economic hardships, difficulties encountered by intermarried couples, as well as problems integrating into an Israeli society, predicated on a more religious ideology—revealed in religiously based legislation—than the Russian-Jewish migrants had expected or were comfortable with (Remennick 2007, 289).

Who is a Jew?

Presenting an informed analysis of Russian Jews from Israel in Toronto requires working definitions of who is a Jew and who is a Russian Jew. Judaism shares some of the characteristics of a nation — an ethnicity, a religion, and a culture — making the definition of who is a Jew vary to some extent, depending on whether a religious or ethnic approach to identity is used. According to Jewish law (Halacha), a child born to a Jewish mother is considered a Jew. Reform Judaism however suggests that persons are Jews if they were born to either a Jewish mother or a Jewish father. For the purpose of this chapter an individual who has at least one Jewish parent and who identifies with Jews will be considered a Jew.

"Russian" is commonly used to describe immigrants from all the republics of the FSU. One can argue this is wrong, because each republic has its own distinctive ethnic character, manifested in language, arts, and customs, and often in a particular accent or dialect of the Russian language. However, the non-Russian communities of all the republics of the FSU went through a process of Russification, i.e., an adoption (voluntary or not) of the Russian language and other Russian attributes. Although the community in Toronto has its origin in multiple FSU republics, it defines itself as Russian Jewish—indeed the name of its largest community institution is the Russian Jewish Community Centre. I use the same definition in this chapter: Russian Jews are Jews born in the FSU.

Ethnic Identity

Allan Anderson (2001, 216) points out that global diasporas have, over centuries and especially in recent decades, contributed to "extremely complex ethnic contact situations. Ethnic identification today has become increasingly complicated by the scattering of ethnic people." The mobility of people of diverse ethnic affiliations could hardly be overstated today. Multiple ethnic and social identities have emerged in modern pluralistic societies. Furthermore, numerous scholars have argued that ethnic identity is not constant and can fluctuate over time (Anderson 2001; Basok 2002; Song 2003). Tanya Basok (2002, 345), who conducted several studies of Russian Jewish immigrants in Toronto, views "identity as being constantly (re)constituted in relation to local and global encounters." She suggests that people may be uncertain about what constitutes their own identities, and the questioning and redefinition of the meanings of ethnic identities of immigrants can result in the fragmentation of these identities. These findings resonate with those by Paul Anisef, Etta Baichman-Anisef, and Myer Siemiatycki (2002, 22), who argue that Russian Jewish youth, especially those who lived in Israel, develop multiple fragmented identities: "Are they Russian? Are they Israeli? Are they Jewish, and if so, what part of their identity does it take?"

Some aspects of identity can be self-imposed and others can be the result of outside influence. According to David Weinberg (1996), identity is multi-faceted; therefore, an individual can identify with more than one group on multiple levels. Issues of identity and belonging to a group might be more complicated for diasporic minorities such as Russian Jews. Historically the formation of the identity of Russian Jews was, to a great extent, affected by their experiences: pogroms, anti-Semitism, the creation of a communist Soviet Union, the Holocaust, the establishment of the state of Israel, etc. Russian Jews had to maintain their collective memory and traditions to keep their Jewish identity and preserve it for future generations (Weinberg 1996, 63). Their identity had to incorporate both traditional Jewish values and modern life. For the majority of Russian Jews, who grew up in an atheist society, being Jewish meant to belong to an ethnic rather than a religious group. But their identities were also influenced by their education and exposure to arts and literature, as well as other experiences, which were based on Russian culture. Consequently, in addition to their Jewish identity, they also identified as Russians.

Diaspora and Transnationalism

Contemporary immigrants often move back and forth (physically, virtually, and otherwise) between their countries of origin and destination, thus creating transnational diasporas. According to Judith Shuval (2000) diaspora is a social construct founded on feeling, memory, history, mythology, group identity, longings, and allegorical and virtual elements, all of which play a role in establishing a diaspora reality. A sense of diaspora can be immediate: a response to the trauma of exile. It can also occur or recur after several generations, when group members are themselves no longer immigrants. When a diaspora group experiences exclusion, social discrimination, or limited opportunities for advancement, an active diaspora culture helps to maintain a sense of belonging to a more welcoming social community (Shuval 2000). What distinguishes a diaspora from other groups of migrants is an ongoing or reawakened attachment and loyalty to an earlier culture and specifically to a space defined as a homeland which has been left.

Before the establishment of the state of Israel in 1948, all Jews were considered to be living in the Diaspora. In this Diaspora, Jews kept their Jewish identity alive for centuries while they could not return to their biblical homeland Israel. The Diaspora has been located all over the world with major concentrations in the USA, Canada, France, the FSU, and Argentina. Diaspora Jews have remained intimately connected to their biblical homeland Israel, and for generations prayed daily for a return to a Holy Land and recited "Next Year in Jerusalem" at the end of Passover Seder.

Common language and cultural heritage are the key cementing factors for transnational diasporas. Nina Glick Schiller, Linda Basch, and Cristina Szanton Blanc (1995, 48) define transnationalism as a "process by which immigrants forge and sustain simultaneous multi-stranded social relations that link together their societies of origin and settlement." There are ongoing and continuing ways in which "current-day immigrants construct and reconstitute their simultaneous embeddedness in more than one society" (49). Below I will demonstrate that Russian Jews from Israel have strong transnational links with both Israel and the FSU.

RUSSIAN-JEWISH IMMIGRATION TO ISRAEL AND TORONTO

Profile of the Russian Jewish Immigrants in Israel

This wave of *olim* (newcomers) is rather unique in scope, socio-economic profile, and impact on the Israeli society. Besides their demographic impact, newcomers from the FSU have greatly contributed to the country's social and human capital. Many of the newcomers had academic degrees and had been professionals or white-collar workers in the FSU. However, despite the state's efforts to smooth the transition of educated immigrants by way of Hebrew training, professional courses, and educational scholarships, only 30 percent found jobs relevant to their qualifications. The majority, especially older and female immigrants, had to make their living by unskilled or semi-skilled work, often in the service sector (Remennick 2003). Thus, the occupational integration of Russian immigrants was rather unsuccessful. As a consequence, they had few direct incentives to improve their command of Hebrew and had few points of contacts with their Israeli co-workers (Lissak and Leshem 1999).

In the cultural context, adult Russian speakers cherished their heritage and resisted attempts at their rapid "Israelization" (Epstein and Kheimets 2000). Having fled one major state-imposed ideology in the FSU, they were cautious in subscribing to another dominant ideology, Zionism, in Israel (Lissak and Leshem 1995). According to Larissa Remennick (2002, 2004, 2007) immigrants sustained their ties with Russian culture via two main channels: transnational links with the FSU and the creation of a versatile cultural media market in Israel. In the 1990s over 300 Russian book/video/music stores opened across Israel and about twenty newspapers and magazines in Russian were published, exceeding the number of Hebrew publications. All pivotal cultural events in the FSU were exported to Israel via Russian TV channels and live tours of Russian artists (Remennick 2004, 433). As Alek Epstein and Nina Kheimets (2000) point out, most Russians held on to Russian cultural traditions and wished to preserve the old ways.

Settlement in Israel

The settlement experience of Russian *olim* in the 1970s and 1980s was rather smooth and expedient. However, by the early 1990s the social and economic context of the settlement of tens of thousands of former Soviet newcomers had changed dramatically. The skilled labour market of Israel provided enough locally trained professionals in almost every field. The political events of that period featured the first Palestinian Intifada and the Gulf War with Iraqi missiles targeting Israeli towns and keeping citizens in shelters. "The country's internal agenda was certainly full and its resources stretched as thin as ever; adding to the strain, the Russian immigrants kept arriving by the thousands" (Remennick 2007, 55). The small country was flooded with newcomers looking for rental houses and jobs.

The occupational adjustment of this wave of newcomers was very difficult. In the early 1990s, the unemployment rate among Russian immigrants reached 40 percent; although, this rate slowly declined and reached the national average of 11 percent by the late 1990s. Yet, throughout this period, just over a quarter of the *olim* holding academic degrees from the FSU worked in their original professions (Remennick 2007, 57). The extent of occupational downgrading was especially dramatic for women and older professionals of either gender, who had often been senior specialists before emigration. It was highly traumatic for educated immigrants to find themselves in the bottom tier of the workforce. Remennick (2007, 58) points out that the feelings of social displacement were "augmented by an overarching sense of insecurity—financial (due to unstable income and mounting debts), physical (reflecting ongoing military conflict and acts of terror), and psychological (reflecting poor command of Hebrew, misunderstanding of local norms, and loss of support networks)."

The economic, social, and mostly political situation in Israel in the 1990s made many *olim* question whether they wanted to continue living in Israel. Even if they had reached a certain economic stability (e.g., well-paid positions, purchased real estate) and felt more or less comfortable in the Israeli society, the constant stress caused by "terrorist" attacks, by the ongoing military threat, and mandatory military service motivated many to leave Israel. According to the Israeli Central Bureau of Statistics the number of immigrants from the FSU who left Israel again in 2000 was 3,022 and climbed to 4,406 in 2002.

Russian Jews from Israel in Toronto: The Receiving Community

Throughout the 1990s and early 2000s, Canada was one of the most appealing destinations for Russian Jews from Israel. "The relative lenience of Canadian immigration policy towards skilled immigrants and high human capital of the Russian Jews reflected in their eligibility under the Point System" (Remennick 2007, 279). A steady stream of applicants has been stalking the offices of the Canadian Embassy in Tel Aviv since the mid-1990s and an estimated 3,000 to 7,000 (including Russian Jews and other Israelis) left for Canada every year (283).

Russian Jews from Israel arriving in Toronto came to a city with a large and vibrant Jewish community. According to the 2006 Census, the Jewish population in Toronto had reached 141,685. There are numerous facilities available to the community, ranging from Jewish day and afternoon schools for students of every background to kosher restaurants and shops, a large number of synagogues of every denomination and three community centres.

Jewish Immigrant Aid Services (JIAS), Toronto, is the agency providing services to all newcomers to Toronto. During the past decade, 85 percent of the agency clientele have been Russian Jews from Israel. The agency provides a variety of settlement and integration services, such as information and referral, English as a Second Language classes, immigration consultations, employment counselling, short-term financial assistance, youth program, programs for seniors, a family matching program, and Jewish Holidays celebrations.

METHODOLOGY

Participants for the study were located by consecutive referrals (snowballing) with the starting point in my own informal networks among Russian Jews from Israel living in Toronto. The study sample consisted of six Russian Jewish immigrants from Israel, three male and three female, ages thirty-five to fifty-five, who had lived in

Israel for ten to twelve years and arrived in Toronto in the late 1990s and early 2000s. To preserve the anonymity of the participants, I have changed their names but kept intact other personal details (age, occupation, length of residence in Canada, etc.). Table 11.1 illustrates the socio-demographic profile of the respondents.

Table 11.1: Socio-Demographic Profile of the Respondents

Name	Age	Occupation Former / Current	Years in Toronto	Family Composition
Anna	48	teacher/settlement worker	7	married+2 (19, 23)*
Alex	55	electronic engineer/same	10	married+2 (18, 25)
Olga	45	system analyst/same	6	married+2 (8, 20)
Lena	40	teacher/student	6	married+2 (10, 15)
Vlad	36	mechanical engineer/same	7	married+2 (7, 10)
Josef	43	programmer/same	9	married+1 (16)

*Number and Ages of Children
Source: Created by Author.

I conducted six in-depth interviews in Russian, lasting on average forty-five minutes. The small sample and thorough interviews allowed greater personal understanding of the phenomenon by giving the respondents an opportunity to elaborate on their answers. The collected information provided a substantial basis for an informed analysis. The questionnaire was composed of open-ended questions to allow for the possibility to expand on questions, to probe, to clarify, and to generate additional data. The interviews were tape-recorded, accurately transcribed, and analyzed using thematic coding (Neuman 2006). Having worked with Russian Jews from Israel for eighteen years and having gone through similar immigration experiences contributes to my in-depth understanding and insight into the participants and the related issues, which in turn added to the credibility of the presented findings and their analysis. The objective of this examination was to explore the essence of the multiple migration experiences of Russian Jews from Israel and their impact on their identities and transnational practices.

FINDINGS

The individual interviews conducted for this study pertained to the four general themes: reasons for immigration to Canada, settlement experiences, identity, and transnationalism. Below, I will discuss each of them separately.

Reasons for Immigration to Canada

All the participants in my study strongly identified the lack of safety and political instability as primary reasons for leaving Israel. They reported leaving Israel to escape the constant stress caused by the ongoing military threat and escalating violence in the region. They had gone through nerve-wracking experiences of warning sirens, wearing gas masks, and hiding in bomb shelters. In addition, all the participants voiced concerns that their children, both male and female, would have to serve in the Israel Defense Forces. Furthermore, they cited additional motives to leave Israel: limited employment opportunities, the country's Middle Eastern cultural flavour, their dislike of native Israelis, the overly religious character of the state, the hot climate, and other reasons. It was reported by the respondents that although they were gainfully employed in Israel, the spouses of some could either not find meaningful employment or were unemployed. Another important issue raised by some respondents was the precarious position in which the non-Jewish spouses, especially women, found themselves. There is no legal separation between the state and religion in many important aspects of Israel's laws and government. Orthodox Judaism dominates all official religious institutions, thus only a person who was born to a Jewish woman is considered a Jew. Though the non-Jewish spouses were granted Israeli citizenship according to the Law of Return, they were denied basic civic rights. The matters of marriage, divorce, registration of newborns, and burial are all controlled by the religious authorities, which exclude non-Jews from their proceedings. This meant that the non-Jews could not get married in Israel, they had more trouble getting divorced, registering their non-Jewish children as citizens, and inviting their non-Jewish parents or siblings to visit or to join them in Israel. As a result, the mixed families often felt as second-class citizens (Remennick, 2007).

Some participants shared that their preferred destination was the United States. However, as immigration to the United States was almost impossible, they decided to immigrate to Canada. Others preferred Canada due to relatively inexpensive higher education, universal access to health care, and a more developed welfare system.

Settlement Experiences

The majority of the respondents named employment as the greatest settlement challenge in Toronto. Only immigrants in a few specific professions experienced a relatively smooth transition from the Israeli to the Canadian labour market; these included programmers, electronic engineers, and computer specialists. For other respondents and their spouses, limited command of English posed a significant barrier to getting Canadian accreditation in their profession. In addition, the respondents named the lack of Canadian experience as a significant obstacle in finding employment. Barriers to career continuity existed mainly for regulated occupations: teachers, nurses, physicians, psychologists, etc. Lena, who was an elementary school teacher in Israel, shared that she could not pass the exams to obtain a teaching licence in Ontario. As a result, she decided to go to college to become a social service worker. Alex, whose wife had worked as a physician in the FSU and then (after licensure) in Israel, recounted that they knew too little about Canadian medical regulations. Upon arrival, they learned that Ontario offered foreign-trained physicians a very limited number of residency slots each year, and those who did not complete a residency had no chance to practice medicine. After taking a professional course, his wife became an imaging technician.

Some participants indicated that the adjustment for their children, especially teenagers, was not easy. Many young immigrants from Israel faced a broad linguistic and cultural gap between themselves and mainstream Canadian society, including their peers in schools and other frameworks. These findings confirm the earlier research on Russian-speaking youths (Anisef, Baichman-Anisef, and Siemiatycki. 2002).

Similar to the findings by Basok (2002) and Remennick (2007), my research shows that Russian Jews from Israel had difficulties finding common ground with "mainstream" Canadian society and the established Jewish community. The participants appreciated Canadians' open attitude towards other cultures and languages; they did not experience any kind of discrimination on the basis of their Jewish origin or immigrant status. However, only one participant mentioned having informal relationships with native Canadians outside the workplace, school, and other institutional context. Most participants perceived Canadians as cold and uninterested in having social ties with immigrants. As one participant mentioned: "Canadians are different from Israelis; they are not interested to know about your life outside of the workplace. They are very formal and reserved. Sometimes I find them superficial" (personal interview).

Asked about their relations with the Canadian Jewish community, the respondents had varied reactions. Some participants felt that Canadian Jews expected them to adapt to the same religious practices of the local Jewish community. They felt unable to meet these expectations and believed they would be excluded from the networks of the Toronto Jewish community. As a participant noted, "In Israel you go to the synagogue if you want to pray. Here, in Canada, if you attend a synagogue you belong to the community. We are not used to this" (personal interview).

Other participants were more inclined to take part in Jewish life and participate in community activities, which they saw as a way to maintain their symbolic connection to Israel. Some believed in the importance of coming of age rituals (bar/bat mitzvahs) and Sunday Jewish schools for their children. Unlike those who arrived directly from the FSU, Russian Jews who had lived in Israel were more inclined to take part in Jewish life and participate in community activities, which they saw as a way to maintain their symbolic connection to Israel. The participants reported that they felt closer to Israelis living in Toronto than to Canadian-born Jews. They felt a broad social and cultural distance between themselves and the members of the Toronto Jewish community.

Overall, however, the respondents considered their settlement in Canada successful. Some of them believed the "Israeli experience" contributed to overcoming the difficulties they had faced. They had already gone through the experience of settling in a new country once and were more resilient to new challenges. As one respondent described, "Upon arrival in Canada I was a seasoned migrant, I have already acquired some basic immigrant's life skills." Nevertheless, they also indicated that it was still a "bumpy road" to adjust to a new country. As noted by a respondent: "Canada is very different from Israel. It takes time to get used to a new lifestyle, make friends and feel at home. It is not so simple to start a new life again" (personal interview).

Identity

This study confirms that "new identities emerge as people come to settle in new places" (Basok 2002, 341). Table 11.2 reflects the participants' responses to the question of their primary identity. It illustrates the multiplicity and flexibility of identities of Russian Jews from Israel in Toronto. These findings resonate with the ones presented by Tara Gilkinson and Geneviève Sauvé in Chapter 9 that an individual can have multiple identities without them conflicting or colliding with each other.

Table 11.2: Primary Identity of the Respondents in their Countries of Residence

	FSU	ISRAEL	CANADA
Anna	Russian Jewish	Russian Jewish	Jewish
Alex	Soviet Jewish	Soviet Jewish	Israeli Jewish
Olga	Russian Jewish	Russian	Russian Jewish
Lena	Russian Jewish	Jewish	Israeli Jewish
Vlad	Jewish	Jewish	Jewish
Josef	Russian Jewish	Russian Jew	Jewish

Source: Created by Author.

Most respondents said that in the FSU they felt Jewish simply because they were born in a Jewish family; yet an additional fragment of Russian or Soviet identity was continuously present. An important experience defining their identity as Jews was anti-Semitism. In the FSU they were constantly reminded of their Jewishness not only by the identification of their ethnicity in their passports, but also by the hatred and animosity of non-Jews. In addition some respondents named the celebration of Jewish traditions, knowledge of Jewish history, and synagogue attendance as experiences that nourished their Jewish identities in the FSU.

The stay in Israel produced a varying effect on the migrants' identities. Some of them said that having lived in Israel made them feel more Jewish because they were able to learn Hebrew and study Jewish traditions. Almost all of the immigrants surveyed indicated that the Israeli experience strengthened their connection with Jewish traditions. Yet, encounters with other Jews in Israel, including Israeli-born Jews, made the respondents feel "Russian" because their fellow Jews perceived the immigrants from the FSU as distinct. Several respondents noted that they were continually called Russians by other Jews in Israel, which made them feel that they were not Jewish enough.

Most participants define their Jewish identity in ethnic rather than religious terms. Here, in Toronto they have adopted behavioural expressions of Jewishness and an affirmative connection to the Jewish traditions and Israel, manifested in celebrating Jewish holidays, such as Passover, Chanukah, Rosh Hashanah, and Yom Kippur. In addition, they do not want their children to forget Hebrew. They continue to show attachment to Israel by participating in activities like the celebration of Israel Independence Day, the annual UJA Federation Walk with Israel, and the Israeli Bazaar.

Transnationalism

In Israel and Canada, Russian Jewish immigrants express transnational identity and lifestyle in multiple ways. These expressions are mainly found in the cultural and psychological domain (rather than, say, in the economic and business domain). Because Russian Jews in Israel created in the 1990s a thriving subculture with local Russian theatres, bookstores, newspapers, schools, and television and radio programs, they had the benefit of an existing transnational orientation when they came to Toronto. Their transnational experience pertains to both the FSU and Israel. On one hand, they feel part of a global Russian-speaking community stretching between the FSU, Israel, and the West; on the other hand, they do not see themselves as just Russians, but rather "Russian Israelis."

The majority of respondents said they would prefer to read both Russian and Hebrew newspapers. Some of them have both Russian and Israeli satellite TV. Almost all of their friends are Russian Jews from Israel; they have little in common with those who came directly from the FSU. As one respondent notes: "It is hard for us to relate to Russian Jews who have not lived in Israel. They are different; they have never experienced living in a Jewish state" (personal interview). Many immigrants of all ages keep close personal ties with their relatives and friends in Israel, the FSU, and the U.S. With the development of cheap and accessible communications, such as e-mail and calling cards, more immigrants maintain these ties. The majority of the study participants have travelled to Israel at least once since their arrival in Canada, mostly to visit parents.

In her study Remennick (2007) highlights the differences in recent findings by Ewa Morawska (2004) among Russian Jews in Philadelphia. Unlike Russian Jews in Toronto, Russian Jews in Philadelphia displayed a strong host-country orientation and few transnational engagements with either the FSU or Israel. According to Remennick, this difference can be explained by the specific composition of the Russian Jewish community in Toronto with a higher share of ethnically mixed families, part of which still live in the FSU, as well as the strong cultural bonds many Russian Jews had developed with Israel. Another possible explanation for greater transnational ties with co-ethnics among Toronto Russians, Remennick suggests, is their relative marginalization in Canada: "Unlike their American counterparts, few of them can call themselves proud

Canadians" (Remennick 2007, 307). Remennick concludes that "Russian Toronto is certainly becoming an important isle on the expanding map of the Russian-speaking post-communist diaspora" (307).

CONCLUSION

"Trading place trading luck," so goes an old Hebrew proverb. Russian Jews from Israel dared to do it twice. This study addressed the causes of their secondary migration to Canada, settlement experiences, identity, and transnationalism. Russian Jews from Israel present a particularly interesting case because of their multiple migrations. Having experienced a variety of push and pull factors they moved around half the globe in search of a better future for themselves and their children.

After leaving a country with a communist doctrine and settling in a country with a dominant Zionist ideology and a strong religious influence, they moved to Canada where an imposed doctrine or dominant religious belief system is absent. In the FSU they were forced to be atheists and to abandon their Jewish roots; in Israel they were expected to leave behind their Russian culture; but in Canada they have joined a society that supports multiculturalism and transnational migration. Moreover, transnational is being viewed as an almost inevitable condition for first-generation immigrants. These experiences shaped their identities.

Being a minority in all three countries, they embrace a hyphenated identity, which includes strong attachment to their Russian and their Jewish background. They were transformed from being a member of Jewish national minority in the FSU to a member of Russian national minority in Israel. However, being a minority in Israel did not prevent them from keeping their Russian culture. Just as in Israel, in Toronto the community of Russian Jews from Israel is sustained by Russian language publications, bookstores, websites, cultural events, etc. Russian culture continues to play a significant role in the lives of Russian Jews from Israel.

While maintaining a strong attachment to Russian culture and language, the participants also demonstrated strong sentimental and cultural ties to Israel. In this way, the concept of homeland acquires an additional connotation. It is not just a place of origin, but a place one is attached to. The Russian Jews from Israel combine their "Russianness" and "Israeliness" as fundamental elements of their identity. Given the diversity of their immigrant experiences they are at liberty to choose the best of their versatile heritage.

REFERENCES

Anderson, A.B. 2001. The Complexity of Ethnic Identities: a Postmodern Reevaluation. *Identity* 1 (3): 209–333.

Anisef, P., E. Baichman-Anisef, and M. Siemiatycki. 2002. "Multiple Identities & Marginal Ties: The Experience of Russian Jewish Immigrant Youth in Toronto." CERIS *Working Paper Series* 19.

Basok, T. 2002. "Fragmented Identities: The Case of Former Soviet Jews." *Identity* 2 (4): 341–360.

Cohen, R. 2001. "The New Immigrants: A Contemporary Profile." In *From Immigration to Integration. The Canadian Jewish Experience: A Millennium Edition*, edited by R. Klein and F. Dimant, 214–221. Institute for International Affairs, Bnai Brith Canada: Malcom Lester.

Epstein, A., and N. Kheimets. 2000. "Immigrant Intelligentsia and its Second Generation: Cultural Segregation as a Road to Social Integration?" *Journal of International Migration and Integration* 1 (4): 461–476.

Glick Schiller, N., L. Bash, and C. Szanton Blanc. 1995. "From Immigrant to Transmigrant: Theorizing Transnational Migration." *Anthropological Quarterly* 68 (1): 48–65.

Lissak, M., and E. Leshem. 1995. "The Russian Intelligentsia in Israel: Between Ghettoization and Integration." *Israel Affairs* 2 (2): 20–36.

Morawska, E. 2004. "Exploring Diversity in Immigrant Assimilation and Transnationalism: Poles and Russian Jews in Philadelphia." *International Migration Review* 38 (4): 1372–1395.

Neuman, L. W. 2006. *Social Research Methods: Qualitative and Quantitative Approaches*. Boston: Pearson Education.

Remennick, L. 2002. "Transnational Community in the Making: Russian Jewish Immigrants of the 1990s in Israel." *Journal of Ethnic and Migration Studies* 28 (3): 515–530.

Remennick, L. 2003. What Does Integration Mean? Social Insertion of Russian Immigrants in Israel. *Journal of International Migration and Integration* 4 (1): 23–49.

———. 2004. "Language Acquisition, Ethnicity and Social Integration among Former Soviet Immigrants of the 1990s in Israel." *Ethnic and Racial Studies* 27 (3): 431–454.

———.2007. *Russian Jews on Three Continents. Identity, Integration, and Conflict*. New Brunswick: Transaction Publisher.

Shuval, J. T. 2000. Diaspora Migration: Definitional Ambiguities and a Theoretical Paradigm. *International Migration* 38 (5): 41–57.

Song, M. 2003. *Choosing Ethnic Identity*. Boston: Polity.

Weinberg, D. H. 1996. *Between Tradition and Modernity: Haim Zhitkowski, Simon Dubnow, Ahad Ha-Am, and the Shaping of Modern Jewish Identity*. New York: Holmes & Meier.

Part Four

HOUSING AND RESIDENTIAL CONTEXT

An immediate concern for immigrants arriving at a new location is having access to shelter and housing. A universal model of how immigrants are sheltered in their first days in the new country does not exist. Some immigrants may have already bought or rented a house or an apartment prior to arrival; some are staying with extended families or friends; while others use shelters provided by faith-based communities, settlement services, and government programs, or stay in hotels and hostels. Similarly, there is no universal housing experience as immigrants settle in a new country and community.

Housing is more than shelter. It frames immigrants' residential context, the people whom they meet on a daily basis, their spatial access to employment, schools, and recreation, and the status and stereotypes they can acquire by living in certain neighbourhoods. The topic of housing and residential context thus intertwines with issues of identity and community, discussed in part three.

Housing and residential context also relate to the economic situation of immigrants. For most immigrants and immigrant families, housing constitutes the single largest expense. Employment income thus defines the type of housing immigrants and their families can afford. Since the earnings of immigrant workers tend to be lower than that of their native-born counterparts, they often spend an even higher share of their incomes on housing while living in crowded circumstances.

The chapters in Part Four address the topic of housing and residential context from policy perspectives and from the viewpoint of the immigrant experience. In Chapter 12, Alfredo Agustoni, Alfredo Alietti, and Roberta Cucca examine social housing as a tool for ethnic integration in Europe. Since WW II, social housing policies have played a crucial role in the process of immigrants' integration in Europe. The application of housing policy as an integration tool, however, has started to transform in most European countries. The public funds invested in social housing have been decreasing in several countries, and have been focused on fighting against ethnic segregation rather than responding to the housing needs of immigrants. Moreover, national housing policies are very heterogenic and lack a common European approach. The chapter analyzes the changing governance of housing policy in Europe, with a special focus on the recent Italian experience. The Italian case outlines the negative consequences related to housing policies oriented towards desegregation and social mix, without improving social housing supply.

In Chapter 13, S. Gopikrishna assumes the perspective of practitioners to explore the problem with hidden homelessness among newcomers in the Greater Toronto Area. Hidden homelessness occurs when families live in overcrowded habitation and are subject to living conditions typical for homeless shelters. Gopikrishna outlines the evolution of hidden homelessness in Toronto, identifies its causes, symptoms, and impacts, and questions why hidden homelessness is "hidden" and not subject to greater public debate.

The final chapter of Part Four also deals with the Toronto context, and with high-rise apartment buildings in which hidden homelessness among newcomers commonly occurs. Sutama Ghosh, however, highlights the agency of immigrant communities and their response to unfavourable housing conditions. Many new immigrants reside in high-rise apartments upon their arrival, and for a variety of interrelated economic and socio-psychological reasons, continue living there for a prolonged period of time. Ghosh therefore asks: how do the vertical structure high-rise apartment buildings affect the life worlds of the residents? How do immigrants develop attachments to these spaces, and how do they make them their own? By drawing on the experiences of thirty Bangladeshi immigrant households in Toronto, Ghosh demonstrates that the residents variously transform functional spaces into unique "Bengali neighbourhoods" that are filled with ambivalent feelings of hope and despair, and a place they can call "home away from home."

Chapter 12

SOCIAL HOUSING AS A TOOL FOR ETHNIC INTEGRATION IN EUROPE: A CRITICAL VIEW OF THE ITALIAN EXPERIENCE

ALFREDO AGUSTONI, ALFREDO ALIETTI, AND ROBERTA CUCCA

INTRODUCTION: SOCIAL HOUSING SUPPLY AND RESIDENTIAL SEGREGATION IN EUROPE

The relation between housing policies and immigrant integration in Europe represents a challenging topic because of the complexity and variety of European policies and regulations governing this relation: different social, economic, and political attitudes regarding the governance of immigration; variable welfare regimes, especially related to housing policies; the multiplicity of prevailing patterns of integration (assimilation versus pluralism) and regulatory policies; and, finally, different histories in terms of immigration flows. These elements interact, producing different patterns that cannot be understood as a common European housing experience for immigrants. It is clear, however, that in many European countries today the role of housing in integration policy is marginal, while labour, health, language, and training are more consistently financed and regulated (Tosi 2010; Edgar 2004, 87–9). Moreover, the housing question has been defined as the "wobbly pillar" of the welfare state in the European context (Torgersen 1987).

In spite of different social and institutional contexts, housing problems of immigrants seem to be similar in European countries. Especially recent immigrants experience a clear disadvantage compared with their native-born counterparts in terms of quality of accommodation, overcrowded housing conditions, and the rate of homelessness (EUMC 2005; Musterd 2005), including "hidden homelessness" (see Chapter 13). In addition, urban areas with a significant presence of foreigners are characterized by growing socio-spatial marginalization and significant segregation. Direct and indirect discrimination in housing allocation are common, limiting the chances of home acquisition and promoting housing solutions for foreigners and migrants that are unattractive for native-born persons. These conditions have been described as "new migrant penalty" (Jayaweera and Choudhury 2008, 17), highlighting the structural obstacles that newcomers experience in obtaining a "good home."

Despite the differences among European policies, since 2000 the attention of most European countries regarding the role of housing policies in the process of immigrant integration has been focused even more than before on combatting residential segregation rather than on strategies to promote better housing affordability for newcomers. Interesting exceptions are the social housing policies promoted in France after the Social Cohesion Plan of 2004, which revived social housing as a "service of general interest." With this exception, generally speaking, a gradual reduction of state intervention and a substantial reconfiguration of the principle of universal welfare in favour of more selective territorial policies have affected the social housing sector since the crisis of the Fordist model of urban integration (with its ability to mediate between social classes through the welfare state).

In this context, the spatial concentration of vulnerable populations is becoming prevalent, and the "social question" is increasingly linked to the social problems characterizing specific places (Simon 2003). In particular the districts with high concentrations of social housing experience negative consequences of economic restructuring and social exclusion, affecting both native-born and immigrant residents. The outcome of this trend is ethnic conflict within deprived environments; this conflict was previously mediated by the integration of newcomers within the contexts of labour and production (the factory and the unions), the local presence of a vast and diverse NGO sector, and political activists who advocated for solidarity and the rights of the workers (Alietti 1998; Lagrange and Oberti 2006). Furthermore, the media and political debates have assisted the emergence of a "toponymy degradation" related to these multi-ethnic urban spaces and expressed in terms such as "ghettos" and "neighbourhoods in crisis." These representations are widespread throughout Europe, reaffirming a sort of inescapable fate in the trajectories of immigrant settlement (Agustoni and Alietti 2009).

In a wide-ranging review of public housing in several European countries and the United States, Michael Harloe notes that since the 1980s a residual pattern of public intervention has begun to address the so-called "new urban poverty" (especially oriented to the lower income groups not able to afford the private rental market); consequently, stigmatization has affected the social housing sector in western countries (Harloe 1995, 523). As exemplified by the Netherlands, the reduction of public and political support has been associated with a greater concentration of lower income groups and a decline in higher income earners in the public housing stock (van Kempen and Priemus 2002). In most European countries, the fiscal crisis has accelerated the neo-liberalization of social housing systems, now characterized by: (a) the withdrawal of the state from providing social housing; (b) the shift to individual ownership; (c) the abolition of rules and limits in the private rental sector; (d) the privatization of public housing stock (European Parliament 1997; Edgar, Doherty, and Henk 2002; Arbaci 2007; Whitehead and Scanlon 2008).

This general tendency is well represented by the case of Copenhagen, a city characterized by vast transformations in its social housing policies over the last decade. Between 1995 and 1996 Copenhagen sold most of the municipal social housing stock (16,000 in 20,000 flats) to tenants interested in buying their apartments and establishing housing associations in the form of cooperatives (Penninx 2007; Municipal Statistics, Copenhagen 2005). This policy has created a significant social divide between the tenants able to take advantage of state efforts to offer affordable mortgages and those without the prerequisites. In addition, the number of homes available at affordable rents was dramatically cut, due also to widespread gentrification of inner city areas (Larsen and Lund 2008). As a result, lower income groups (often immigrants and refugees) now concentrate in the few areas of remaining social housing (Andersen 2002). Today, local authorities identify several types of ethnically segregated areas: vulnerable areas, in which at least 7 out of 10 inhabitants are immigrants (at least 14,000 people now reside in these areas); areas of "high risk," where 5 out of 10 residents are immigrants (18,000 inhabitants); areas "at risk," in which 3 out of 10 residents are immigrants (40,000 inhabitants) (Penninx 2007). Public debate represents these areas, in some cases, as ethnically homogeneous (Andersen 2007), and as linked to segregation in school and the labour market (Schindler Rangvid 2007).

Although the case of Copenhagen is extreme, it is helpful to illustrate the relations between social housing supply and segregation in many European cities. The aim of this chapter is to further explore this relation, and assess the thesis that effective desegregation policies should deal with general housing affordability. However, these policies can also achieve the opposite, as the analysis of the Italian case suggests. In the next sections, we first discuss the European "ghetto" panic and policies against segregation. Then we examine the Italian case of immigration, residential segregation, and housing policies, followed by a conclusion.

THE "GHETTO" PANIC IN EUROPE

The issue of socio-spatial segregation of ethnic minorities and immigrants in Europe has become significant not only in academic debate, but also in mass-media representations and in political discourse on *ghettos*, normally labelled as "ethnic." The focus of these representations and discourses is often on the potential negative effect of spatial segregation on the chance to escape from a cycle of poverty and from exclusion and isolation, owing to poor availability of local resources, job opportunities, and social capital (Musterd and Andersson 2005; Bolt, Özüekren, and Phillips 2010; Bolt, Phillips, and Van Kempen 2010). The European Commission, in a document on the promotion of sustainable urban development, stresses as a special challenge the preventing of spatial concentrations of ethnic minorities in cities (Musterd 2003, 625).

In the European context, different patterns of integration exist between cities of northern and southern Europe (Allen et al. 2004; Musterd 2003; Arbaci 2007). Generally, in metropolitan areas of southern Europe, the situation can be summarized as follows: housing conditions of immigrants are generally modest; high levels of informality exist in the real estate market (e.g., undocumented rents, bed-sharing); low levels of spatial segregation combine with complex patterns of spatial fragmentation and significant suburbanization (especially with regard to non-European groups) (Malheiros 2002,108; Arbaci and Malheiros 2010). In northern Europe, immigrants also experience modest housing conditions and informal housing arrangement; however, there is a trend towards spatial concentration of the migrant population and a more widespread presence of minorities in central areas (inner cities). Because of these differences, understanding the relationship between spatial segregation and social integration in Europe is a complex task.

Nevertheless, the vast empirical literature paints a picture of the spatial concentration of migrants as a sign of trouble. This picture relates to the reason why migrants fail to obtain adequate housing: their low socio-economic status; discriminatory mechanisms working at the housing market level; the mechanisms of selection operated by the bureaucracy of the public housing sector; the regulatory framework of the social housing sector; the outflows of the autochthonous middle class from the social housing areas; and, last but not least, the voluntary choice to live with others of the same ethnic background. Regarding the latter, ethnic self-segregation may meet special needs of immigration, including the need for a network to help find housing or access to a job in an ethnic business (see Chapter 14). An interesting case is the United Kingdom. Following the Dutch system of housing allocation, many parts of the United Kingdom have tested a method that provides more choice for applicants than the traditional waiting list. According to his model, applicants for social housing, or tenants of social housing who want to move, can apply for accommodation that best meets their needs by choosing from that reported by newspapers and specialized websites. Unlike in the Dutch cities that applied a similar model, in the United Kingdom this model has, in some cases, encouraged self-segregation among ethnic groups (van Ham and Manley 2009). The different outcomes of a similar policy illustrate the importance of context, in this case the different models of cultural integration that characterize the two countries (Rutter and Latorre 2009).

POLICIES AGAINST RESIDENTIAL SEGREGATION IN EUROPE: PATHS AND MECHANISMS

The mechanisms of segregation and self-segregation in Europe are diverse; likewise, the policies intended to counter segregation differ significantly between EU countries

(Bolt 2009; Cucca and Pologruto 2011). According to the Cities for Local Integration Policies (CLIP) project (2007) there are three main overlapping policy directions: (1) policies to reduce or prevent spatial segregation; (2) policies to reduce the negative effects of spatial segregation; (3) policies making positive use of the opportunities that ethnic segregation presents.

Throughout Europe, policies to reduce or prevent spatial segregation are the most frequent; they are strongly entangled with the aim of creating a so-called social and ethnic mix. The other two policies take into account the difficulty of achieving real and effective desegregation; consequently they focus on programs to improve living conditions and opportunities through integration and urban regeneration of deprived neighbourhoods. Many European countries have developed such urban policies, known as area-based policies, at different times. The various measures and instruments used to implement these policies are action-oriented, interactive, and multi-purpose in their nature. Often they focus both on the renovation of housing facilities and on the dynamics of social inclusion, while incorporating training and employment programs. In areas with a strong ethnic concentration, actions are oriented towards strengthening the resources available locally (see Chapter 13), for example, by consolidating ethnic economies, providing opportunities for vocational training, offering language courses, opening channels of trade with the rest of the city, fostering appreciation for the contribution of ethnic institutions, and facilitating the participation of foreign families in design of housing choices (Edgar 2004). Often these different strategies are integrated with each other. An interesting case is Sweden, where housing segregation has been declining, owing to two intervention strategies (Holmqvist and Bergsten 2009). The first strategy consisted of instruments of urban planning oriented towards increasing the heterogeneity of the housing stock. The second strategy concerned the promotion of a "right to buy," establishing housing associations in the form of cooperatives, avoiding speculation, and providing access to credit for disadvantaged households. This strategy has been applied to neighbourhoods considered "less attractive." In addition, over the past decade, social policy interventions have been applied to districts with high concentrations of disadvantaged groups. In 1998 the Swedish government launched the "Metropolitan Development Initiative," a project intended to improve the quality of public spaces and facilities, to combat early school leaving, and to support the acquisition of professional skills. The goal was not to transform the housing mix but to promote the overall development of people living in the area, with a focus on fighting unemployment and improving social mobility.

Another interesting example of area-based policy has recently been implemented in the Netherlands. After the terrorist attacks in New York and Washington DC in 2001, the line of action had turned more and more against ethnic segregation to prevent radicalization. In 2007 the national government promoted the program "social cohesion and housing mix." This program has a strategy of urban renewal and social interventions based on five pillars (home, work, education, integration, and security), and is explicitly designed to encourage social mix. It has targeted 40 urban districts, known as "action areas." These areas were selected on the basis of indicators, including around 100 percent social housing stock, high percentage of households with low income, bad living conditions in terms of personal security, high percentage of immigrants, deteriorating building structure, and poor infrastructures. Since the term *social cohesion* is essentially ambiguous (Ranci and Torri 2007; Alietti 2009), it is interesting to consider the definition within this program: social cohesion here means the "feeling of living in an area that is your home and where you have control over the environment" (Van Kempen and Bolt 2009). Often municipalities participating in the program defined spatial concentration in terms of socio-economic segregation rather than ethnic concentration.

Interestingly, the plans implemented by the municipal governments that joined this program have had very different effects in the districts where they were deployed (Van Kempen and Bolt 2009). In some cases, social mix was a minor aim, and the centrality of the projects shifted towards social integration; in many cases in which social mix was one of the objectives, socio-economic rather than ethnic mix was pursued; in other cases, social mix was at the centre and pursued through the demolition of entire complexes of social housing to promote greater attractiveness to the middle and upper classes; finally, there were plans without the slightest intention of creating social mix, focusing solely on actions improving social life and the socio-economic conditions of local residents.

The association between desegregation and social mixing reflects the urban and housing policies of most European countries, despite their different traditions of migration and welfare regimes (Musterd and Andersson 2005; Bolt 2009; Bolt, Özüekren, and Phillips 2010; Bolt, Phillips, and Van Kempen 2010). Apparently, policy-makers are convinced that social mixing will help to reduce the most serious outcome of segregation and neutralize the threat to social cohesion. This goal becomes possible by setting up ad hoc programs that ensure the coexistence of individuals and social groups of different social status and ethno-national origin to enable a wider range of social engagement and a general improvement of living conditions. In Europe social policies have long been framed in the context of urban works and housing. In Sweden this tool has been adopted since 1974; in Britain programs to create socially mixed neighbourhoods were already present in the 1950s and experienced resurgence in the mid-1990s with New Labour's urban regeneration projects (Bolt 2009; Launay 2010).

Two approaches often coexist in a country, forming the basis for a balance between residential, social, and ethnic inclusion: first, the diversification of housing (type of housing and employment status) in disadvantaged areas and/or in new buildings; and, second, procedures of allocation, specifically in the social housing sector, as a tool to disperse low-income earners and immigrant families. The first approach consists of upgrading housing stock through the demolition of old buildings and the reconstruction of new and more adequate housing. The aim is to attract a proportion of the middle class or other groups (e.g., students), and to achieve a tenure mix (home ownership, market rent, and capital). The second approach aims at an acceptable social and ethnic mix, through a policy of allocation oriented to prevent the concentration of immigrant families, and therefore, the possibility of "ghettoization."

In some cases local authorities have stated a maximum quota of foreign presence in a specific area that may not be exceeded. In an experiment in Rotterdam in 1972 the limit was set at 5 percent—although it was later abandoned because it contradicted national guidelines on anti-discrimination. In 2003, however, the urban plan "Rotterdam Perseveres" aimed to regulate inflows of low-income people, some of them belonging to ethnic minorities, in sensitive areas through stricter allocation rules, for example, by increasing the average income required for potential tenants (Kleinhans 2004, 373). Another example is the United Kingdom guidelines on housing strategies of 2000, which aimed to diversify the existing housing stock in residential neighbourhoods and prompted local authorities to achieve diversity through changing allocation policies (DETR 2000, cited in Kleinhans 2004, 371). In France, administrators can act to prevent the concentration of "problematic" families in areas considered "at risk." Similarly, in some German municipalities, such as Stuttgart, the proportion of foreign inhabitants in the public housing neighbourhoods is limited to 30 percent (Simon 2003; Munch 2010).

The historical experience and dissemination of policies against segregation focused on the idealization of social mix as a principle of intervention has caused, and continues to cause, a long history of analysis and critical opposition. A critical issue related to the policies of social mix centres on the questionable belief that the spatial proximity between groups or classes contributes to the social proximity of these groups or classes. The weakness of this sociological determinism has long been highlighted by authors such as Herbert Gans (1961) who, in his pioneering reflection on the creation of "balanced communities" through urban planning, emphasized that the homogeneity of socio-cultural background and their similar interests and values make it possible to develop social relationships that are deeper than a polite exchange of greetings between people regardless of their different backgrounds (Gans 1961, cited in Bolt 2009). Norbert Elias draws the same conclusion in fundamental research conducted in the late 1950s and early 1960s on the relationship between old (established) and new residents (outsiders) in England (Elias and Scotson 2004). This research suggests that the assumption of the policies of social mix may collide with a substantial lack of willingness among the different social groups to make contact and build cohesive relationships (Atkinson and Kintrea 2001; Bolt, Özüekren, and Phillips 2010; Bolt, Phillips, and Van Kempen 2010). Indeed, in certain circumstances, specifically when people live together against their will, proximity can exacerbate conflicts and enhance their membership of class and status (De Rudder 1989; Blanc 2010). In addition, if the majority of countries try to achieve a balance of socio-ethnic population structure at the neighbourhood level, it is not completely clear what exactly constitutes a "fair mix" (Bolt 2009). There are no statistically significant correlations that would justify the identification of an appropriate level of foreign families in a neighbourhood, or in a building, to prevent conflict and promote a "reasonable integration." A hypothetical "threshold of tolerance" in inter-ethnic cohabitation lends itself as an ideological instrument that reinforces the stigmatization of ethnic neighbourhoods and immigration, largely in a negative way (De Rudder 1991).

These criticisms tend to reveal a model of social engineering. In addition, the policies cannot be fully justified in light of the lack of research on the impacts of policies of social mixing in European cities. It is beyond question, however, that the conditions of spatial confinement and social isolation experienced by the poorest social groups have many negative effects. The same reasoning regarding the potentially positive effects of mixed neighbourhoods should not be dismissed out of hand. The mixing of social classes and ethnicities can be a desirable goal and used as a strategy to fight against territorial isolation and stigmatization (Lagrange and Oberti 2006). However, policies of social mixing focusing on spatial segregation do not address the most important problem: the growing unequal distribution of wealth between different social groups (Blanc and Bidou-Zachariasen 2010; Cucca 2010). Therefore, without a proper macro socio-economic inclusion program accompanying desegregation efforts, the result appears weak, ineffective, or even counterproductive (Arbaci 2007), as the Italian case in the next section testifies.

IMMIGRATION, RESIDENTIAL SEGREGATION, AND HOUSING POLICIES: THE ITALIAN CASE IN THE "MEDITERRANEAN MODEL"

As an introduction of our analysis of the Italian case, we first examine the political struggle about welfare benefits in an age when the short-sighted idea of the foreigner as a competitor for welfare benefits (and the idea of the foreigner as a danger to public order) has achieved increasing importance in mobilizing the electorate. With reference to housing policies, the scarcity of resources is particularly evident, facilitating a "common sense" representation of immigrants "stealing" the house of the Italian lower classes. This lack of resources is related to what some scholars (Minelli 2004; Poggio 2006) have called the "Mediterranean model" of housing, referring to the relative lack of public or social housing and an abundance of private home ownership. This model is associated with Spain, Portugal, Greece, and (partially) also Italy (Allen et al. 2004). Rather than reflecting the widespread cultural emphasis on the family and family-centred values, this model is the result of housing policies that concentrated on access to ownership. Due to these policies, home ownership has increased over the last decades, while renting has declined and stood at 20 percent in 2001 (Table 12.1).

Table 12.1: Families Occupying their Home in Italy (percent)

	Ownership	Rent	Other
1961	45.8	46.6	7.6
1971	50.8	44.2	5
1981	58.9	35.5	5.6
1991	68	25.3	6.7
2001	71.4	20	8.6

Source: Census data from the Italian Statistical Institute (ISTAT 2001).

With more than 70 percent of families living in a house of their own, the Mediterranean model applies also to Italy. On the other hand, its 4.5 percent of public dwellings distinguishes Italy from other Mediterranean countries, such as Spain and Portugal, where public housing constitutes an even lower percentage of total dwellings (Table 12.2).

Table 12.2: Social Housing on Total Housing Stock (percent)

	Total dwellings	Total rented dwellings
Netherlands	34.6	76.8
Sweden	21	45
United Kingdom	21	66
Denmark	20	43
France	17.5	45.5
Finland	17.2	50
Austria	14.3	35.4
Ireland	8	45
Belgium	7	23
Germany	6.5	12.5
Italy	4.5	23
Portugal	3.3	15.8
Spain	0.9	12.6

Source: National Board of Housing, Building and Planning 2005.

A Short Inquiry into the Italian Public Housing System from the "Golden Age" to the Present Day

Despite the current weakness of Italian social housing, data provided in the previous section, if interpreted with reference to urban and housing policies, reveal a favourable attitude toward the public housing system, particularly during the "golden age" (1944–1971). During this period, with the INA-Casa plan and GesCaL[1] administration,[2] Italian public housing performed various tasks. First, within the context of Keynesian economic policies, it helped to strengthen the impact of the housing sector on economic growth during the 1950s and 1960s. Second, from the viewpoint of the centrist and centre-left government coalitions ruling Italy from the 1940s to the 1980s, it played an important role in gathering electoral consensus in the contexts of the Cold War and what some scholars call the "Keynesian class agreement" that characterized "organized" postwar capitalism (Harvey 1990, 2005; Hobsbawm 1994). Third, concerning the major urban areas, it accompanied the urbanization of rural populations that came from all regions of Italy and converged toward the industrial towns of the North-West (especially in Milan, Turin, and Genoa).

Between 1 and 2 million public dwellings were completed from 1949 to 1984. Although this figure seems small for a country with 50 million inhabitants, it is considerable in comparison with the following decades: in 1984 only about 34,000 public dwellings were built, and 20 years later the number had fallen below 2,000. Currently, Italy has one of the lowest percentages of GDP spent on housing policies in the EU: at the same time, the number of public housing units has decreased, as a consequence of a 1993 law that encouraged the sale of public apartments to tenants (following the British example of the "right to buy"). Although this measure was justified by the aim to earn money to further boost public housing, it was not able to achieve this aim because the special prices negotiated for tenants required the sale of four dwellings for the construction of one new dwelling. In 1996 another reform that dismantled the public housing system created under fascism in 1938, identified responsibility for public housing as resting with national government, and initiated the transfer of responsibility to the regions. After the 1996 reform, much of the authority in the field of public housing was transferred to the regions.

These measures can be interpreted as the retreat of the state from social policies as a consequence of the "fiscal crisis" that hit Western countries in the late 1960s (O'Connor 1971) and the drastic change in political agendas, at national and global scales, starting with the "libertarian" revolutions in Great Britain and the United States between the late 1970s and the early 1980s (Harvey 2005). Furthermore, the emphasis on the local scale, the growing involvement of private actors, and the strong international ties of several actors in the housing sector reflect the spatial rescaling by globalization processes and relativization of the monopolistic role of the national state as an actor (Sassen 2007). The new social philosophy can explain the shift in emphasis of Italian housing policies away from the traditional concept of public dwelling towards a wider and more "modern" concept of "social housing." The "modernity" of this concept refers to the acceptance of a particular "libertarian" point of view and the minimization of state intervention.

Unlike what happened in other countries, in Italy, where housing support for the lower classes had been chiefly achieved by means of public housing, the new philosophy's success produced a deep housing crisis, in particular regarding the allocation of resources. Nevertheless, some local virtuous initiatives of cooperation between public institutions and other actors from "civil society" were successful.

Former Migrants: Milan under the Miracle

We now examine the legacy of public housing of the "golden age" in urban Italy today. In particular, we consider the case of Milan, the chief city of Lombardy, and together with Turin, a centre of the industrial growth of the "golden age" (Cucca 2010). In addition to suffering a housing emergency due to heavy destruction from bombing in WW II, Milan and its surroundings received important migration from other regions of Italy. There had been a continuation from the postwar emergency to the migration crisis, which became visible during the 1950s in the phenomenon of the *coreas* (squats or *favela*-like settlements that grew at the margins of the city). The subsequent building efforts by the private and public sectors suddenly gave life to a nameless "new periphery," consisting of rationalistic-style quarters placed within or immediately outside the municipal borders (Foot 2001; Agustoni and Rozza 2005).

Those quarters often took the shape of isolated "forgotten suburbs," where settlement was not followed by transportation and services, generating during the 1970s a decade of urban struggles for improved quality of housing and services, alongside similar struggles by traditional neighbourhoods reacting against gentrification measures. The capacity to mobilize can be considered an indicator of the strength of local networks, related to the social physiognomy of the "Fordist" town, in which social capital of trust and solidarity was built around trades unions, cultural and recreational associations (with either religious or political traits), local left-wing party headquarters, and rising new political movements. This kind of network contributed to a particular process of social integration of migrants from other regions, both in old neighbourhoods and the "new periphery" (Agustoni and Alietti 2009). In this context, migrant workers assimilated to neighbourhoods that were partially segregated by class. Paradoxically, while social change was vapourizing class borders for example through a consumption-oriented individual identity, political mobilization of local *issues* worked as an "equal-but-opposite" force that reinforced a symbolic working-class collective identity (Agustoni and Rozza 2005).

The last decades, during which immigrants arrived from abroad, constitute a completely different context. Often, the same neighbourhoods where fifty years ago people from other parts of Italy settled now accommodate foreigners coming to Milan. These foreigners frequently settle in the older and rundown neighbourhoods, and present established residents with the opportunity of renting apartments without any maintenance responsibility. In the last decades, these neighbourhoods have been characterized by a phenomenon that Loïc Wacquant (2006) has called "deproletarization," i.e., the weakening, if not the complete disappearance, of solidarity networks characteristic of many working-class quarters that facilitated the assimilation of former Italian migrants. Residents of old neighbourhoods are often interested in gentrification whereby urban renewal can coexist with a vicious circle of degradation.

Italian Housing System and Mechanisms of Segregation

The previous section outlined the dwelling conditions of immigrants not only in Milan but in Italy as a whole. These conditions are generally characterized by a "residual" way of settlement (Agustoni 2003): immigrants generally occupy dwellings abandoned by Italians and in a state of disrepair. Their presence often reduces the perceived desirability of a neighborhood, slashing real estate prices (and reinforcing local resistance to their settlement). Contributing to this situation, the poor "symbolic capital" in terms of widespread mistrust makes it difficult for immigrants to find a decent place to live. As surveys of estate agents show, renting a house to immigrants is perceived as a risk due to possible damage to the property, potential arrears with the rent, and possible problems with the neighbours (Agustoni 2006).

These factors explain at least two phenomena: first, if renting to immigrants is considered a risk, then the landlord will request compensation in the form of "particular" fees for foreign renters. A survey produced by an important tenant union shows that fees for foreigners are indeed higher than for Italians (SUNIA 2010). Second, immigrants tend to concentrate in urban areas characterized by poor dwelling conditions, where it may be more difficult to find Italian tenants. Their presence generally reinforces the feeling of poverty and therefore represents a "push factor" for "established" residents—with the exception of marginal groups (elderly, poor, etc.)—to leave the area. The result is the concentration of marginalized groups.

Two additional implications need to be considered: immigrants' access to ownership and their access to social housing. The issue of home ownership among immigrants is mostly relevant in Northern Italy and less so in the South (Table 12.3). The immigrants arriving in Southern Italy are often introduced to a world of undocumented work and accommodation. Many "life accounts" report of immigrants in the South working irregularly in agriculture or performing other menial tasks (Agustoni 2008). In some cases, this irregular situation can help immigrants in their way towards integration (Tumminelli 2010).

Table 12.3: Immigrants' Homes (percent)

	Central and Northern Italy	Southern Italy	Italy
Ownership	11.8	3.4	10.9
Rent (alone or with family)	48.8	49.2	48.8
Rent (with other people)	22.3	24.4	22.5

Source: Menonna et al. 2006.

Conversely, Northern Italy represents a place of relative stability and regularity in respect to employment and housing—although this may not mean a better situation in terms of housing quality (due to the high costs of rentals). Nevertheless, territorial stability implies a stronger motivation to home ownership, despite the fact that it often represents an obliged choice, as a consequence of obstacles immigrants face in the rental market. Since 2000 many immigrants have been encouraged to take out mortgages, often with dramatic consequences after the advent of the international banking crisis. Moreover, immigrants often buy their dwelling in segregated places inhabited by other immigrants because housing in these places is cheaper (Agustoni and Alietti 2009). Thus, immigrants often invest money in an estate subject to devaluation as a consequence of migrant concentrations and local reactions to their presence (Agustoni 2011).

Another case is public housing. Table 12.4 shows that public housing for immigrants increased while it declined for Italy and its regions as whole. To access public housing, immigrants must have access to adequate "cognitive capital," i.e., a satisfactory level of knowledge about institutional opportunities and welfare benefits in the host countries. With the possibility of "housing welfare" benefits, more and more foreigners have asked for a "public dwelling," joining the long waiting list. The demand for public housing suddenly increased since 2000, particularly among people from Northern Africa and Eastern Europe, perhaps because of their relative familiarity with trades unions (and tenant unions) or perhaps because of their relatively frequent employment in the building sector, both raising their "cognitive capital." Similar to the private rental market, in public housing immigrants tend to concentrate in the older, more rundown, and socially problematic quarters, where Italian families generally refuse to settle. This situation creates a vicious circle, making these quarters less desirable, as shown in the above example of Milan (Alietti 1998; Agustoni 2003).

Table 12.4: Public Housing Tenants in Italy and its Regions (total and immigrants)

	2001	2004	Difference%
Italy	2,057,704	1,835,922	- 10.8%
Northern Italy	790,036	727,135	- 0.8%
Central Italy	457,567	358,138	- 21.7%
Southern Italy	810,101	750,649	- 7.3%
Immigrants	47,287 (2.3%)*	73,761 (4%)	+ 35.9%
Northern Italy	30,443 (3.9%)	51,999 (7.2%)	+ 70.8%
Central Italy	16,432 (3.6%)	20,357 (5.7%)	+ 23.9%
Southern Italy	412 (0.051%)	1,405 (0.19%)	+ 24.1%

Source: Ministry of the Interior 2007. (* percentage of immigrants in relation to the total)

The image of foreigners as rivals for meagre resources, as well as the representation of immigrant concentration in some areas of public housing as a danger for social cohesion, could easily be exploited for political gain. At a regional scale, in Lombardy and Friuli (the two Northern Italian regions, the former including Milan), measures were implemented to restrict the access of public housing to foreigners, worsening the housing conditions of immigrants. In addition, these measures paved the way for a very restrictive national law enacted in 2008. Currently, this national law demands

5 years of residence in the same region and 10 years in Italy as conditions of eligibility for public housing. Despite the widespread feeling of dispossession of Italian people needing a home, the decline of public housing (see Table 12.4) seems to be the result of the disinvestments in the 1980s, when the increasing emphasis on alternative measures towards "social housing" were unable to substitute for the traditional public approach to provide housing for the needy. Despite the need for the state to pay more attention to issues such as social mix and to support local governance experiences in the field of social housing, the direct intervention of the state in financing and managing the social housing system was impossible to replace.

CONCLUSION

In this chapter we dealt with the complex issue of segregation and social housing availability in Europe, with a particular focus on the Italian experience. A general tendency to promote social mix is present in most European countries; although, both the concept of "balanced social mix" and the policies to achieve this mix are ambiguous in definitions and results. With the exception of France, social housing policies are generally too weak to satisfy the housing needs of most disadvantaged social groups, which include in all European countries a large percentage of immigrants. At the same time, the subsidies to make rents more affordable and ownerships accessible are not very congenial for the very lowest income groups, especially in this period of financial crisis, as the Italian experience clearly testifies. In countries such as Italy, where immigrants tend to be disadvantaged and unable to afford private market housing, a strong public subsidy to the housing sector is still needed. The contemporary lack of public housing is due to the disinvestments that occurred in the 1980s. In short, immigration flows seem to have worsened the situation of an already suffering housing sector.

In Italy, as in other European countries, the increasing emphasis on alternative measures of "social housing," in particular attention to the problem of segregation, was unable to substitute the traditional approach of public housing provision. Segregation has been caused by two main factors: first, the shortage of affordable rents for the very low-income newcomers, and second the mistrust toward immigrants as neighbours or tenants. The combination of these two processes increased the concentration of immigrants in the most degraded housing sector, both public and private. At the same time, the few and weak Italian policies aimed to achieve an ambiguous "balanced social mix" seemed only to increase this phenomena, especially for newcomers who are not allowed to have access to the social housing stock. In light of these problems, only a strong housing policy would be able to reduce segregation. Despite the attention to social mix and local governance support in the field of social housing, the direct intervention by the state in developing and managing social housing has been difficult to substitute.

ENDNOTES

1. The INA-Casa plan built houses managed by the INA (National Institute for Insurances); GesCaL refers to *Gestione Case per I Lavoratori* (Workers Housing Management).
2. The INA-Casa Plan (1948–1962) and the GesCaL administration (1963–1978) foresaw the construction of public dwellings and the financing of housing cooperatives with money from soft taxation of working revenues. These actions were strongly opposed by the left-wing opposition.

ACKNOWLEDGEMENTS

We wish to thank the ISMU Foundation for financing, in 2009, the project "Radici-Roots" on immigrants and housing in Lombardy, as well as Paola Pologruto and Veronica Riniolo for their precious help. Although this article is a collaborative effort, it is possible to attribute to the writing of sections four and five to Alfredo Agustoni, sections one and two to Alfredo Alietti, and sections three and six to Roberta Cucca.

REFERENCES

Agustoni, A. 2003. *I vicini di casa*. Milano: FrancoAngeli.
Agustoni, A. 2006. "Abitare e insediarsi," in XII *Rapporto ISMU sulle migrazioni in Italia*. Milano: FrancoAngeli.
Agustoni, A. 2008. "Globalizzazione, migrazioni e territori marginali." In *Aspetti del mutamento sociale sontemporaneo*, edited by A. Agustoni, 176–192. Roma Aracne.
Agustoni, A. 2011. "Abitare e Insediarsi," in *XVII Rapporto ISMU sulle migrazioni in Italia*. Milano: FrancoAngeli (forthcoming).
Agustoni, A., and A. Alietti. 2009. *Società urbane e convivenza interetnica*. Milano: FrancoAngeli.
Agustoni, A., and C. Rozza. 2005. *Diritto alla casa, diritto alla città*. Roma: Aracne.
Alietti, A. 1998. *La convivenza difficile: Coabitazione interetnica in un quartiere di Milano*. Torino: L'Harmattan Italia.
Alietti, A. 2009. "Quei soggetti spinti ai confini della società. Note critiche sul concetto di coesione sociale." *Animazione Sociale* 234: 12–19
Alietti, A., and A. Agustoni, eds. 2011. *Migrazioni, politiche urbane e abitative: dalla dimensione europea alla dimensione locale*. Milano: Fondazione Ismu, Regione Lombardia: Commisioned by Osservatorio Regionale per l'integrazione e la multietnicità.
Allen, J., J. Barlow, J. Leal, T. Maloutas, and L. Padovani. 2004. *Housing and Welfare in Southern Europe*. Oxford, Blackwell
Andersen, H. T. 2002. "Globalisation, Spatial Polarization and the Housing Market." *Danish Journal of Geography* 102 (1): 93–102.
Arbaci, S. 2007. "Ethnic Segregation, Housing System and Welfare regimes." *European Journal of Housing Policy* 4: 401–433.

Arbaci, S., and J. Malheiros. 2010. "De-Segregation, Peripheralisation and the Social Exclusion of Immigrants: Southern European Cities in the 1990s." *Journal of Ethnic and Migration Studies* 36 (2): 227–255.

Asselin, O., F. Dureau, L. Fonseca, M. Giroud, A. Hamadi, J. Kohlbacher, F. Lindo, J. Malheiros, Y. Marcadet, and U. Reeger. 2006. "Social Integration of Immigrants with Special Reference to the Local and Spatial Dimension." In *Migration and Settlement in Europe: A State of the Art*, edited by R. Penninx,M. Berger and K. Kraal, 133–170. Amsterdam: Amsterdam University Press.

Atkinson, R., and K. Kintrea. 2001. "Disentangling Area Effects: Evidence from Deprived and Non-deprived Areas." *Urban Studies* 38 (1): 2,277–2,298.

Blanc, M. 2010. "The Impact of Social Mix Policies in France." *Housing Studies* 25 (2): 257–272.

Blanc, M., and C. Bidou-Zachariasen. 2010. "Éditorial: Dossier Paradoxes de la mixité sociale." *Espaces et Sociétés*. 140–141: 9–20.

Bolt, G. 2009. "Combating Residential Segregation of Ethnic Minorities in European Cities." *Journal of Housing and the Built Environment* 24: 397–405.

Bolt, G., S. Özüekren, and D. Phillips. 2010. "Linking Integration and Residential Segregation." *Journal of Ethnic and Migration Studies* 36 (2): 169–186.

Bolt, G., D. Phillips, and R. Van Kempen. 2010. "Housing Policy, (De)segregation and Social Mixing: An International Perspective." *Housing Studies* 25 (2): 129–135.

Cities for Local Integration Policy (CLIP). 2007. *Housing and Integration of Migrants in Europe*. European Foundation for the Improvement of Living and Working Conditions, Strasbourg Council of Europe. Accessed August 6, 2011. www.eurofound.europa.eu/pubdocs/2007/94/en/1/ef0794en.pdf.

Cucca, R. 2010."Crescita diseguale. Gli impatti sociali della transizione al post-fordismo nelle città europee." In *Ranci Costanzo*, edited by *Città nella rete globale. Competitività e disuguaglianze in sei città europee*, 79–115. Milano: Bruno Mondadori.

Cucca, R., and M. P. Pologruto. 2011. "Azione pubblica e modelli empirici: una riflessione su alcuni casi studio." In *Migrazioni, politiche urbane e abitative: dalla dimensione europea alla dimensione locale*, edited by A. Alfredo and A. Agustoni, 51–80. Milano: Fondazione Ismu Regione Lombardia, Osservatorio Regionale per l'integrazione e la multietnicità.

De Rudder, V. 1989. "De la question du l'aogement à la question ethnique." In *Banlieues, immigration et gestion urbaine*, sous la direction de N. Boumaza, 15–75. Grenoble: Université J. Fourier.

De Rudder, V..1991. "Seuil de tlerance et cohabitation plurietnique." In *Face au racisme, La Découverte*, sous la direction P. A. Taguieff, 2: 154–166.

Department of Environment Transport and the Regions (DETR). 2000. *Quality and Choice: Decent Home for All: The Housing Green Paper*. London: The Stationery Office.

Edgar, B. 2004. *Policy Measures to Ensure Access to Decent Housing for Migrants and Ethnic Minorities*. Dundee and St. Andrews: Joint Centre for Scottish Housing Research.

Edgar, B., J. Doherty, and M. Henk. 2002. *Access to Housing – Homelessness and Vulnerability in Europe*. Bristol: Policy Press.

Elias, N., and E. Scotson. 2004. *The Established and the Outsiders*. Bologna, Italy: Il Mulino..

European Monitoring Centre on Racism and Xenophobia (EUMC). 2005. *Migrants, Minoritiesand Housing: Exclusion, Discrimination and Anti-Discrimination in 15 Member States of the European Union*. Bruxelles: EUMC.

European Parliament. 1997. "Housing Policy in the EU Member-States." *Directorate General for Research, Division for Social Affairs*, Working Document W.14: Luxembourg.

Foot, J. 2001. *Milan since the Miracle: City, Culture and Identity*. Oxford: Berg.

Gans, H. J. 1961. "The Balanced Community: Homogeneity or Heterogeneity in Residential Areas?"*American Institute of Planners Journal* 27 (3):176–184.

Jayaweera, H., and T. Choudhury. 2008. *Immigration, Faith and Cohesion: Evidence from Local Areas with Significant Muslim Populations*. York, UK: Joseph Rowntree Foundation.

Harloe, M. 1995. *The People's Home? Social Rented Housing in Europe & America*. Oxford: Balckwell.

Harvey, D. 1990. *The Condition of Postmodernity*. Oxford: Blackwell.

Harvey, D. 2005. *A Brief History of Neoliberalism*. Oxford: Oxford University Press.

Hobsbawm, E. 1994. *Age of Extremes: The Short Twentieth Century*. London: Abacus.

Holmqvist, E., and Z. Bergsten. 2009. "Swedish Social Mix: A General Policy without an Explicit Ethnic Focus." *Journal of Housing and Built Environment* 24: 477–490.

Kleinhans, R. 2004. "Social Implications of Housing Diversification in Urban Renewal: A Review of Recent Literature." *Journal of Housing and the Built Environment* 19: 367–390.

Lagrange, H. and M. Oberti. 2006. *Emeutes urbaines et protestations. Une singularité française*. Paris: Presses de la Fondation des Sciences Politiques.

Larsen, H. G., and H. A. Lund. 2008. "Gentrification: Gentle or Traumatic? Urban Renewal Policies and Socioeconomic Transformations in Copenhagen." *Urban Studies* 45: 2429-2448.

Launay, L. 2010. "De Paris à Londres: La défi de la mixité sociale par les acteurs clés." *Espaces et Sociétés* 140–141:111–126.

Malheiros, J. 2002. "Ethni-cities: Residential Patterns in the Northern Europeans and Mediterranean Metropolise — Implications for Policy Design." *International Journal of Population Geography* 8:107–134.

Minelli, A. R. 2004. *La politica per la casa*. Bologna: Il Mulino.

Munch, S. 2009. "'It's All in the Mix': Constructing Ethnic Segregation as a Social Problem in Germany." *Journal of Housing and Built Environment* 24: 441–455.

Musterd, S. 2003. "Segregation and Integration: A Contested Relationship." *Journal of Ethnic and Migration Studies* 29 (4): 623–641.

Musterd, S. 2005. "Social and Ethnic Segregation in Europe: Levels, Causes and Effect." *Journal of Urban Affairs* 27 (3): 331–348.

Musterd, S., and R. Andersson. 2005. "Housing Mix, Social Mix and Social Opportunities." *Urban Affairs Review* 40 (6): 1–30.

Musterd, S., and A. Murie. 2006. "The Spatial Dimensions of Urban Social Exclusion and Integration." In *Neighbourhoods of Poverty — Urban Social Exclusion and Integration inEurope*, edited by S. Musterd, A. Murie, and C. Kesteloot. New York: MacmillanPalgrave.

National Board of Housing, Building and Planning. 2005. *Housing Statistics in the European Union 2004*. Sweden. Accessed August 2, 2011. www.iut.nu/EU/HousingStatistics2004.pdf.

O'Connor, J. 1971. *The Fiscal Crisis of the State*. New York: St. Martin Press.

Penninx, R. 2007. *Case Study on Housing, Copenhagen, Denmark*. CLIP Network Paper.

Poggio, T. 2006. "La casa come area del welfare." *Polis* 2: 279–308.

Ranci, C., and R. Torri. 2007. *Milano tra coesione sociale e sviluppo*. Milano: Bruno Mondadori.

Rutter, J., and M. Latorre. 2009. *Social Housing Allocation and Immigrant Communities*. Research Report 4, Equality and Human Rights Commission UK. Accessed August 6, 2011. www.equalityhumanrights.com/uploaded_files/4_social_housing_allocation_and_immigrant_communities.pdf.

Sassen, S. 2007. *A Sociology of Globalization*. New York: Norton.

Schindler Rangvid, B.. 2006. "Living and Learning Separately? Ethnic Segregation of School Children in Copenhagen." *Urban Studies* 44 (7): 1,329–1,354.

Simon, P. 2003. "Le Logement Social en France et la Gestion des 'Populations Risques'." *Hommes & Migrations* 1246: 76–91.

SUNIA. 2010. *L'Offerta di Abitazioni in Affitto nelle Aree Metropolitane*. Research Report. Roma. www.sunia.it.

Torgersen, U. 1987. "Housing the Wobbly Pillar Under the Welfare State." In *Between State and Market: Housing in the Post Industrial Era*, edited by B. Turner, J. Kemeny, and L. Lundquist, 116–126. Stockholm: Alquist and Wicksell International.

Tosi, A. 2010. *Le condizioni abitative. In dieci anni d'immigrazione in Lombardia*. Rapporto 2009, a cura di Fondazione Ismu, Regione Lombardia, Osservatorio Regionale per l'Integrazione e la multietnicità. 353–64. Milano: Fondazione Ismu.

Tumminelli, A. 2010. *Sovrapposti. Processi di trasformazione degli spazi ad opera degli stranieri*. Milano. FrancoAngeli.

van Ham, M., and D. Manley. 2009. "Social Housing Allocation, Choice and Neighbourhood Ethnic Mix in England." *Journal of Housing and the Built Environment* 24: 407–422.

Van Kempen, R., and G. Bolt. 2009. "Social Cohesion, Social Mix, and Urban Policies in the Netherlands." *Journal of Housing and Built Environment* 24: 457–475.

Van Kempen, R., and Hugo Priemus. 2002. "Revolution in Social Housing in the Netherlands: Possible Effects of New Housing Policies." *Urban Studies* 39 (2): 237–253.

Wacquant, L. 2006. *Parias urbains. Ghetto, banlieues, Etat*. Paris: La Découverte.

Whitehead, C., and K. Scanlon, eds. 2008. *Social Housing in Europe II*. London: LSE London.

Chapter 13

HIDDEN HOMELESSNESS IN THE GREATER TORONTO AREA'S NEWCOMER COMMUNITIES: SIGNS, SYMPTOMS, AND SOLUTIONS

S. GOPIKRISHNA

INTRODUCTION

The issue of "hidden homelessness" among newcomers to Canada has received increasing academic attention in the recent past. Hidden homelessness refers to multiple families inhabiting space meant for a single family; it can spatially concentrate and propagate "ghettos" of this particular form of homelessness. Hidden homelessness exists throughout urban areas of Canada. In the Greater Toronto Area, it has "crept" outwards from the City of Toronto in the last decade, and now is a common phenomenon in Toronto's surrounding regions (Peel and York in particular). The dominance of Toronto in the academic literature on this phenomenon suggests that how this issue is addressed in Toronto will have policy implications for other urban centres in the country.

To understand the impact of hidden homelessness on the lives of affected people and to develop possible solutions to this problem, the experiences and insights of front-line workers and staff of non-profit organizations are extremely valuable. The perspectives of these "practitioners" enrich our current understanding of hidden homelessness. In this chapter, I assume this perspective to concentrate on documenting aspects of hidden homelessness and to link these aspects to social phenomena such as immigrants' priorities during settlement processes, constructs of "model minorities," and the self-imposed desire among newcomers to fulfill the associated expectations.

Research on the issue of hidden homelessness is complicated by the lack of statistical data. The chapter therefore draws on practical experience of front line workers and anecdotal information. It commences with brief discussions of the settlement context of newcomers in the Greater Toronto Area, how hidden homelessness falls into the scope of the official definition of homelessness in Canada, and why "hidden" homelessness is eclipsed by discussions of "real" homelessness. Furthermore, I explore the lack of statistical data and the underlying reasons for this lack. Thereafter, I address the symptoms and impacts of hidden homelessness, including the possible effects on the children and youth, health, and social relations. A separate section deals with possible solutions at both policy and practical levels, including strategies for the non-profit sector and various levels of government, as well as prevention through improved knowledge of tenants' rights. Finally, I present recommendations for future research.

CONTEXT

The Greater Toronto Area has proved to be a magnet for newcomers to Canada. Between 2000 and 2009, the Toronto urban area welcomed between 33 percent and 50 percent of all immigrants to Canada (Citizenship and Immigration Canada 2011). Newcomers have to overcome numerous difficulties in finding adequate housing and have varying degrees of success in achieving their housing dreams (Murdie 2002). Over the last decade, the phenomenon of multiple newcomer families crowding into an apartment meant one family has been observed in various regions within the Greater Toronto Area (Kilbride and Webber 2006; Preston et al. 2009). This phenomenon seems to have become so commonplace that it is also discussed in the media (*Toronto Star*, 2009).

The tendency among newcomers in Toronto to concentrate in specific geographical areas and the resulting impact on housing has been documented in great detail (Ghosh 2005). Overcrowding has further resulted in the need to apply appropriate standards of habitation to newcomer housing (Murdie and Texeira 2000) and address the issue of hidden homelessness (Kilbride and Webber, 2006). As geographical concentrations and consequent housing challenges are increasingly suburbanizing, hidden homelessness has become synonymous with immigrant suburban homelessness.

Notwithstanding the academic and media attention that hidden homelessness among newcomers recently received, there are significant barriers to understanding the scope of this problem. Counting the numbers of homeless people is challenging and controversial (Shapcott 2006). It is conventionally accepted that enumerating people in situations of hidden homelessness is unfeasible. Although ideas exist about how the numbers of people in hidden homelessness can be estimated through census data, these ideas have not been thoroughly explored (City of Toronto 2002). Institutional barriers, employment, and other "secondary characteristic barriers" are significant causes of hidden homelessness (Chambon et al. 1997). Studies in Ottawa, for example, show the significance of employment in determining the attainability of housing (Klodawsky et al. 2005). Furthermore, the impact of hidden homelessness on newcomer children appears to be similar to the impact on children living in shelters, as can be inferred from a study by Samantha Sherkin (2006).

DEFINING HIDDEN HOMELESSNESS

The Housing and Homelessness Branch of the Department of Human Resources and Social Development Canada (HRSDC) defines as "homeless" any person, family, or household with no fixed address or security of housing tenure. This definition includes those at risk of homelessness, which is different from the conventional understanding and literal definition of homelessness referring exclusively to people without a home. Homelessness can therefore be divided into two categories: "real" homelessness and "hidden" homelessness, alternately called "concealed" homelessness (Hulchanski 2003). Real homelessness refers to people who live on the street and do not have a home or a roof over their heads; this type of homelessness corresponds to the popular picture of homelessness. Hidden homelessness is more difficult to define and can refer to overcrowding, couch surfing, or temporary accommodation in shelters. In addition, different populations experience different types of hidden homelessness: for example, among youth hidden homelessness manifests itself in the form of couch surfing; homelessness among victims of family violence may reveal itself in the form of staying with friends and family for short periods of time. In these forms of hidden homelessness the population of interest may have the roof over the head, but the roof is temporary and changes on a regular or daily basis.

Yet a different type of hidden homelessness applies in the cases of both newcomers to Canada and Aboriginal populations. Homelessness among these populations can be defined as overcrowding, with multiple families living in a space meant for one family. A vivid description of hidden homelessness was provided by an anonymous immigrant who lived in this situation:

> Enough people to populate a floor of an apartment building living in a single apartment; enough people to populate an apartment building crowding onto a floor; enough people to populate a small town in rural Ontario packed into an apartment complex.

This form of hidden homelessness differs from other kinds of homelessness experienced, for example, by youth and victims of family violence in that the roof over peoples' heads is permanent. However, while this population may have a roof over its head, it is homeless for all practical purposes, lacking privacy, hygiene, and dedicated space for specific activities. This "permanent" hidden homelessness is common especially among newcomers in urban and suburban areas.

WHY IS HIDDEN HOMELESSNESS HIDDEN?

The reasons for homelessness to remain hidden are numerous. They include the following:

Governmental Priorities

The term hidden homelessness signifies the invisibility of the living conditions associated with extreme overcrowding; it may also indicate a lack of debate on this form of homelessness relative to "real" homelessness. In public and academic discourse, real homelessness has received much more attention than hidden homelessness. This difference is also discernible in the funding allocated to address the two forms of homelessness. Funding to combat homelessness targets real homelessness, as exemplified by the last major federal investment in addressing homelessness, the Supporting Communities Partnership Initiative (SCPI) of 2000. While SCPI was laudable for the envelope of funding of $305 million and its efforts to address homelessness on an unprecedented scale, almost all of it was directed at real homelessness. When SCPI was renamed Homelessness Partnership Initiative (HPI) in 2006–2007 and the budget was reduced to $270 million over a three-year period, the priorities of the funding continued to focus on real homelessness. Notwithstanding the increasing public and academic attention to hidden homelessness among newcomers, there is no designated funding of any significant magnitude to address this problem.

Lack of Awareness

Hidden homelessness is also caused by the lack of awareness among newcomers about norms, practices, and legal requirements in Canada. The orientation of newcomers towards Canadian practices and requirements often occurs in the period during which they look for their first rental apartment. Given many newcomers' lack of knowledge and the need to have a roof over their heads, they often comply with the landlords' demands irrespective of the outrageousness and illegality of these demands. Landlords in Ontario conduct three tests before admitting renters: the renter has to demonstrate proof of employment, pass a credit check, and show references from previous landlords. Many newcomers fail to pass one or all of these tests; they lack employment, references, and/or a credit history. There are many recorded instances where the landlord subsequently suggests an "informal arrangement" where the renter can circumvent the aforementioned tests through a deposit of six months' worth of rent or more (*Toronto Star* 2001; CBC 2003). Notwithstanding the legal requirement of providing only the first and last month's rent, many newcomer families are willing to enter into the arrangement in the belief that they can move out after employment is secured.

Given their paucity of financial resources, many newcomer families have to pool their resources with other newcomer families faced with a similar predicament to come up with the required deposit. While this approach may help the families secure a roof over their heads, it also results in a situation where two or more families have to live in a space meant for a single family. In other words, hidden homelessness is created on the day these newcomer families secure their first apartment.

Newcomers who are aware of the less-than-acceptable quality of their housing arrangement often hope that employment will eventually ameliorate this situation. However, many newcomers fail to enter the job market due to barriers such as the lack of Canadian experience or the non-recognition for foreign credentials (see Part Two of this volume). Other newcomers remain unemployed or underemployed for many years after arriving in Canada. The decision to predicate the process of settlement (including housing) on employment, works against the newcomers: failure to secure decent employment consigns them to hidden homelessness for the foreseeable future.

Immigrants often internalize the logic that lack of access to habitable housing is the outcome of the lack of employment; they often do not see housing as an issue separate from employment. While habitable housing may be resolved through employment, it can also be resolved through accessing existing community resources. Thus, they rarely seek solutions to hidden homelessness in the community by accessing help from non-profit agencies.

Social Factors

The invisibility and longevity of hidden homelessness is assisted by social factors and behaviours, some of which are ironically rooted in the need to protect the collective reputation of the newcomer community. A popular reaction to hidden homelessness from newcomer communities is defensiveness: the practice of crowding and cohabitation is defended as adherence to cultural practices from the country of origin. For example, cohabiting with the extended family is a common practice in many parts of Asia (where the majority of current immigration to Canada originates). In these contexts, living space is shared with extended family; it would be unusual to cohabit with strangers who are not relatives. In Canada, however, cohabitation is often shared with non-family and between people who speak different languages and who practice different religions and culture. The defence of hidden homelessness as cultural tradition is glaringly contradicted in cases in which men and women belonging to communities that traditionally practice gender separation share living space.

Some communities question and contest social issues that may tarnish their collective image. Some newcomer communities are unwilling to concede the existence of poverty, homelessness, or social conflict amongst themselves. Such denial contrasts with the pride and a record of achievement which newcomer communities sometimes project of themselves. For example, academic achievement by younger members of the community is often played up as evidence of the community's "model minority" status. Apparently, the model minority status is sacrosanct and has to be defended, even when the community faces severe social problems.

The desire of a newcomer community to achieve and retain the image of a model minority deserves further attention in the context of hidden homelessness. The notion "model minority" was first mentioned by American sociologists like William Petersen (1966) to differentiate between Japanese-Americans and African-Americans. Japanese-Americans supposedly distinguished themselves through hard work, academic achievement, obedience, and loyalty. The meaning of the term seems to point towards behaviour where the minorities unquestioningly fulfill their duties, uphold contemporary social structures, and provide selfless services without any expectations of reward notwithstanding their low social status. The perception of being a "model minority" in the immigrant community seems severely distorted, prima facie, by the complimentary sounding nature of the term. The resulting pressures on such communities as well as the lack of factual evidence to back up such claims have been well documented in an American context (Chou and Feagin 2008). Similarly, in a Canadian context, the denial of poverty and hidden homelessness likely relates to the need to uphold the self-imposed image of being a model minority and the associated unrealistic and mythical expectations.

SYMPTOMS AND IMPACTS OF HIDDEN HOMELESSNESS

Practical experience and knowledge generated through discussions with housing workers, illustrate some of the symptoms of hidden homelessness. When hidden homelessness occurs in apartment complexes it is often accompanied by balconies overflowing with household goods, multiple apartments with clotheslines overflowing with clothes (especially in the summer), constant state of repair (e.g., broken down elevators, lack of adequate water) due to excessive wear and tear, and a rundown look (e.g., paint peeling off the exterior). Hidden homelessness can also be found in rental basement apartments. In a part of Toronto known as Northern Scarborough, for example, it is not surprising to see an elegant Victorian mansion with an untended garden and multiple cars on the driveway. The mansion's impressive exterior provides a shocking contrast to a dingy interior with little but drywall to separate what should be the living room, kitchen, and bedrooms. "Rooms" in this context are merely enclosures, each "room" occupied by a different newcomer family.

The impact of hidden homelessness is difficult to quantify due to challenges in identifying and counting the affected populations. However, anecdotal information from front-line workers coupled with known impacts on populations sharing similar traits enabled me to identify the impacts that follow.

Impact on Children and Youth
The competition for space results in situations where children and youth do not have a suitable environment to complete their homework or concentrate on their studies.

This issue is compounded if the family is periodically or continuously transient. Studies conducted by Social Planning Toronto (Sherkin 2006) on children residing in shelters clearly demonstrate that school transfer adversely impacts the education of children.

Impact on Health

Notwithstanding the reluctance to discuss, let alone admit, the existence of mental health–related issues among newcomers impacted by hidden homelessness, there is a continuous stream of anecdotes about depression and other mental health problems caused as a result of sharing living space with many strangers. In addition, newcomers living in situations of hidden homelessness tend to have limited and fixed incomes; any increases in rent—which happen relatively often—have to be compensated through savings on food. A diet of cheap, low-quality food reverses the "healthy immigrant effect" (Newbold 2005) and creates a wide range of health-related problems. Furthermore, buying medication becomes a luxury, resulting in many minor ailments remaining untreated, often becoming chronic. Hidden homelessness therefore promotes physical and psychological degeneration in the long term.

Social Issues

Social tensions develop between families living in the same confined space. Such tensions can be especially problematic for families of cultures disapproving of interactions between members of the opposite gender who are not related. Furthermore, the lack of access to adequate recreational resources and space can create stress and foster problematic behaviour among adults and youth alike. Moreover overcrowded housing arrangements are not conducive to youth supervision, resulting in problem behaviour outside of the home. Discussions with officials of the York District School Board about the possible impact of zero-tolerance policies on South Asian immigrant youth revealed that suspensions from school were possibly caused by the lack of adequate supervision at home.

SOLUTIONS TO HIDDEN HOMELESSNESS

Possible solutions to hidden homelessness include improved linkages between the Housing Help sector and agencies serving the newcomer community. There are 74 Housing Help Centres throughout the province of Ontario, each of which is funded by the local municipality to help local community members access habitable housing and achieve housing stability. The Province of Ontario also has more than 200 agencies funded by the federal and provincial governments to respond to the settlement and employment needs of newcomers. The lack of adequate interaction and awareness about each other's programming is a major gap that is detrimental to the long-term housing goals of newcomers. It is therefore important that housing help centres and immigrant serving agencies network and interact closely with each other and devise ways to jointly help newcomers address their housing needs. In addition, service providers should help newcomers distinguish between housing and employment components of their overall settlement trajectory.

A second aspect of solving the hidden homelessness program is awareness-raising among newcomer communities. As discussed above, many newcomers are not aware of their rights and the Residential Tenancies Act that governs renter-landlord duties and obligations. This objective of raising awareness of rent and habitability standards may be accomplished through increased targeted funding with the specific objective of disseminating information and providing one-on-one services where appropriate.

Third, it would be important to change the focus of debate from real to hidden homelessness. Since the Homelessness Partnership Initiative is currently under reviewed by the federal government there may be an opportunity for activist and advocates to influence the policy and associated debate of homelessness. The fact that all political parties are trying to court the urban newcomer vote may help in drawing attention to an issue that significantly impacts the urban newcomer community.

A final solution is to recognize the impact of hidden homelessness on intergovernmental transfer payments. Since the level of intergovernmental transfer payments depend on enumerated populations, municipal governments are likely underpaid as a result of inaccurate statistics about hidden homelessness. Across the province, policy-makers at the municipal level should be interested in this argument as their governments find it difficult to balance their budgets.

RECOMMENDATIONS FOR FURTHER RESEARCH

There are significant methodological challenges to count the hidden homeless population, including access to private homes or apartments, establishing guidelines for temporary and permanent residents, and issues related to multiple-counting or not counting residents. The lack of accepted enumeration methods is a major barrier in the capacity of advocates and non-profits to paint a comprehensive and compelling picture of hidden homeless. It is therefore important to estimate (as opposed to accurately count) the number of people affected by hidden homelessness on the basis of other available information. Some ideas include establishing income cut-offs for identifying hidden homelessness. Banks routinely advise clients applying for mortgage loans to limit monthly mortgage payments to one-third of their net income. Based on this rule of thumb, it could be concluded that a family spending significantly more than one-third of their income on housing is at risk of homelessness and of sharing accommodation with other families in order to make ends meet. A family that spends 40 to 50 percent or more of its net income on housing could possibly be in a situation of hidden homelessness. If this assumption were applied to the average rent of at least

$1,500/month in 2008 for a two-bedroom apartment in Toronto (Toronto Real Estate Board 2009), then it could be argued that a family with at least one adult and one child earning less than $3,000/month and renting a two-bedroom apartment is at risk of hidden homelessness.

A different way of identifying potential spots of hidden homelessness would be to utilize Toronto's Municipal Property Standards Act. This act specifies that every individual should have a minimum of nine square metres of living space. The head count per apartment complex could be ascertained through interviews with property management or access to the apartment complex's electricity and water bills. The estimates of the numbers of residents, in conjunction with details of habitable space, can help determine whether a given house or apartment complex has issues related to hidden homelessness.

ACKNOWLEDGEMENTS

I wish to acknowledge the financial support of Citizenship and Immigration Canada through an Immigration Settlement Adaptation Program (ISAP) – Stream B grant ET01392911 for the year 2010–2011. I would like to thank my colleagues Sara C. Jones and Glen Gifford at the Scarborough Housing Help Centre for discussion and comments. Sincere thanks are due to Harald Bauder whose patient and extensive editing is responsible for clarity of information and development of arguments and ideas in this chapter.

REFERENCES

Canadian Broadcasting Corporation (CBC). 2003. "Discriminatory Housing Practice Preys on New Canadians." January 21. Accessed August 6, 2011. www.cbc.ca/marketplace/pre-2007/files/home/housing_discrimination/index.html.

Chambon, A., D. Hulchanski, R. Murdie, and C. Teixeira. 1997. "Access to Housing in a Canadian City." Paper presented at the Urban Affairs Conference, Toronto.

Chou, R. S., and J. R. Feagin. 2008. *The Myth of the Model Minority: Asian Americans Facing Racism*. Boulder, CO: Paradigm Press.

Citizenship and Immigration Canada. 2011. "Permanent residents by province or territory and urban area." *Facts and Figures 2009*.

City of Toronto website. 2010. Accessed October 30, 2011. www.toronto.ca/toronto_facts/diversity.htm.

City of Toronto. 2002. Rule 629–25, Occupancy Standards, Sections C-F:31.

Ghosh S. 2005. "'We Are Not All the Same,' The Differential Migration, Settlement Patterns and Housing Trajectories of Indian Bengalis and Bangladeshis in Toronto." Doctoral Thesis, York University.

Hulchanski D. 2003. Living on the Ragged Edges — Immigrants, Refugees and Homelessness in Canada, Forum Summary. March 28.

Kilbride, K. M., and S. Webber. 2006. "Plug Them In and Turn Them On: Homelessness, Immigrants, and Social Capital." Report submitted to the Housing and Homelessness Branch of the Department of Human Resources and Social Development Canada.

Klodawsky, F., T. Aubry, B. Behnia, C. Nicholson, and M. Young. 2005. "Findings and Conclusions from the Panel Study on Homelessness in Ottawa: Secondary Analysis of Responses of Participants whose Country of Origin Is not Canada." A Report Prepared for: National Secretariat on Homelessness. Accessed August 5, 2011. canada.metropolis.net/Virtual%20Library/homelessness/Panel.pdf.

Murdie, R. A. 2002. "A Comparison of the Rental Housing Experiences of Polish and Somali Newcomers in Toronto." *Housing Studies* 17 (3): 423–444.

Murdie, R. A., and J. C. Texeira. 2002. "Toward a Comfortable Neighbourhood and Appropriate Housing: Immigrant Experience in Toronto." Working Paper Series of the Joint Centre of Excellence in Research and Settlement, Toronto.

Newbold, K. B. 2005. "Self-Rated Health within the Canadian Immigrant Population: Risk and the Healthy Immigrant Effect." *Social Science and Medicine* 60: 1,359–1,370.

Petersen, W. 1966. "Success Story, Japanese American Style." *New York Times Magazine*, 20–21, 33, 36, 38, 40–41, 43.

Preston, V., R. Murdie, S. D'Addario, J. Logan, A. Murnaghan, J. Wedlock, S. Agrawal, and U. Anucha. 2009. "At Risk in the Suburbs? Immigrants' Housing Needs and Challenges in York Region." Report submitted to Homelessness Knowledge Development Program, Homelessness Partnering Secretariat, HRSDC: 2.

Shapcott, M. 2006. "Toronto's 2006 Street Needs Assessments: Moving to Action." Wellesley Institute.

Sherkin, S., 2006. "Supporting the School Success of Children in Scarborough." Kid Builders Project Phase II Social Planning Toronto: 1–50. Toronto Real Estate Report, Report 2009.

Toronto Star. 2001. "Landlord Demands Up to Year's Rent from Newcomers." June 29.

Toronto Star. 2009. "York Region Hit by 'Hidden' Problem." January 14.

Chapter 14

EVERYDAY LIVES IN VERTICAL NEIGHBOURHOODS: EXPLORING BANGLADESHI RESIDENTIAL SPACES IN TORONTO

SUTAMA GHOSH

INTRODUCTION

A residential neighbourhood has two intertwined components: the built form and the people. Ideally, the built form facilitates social interaction, and in the process, pulsating neighbourhoods emerge with their characteristic sights, smells, colours, and meanings. Of course not all built forms are so ideally created. Many residential high-rise buildings were developed according to the utopian visions of planners and bureaucrats to "look like" regimented and ordered places, but routinely ignored the "desires, histories and practices of those who occupied them" (Hubbard and Lilley 2004, 274; also Harloe 1995; Sandercock 1998; Forrest 2002). Often occupying distinct and discrete neighbourhoods (Power 1999), "the high-rise was the form to which a tightly scripted story of the life and death of the monster of modernist planning and architecture attached itself" (Jacobs 2006, 8). Over time, many such neighbourhoods of aged and ill-maintained buildings emerged as sites where "deprivation coincided with housing" (Jacobs 2006), producing hidden homelessness conditions which S. Gopikrishna highlighted in the previous chapter. Under neo-liberal governance, in particular, not only the structural conditions of the rental high-rises further deteriorated, but also the occupants were marginalized on several fronts, including declining incomes and rent increases (Glynn 2009; Hackworth, 2009b). As a remedial measure, some policy-makers and planners advocated for the renewal of such housing, including public housing projects. These renewal efforts have demonstrated mixed outcomes in North American cities, such as Chicago and Los Angeles (Hackworth 2009a), and European[1] cities. In some cases, demolition and reconstruction of the built form has improved the occupants' quality of life; in other cases, this form of gentrification has ruptured the socio-cultural and economic rhythm of low income communities (Walks and Maaranen 2008), with the result that "modernity" is being "unevenly experienced" (Appadurai 1996, 3).

The purpose of this chapter is to shed light on the "the small, the minor, and the exceptional" (Jacobs 2006, 22) rhythms of everyday life of a visible minority group—the Bangladeshis—living in high-rise buildings in downtown Toronto and Toronto's inner suburbs of East York, North York, and Scarborough. In particular, I explore how the tall buildings are "fully lived" (Lefebvre 1991, 38) and transformed into vibrant spaces: "vertical neighbourhoods." Through an examination of residents' spatial practices, I conclude that vertical neighbourhoods are produced both consciously and subconsciously through bonds that are created locally and transnationally. It is the transnational habitus[2] that provides the immigrants with a dual lens of reference, affecting the evaluations of their circumstances in the migrant city as well as influencing their housing needs and satisfactions. In the following sections, I explain the Toronto context, followed by a discussion of the research methods, and the detailed presentation of results. The chapter ends with a discussion and conclusions.

THE TORONTO CONTEXT

In the Toronto Census Metropolitan Area (CMA), rental high-rises have a formidable presence. There are more than 1,000 high-rise residential buildings,[3] comprising about 27 percent of the total housing stock (Statistics Canada 2006). A majority of Toronto's public and private rental[4] accommodations are in high-rises. Although it seems that the high-rises are geographically dispersed in the Toronto CMA, in reality, a majority (60 percent) of them are located in the inner suburbs (East York, Etobicoke, North York, and Scarborough) comprising of more than 126,000 units. Downtown Toronto has the other 40 percent of the stock with about 86,000 units. Constructed primarily in the 1960s and 1970s (Statistics Canada 2006), most rental high-rises in Toronto are between 8 and 29 storeys high. Some noted high-rise neighbourhoods are St. James Town, Moss Park, and Regent Park in downtown Toronto. Other high-rise concentrations are in the suburban "Jane and Finch" corridor in North York and Crescent Town in East York. At the time of construction, it was envisioned that the occupants of these high-rises would be primarily middle-income singles and couples. As their economic conditions improved, they would move out of the rental apartments and into their own homes (Caulfield 1994, 26).

Since the early 1990s, however, the geography of Toronto's "big things" (Jacobs 2006) has dramatically changed. Large volumes of immigrant and refugee families gravitated towards the high-rise apartment buildings in Toronto's inner suburbs for several reasons, including, the presence of relatively low-cost units, larger-sized apartments, nearness to work, and ethnic institutions (retail businesses, places of worship) (Rose and Ray 2001; Murdie and Ghosh 2010). As more new immigrants gravitated towards these enclaves, ethnic clusters enlarged (Ghosh 2007; Murdie and Ghosh 2010). The more disturbing part of this scenario, however, is that over time the interrelations between "race," poverty, and high-rises also strengthened particularly in the inner suburbs (United Way 2011).

Increasing demands for low-cost rental units, together with a socially induced scarcity of housing supply (i.e., removal of rent control and no new construction of affordable rental units) put many new immigrants in a vulnerable state (Engeland, Lewis, and Ehrlich 2004; Hibbert 2009). As a result of having to compete over residual housing, with little knowledge about the housing markets, many newly arrived families paid substantial deposits to secure a roof over their heads and exorbitant rents, even exceeding 50 percent of their gross income. As the previous chapter illustrated, this situation can lead to hidden homelessness. In addition, fluctuating labour market situations have slowed down their progress toward home ownership (Preston, Murdie, and Murnaghan 2007), prolonging their stay within these structures. Consequently, even those units that would be difficult to rent out due to their low quality have become "source[s] of productive wealth for the capitalist class" (Merrifield 2002, 139).

RESEARCH GROUP AND RESEARCH METHODS

The field research was conducted in Toronto, the home of more than 70 percent of Bangladeshis in Canada. Bangladeshis are one of Canada's most recent immigrant groups, arriving primarily between 1996 and 2006 (Statistics Canada 2006). Most came as economic migrants, and therefore, by virtue of immigrant selection criteria, they are primarily "designer immigrants": young, well educated, and with professional skills. Despite these traits, Bangladeshis in Toronto are among the most impoverished and residentially segregated groups.[5]

Fifteen key informants, including housing workers and counsellors, were consulted for this study, using a purposive sampling method. In addition, 30 Bangladeshi households (husband and wife) participated in this study; they were Bangladeshi by birth, Muslim by religion, had lived in Toronto for at least five years, at which they developed a housing trajectory (Murdie 2003, 2005), and were either currently living or had previous lived experiences in a high-rise apartment building in Toronto. Since all interviews were conducted in the residence of the respondents, I was able to visit 14 high-rise buildings, of which 11 were located within three areas of Bangladeshi concentration: Victoria Park, Regent Park, and the Eglinton Avenue and Markham Road area (indicated hereafter as EM area).

The information presented in this chapter was collected during face-to-face semi-structured interviews, informal conversations with respondents before and after the interview, and participant observations. To guarantee confidentiality, the names of the respondents have been changed.

TORONTO'S BANGLADESHI NEIGHBOURHOODS

Three criteria were used to identify the Bangladeshi neighbourhoods in Toronto: concentration of the group, degree of institutional completeness, and self-identification. Victoria Park has the largest concentration of Bangladeshis in Toronto, followed by Regent Park, and the EM area (Statistics Canada 2006). There are many similarities among these three areas. First, the concentration of Bangladeshis is high in all three areas. Bangladeshis are the single largest immigrant group in Victoria Park and Regent Park, and the second largest group in the EM area. Secondly, not only are all three neighbourhoods primarily immigrant areas, but two of the three neighbourhoods are also immigrant "reception" areas.[6] Recent immigrants comprise more than 75 percent of the residents of Victoria Park, and more than 60 percent of those living in the EM area. The remaining quarter of the population of Victoria Park and about two-fifths of the EM area were from Pakistan, India, and Sri Lanka (Statistics Canada 2006). Since it takes longer to access social housing, the percentage of recent immigrants in Regent Park is relatively smaller (Statistics Canada 2006). Thirdly, the median household income in Victoria Park was just under $40,000, it was close to $30,000 in the EM area, and less than $20,000 in Regent Park, compared to $59,500 for Toronto as a whole (City of Toronto Neighbourhood Profiles 2006).

Fourthly, the housing stock in Victoria Park and EM area are similar, in terms of structure, tenure, cost, quality, and size. Built in the 1960s and 1970s, at a time when Toronto was becoming a "Working City," most of the apartment buildings in Victoria Park and the EM area are more than 20 storeys high. The social housing complex of Regent Park is structurally 'mixed'. Predominantly, low-rises in the North and high-rises in the South. The high-rises in Regent Park South were also built in the late 1960s and early 1970s. The buildings in all three areas are ageing and lacking proper maintenance, and those in Regent Park in particular are of the poorest quality (Statistics Canada 2006). In terms of tenure, whereas most high-rises in Victoria Park and the EM area are private rental buildings, all in Regent Park are social housing, rent geared to income (RGI), units. With respect to cost, the average rent of a two-bedroom apartment in Victoria Park is about $1,200 and $1,400 in the EM area. The sizes of the dwellings are relatively spacious in all three areas. This particular feature may have attracted Bangladeshis who typically have relatively larger families (about 4 persons), compared to the Toronto average (3.1 persons).

Fifthly, all three areas are institutionally complete, albeit to varying degrees. Of the three neighbourhoods, Victoria Park is the most institutionally complete. The area contains several Bangladeshi retail stores and services; it includes grocery and clothing stores, beauty parlours, photo studios, entertainment stores, remittance centres, and immigration consultants. In addition, it houses the main offices of two Bengali newspapers and community agencies serving Bangladeshi-Canadians. Several mosques, including the "Baitul Mukarram" mosque built in the late 1990s, are located in the immediate vicinity. In the EM area, there are Bangladeshi grocery stores and a mosque that caters to Sunni Muslims in general. Regent Park is the least institutionally complete. Planned in the 1950s as a massive residential complex, little provision was made for retail stores within the development or its immediate surroundings. In recent years, however, some Bangladeshi retail stores (grocery, convenience, and audio-video) and institutions (Islamic study circle and mosque) have been established in this neighbourhood.

Finally, in all three areas, the settlements of Bangladeshis have followed the "invasion-succession" pattern. Victoria Park was first settled by eastern Europeans, followed by Sylheti Bangladeshis from Montreal, and most recently new immigrants from a variety of sending countries. In Regent Park, Bangladeshis from Sylhet began to settle the late 1980s, joining existing First Nations and Caribbean communities. The EM area was also initially inhabited by European immigrants and was only recently settled by Caribbeans, Sri Lankan Tamils, Pakistanis, Afghanis, and Bangladeshis.

THE HIGH-RISE BANGLADESHI "NEIGHBOURHOODS"

Tall buildings dominate the built form of Victoria Park (97 percent), the EM area (75 percent), and Regent Park (66 percent). A majority of the buildings were constructed from a modernist functional perspective, are almost identical in their layout, and remain highly regimented spaces. On the ground floor, beyond the unwelcoming main entrance, are the rental office and the lobby. Even though in most buildings these two areas are under surveillance, the main entrance is often unsecured. Also located on the ground floor are the mailroom and few private apartments (usually occupied by the building supervisors and managers). Narrow passages—just over a metre wide—provide access to the apartments. Usually, there are between 12 and 14 apartments of varying sizes on each floor. Two garbage chutes run through the vertical length of the building, emptying into massive vats seated on the ground floor, making the ground floor smelly and unattractive. The common laundry room (with about 15 dryers and 10 washers), is located in the basement. There are no ramps to these facilities or anywhere else in the buildings. Although all buildings have central heating, there is no central air conditioning.

In these high-rises, the line between "public" and "private" spaces is blurred. Some "public" spaces such as the lobby area, where social interaction is meant to occur, are under surveillance and signs state that "loitering is strictly prohibited." The "private" apartments are also under constant scrutiny. Routine checks are performed to ensure that the occupants are not using "heavy" electrical appliances (such as a dishwasher, washing machine, air conditioners, or heaters), windows are not opened more than a few centimetres, and there are no undeclared guests (i.e., hidden homelessness, see Chapter 13). Not being able to control air temperatures within their privately rented apartments often adversely affects those families with infants, children, and the elderly.

Rules and regulations were set up to ensure continuous profit from the decaying apartments. For instance, in addition to the first and last month's rent, potential renters often paid a hefty non-refundable security deposit (Preston, Murdie, and Murnaghan 2007; Preston et al. 2009). If the occupants wish to move into another apartment within the same building, they have to pay the "new market rent" for that unit. With the removal of rent control in Ontario in the 1990s, this notorious rule has enabled owners to limitlessly increase rents.

All three areas are racialized spaces. Regent Park, in particular, has been referred to as "Canada's largest ghetto" (Sahak 2008), where the "bodies of colour [are kept] in bounded spaces in order to secure white spaces of dominance" (Rosa 2006; Sahak 2008). Located in the central part of the city, this massive social housing complex was deliberately constructed as a "periphractic space" (Goldberg 1993), where the residents' access to power, rights, goods, and services were routinely denied, by keeping them isolated from the rest of the city (Sahak 2008, 46). Unlike Regent Park, the high-rise complexes in Victoria Park and the EM area were not deliberately planned to huddle the working poor; yet, the poorly maintained buildings, unkept grounds, and ill reputation of the neighbourhoods reflect socio-economic exclusion. In all three areas, the natural ageing process of the buildings combined with the owners' profit motivation, disinvestment, and mismanagement, systemically and synchronously intimidates the residents and denies them one of the most fundamental human rights: access to adequate housing.

THE MAKINGS OF A VERTICAL NEIGHBOURHOOD *"PARA"*

The rental high-rises are more than just a place to live for the occupants of these spaces. Some Bangladeshi respondents identified particular buildings in all three areas as a "Bengali *para*" (translated into English as "neighbourhood"). Upon inquiring what makes a building a para, one respondent, Altaf, said: "Where most tenants were Bengali Muslims." Shaira, another respondent, added that acquiring an apartment in such a building was "like you got a prize [and] ... you need to have connections to get in."

While conducting interviews in the respondents' residences, I often found that the front door to the individual apartments was left unlocked. Rehana, a Bangladeshi mother revealed:

> Oh I keep the door opened, otherwise, I will have to open it every minute.... [T]hey [her and her neighbours' children] are always coming and going ... this house, this fridge is theirs and theirs' is mine.... [W]ho will rob us?... [I]f I closed the apartment door, the neighbours will feel hurt. (personal interview)

This "open door policy" was not just limited to families living on the same floor, but the entire building. Families know each other and keep an eye on each other's children. Living in close proximity has allowed the households to live like "back home as one family," said Jaigir, thereby considerably reducing the tensions of settling in a new country. As Elora remarked, "I didn't feel that I came to a foreign country, this was like, maybe, going from Khulna to Dhaka, that's all."

Although the desire to recreate a home in the destination country is not a unique experience among diasporic communities, how it is recreated within a high-rise building is noteworthy. In their habitus (Bourdieu 1984, 1986, 1990, 1998, 2002; for a migration context see Bauder 2003, 2004; Kelly and Lusis 2006) "back home," it is customary to leave the front door of the house open. The cultural practice of providing a welcoming atmosphere to neighbours has been transposed from a neighbourhood with individual houses on the same street in Bangladesh to almost seamless vertical social spaces in Toronto.

TRANSFORMATION OF SPACE

Despite the meticulous scrutiny of the building supervisors, Bangladeshis manage to variously transform functional spaces into their own social, sacred, economic, and political spaces. Below I review some of these transformations.

From a Functional to a Social Space

Applying their modernist approach, the planners and the developers who constructed the high-rise buildings in the 1970s ensured that each part of the building performed its function efficiently. Bangladeshi women, however, variously transformed these functional spaces into social spaces through their daily routines. Many recent Bangladeshi immigrant women spent much of their daily lives within the confines of the high-rises, particularly during the long winter months. Canadian social norms and the building rules, however, direct them to socialize either within their apartments or in other public places (e.g., parklands or community centres). For many Bangladeshi women, this arrangement is inconvenient. Therefore, as Shipra explains, they often "coordinate their chores ... like doing laundry to catch up with another." When I reminded them of the building "rules," that they are not supposed to loiter in the common areas, Soha said, "I know they have all these signs, oh, but we do anyways."

Some Bangladeshi parents complained that without a playroom or even a common area inside the building, their children are physically inactive, particularly during winter. To alleviate this issue, despite strict regulations, the narrow passages are often transformed into mini play areas. When the building supervisor is alerted, the activities are temporarily halted.

The above examples demonstrate that the actors—Bangladeshi women and children living in the regimented high-rises—are able to transform functional spaces into social spaces by playing the "game" *of* and *with* the authorities. In order to fulfill their needs for social living, these individuals—who are often perceived as powerless—routinely ignore and transform regulations. Although their activities may be interpreted as a form of resistance, their objectives are seldom politically motivated or necessarily achieved through conflict.

From the Residential to the Sacred, Economic, and Political Space

The occupants had also transformed their residential spaces into sacred, economic, and political spaces. Numerous religious and cultural activities are informally organized in the buildings. These include conducting daily public prayers, weekly Quran classes, music, dance, and Bengali language classes, informal daycares, at-home beauty parlours, and catering services. In some buildings, an apartment is transformed into a mosque for offering daily prayers and weekly Quran classes. For this purpose, the rent of the apartment and the salary of the *moullavi* (preacher) are shared by the users of the facility. As noted by the following respondents, women and children particularly benefit from this arrangement.

> In Bangladesh and Toronto it is a recent phenomenon that women are encouraged to go to the Mosque to read *namaz* [prayer] every week; … for us [women] and children it is important to have a mosque nearby. (Shahana, personal interview)

> We have a mosque on the *** floor of this building, yes it is rented but we all pay you know. It is so cold here in the winter months and I cannot drive.... [T]his is a good place for us to go and pray, I can take my children as well. Their father goes to the Baitul mosque. (Nelofar, personal interview)

Bangladeshi women in particular have recently been encouraged to express religiosity more publicly. This meant that in addition to wearing the hijab or the naquab, they are encouraged to pray at mosques. Even though the Baitul Mosque is close to Victoria Park, it is not within walking distance. For many women who did not have access to a car, praying at Baitur was impossible. As an alternative, therefore, they consciously revised the rules of the original habitus to fit with the convention in the migrant country: prayers were allowed at transformed residential spaces.

Photo 14.1 indicates that a ground-floor apartment has been converted into a grocery store. Although there are a number of Bangladeshi grocery stores in the vicinity, having one within the building is particularly convenient for the occupants. Although the building supervisors were aware of this store, there seemed to be a lack of effort to enforce building regulations in this regard.

When choosing a particular building to live in, many Bengali women revealed that they would "target" those buildings where their friends and relatives were. In addition to "feeling at home," friends and relatives often provide informal daycare services, at-home beauty parlours, and cultural centres (music and dance classes). Sumaya, a new mother, revealed:

> When I go for my ESL classes, I leave her [daughter] with Bhabhi [no blood relation].[6] ... I go with a peace of mind. I know that she will be well cared for. Also, she will learn our language, our culture.... I pay her $5 an hour. (personal interview)

Some Bengali men revealed that "it is not necessary for them to have these facilities in the building but definitely in the neighbourhood" (Akram). In addition to convenience, these retail spaces also provide a space for social interactions. Muzaffar, a computer engineer working as a quality control supervisor in a small factory, stated:

> I work long hours and shop only Sundays in Sarkar foods.... As soon as I enter the store, he [the manager] says *"ashun bhai"* [*come in brother*]; it feels good you know. Can you imagine this welcome in No Frills [a Canadian grocery chain].... [E]ven if one day I go away

from here, I will keep coming back to shop here—otherwise I will not be able to digest my rice.

Although retail activities within high-rise residential buildings are not a part of the Bangladeshi habitus, such activities and associated transformations of space may be understood as a product of the *transnational habitus*. In Bangladesh, the households are used to having retail stores and services in their para or neighbourhoods. There they have personal connections with the retailers and the service providers, something they cannot ordinarily expect in Toronto.

The transformation of residential spaces into informal economic spaces further demonstrates the existence of a transnational habitus, regulating the everyday practices of these immigrant families. The households made these adjustments based on their own financial circumstances in Toronto (e.g., unemployment and underemployment), as well as the increasing demand for specific "Bengali" services within their buildings. In doing so, they not only gained economically but they also forged new social bonds. Reciprocity towards community members (however imagined) also seemed to have motivated Bangladeshis to patronize businesses in their neighbourhoods.

SPACES OF HOPE AND DESPAIR

When describing how they were "lucky" to have "a place of their own" in this "Bengali para" in a foreign land, many Bangladeshi men and women viewed their apartment buildings as spaces of hope. Often the households viewed the Bengali neighbourhoods and particular buildings in such a way even before they had arrived in Canada. It was a common practice among the Bangladeshi households I interviewed to have started a housing career in Toronto long before they had actually landed at the Pearson airport. They were almost always greeted by "family friends"[7] at the airport and lived with them for a while (even months) until they found their own apartment, usually in the same building.

Although in many buildings women run informal businesses, they also provide "free" services, especially when another family is in a crisis.

> When we had my child, I became very sick. The doctors told me to rest. I could not even take care of my child, my mother could not come here and my relatives were in the States.... I didn't want to put her in a daycare. At the time, Tulika *Bhabi* [sister-in-law; no blood relation] ... our next-door neighbour actually took care of her. (Noor, personal interview)

> If we move from here I would not get small jobs here and there. When I first came, I used to cook for *** restaurant.... I don't have to ask my husband all the time for little things. I also worked in *** store, the man ... used to treat me like a servant. (Rehana, personal interview)

> When her [wife's] father passed away, she left everything, me the children and went back home. Our friends here told me, let Aisha go, we will take care.... [W]here else can I get this in Toronto? (Aslam, personal interview)

As noted in these quotations, the respondents depend on the social networks forged with other residents of the building for various practical purposes. These networks provide them with various kinds of facilities, including psychological support. Whereas physical proximity enhanced by the buildings' structure increases interdependence among the occupants, many Bangladeshi households revealed a strong desire to self-segregate from Europeans (including British-Canadians) and other "South Asians" (particularly Pakistanis and Indians). I will discuss the effects of these "choices" in detail further below.

Some Bengali households expressed a sense of despair when conversing about their life in Toronto in general and within the "vertical neighbourhoods" more specifically. Toronto was often described as a place that was once filled with many hopes and promises, but in reality, has given them despair. Since arriving in Toronto, the financial capital of these Bengali families, which they brought with them, quickly vanished, and with each passing year, the dream of finding a well-paid job is becoming more distant. Even when searching for a place to live, they are treated unfairly. Noor reported how the landlords took advantage of their "ignorance" about the system:

> When my husband came to see the apartment ... they said, you can see a similar apartment but not the one you are about to get because it was not vacant. The one he saw was nice and airy; ... the day we reached here, they gave us a horrible apartment directly over the garbage room.... [W]hen we complained to the manager, he claimed that he had showed my husband this very apartment.... [Since he had] signed the lease ... nothing more could be done. (personal interview)

When these households attempted to move out of the poor quality apartment buildings, they often met with covert and overt discriminatory practices. In Khairul's case, the manager of a Victoria Park building with primarily non-Bangladeshi tenants, discriminated against him:

> There were no apartments empty here [in Teesdale and on Dawes Road]. In one building, on that side [the east side] I knew there some apartments *were* available. The supervisor will not give me the place. She is a white lady.... [S]he looked right in my eyes and said nothing was vacant. (personal interview)

238 *Immigration and Settlement*

Despite spending a large amount of their income on rent (from 30 percent to over 50 percent), the occupants could not control the air temperature in their units nor were they allowed to open bedroom windows beyond a few centimetres. As a result, many respondents referred to their apartments as "prison cells" (Noor), where they "could not even breathe" (Ayub). These experiences also led to intense feelings of dissatisfaction and despair with their dwelling in Toronto, as Shaira and Jahangir explain:

> See the apartment yourself ... we pay $850 for a one-bedroom and see how it is ... there are cockroaches and insects everywhere.... [T]hey [the supervisors] will come and promise they will do something but eventually nothing will happen. The roof of our bathroom is leaking, one day my son was playing in this area when a huge chunk of building material fell; ... it almost hit him. (Shaira, personal interview)

> I am ashamed to invite anyone like you to my home. We have become like beggars here. In Bangladesh, no one of my stature, not even our relatives will believe that we are living like this. (Jahangir, personal interview)

Although most respondents held the "building supervisors ... responsible for the lack of maintenance" (Shaira) of their buildings, in reality many building supervisors are themselves new immigrants, with limited grasp of conversational English and without necessary technical qualifications required to run and manage about 130 units. They are often hired contractually and for a limited term. Some supervisors lamented that they, "too, are in a precarious state ... listening to complaints [tenants and managers] all day and hearing them [tenants] swear in their own language" (Rajan, building supervisor). They accepted this position because they could not find suitable employment in their field of expertise, and as building supervisor they can live in one of the apartments free of charge. Also, at the time of joining, the owners had not informed them of the challenges associated with running such a large operation on a daily basis. As a result, supervisors and managers are simply unable to provide essential services, such as maintaining the basic cleanliness of the public places within the buildings.

SPATIAL IMAGINATIONS AND CONTESTATIONS AND GEOGRAPHIES OF FEAR

Most Bangladeshis participants agreed that an ideal neighbourhood should have a Bengali identity.[7] Respondents further articulated that when they enter into home ownership, they would still search for a place that was Bengali. Despite such assertions of "Bengaliness," however, there were some social and ideological divisions within the community, their spatial imaginations, and associated "struggles and debates over the distribution of scarce resources" (Eade 1991, 32; Ahmed 2001).

In contrast to the Bangladeshis of Tower Hamlets in east London, Sylhetis are a minority in Toronto.[9] As in London, however, in Toronto, Sylhetis distinguish themselves from other Bengalis and have formed their own regional organizations (Eade 1994, 386.), e.g., the Sylheti Jalalabad Association. Similarly, non-Sylhetis do not consider Sylhetis to be Bengalis. When describing the history of Bengali settlement in Victoria Park, a Sylheti key informant claimed that Sylhetis "created Victoria Park as a Sylheti place, and [non-Sylheti Bangladeshis] just came and enjoyed it" (Chowdhury). Several non-Sylheti key informants and respondents, on the other hand, complained that Sylhetis were nepotistic and restricted Bengalis from accessing apartments in particular buildings. As Sumaya explains, "Sylhetis are always like that you know, very village like, looking after their own people." Nevertheless, even though in Bangladesh, Sylhetis would not socialize with other Bengalis, in Toronto they do so for two reasons: first, here they are all a minority, which necessitates bridging socio-cultural gaps. Second, living in the same building, has helped them to come closer. As Mosharef elaborates, "When you are in a house, you first play with your own brothers and sisters.... But this is not home; ... we have to be one. They are my neighbour, so you are friendly."

In addition to their national and regional identities, the spatial practices of Toronto's Bangladeshis were also influenced by significant historical and contemporary events, in their home country and the "West" at large. The memories of and reactions to these events created unique "geographies of fear" towards the charter group, other South Asians and Caribbeans. During discussions about "an ideal neighbourhood," "neighbourhood choice," and "neighbourhood satisfactions," many Bangladeshis alluded to 9/11 and discussed specific media reports and anecdotes of atrocities against Muslim men in other Western countries (particularly Britain), while explaining why Bangladeshis would refrain from living in "White neighbourhoods" in Toronto. It was also evident in these conversations that it was primarily the information communicated over transnational social spaces (e.g., telephone conversations, emails) and not always peoples' first-hand experiences that created the geographies of fear. For instance, Choudhury (who came to Canada in the 1980s from England) recollected the 1980s race riots in Britain: "Bangladeshis are wary of 'white' people in Toronto, so they keep away"; while Mujaffar had never lived in Britain, yet expressed similar sentiments, saying: "I know what happened in Britain.... Exactly the same thing can happen anytime here ... they may be polite but the British people don't like us." Ayub on the other hand, deliberated upon the global and the local contexts and concluded: "[W]e [Bangladeshi men] are targeted and rounded up for questioning [in other cities] ... and similar things have started in Toronto.... [It is] better we live in our own neighbourhood."

Thus the post 9/11 circumstances attracted many families to Muslim neighbourhoods of Toronto, particularly in Scarborough and East York. This also resulted in

Bangladeshis sharing neighbourhoods with Pakistanis, sometimes causing a different kind of insecurity and dissatisfaction with their neighbourhoods. Despite their physical proximity, memories of the war[10] became a formidable barrier in the path of compressing pre-existing social distances between Pakistanis and Bangladeshis. As Shahana remarks:

> If in a condition where a Bangladeshi must choose between living near an Indian or a Pakistani, most would prefer to live near an Indian.... [W]e remember what we have faced and there is always this uneasiness which is difficult to overcome. (personal interview)

A few Bangladeshis revealed that although they were currently somewhat satisfied with their neighbourhood, if Pakistanis became a majority, they would move. As Ayub noted: "Yes we are happy living here [EM area]—but if too many Pakistanis continue to come in, it will no longer be good for us, then I will move."

In the Bangladeshi imaginations, an ideal neighbourhood would also be free of drugs and crime. In this context, Bangladeshis were eager to distinguish themselves from the "Black people" in their neighbourhoods. Some respondents even expressed racial aversion towards lone parent Caribbean families, in particular, holding them responsible, as Ayub believes, for "spoiling the image of [their] area." When spatial contestations ensued between the two opponent groups, Bangladeshis, more aware of the game, took actions in advance. As Haque explained: "We have to be active if we want this place to be what we want.... Bengalis are politically very conscious you know, so we ran a very successful campaign and got all our candidates elected."

The dual lens of the transnational habitus also led them to evaluate Toronto as *desh* and *bidesh*. For many Bangladeshis, while Toronto was the foreign land or *bidesh*—a place where one goes to make money—the "Bengali para" was their *desh* or homeland, the locus of individual and collective identity. Sajida, for example, remarks:

> For me, Toronto is like a place you go to, you work and then come back home. Nowhere in Toronto, do I feel the way I feel when I come here. It is just different. When you go out of here you actually know how it feels. (personal interview)

Similarly, Maqboor said:

> Where I will live all of my life does not necessarily have to be a place with big houses, cars, [and] well-dressed people—it has to be a para—when I enter it, I can say oh this is my home.

DISCUSSION AND CONCLUSIONS

High-rise rental buildings are an enduring feature of Toronto's cityscape, particularly in the ethnic enclaves in the suburbs. Although there is much debate among planners, policy-makers, and academics with respect to how to change these spaces of exclusion into spaces of inclusion, little is known about the daily lives of the households living within these "big things" of brick and mortar. In the Toronto CMA, almost a third of the total housing stock is comprised of high-rise apartment buildings. Not only do most new immigrants reside in these structures upon their arrival, they often continue living here for a prolonged period of time, for a variety of interrelated economic and socio-psychological reasons.

Based on the experiences of thirty Bangladeshi households, the purpose of this chapter was to explore the everyday lives of this new immigrant group in Toronto's high-rise rental buildings. My aim was to understand how aged, regimented, and dilapidated mass-produced housing complexes were transformed into vibrant vertical neighbourhoods. During fieldwork, I visited 14 high-rise buildings located in three Bangladeshi neighbourhoods, all of which can be regarded as "ethnic enclaves," due to the presence of a large number of immigrants and recent immigrants, and institutional completeness. My research showed how Bengali spaces are produced through complex processes of place-making. Although the fourteen buildings I visited were planned as functional spaces for middle-class, young, singles and couples of Western European origin, the social identities of the occupants had changed dramatically since the mid-1990s. Yet, authorities had made few adjustments to accommodate the needs of these new occupants: young, highly educated, yet low-income, ethnic minority families. For instance, the green areas around the buildings were not maintained, or secured, so that mothers and children could have a safe space in which to socialize.

Although within the high-rises, the authorities attempted to draw clear boundaries between "public" and "private" property, the residents blurred these lines. By installing (sometimes contradicting) "rules and regulations," public places were made quasi-private and private apartments had become quasi-public. In most buildings, there were hardly any non-surveillanced common areas for people to gather for conversations or festivities, and by installing surveillance cameras and signs the owners and supervisors made sure that the occupants' social interactions were restricted. Furthermore, by inspecting private apartments in search of "illegal activities," at the same time as not providing a clean and healthy environment, the building supervisors routinely denied the occupants' rights to adequate housing. Additionally, taking advantage of their naivety and ignorance, households were "caught up in the lease" and economically exploited, further constraining their residential upward mobility.

Despite these problems, however, the Bangladeshis' sense of community was strengthened by the built form. Living in the same building enabled them to develop close familial bonds and to some extent empowered them to overcome the many challenges of settling in a new country. By simply living their lives, consciously and subconsciously, Bangladeshis were able to transform spaces: from functional to social, sacred, economic, and political. Living in the confines of concrete walls, women and children in particular had learned to "play the game" *with* and *of* the authorities. They successfully achieved their objectives to socialize while working, and playing in the corridors, not through friction, but through tact and improvisation of the same rules that restricted them.

The residential spaces were also transformed into economic spaces. Although retail activities within dwellings were not a part of the Bangladeshi habitus, perhaps financial needs (i.e., the position of the actor in the society) together with increasing demand for specific cultural services (i.e., the circumstances in the migrant society) encouraged them to open their own private apartments as "shops" (i.e., spaces of informal economic activities). Such adjustments made to the original habitus demonstrate the presence of a transnational habitus, greatly influencing the everyday practices of the occupants and their associated spatial transformations in the migrant city.

The transnational habitus also helped Bangladeshis to develop a sense of place and emotional attachments to the vertical high-rises. Although from the outside, these rental high-rises seem lifeless, they are in fact lively spaces, imbued with ambivalent feelings of hope and despair, as well as spatial imaginations and contestations. Many Bangladeshis were aware of these "vertical neighbourhoods," even before they arrived in Canada. An apartment in one of the buildings in one of the three Bangladeshi enclaves was like a highly sought-after prize. To the study participants, the buildings were places where they hoped to find a sense of community—to be able to depend economically and socio-psychologically—while adjusting to a new life, and at the same time develop a sense of belonging. These were also spaces that disillusioned them, however. In addition to not finding a job in their area of expertise, they were also variously taken advantage of and exploited by the housing providers and managers. Thus, full of despair, they evaluated their current living situations in Toronto very poorly.

The complex habitus of Bangladesh, of Toronto, and of Bangladesh and Toronto constructed Bangladeshis' imaginations of ideal neighbourhoods, which were not necessarily in harmony with those of the other immigrant groups, occupying the same residential buildings. Their perceptions about Caribbeans (whom they had only encountered in Canada), the stories of racism encountered by Bangladeshis in Britain, and the past and current conflicts in the Indian subcontinent (between India, Pakistan, and Bangladesh) created and reproduced "geographies of fear," restricting them to specific geographical locations. Whereas, on one hand, this restriction strengthened their existing enclaves, on the other, it discouraged them from trying new residential neighbourhoods.

The dual lens of the transnational habitus also led Bangladeshi newcomers to evaluate Toronto as "*bidesh*" (foreign land) and the vertical neighbourhoods as "*desh*" (homeland). The connotation of "*bidesh*" was more than just a site of economic activity. It is seen as a space, which did not represent the Bangladeshis socio-economically and/

or culturally. It is a non-Bengali, non-Muslim environment, where they were racially marginalized and alienated. The high-rise apartment buildings, on the other hand, although regimented and restrictive, had become "*desh*," through various transformations, made consciously and subconsciously. Through daily living routines these sites become filled with symbols, smells, colours, and meanings, thus providing a unique normality—a transnational habitus.

ENDNOTES

1. Restructuring Large Scale Housing Estates in European Cities (RESTATE) project, for instance, was started in 2005. This research involves a study of 29 housing complexes in 10 EU countries.
2. Habitus (Bourdieu 1984, 1986, 1990, 1998, 2002; for a migration context see Bauder 2003, 2004; Kelly and Lusis 2006) is a way of being in the society. Guarnizo (1997) suggests that the transnational habitus is "a particular set of dispositions that inclines migrants to act and react to specific situations in a manner that can be, but is not always, calculated, and that is not simply a question of conscious acceptance of specific behavioural or socio-cultural rules.… The transnational habitus incorporates the social position of the migrant and the context in which transmigration occurs" (Guarnizo 1997, 7). The duality of the transnational habitus also leads to the construction of ambivalent feelings about home and migrant life in the foreign land.
3. Slightly more than 10 percent of all rental housing in Toronto is under the public (or social) sector. Toronto Community Housing is the largest owner and provider of social housing in Toronto (64 percent of all social housing, and over 160 high-rise buildings). Other providers of non-profit housing are community-based organizations, such as faith based and ethno-racial groups. In addition there is cooperative housing. The city of Toronto also runs private rent supplement programs and housing allowance programs to assist people with rent payments. However, during the conservative Tory government, subsidies for 17,000 planned new affordable units were cut, and the private sector was deregulated by removing rent controls.
4. The average cost of private rental apartments in Toronto is one of the highest, among all other Canadian CMAs (CMHC 2009, 2010). In 2009 the average cost of a one-bedroom apartment in a private rental building was $900, two bedrooms cost $1,061, and average rent for a three-bedroom apartment was $1,252 (CMHC 2009).
5. The Index of Segregation was 72 among Bangladeshi immigrants vs. non-immigrant population by census tract, 2006—a level of segregation corresponding to Peach's (1997) findings in Britain.
6. When this study was undertaken the revitalization project in Regent Park was just beginning. As a result, the findings of this research do not reflect the effects of the revitalization project.
7. The idea of "family friends" is different in the context of Bangladeshis. Even when they are not related by blood, Bangladeshis address their neighbours and friends as their relatives—such as Uncle (*chacaha*) Aunt (*khala*), brother (*bhai*), Sister (*apa/bon*), brother-in-law (*dulha bahii*), and sister-in-law (*bhbhi*).
8. A Bangladeshi Bengali identity as explained by several key informants and Ahmed (2001) is comprised of three major elements: Bangla or Bengali language; faith (Muslims are a majority, fol-

lowed by Hindus and Buddhists); and political ideology (pro Indian Awami League, Bangladesh National Party or BNP, and an Islamist group known as the Jamat-e-Islami Bangladesh. Incidentally this third party was opposed to independence of Bangladesh from Pakistan. For many Bangladeshi Hindus and Muslims it is the linguistic bond that makes them one nation—and this often supersedes the other two axes of cultural identifiers.

9. Bangladeshi migration to Toronto is different from that to London (Britain) where Bengalis have a long history of settlement (Peach 1990; Gardner 2002). In contrast to London, where almost 90 percent of Bangladeshis are from Sylhet, most Bangladeshis in Toronto were from various districts of Bangladesh such as Dhaka, Mymensingh, Chattagram, Khulna, Faridpur, and Noakhali.

10. At the time of India's partition in 1947, although Bengali Muslims preferred to join East Pakistan, soon thereafter it was realized that they were discriminated against by the Pakistani government, both socio-economically and culturally (Ahmed 2001). This disappointment led to the Bangladesh war of independence in 1970, during which time, many Bangladeshis currently living in Toronto lost family members. "The war raged for 10 months, cost the lives of millions of people, and incurred much destruction to property. Over 10 million people had to flee the country and take shelter in India. Bangladesh was born as a sovereign state in December 1971 amidst blood and tears" (Ahmed 2001, 23).

REFERENCES

Ahmed, R. 2001. *Understanding the Bengal Muslims: Interpretative Essays*. Oxford, UK: Oxford University Press.

Ahmed, S. 1993. "Discrimination in Employment and Adaptation of Immigrants: Dimensions of Bangladeshi Experience." Unpublished Master's Thesis, York University.

Appadurai, A. 1996. *Modernity at Large*. Minnesota: University of Minnesota Press.

Bauder, H. 2003. "'Brain Abuse,' or the Devaluation of Immigrant Labour in Canada." *Antipode* 35 (4): 699–717.

———. 2004. "Habitus, Rules of the Labour Market and Employment Strategies of Immigrants in Vancouver." *Social and Cultural Geography* 6: 81–97.

Bourdieu, P. 1984. "The Choice of the Necessary." In *Distinction: A Social Critique of the Judgement of Taste*, 372–396. Boston: Harvard University Press.

———. 1986. "Forms of Capital." In *Handbook of Theory and Research for the Sociology of Education*, edited by J. G. Richardson, 241–257. New York: Greenwood Press.

———. 1990. *The Logic of Practice*. UK Cambridge: Polity Press.

———. 1998. *Practical Reason: On the Theory of Action*. Stanford: Stanford University Press.

———. 2002. "Habitus." In *Habitus: A Sense of Place*, edited by J. Hiller and E. Rooksby, 27–33. Aldershot: Ashgate.

Caulfield, J. 1994. *City Form and Everyday Life: Toronto's Gentrification and Critical Social Practice*. Toronto: University of Toronto Press.

City of Toronto. 2006. "Neighbourhood Profiles: Crescent Town and Oakridge." Accessed August 5, 2011. www.toronto.ca/demographics/neighbourhoods.htm.

CMHC. 2009. *Rental Market Report: Greater Toronto Area*. Ottawa: Canada Mortgage and Housing Corporation. Accessed August 8, 2011. www.cmhc-schl.gc.ca/odpub/esub/64459/64459_2009_A01.pdf?fr=1312805389040.

CMHC. 2010. *Rental Market Report: Greater Toronto Area*. Ottawa: Canada Mortgage and Housing Corporation. Accessed August 8, 2011. www.cmhc-schl.gc.ca/odpub/esub/64459/64459_2010_A01.pdf?fr=1312805607925.

Eade, J. 1991. "The Political Construction of Class and Community: Bangladeshi Political Leadership in Tower Hamlets, East London." In *Black and Ethnic Leadership in Britain: The Cultural Dimensions of Political Action*, edited by P. Werbner and M. Anwar, 66–83. London and New York: Routledge.

Eade, J. 1994. "Identity, Nation and Religion: Educated Young Bangladeshi Muslims in London's East End." *International Sociology* 9 (3): 377–394.

Engeland, J., R. Lewis, and S. Ehrlich. 2004. *Evolving Housing Conditions in Canada's Census Metropolitan Areas, 1991–2001*. Ottawa: Canada Mortgage and Housing Corporation and Statistics Canada.

Forrest R. 2002. "Neighbourhood in a High-Rise, High Density City: Some Observations on Contemporary Hong Kong." *The Sociological Review* 50 (2): 215–240.

Gardner, K. 1995. *Global Migrants Local Lives*. Oxford, UK: Clarendon Press.

———. 2002. "Desh-Bidesh: Sylheti Images of Home and Away." *MAN* 28 (1): 1–15.

Ghosh, S. 2007. "Transnational Ties and Intra-Immigrant Group Settlement Experiences: A Case Study of Indian Bengalis and Bangladeshis in Toronto." *Geojournal* 68: 223–242.

Glynn, S. 2009. *Where the Other Half Lives: Lower Income Housing in a Neoliberal World*. London and New York: Pluto Press.

Goldberg, D. T. 1993. *Racist Culture: Philosophy and the Politics of Meaning*. Oxford, UK: Blackwell.

Guarnizo, L. E. 1997. "The Emergence of Transnational Social Formation and the Miracle of Return Migration among Dominican Transmigrants." *Identities* 4 (2): 281–322.

Hackworth, J. 2009a. "Destroyed by HOPE: Public Housing, Neo-Liberalism and Progressive Housing Activism in the US." In *Where the Other Half Lives: Lower Income Housing in a Neoliberal World*, edited by S. Glynn, 232–256. London and New York: Pluto Press.

———. 2009b. "Political Marginalisation, Misguided Nationalism, and the Destruction of Canada's Social Housing." In *Where the Other Half Lives: Lower Income Housing in a Neoliberal World*, edited by S. Glynn, 257–319. London and New York: Pluto Press.

Harloe, M. 1995. *The People's Home? Socially Rented Housing in Europe and North America*. Oxford, UK: Oxford.

Hiebert, D. 2009. "Newcomers in the Canadian Housing Market: A Longitudinal Study, 2001–2005" *The Canadian Geographer* 53 (3): 268–287.

Hubbard, P., and K. Lilley. 2004. "Pacemaking the Modern City: The Urban Politics of Speed and Slowness." *Environment and Planning D: Society and Space* 22: 273–294.

Jacobs, J. M. 2006. "A Geography of Big Things." *Cultural Geography* 13: 1–27.

Kelly, P., and T. Lusis. 2006. "Migration and the Transnational Habitus: Evidence from Canada and the Philippines." Environment and Planning A 38: 831–847.

Lefebvre, H. 1991. *The Production of Space*. Translated by D. Nicholson-Smith. Oxford, UK: Blackwell.

Merrifield, A. 2006. *Henri Lefebvre: A Critical Introduction*. New York: Routledge.

Murdie, R. A. 2003. "Housing Affordability and Toronto's Rental Market: Perspectives from the Housing Careers of Jamaican, Polish and Somali Newcomers." *Housing, Theory and Society* 20 (4): 183–196.

Murdie, R. A., and S. Ghosh 2010. "Does Spatial Concentration Always Mean a Lack of Integration? Exploring Ethnic Concentration and Integration in Toronto." *Journal of Ethnicity and Migration* 36 (2): 293–311.

Peach, C. 1990. "Estimating the Growth of Bangladeshi Population in Great Britain." *New Community* 16 (4): 481–491.

———. 1997. "Contrasting Patterns of Indian, Pakistani and Bangladeshi Settlement in Britain." *Migracijske Teme* 13: 1536.

Power, A. 1999. "High-Rise Estates in Europe: Is Rescue Possible?" *Journal of European Social Policy* 9 (2): 139–163.

Preston, V., R. Murdie, and A. M. Murnaghan. 2007. "The Housing Situation of Recent Immigrants in the Toronto." CMA CERIS Working Paper No. 56. Toronto, ON: Centre of Excellence for Research on Immigration and Settlement.

Preston, V., R. Murdie, J. Wedlock, S. Agrawal, U. Anucha, S. D'Addario, M. J. Kwak, J. Logan, and A. M. Murnaghan. 2009. "At Risk in Canada's Outer Suburbs: A Pilot Study of Immigrants and Homelessness in York Region." In *Finding Home: Policy Options for Addressing Homelessness in Canada*, edited by J. D. Hulchanski, P. Campsie, S. Chau, S. W. Hwang, and E. Paradis, Chapter 5.3. Toronto: Cities Centre, University of Toronto.

Rosa, V. 2006. "Producing Race, Producing Space: The Geography of Toronto's Regent Park." Unpublished Master's Thesis, OISE, University of Toronto.

Ray, B. K., G. Halseth, and B. Johnson 1997. "The Changing 'Face' of the Suburbs: Issues of Ethnicity and Residential Change in Suburban Vancouver." *International Journal of Urban and Regional Research* 21 (1): 75–99.

Rose, D., and B. K. Ray. 2001. "The Housing Situation of Refugees in Montréal Three Years after Arrival: The Case of Asylum Seekers Who Obtained Permanent Residence." *Journal of International Migration and Integration* 2 (4): 493–527.

Sahak, J. 2008. "Race, Space and Place: Exploring Toronto's Regent Park from a Marxist Perspective: A Major Research Paper." Unpublished MRP in Immigration and Settlement Studies, Toronto: Ryerson University.

Sandercock, L. 1998. *Towards Cosmopolis: Planning for Multicultural Cities*. New York: John Wiley.

Statistics Canada. 2006. Community Profiles. Accessed September 8, 2011. www12.statcan.ca/census-recensement/2006/dp-pd/prof/92-591/index.cfm?Lang=E.

United Way of Greater Toronto and The Canadian Council on Social Development. 2011. *Vertical Poverty, Poverty by Postal Code 2*. Toronto: United Way of Greater Toronto. Accessed August 5, 2011. www.unitedwaytoronto.com/verticalpoverty/report/introduction/

Walks, R. A., and R. Maaranen. 2008. "Gentrification, Social Mix, and Social Polarization: Testing the Linkages in Large Canadian Cities." *Urban Geography* 29 (4): 293–326.

Part Five

EMERGING OPPORTUNITIES

While the previous parts of this volume engaged with some of the most widely debated and hottest topics related to immigration and settlement, this final part moves beyond these established themes and highlights emerging topics and opportunities for future research and policy development. In this way, the individual chapters point towards important gaps in the current debate and the need to gain a better understanding of these particular areas of immigration and settlement.

In the opening chapter of Part Five, Hannah Allerdice examines the role of refugee organization building programs in shaping the political activities of refugees. Using evidence from semi-structured interviews with Sudanese refugees, service providers, and government officials in the USA and Australia, she demonstrates how settlement policies in these countries not only politically mobilize the refugees, but also channel them towards particular country-specific political aims. Examining the broader implications of refugee political activities and political self-determination, Allerdice concludes that settlement policy agents may indirectly and inadvertently disempower refugees. This chapter draws attention to the understudied link between settlement services and the political activities of newcomers, presenting opportunities for further research on how to mitigate the problematic practices that disempower newcomer communities.

Chapter 16 by Erika Gates-Gasse examines international students as potential immigrants to Canada. International students are "designer immigrants" whose Canadian education, work experience, and social integration are supposed to increase their successful integration into the Canadian labour market. In an effort to retain these students, federal and provincial governments have created simplified paths to permanent residency, such as the Canadian Experience Class. However, successful immigration is not only a function of simplified and accelerated immigration procedures, but also it begins with supporting international students during their studies. In her chapter, Gates-Gasse reviews the available literature on international student retention, examines existing programs aimed at international students at the federal, provincial, municipal, and university levels, and considers international approaches to supporting these students. Attracting and harnessing international students as immigrants is an emerging policy issue beyond Canada.

Finally, in Chapter 17, Judith Colbert addresses another under-researched topic: the settlement of young newcomer children. Colbert argues that the distinctive settlement needs of young newcomer children have not been fully recognized, although cross-cultural psychologists tell us that acculturation begins in infancy, and data indicate that many kindergarten children who are second language learners are disadvantaged. Focusing on Canada, she demonstrates that much remains to be learned about early intervention as an important settlement service. Progress is slow in part because programs continue to focus on Western ideas of development and childrearing. Colbert's work suggests that more effort by governments, academics, and community-based organizations is needed to ensure that current programs address the settlement needs of young children more effectively.

Chapter 15

CREATING AND CHANNELLING REFUGEE POLITICAL ACTIVITIES: THE ROLE OF REFUGEE ORGANIZATION BUILDING PROGRAMS

HANNAH ALLERDICE

INTRODUCTION

Many host countries manage the political organization of refugee communities through programs that I call "refugee organization building programs," or ROBs. These programs aim to accomplish two goals: to empower refugee communities and to deliver necessary settlement services. Host country policy-makers assume that by encouraging refugees to help themselves, they can meet their own goals. This assumption derives from community capacity initiatives that became popular in the 1990s (Verity 2007). In the United States and Australia, the federal governments fund settlement organizations (what I refer to as service providers) to provide these services for newly arriving refugees.[1] Building refugee community capacity in general, and their organizational capacity in particular, is now commonly advanced by community-based advocates as the best way to provide services and expand refugee capacity. Yet, these efforts ultimately have positive and/or negative effects, depending on how these programs are implemented.

My research starts from an empirical puzzle. On the whole, Sudanese refugees are deeply concerned about transnational issues because of their life experiences and the current conditions in southern Sudan. Yet, despite this transnational political drive, the Sudanese refugee community in Australia is much less likely than the Sudanese refugee community in the United States to organize collectively toward transnational ends. In the Unietd States, the Sudanese community channels 70 percent of their collective efforts toward the social and economic development of southern Sudan. In contrast, 35 percent of Australian-based Sudanese organizations engage in similar transnational political activities.

In this chapter, I pursue three broad objectives. First, to present the case that empirical differences in Sudanese refugee political activities in the United States and Australia are partly due to how each host country manages refugee political organization through specific refugee organization-building programs. My second objective is to demonstrate how these programs channel refugee political activities towards domestic-oriented or transnational agendas. Refugees who participate in ROBs receive material and social benefits. In order to receive these benefits, refugee leaders must engage in activities that are suitable to funding agents of the host country. As political learners and strategic actors, refugees adapt to these constraints and go after these program benefits. Third, I discuss the unintended consequences of channelling refugee political activities, and how programs may undermine the essential purposes of community capacity building.

The plan of the chapter is as follows. First, I detail the research design and methods. Second, I define more fully what I mean by Refugee Organization Building programs. I demonstrate that most characteristics of these programs—their purpose, eligibility requirements, and other design components—are actually very similar in the United States and Australia. In the third section, however, I describe the key national difference of this policy. In Australia this policy is a key tool to engender self-reliance of refugee communities, while in the United States other activities, such as finding early employment for refugees, take precedence. Essentially, Australia manages refugee political organization more extensively than the United States. In the fourth section, I demonstrate how, through the material and social incentives of these ROB programs, Australian- and United States–based Sudanese refugees are guided toward domestic-focused political activities. In section five, I discuss the unintended consequences of channelling refugee political activities. The conclusion follows.

RESEARCH METHODS

I used three research methods to collect data. First, I collected descriptive data on Sudanese-created organizations in both of these national sites to determine the "target," or direction of their political activism. Second, I conducted an in-depth analysis of United States and Australian settlement policies, procedures, and programs, utilizing policy and programmatic documentation collected during fieldwork and through Internet research. Third, I conducted semi-structured interviews with key players in both countries involved in creating policy (government officials), and implementing policy (government officials, settlement administration and staff) as well as those who were the subjects of the policies (refugees).

REFUGEE CAPACITY BUILDING PROGRAMS

In Australia and the United States, ROBs are used to encourage the integration of refugee communities into society. Despite differences in the general social policy character of each country, ROB programs in these countries have common features.² Each country's objective with this program is to integrate refugee communities that are struggling to connect with resources and communities of the host country, to encourage self-reliance, and to perpetuate mutual assistance for resettled refugees. Further similarities between the programs in both countries are, first, that the policies in each country are targeted toward refugees who are new arrivals; second, each country funnels federal funds toward established refugee-led organizations, service providers, and through local or state-level governments. Below, I describe these characteristics in more detail.

The Purpose of Building Refugee Organizational Capacity

In both countries, community capacity building tools have two interconnected objectives aimed at fostering the broad goal of integrating refugee communities. The first objective is to ensure that refugee communities are able to identify their collective needs (including long-term settlement needs such as housing, employment, health, and education) and get linked into local services to meet these needs. Second, as refugees get linked into mainstream services, their level of participation with the host society should increase.

In the United States, these programs are implemented through the Department of Health and Human Service's Office of Refugee Resettlement discretionary grant, the Ethnic Self-Help Grant. The grant tender stipulates: "the objective of this program is to strengthen organized ethnic communities comprised and representative of refugee populations to ensure ongoing support and services to refugees after initial resettlement" (US Office of Refugee Resettlement 2008). A national United States advocate noted: "[E]thnic community-based organizations fill in the gaps when funding for VolAgs [i.e., voluntary agencies] run out."³ Additionally, many settlement service providers stated that building refugee organizations was the best way to build refugee capacity.

In Australia, building refugee community organizations falls under the Developing Communities pillar, one of the three domestic priorities of the Department of Immigration and Citizenship's broader Settlement Grants Programme. This pillar aims to "help newly arrived humanitarian communities to identify common goals and interests and develop a sense of identity and belonging" through initiatives to build their organizational capacity (Australia Department of Immigration and Citizenship 2010a). In practice, community development is essentially about creating organizations. As one service provider's grant proposal stated: "Successful settlement is fostered through the development and funding of refugee community organisations to deliver projects to communities" (STARTTS 2008). A representative of the Australian federal government's Settlement Grants Program seconded this strategy: "Community development strategies for some groups have consisted of helping people establish CBOs [Community Based Organizations] to help people organize, and advocate for their own needs" (personal interview). Another Settlement Grant's Programme official notes: "We recognize that it is still important to fund small organizations because of the depth of support they can provide—so we try to do this, so long as new refugees are still coming in" (personal interview).

Eligibility Requirements

The grants target refugee communities with newly arrived populations. In the United States, refugee communities originating from countries from which refugees are currently being resettled, who are "slow to integrate," and who meet citizenship requirements are eligible to receive services through the Ethnic Self-Help Grant (US Office of Refugee Resettlement 2001, 2004, 2008). For Australia's Settlement Grants Programme, only communities that have arrived in the last five years and continue to receive refugees are eligible (Department of Immigration and Citizenship 2010a; Department of Immigration and Multicultural Affairs 2003). These eligibility requirements are essentially identical.

Additionally, while eligibility requirements in both countries have changed over the last 10 years, they have grown to mimic one another. Eligibility requirements in Australia have shifted over the last decade to centre on newly arrived, "emerging" refugee communities, who have the "greatest need." Before 2005–2006, Australia did not have time-specific targets. In fact, established communities, such as the Greek and Italian, were receiving funds to build the capacity of their organizations. After a 2003 review of settlement services, it was recommended that the focus of these funds should be solely on the newly arrived (Department of Immigration and Multicultural Affairs 2003). In the United States, while priorities have generally been on the newly arrived, in 2001 the program specified particular communities, including the Sudanese. In 2004 the program was restricted to populations who have arrived in the last 10 years. Since 2008 only newly arrived communities with significant populations are eligible.

The rationale to focus on newly arrived populations derives from the notion that new arrivals have more needs and are less able to fulfill them due to lack of organization, knowledge, and connections. The Sudanese are included in this "emerging" designation. In both countries, the first decade of the 2000s has been the height of their resettlement. Settlement actors help these new communities through capacity building initiatives. An Australian settlement service provider explained: "[T]he best way to [help refugee communities] is to have the assistance of another organization that has already gone through that process, that can be supportive through that process" (personal interview). In both countries, many "types" of organizations are allowed to apply for these grants. Both countries encourage established refugee community organizations, settlement actors, and local and state government entities to apply.

Organization Building Activities

Building refugee organizational capacity includes many tasks and varies from one refugee community to another. Generally, however, it involves extending resources to refugee communities to create their organization, linking them into service provider networks, socializing leaders, and supervising their efforts. In its most basic form, this work involves educating the community about what is involved in starting an organization in a Western industrialized context. A United States state-level service provider explained: "Capacity building with Sudanese was basically how to set up an MAA [Mutual Assistance Association], how to receive 501(c)3 status, create bylaws—it was basically a 101 set up not-for-profit" (personal interview). But, it also involves finding or cultivating leadership, getting refugee organization funding, and helping communities to meet reporting requirements when funded. The executive director of an Australian settlement service organization described this process in the following way:

> As the community becomes established, that's when they start to come to you.... They get incorporated; can you help us with this funding application? They get the money. They suddenly realize that they have to do a financial report, so you can see them slowly moving through the stages of development as a community becomes established. (personal interview)

Australia's Settlement Grants Programme guides settlement actors by outlining suitable program functions, including helping leaders and community members organize, promote activities and their communities, find spaces for gatherings, and teach and connect leaders to other providers and communities for support and funding (Australia Department of Immigration and Citizenship 2010b). The United States–based Ethnic Self-Help Grant spells out similar programmatic tasks such as organizing refugee communities, leadership and organizational development, assisting refugee organizations in connecting with community resources, and for specific settlement activities that extend beyond previously established services (Office of Refugee Resettlement 2008).

In practice, as is implied above, the program involves an extensive amount of education about logistics. Settlement actors are educating refugees about the utility of organization. An Australian mid-level settlement service provider remarked: "The way to access these services is if you form yourself into a structure where there is someone who can organize, or advocate, someone you can go to, and then they can go to whoever the service providers are" (personal interview). Another Australian mid-level settlement service provider says: "We provide info sessions, letting them know what is available" (personal interview). These activities involve a certain degree of socializing them into Western ways, as an Australian settlement service provider explained: "So sometimes, it is a whole new ball game. So, it's not something you [the refugee leader] can compare and say, oh, I have seen this before. It's new" (personal interview).

For refugee community organizations to receive grant funds and/or donations to provide community services, funding bodies often require organizations to have formal non-profit status, and pre-set governing and financial structures. At the refugee organization's inception, service providers often act as an "auspicing" agent, meaning that they manage any procured funding, thereby lowering the perceived risk to fund these new organizations. To paraphrase one Australian federal grants manager:

"Communities don't have skills to manage funds, so large organizations auspice these organizations. These [refugee] organizations then get experience.... One of my roles is to train organizations who are funded.... The primary goal is to see that funds are used efficiently and for the clients" (personal interview).

Another key practical aspect of ROBs is that settlement service providers coordinate most of the work through refugee leaders. Refugee leaders are able to straddle linguistic and cultural divides between refugee and host communities and their institutions. An Australian service provider remarked: "Most leaders speak English.... And they are people who understand the culture, the way of life here, much better. [The service providers] might not understand community ... [so] ... it is better to go through a leader ... [and it is] easier to build rapport with a leader rather than with the entire community" (personal interview). The strategic benefits for providers to work with refugee leaders are similar for all settlement services, including building organizations.

In both countries, as is evident above, there are a variety of activities that grant recipients can undertake to build refugee organizational capacity. Within both countries, there are also specific activities that are barred, including anything that is considered political, activities that are geared toward cultural preservation for a specific ethnic community, and transnational activities. These are specifically stated in the program funding announcements. These restrictions aim to result in specific outcomes: that refugee community organizations develop structures that fit Western standards, are headed up by Western-like leaders, and can receive funding by Western bodies.

In this way, the effect of this social policy tool is functional and straightforward: refugees develop the ability to help themselves within the host country. In this section, I found that the specific qualities, or characteristics, of ROBs in Australia and the United States do not vary significantly. Yet, as I describe in the following section, the tool is used so extensively in Australia and not as much in the United States, shaping two distinct refugee political paths within these two countries.

DIFFERENCES IN POLICY PRIORITIES

As I illustrated in the previous section, the overarching objectives and practices of creating, building, and sustaining refugee community organizations are similar in the United States and Australia. One key difference, however, stands out sharply: Australia prioritizes this program much more than the United States. This difference matters greatly because when this program is used more often, refugee community organizations and the projects they implement, are managed, or nudged, by settlement actors toward long-term settlement benchmarks and other goals. Furthermore, in Australia, refugee community groups are managed through organizations that have strong financial and historical ties to the government.[4]

Show Me the Money: Differences in Funding for Refugee Organizations

How are these policy priorities playing out, given that each country has different types of services and means of funding settlement programs? Each country's level of spending on specific Refugee Organization Building programs is a clear indicator.

Table 15.1: Funding for Refugee Community Organization Building Tools (2000–2007)

Year	Australia	United States
2000	$7,759,667	$2,680,866
2001	$8,024,000	$4,025,994
2002	$8,225,000	$7,781,202
2003	$8,869,000	$8,011,363
2004	$9,044,000	$9,491,874
2005	$9,190,667	$8,011,363
2006	$9,931,000	$7,258,667
2007	$10,277,667	$8,481,926

Sources: Australia Department of Immigration and Citizenship (former Department of Multiculturalism and Immigration Affairs); Portfolio Budgets for Australia Department of Immigration and Citizenship, annual reports (years 1999–2000 to 2010–2011; www.immi.gov.au/about/reports/budget); *US Office of Refugee Resettlement's Annual Report to Congress* (www.acf.hhs.gov/programs/orr/data/arc.htm).

As is evident in Table 15.1, each country spent millions of dollars throughout the 2000s on these initiatives. At first glance, Australia's spending is significantly higher than United States' spending in only two years: 2000, 2001. In the early 2000s, Australia's initiatives to develop refugee organizations included funding well-established organizations, such as the Greek and Italian organizations (Department of Immigration and Multicultural Affairs 2003). After a 2003 review of United States settlement services, new and emerging communities were specifically targeted for these funding resources and long-standing communities were no longer eligible.

Yet, these figures hide the fact that the United States must distribute these funds to a much greater number of incoming refugees. The flow of refugees into the United States is much higher than in Australia (Figure 15.1). The lowest number of refugees (26,807) was resettled to the United States in 2002, the year following the terrorist attacks on September 11, 2001—when the United States almost entirely shut down its resettlement program. Australia's highest number of refugees resettled during this period (13,061 in 2004) is still less than half of the United States' lowest number. Australian settlement policy-makers and service providers often boast that Australia accepts more refugees relative to their overall population than any other country.

In addition, refugee organization building funds are much greater on a per-capita basis in Australia than the United States (Figure 15.2). Because "developing communities" is a pillar of Australian refugee services, the government funds it more extensively. Each refugee community in each settlement site is more likely to participate in these activities. This is not the case in the United States, where a smaller amount of funds are scattered throughout many more sites.

256 *Immigration and Settlement*

Table 15.1: Refugees Resettled in Australia and the United States (2000–2007)

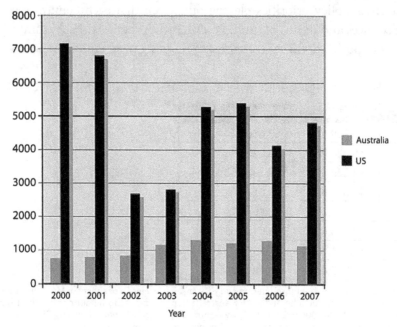

Source: Created by Author.

Table 15.2: Refugee Community Organization Funds per Refugee (2000–2007)

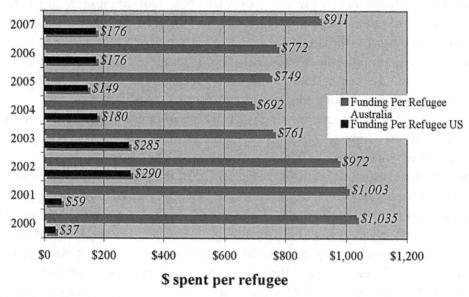

Source: Created by Author.

Service provider comments confirm how the United States' federal government is not prioritizing refugee community organization capacity building. In Australia the act of building refugee organizational capacity was almost taken for granted, and all providers went to great lengths to describe their programs to me. Conversely, in the United States it was rare to hear about similar key initiatives. One United States provider noted that federal funding is not for capacity building but "they are just program funds." The overwhelming majority of settlement actors I interviewed in the United States reiterated that the United States program is geared toward refugee self-sufficiency by means of employment.

Systems to Sustain Building Refugee Community Organizations

Outside of basic differences in funding, policy priorities are also demonstrated in the ways in which these two countries create the necessary mechanisms to a) keep refugee community organizations functioning through small grants, and b) keep service providers funded specifically for these programs. The former mechanism ensures that inexperienced refugee organizations gain experience by receiving small grants to implement programs. The latter serves to maintain and perpetuate institutional knowledge about the quotidian practices of organizing refugee communities and leaders.

In Australia, refugee organizations, once they are established, often acquire new funds through local government funding. The federal government and local service providers often work in sync with local governments to help build refugee community capacity. The federal government supplements local government funds, and requires service providers to work closely with these entities. Consequently, local governments along with settlement service providers end up providing much-needed resources to emerging refugee community organizations. A settlement service provider who works specifically on developing Sudanese refugee organizations illustrates this situation:

> [The] Kingston government, another local government in the area, provided the [settlement service provider] with a number of buildings that community groups could use free of charge—so [a refugee leader] was provided access to office space where they could meet—and then [the refugee organization] got incorporation status, and we helped [the refugee leader] write funding submissions to the state government ... and to local councils in the area—particularly Monash and Kingston—and as a result they got more sums of money: $3,000–$5,000 to do particular projects. (personal interview)

In the United States context, after organizations are established (i.e., incorporated and with a leadership structure), they cannot always remain financially afloat. A representative of a United States state agency servicing refugees stated: "We developed an umbrella organization for Africans—[but] it was hard to fund" (personal interview). The Ethnic Self-Help grant is a discretionary grant. Unlike cash, medical, and employment assistance funds, these programmatic resources are neither distributed through states nor do they reach local-level institutions. In general, local-level institutions, such as city and municipal governance bodies, are generally not involved in funding refugee organizations or settlement services.

Australia's extensive federal funding for refugee organization building has established the necessary institutional structures and experiential know-how to sustain these programs. Many organizations have specific staff whose sole purpose is to build refugee community capacity. For example, several organizations I interviewed had community development workers or specialists. This is not the case in the United States, where core funding for staff members with the sole task of refugee community capacity building is unavailable.

Trade-Offs

United States advocates, service providers, refugee scholars, and policy activists point out that there are essential trade-offs. Due to the large number of individuals receiving refugee status in the United States, there can neither be the same level nor the variety of services (including refugee organization building) that are provided in Australia. One United States advocate explained:

> When you are looking at the federal government's definition of success, we need to be fair and look at the big numbers. The only country that is even close to this number is Canada. There is a huge gap in numbers: US is by far the largest. When that many numbers are being resettled, other countries may be providing more, but it is a tradeoff. (personal interview)

On the whole, a supportive culture of refugee organization building is present in Australia and lacking in the United States. The funding and institutional support for these programs has reinforced and perpetuated programs in Australia, while these elements are missing in the United States. In the next section, I examine differences in the management of ROB programs in Australia and the United States, and how refugee leaders are channelled, or guided, toward domestic-focused political activities.

MANAGING REFUGEE LEADERS

Australian and American bureaucrats attempt to shape refugee political activities with programs that cultivate refugee organizations, especially for purposes they believe are suitable to both the host country and to incoming refugee populations. They seek to create better conditions in which refugee leaders can carry out ongoing settlement activities involving refugee communities. Yet, bureaucrats and providers are not the only decision-makers in this social process. Savvy refugee political leaders seek to secure the material and social goods provided through ROBs. As one refugee leader describes: "We worked with [a service provider], who connect[ed] us with others, [and who] helps us with grants, trainings" (personal interview). That these are necessary political prerequisites is no mystery to refugee leaders, many of whom had prior leadership experience in Kakuma refugee camp. For example, some were "Zone leaders," looking after groups of young boys, ensuring their needs were met. Others were leaders of drama, conflict resolution, and HIV training programs. Still others were church leaders and even teachers. These experiences, as well as just generally living in a refugee camp, served to teach them valuable skills about acquiring resources and building relationships to meet their needs. Below, I describe the material and social incentives provided through ROBs.

Material Incentives

The material wherewithal for newly developing refugee organizations and leaders includes in-kind support and funding for programs and salaries. These material benefits present incentives for refugee leaders to engage in certain domestic activities over others, and draw them away from transnational political activities. In particular, these benefits provide support for refugee organizations' infrastructure, including places to work, a mailing address, and office supplies and support. For example, when one leader came to the Ecumenical Migration Centre, a non-profit settlement service organization in Melbourne, in the mid-2000s, a mid-level settlement service worker noted that they realized "the need for him to have an office … and then it was a question of, how can we best support him and his organization. And that's when we offered him space" (personal interview). Another Sudanese refugee leader commented on how "one [Australian] person has offered a building in Dandenong for free" (personal interview), and how another community supporter he met through Springville Aid, a settlement organization in Melbourne, provided the furniture.

Settlement organizations guide refugee leaders through the development of their refugee organization. This involves helping them receive funding. During this guiding process, refugee leaders are often nudged to pursue certain goals, and not others. Many providers see this "translation" of the goals of eager refugee leaders into aims that are more doable and activities that are more fundable, as a necessary element of building refugee organizations. An Australian settlement service provider stated: "[T]he communities, they are really keen, but it's a challenge to translate that keenness into actually where you want [them] to go" (personal interview). This is no surprise: settlement service providers are mandated to implement the policies for which they receive funding.

This act of channelling includes shaping what "type" of domestic activity the refugee community organizations undertake. One Melbourne-based provider's comments reflect a common provider sentiment. She noted that refugee organizations need to strategically propose projects suitable to donors and therefore redirect refugee leaders away from their original funding proposal ideas. "It might be great to do a cultural event, but increasingly it's difficult to get funding for that—maybe look at issues of positive parenting" (personal interview). In Australia, the "donors" are generally local and state governments, who often receive larger grants from the federal governments for refugee organizational activities.

Provider channelling also shifts refugee political leaders' foci from transnational goals towards domestic-related goals. The story of the development of one prominent Australian-based Sudanese organization epitomizes this process. A refugee leader initially approached a settlement organization provider stating: "We are very worried about our community back home, how can we help?" The provider comments:

> [We] explained that as an agency, our focus is on refugees in Australia, so you know, we talked about that with him. We said we understood his concerns with the community back home, but he wasn't going to be able to—it would be difficult to attract funding for money back home because there were also very high needs within the immediate community here, within the southern region [of Sydney]. (personal interview)

This leader "listened to that, and acknowledged that and agreed that there was also a lot of worthwhile work that he could be doing here" (personal interview). The settlement organization went on to guide this leader through the organizational incorporation process, finding office space, linking him up to other leaders in refugee service provision, and writing funding applications. Over several years, the organization became more established and was able to slowly procure larger grants. This story is not unique. In order to create a viable organization, refugee leaders are encouraged to follow the funding. They are also nudged by the work opportunities that arise from engaging in domestic settlement and fundraising activities. This includes traineeships with service providers, and as a mid-level Australian service provider stated, "funding for them to work in their own communities" (personal interview).

A final source of channelling refugee leaders through material benefits is when settlement actors "auspice," or manage, the finances of grants that refugee organizations procure. In Australia, donors are more likely to provide funding to new organizations when the funds are secured by an established Australian organization. This is a critical benefit provided during the community capacity building process and one way that organizations are nudged. The executive of a settlement organization noted: "Although [the Women's Refugee Network, a refugee community-based organization] have their own funds, and they are incorporated, basically our organization handles the money for them and [we] point them in the direction that this is a better way" (personal interview).

Channelling is a necessary part of the current model of building refugee organizations, especially given specific funding constraints in regard to both funding for settlement actors and upcoming refugee organizations. Helping refugees engage in transnational work is not a part of the mission of settlement organizations. For example, when I asked a United States provider about her experience working with Sudanese refugees to engage in transnational activities, her comment echoed numerous other providers: "I'm focused on America" (personal interview). Instead, she suggested that refugees are better served partnering with organizations already involved in transnational work. This is a difficult task, especially when the refugees have not developed strong social networks. Nevertheless, this channelling process does not entirely preclude refugee organizations from engaging in transnational activities in the long term. Although it is not in the "brief" of settlement actors, one service provider noted that once refugees are "on their own, they can look at how they can help others at home. If those groups can on their own decide they want to do something specific to their country, they raise funds for building schools over there" (personal interview).

Social Incentives

Another seminal political requirement for refugee leaders is a large social network. Through ROBs, refugee leaders are linked into such broad social networks, which lead to more resources. A Sydney Sudanese refugee organizational leader explained: "In Australia, we have agencies, and so you connect [with them]—so if I have an idea—these people connect me—they show me the agency—or the way you get the funding" (personal interview).

Effective capacity building expands refugee social networks in many ways. Refugee leaders are encouraged to attend interagency meetings with multiple social service providers (in one case over 80), including the police, fire department, legal offices, and the media. They discuss issues such as crime, discrimination, and cultural misunderstandings. Other interagency meetings involve local and state government officials and health care service providers, where participants discuss ways to better work together. Settlement organizations arrange these meetings with the specific objective of making social connections for refugee leaders, as they see themselves as an intermediary between refugees and mainstream service providers. A mid-level settlement service provider in Australia explained: "So, I actually started a meeting called the Sudanese Community Action Network—the purpose is to bring leaders together to meet with service providers—so leaders, fire brigade, police, different welfare organizations, the state government, the local government are represented" (personal interview).

These connections foster relationships between refugees and "mainstream" actors and deepen cross-cultural understanding. One Australian service provider established the "Sudanese Leadership Dialogue," involving refugee leaders and Australian local and state officials. This network facilitated discussion between leaders on key domestically related topics such as consequences of not understanding family law and driving regulations. This resulted in identifying key settlement needs, and finding innovative solutions. For example, one family court justice, after attending one of these Leadership Dialogue sessions, took dowry into account in a court ruling. Due to these expanding social networks, refugee leaders are able to get increasingly involved with new domestic projects and political activities.

Due to different service environments, refugee social connections varied between host countries. In the United States, because of the public-private structure of settlement services (where financial and in-kind resources and social support are provided by governments and private groups), settlement providers rely heavily on the work of volunteers. When I asked in an interview if the staff assistant to one United States state refugee services agency was involved in capacity building, the participant responded: "The people who really built their capacity were really some of the groups that came alongside of them: American volunteers" (personal interview).

Generally speaking, refugees in the United States find themselves connecting with a wider range of people, including church members. In Australia, where federal and local governments fund the program almost entirely, providers do not rely on volunteers to implement their projects. The Australian government more tightly manages refugee settlement. This reduces the scope of refugee social networks. While ROBs facilitate the development of social networks, they also shape the target of refugee political activities. For example, when leaders work with "mainstream" service providers, they must engage their communities in projects that these providers want to pursue.

Positive results of the formation of refugee social networks include the education and socialization of refugees (as well as mainstream social providers). Refugee leaders need these political resources and skills and use them to their benefit. Moreover, I found that in this process refugees are subtly channelled toward domestic-related political activities. In this next section, I examine the unintentional consequences of capacity building policy tools that run contrary to the basic purposes of these tools.

UNINTENDED CONSEQUENCES

The ROB building program, which establishes a refugee community organization from a group of unorganized but spirited people, has multiple consequences. On the one hand, as I have described above, it has tangible effects on refugee political participation. It provides refugee leaders with technical skills, resources, and social networks. It channels these same leaders' efforts toward productive domestic-related settlement activities. These are intentional consequences. Yet, on the other hand, two particularly salient inadvertent impacts are: a) the creation of barriers to refugee self-determination through messages such as, "we know better than you"; and b) the generation of distrust and animosity between refugee leaders and settlement actors when refugees perceive that settlement actors are more concerned with getting funding than with the overall well-being of the refugee community.

Who Knows Best?

Settlement actors consciously and unconsciously inhibit the evolvement of self-determination in the refugee community by limiting input from this community during the refugee organization building process. This practice undercuts the broader purpose of building refugee capacity. In their role as policy implementers, professional service providers wield considerable power over the refugees. Rather than sharing decision-making power, settlement actors often dominate and even dictate rather than motivate, thereby maintaining control over the projects refugee organizations will pursue and the process of capacity building.

As I illustrated in the previous section, settlement actors are often constrained by the demands of donors, such as the Australia Department of Immigration and Citizenship and local governments and the United States Office of Refugee Resettlement. In addition, several refugee leaders in Australia expressed a concern that settlement organizations do not involve them in the more practical decision-making processes, such as choosing projects for specific settlement issues. This can unintentionally send the message that refugees do not have their own ideas about how to solve prickly settlement problems and that the service providers know the needs of the refugees better than the refugees themselves. One provider sought to confront these issues and has therefore assisted in the establishment of new systems in which the settlement actors would guide rather than control projects. This example will be examined fully later.

This unintended dynamic also plays out in regard to refugee leaders pursuing domestic rather than transnational activities. Several refugee leaders noted that often providers do not understand the importance of transnational responsibilities. Settlement actors often view these concerns as a "mental health" issue, something for the refugees to "get over." Conversely, the refugee leaders see them as a socio-political problem, one of major concern to themselves and their communities. The act of channelling refugees solely toward specific domestic-related, donor-approved activities and away from activities directed at dealing with situations in their native land can send the message that "we—not you—know what's best for you and your community."

This message may be sent even more regularly through the daily interactions between settlement actors and refugee leaders. Settlement actors teach refugee leaders the legal and bureaucratic logistics of creating an organization. This means, as the executive director of one Australian settlement organization noted: "[Setting] up an organization according to Australian norms and the Australian legal system" (personal interview). A United States state-level service provider explains that technical know-how includes "what it means to work with the community, [establishing] a board of directors, responsibilities ... then [how to handle] fiscal management, measuring results, [and] raising money" (personal interview). Refugee leaders are also socialized through training sessions on how to engage in "appropriate" organizational practices according to Western values and models (such as democratic governance, transparency, and accountability).

While Sudanese refugees often come to Western countries with little or no experience in dealing with Western institutions, they are not "uncivilized"—a term that one settlement provider use to describe them (in front of a Sudanese refugee who worked in the same organization). In my interviews, I got the sense that some settlement providers saw the Sudanese communities as incapable. The executive director of a settlement organization commented four times about the lack of appropriate leadership in the Sudanese community—saying that they needed to realize that one person cannot be "El Supremo" or "El Presidente." This same person was frustrated with what she saw as a lack of ability on the part of Sudanese community leaders to engage in "appropriate" dialogue among its members. Instead, she suggested, Sudanese leaders were either making all the decisions on their own, or taking "10 hours" to discuss every detail with other organizational members. Helping refugee leaders master these leadership and organizational skills is vital. The attitude with which policy implementers approach their clients is also key to effective capacity building.

The comments of one mid-level settlement service provider are worth quoting at length because they show that the manner in which capacity building was implemented by this organization was unintentionally demotivating refugee leaders.

> So we've been in this room, and we're having meetings and we're talking and they are listening. To the point where I had to stop and say, "What is going on here?" And they would say, "We don't know what you're talking about." And the Western, or Anglo, the professional way of approaching a meeting is that you go through this, this [pointing, like at agenda items], and this to go through, and if there are no objections, you move on. Whereas I think their way of—a cultural difference, that needs to be respected, and acknowledged, and I think we have a lot to learn from them. Because the feedback … was that we weren't actually listening and we weren't on the same page. So one of their committee members that was present had not said anything at all and the feedback was that he was the most vocal out of all of them, but the way that the meeting had been run, he had been disempowered. And that's how they feel out in society, out there—they feel that the power—they felt that the power was with us—we had the power without even realizing. We were thinking, this is for them, this project. But the way the meeting was run, it was saying the opposite. (personal interview)

This service provider's power came from having a better command of the English language and using terminology unrecognizable to Sudanese. Setting the agenda and the practices of the meetings and controlling the process were additional acts of power. Unbeknownst to the provider, these actions served to exclude the refugee participants. After reflection and extensive feedback from the Sudanese refugees of this group, this same provider became aware of the "cross-cultural aspect" and the power inequities of community capacity building, and worked toward "mak[ing] space for them—not in a patronizing way" (personal interview). This new approach was accomplished when the provider consciously chose "not [to] assume that things should be done in a particular way. That's been a learning experience for *us* [my emphasis]" (personal interview). This new approach involves a continual process of negotiation in which refugees' practices are respected: "[T]he negotiation aspect is really important, and it's about the parties having equal power—so they are a subject of that negotiation—rather than an object of that negotiation." In the end, this approach may not meet the expectations of efficiency of organizational practices in Australia and other Western industrialized countries, but it could be a more effective capacity building strategy. As the same service provider noted: "So, it's respecting that the decisions may take longer, but the process was more important than the outcome" (personal interview).

Before this particular provider established new power-sharing practices, refugee leaders received the message: "We know better than you." Creating a new modus operandi took effort on the part of the provider—asking for and accepting feedback, and significantly changing attitude and methods. It required that the refugee participants give honest feedback, despite power differences.

Whose Side Are You On?

Refugee settlement actors are constrained by the objectives and regulations of their donors. The concern with donor wishes can overshadow the concern for refugee needs. I found that this situation bred suspicion about whose "side" settlement actors were actually on, or in other words, whose interests most concerned them. One particular example was quite important to many in the Sudanese community. Former Australian immigration minister Kevin Andrews publicly stated on October 1, 2007, that Sudanese refugees were unable to integrate (Farouque, Petrie and Miletic 2007). Most settlement service providers did not speak out against these negative comments. Some providers stated that responding to such remarks was the role of Sudanese organizational leaders. Providers mentioned that they should not speak out against the minister's comments to avoid going beyond their organization's mission (or mission creep). Other providers pointed to specific regulations in their funding contracts that barred them from "political" activity.[5] Many Sudanese leaders interpreted this inaction as an indication that providers were more interested in keeping their funding than supporting Sudanese refugees. Given that providers are usually closer to refugee populations than other citizens of the host country and expected to be allies of the refugees, this was a particularly hard blow to the Sudanese community. One former African refugee noted that if providers are not on refugees' sides, "then who is" (personal interview).

One other example, recounted by an interviewee who was troubled by the extent to which providers were too focused on funding, highlights this same concern. In an effort to promote an upcoming event, a service provider called another organization saying, "we need black faces" (personal interview). For the interviewee recounting the story, this request stemmed from the desire to appear to be "in good graces" with Sudanese in order to win another federal government grant. This dynamic is not solely created by less-than-thoughtful service providers; it stems from several interrelated factors including a competitive funding system and the targeting of particular refugee and migrant groups. Nevertheless, such statements do not bode well for relationship or capacity building, and reduce the effectiveness of the program's original intention.

CONCLUSION

In this chapter, I have demonstrated how settlement policies such as the funding of refugee organization building programs shape the political activities of refugees in receiving countries. In essence, through these programs, service providers not only educate, but also channel refugees towards particular political goals. Through specific refugee organization building programs, settlement policies provide necessary political requisites for refugees, including financial and other types of resources, skills, and access to social networks. But they also channel them towards particular country-specific political aims, particularly domestic-focused activities. Additionally, I find that settlement policy agents also disempower refugees through such processes of channelling.

The findings suggest recommendations for policy-makers in each of these countries, as well as those dealing with global refugee protection. First, policy-makers should review the unintentional consequences of the use of professional and volunteer policy implementers. This includes a pointed look at how policies and service provider–refugee interactions foster or impede refugee social, political, and economic activities and their effects on refugee self-determination. Second, evaluation and dialogue about refugee resettlement should be markedly ramped up. In so doing, new and older refugee settlement countries will benefit. These efforts are likely to enhance integration efforts by supporting refugees toward self-sufficiency.

This project has demonstrated that refugees respond to their interactions with policy implementers. Through these settlement-refugee interactions, policy implementers have multiple inadvertent influences on refugee leaders. These can alter the paths of their activities and their political efficacy and hinder the development of overall self-esteem and self-determination. I recommend that each country sincerely examines these unintended consequences. With regard to the former, the United States and Australia would benefit from acknowledging and evaluating how their programs and policy implementers influence refugee social and political practices and how these in turn impact paths to and levels of integration. For example, given differences in centralization and institutionalization of national social policy, will refugee political, social, and economic activity be more individualistic in some countries than in others? Will more individuals, rather than groups, within a community enact political activities? Unfortunately I was not able to assess this aspect with the data I collected. Yet, these questions are important for policy-makers and service providers alike and should be a focus of future research.

With regard to the second unintended consequence, I find two specific outcomes of refugee–policy implementer interaction that should be remedied: a) the creation of barriers to refugee self-determination through messages that "we know better than you"; and b) the generation of distrust and animosity between refugee leaders and settlement actors when refugees perceive settlement actors to be more concerned with their funding than refugee well-being. In order to reduce the "harm" done to newcomers, American and Australian settlement service providers can become more mindful during interpersonal exchanges and when channelling or guiding newcomers toward specific activities. These effects are related to limitations of resources available to settlement policy implementers. Some providers would aptly explain that their time is short, and they cannot always spend additional time explaining things, and reflecting on their own interactions. This is understandable. Nevertheless, the importance of building rapport, ensuring critical information is conveyed, and building the esteem of refugees cannot be overstated. I recommend that providers receive ongoing training in creating proper boundaries with refugees and help in developing coping mechanisms to deal with stress.

Furthermore, I suggest that settlement countries consider seeking creative ways to empower newcomers' transnational endeavours by combining them with their own international development initiatives. Canada, and some European countries, have already begun to make this link and develop the appropriate institutional mechanisms to enact it. With South Sudanese refugees' overwhelming support of Independence from Sudan, this development-migrant link is only more vital. Transnational political action on the part of Sudanese refugees has not yet reached its fullest potential. Host countries could mobilize these efforts even more and serve their own interests in seeing to the healthy development of future South Sudan.

My research suggests that the policy-makers and implementers of these two refugee settlement programs could benefit immensely from a cross-dialogue with one another and that the strengths of these programs combined could be offered as a new "model" of refugee settlement services. To this end, I recommend that the Office of the United Nations High Commissioner for Refugees (UNHCR) increase its evaluative and information exchange resources in the specific area of Third Country Resettlement, and specifically at the level of domestic assistance following the refugees' arrival in the new host country.

ACKNOWLEDGEMENTS

I thank my advisor Kristi Andersen for her pointed suggestions and motivation. I am grateful, too, for the financial and academic assistance provided by the Political

Science Department of Syracuse University. The support I received from interview participants and colleagues is also greatly appreciated. Finally, I extend a special thanks to my father, John Allerdice, for his unwavering guidance throughout this doctoral experience. Any errors are my own.

ENDNOTES

1. In the United States, 10 voluntary agencies and national networks of their affiliate organizations provide the bulk of refugee services along with a great deal of volunteer support. In Australia, more than 160 non-profit organizations provide these refugee services, with much less help from volunteers. In Australia, local government councils are also often key players in programs to build refugee organizations.
2. This is reflected in the general policies to settle refugees as well. In the Australian system funds are administered at the federal government level, while in the United States, funds are distributed through states. Additionally, the Australian program provides more extensive services relative to the United States. The former focuses more on building refugee capacity to access services as all Australians do, while in the United States, the program is more geared toward getting refugees employed quickly.
3. *Ethnic community-based organizations* is a term generally used to connote community organizations comprised of members from the same nationality or ethnicity. It is used more in the United States. In Australia, refugee-led organizations are often called refugee community-based organizations.
4. These settlement organizations are comprised of many non-profit organizations, including (but not limited to) larger ones such as Anglicare, "Vinnies", and Migrant Resource Centres scattered throughout Australia.
5. Not every settlement organization refrained from speaking out. Some were signatories on a letter sent to Kevin Andrews, for example.

REFERENCES

Department of Immigration and Citizenship. 2010a. "Settlement Grants Programme Application Information." Australian Government. No longer available on line.
———. 2010b. "Settlement Grants Programme Services Funded." Accessed August 2010. www.immi.gov.au/living-in-australia/delivering-assistance/settlement-grants/what-sgp-services.htm.
Department of Immigration and Multicultural Affairs. 2003. "Review of Settlement Services for Migrants and Humanitarian Entrants 2003." Accessed August 2010. www.immi.gov.au/living-in-australia/delivering-assistance/government-programs/settlement-policy/review-settlement-services.htm.
Farouque, F., A. Petrie, and D. Miletic. 2007. "Minister Cuts African Refugee Intake." *The Age*, October 2. Accessed December 13, 2010. www.theage.com.au/articles/2007/10/01/1191091031242.html.

Office of Refugee Resettlement. 2001. "Standing Announcement for the Ethnic Community Self-Help Program." In *Federal Register*, May 9 Accessed August 20, 2010. frwebgate.access.gpo.gov/cgi-bin/getpage.cgi?position=all&page=23714&dbname=2001_register.

Office of Refugee Resettlement. 2004. "Standing Announcement for the Ethnic Community Self-Help Program." In *Federal Register*, April 23. Accessed August 7, 2011. edocket.access.gpo.gov/2004/pdf/04-9183.pdf..

Office of Refugee Resettlement. 2008. "Standing Announcement for the Ethnic Community Self-Help Program." Accessed August 20, 2010. www.acf.hhs.gov/grants/open/HHS-2008-ACF-ORR-RE-0117.html.

STARTTS. 2008. "STARTTS' Submission to DIAC's 2008/09 Refugee and Humanitarian Intake Program, March 2008." Accessed August 2010. www.startts.org.au/ContentFiles/Startts/Documents/DIAC%20intake%20submission%2008-09%20final.pdf.

Verity, F. 2007. "Community Capacity Building: A review of the Literature." For the South Australia Department of Health, Health Promotion Branch. Accessed August 2010. www.publications.health.sa.gov.au/wplan/1/.

Chapter 16

INTERNATIONAL STUDENTS AS IMMIGRANTS

ERIKA GATES-GASSE

INTRODUCTION

With the swelling of international student numbers in Canada and the push by the federal and provincial governments to encourage their immigration, the settlement needs of international students are becoming an increasingly important policy issue that is receiving very little public attention. What kinds of services and supports do international students considering immigration require? What kinds of services and supports will increase the likelihood that they will choose to immigrate? What are national and international examples of good practices? These are questions that I consider in this chapter, with the hope of energizing discussion at both the public and policy levels. There are important factors that support the integration of international students and influence them in their decision to remain permanently. This chapter demonstrates that by supporting international students with services, governments demonstrate how they value them both as individuals and as possible immigrants, therefore increasing the likelihood that they will choose to immigrate.

In the next section, I present the context of international student mobility, their pathways to immigration, and their eligibility for services. Thereafter, I review the existing literature, followed by a section in which I examine good practices. In the final section, I present key challenges and recommendations. This research was undertaken under the auspices of World Education Services as part of its ongoing commitment to exploring this emerging policy area.

CONTEXT

International Student Trends

Over the last 20 years, international student mobility trends have changed profoundly as higher education has become a growing export industry. Globally, from 2000 to 2008, the number of international students has doubled from 1.8 million to 3.3 million (OECD 2010). In Canada, international student numbers at all levels of education have more than doubled in 10 years, from 114,046 in 2000 to 218,161 in 2010 (CIC 2009, 2011b1). At a post-secondary level, numbers have increased by 96 percent from 78,710 in 2000 to 154,199 in 2009 (CIC 2009). Ontario, the province with the largest number of international students, experienced an increase of 188 percent at the post-secondary level, from 19,934 in 1999 to 57,535 in 2009.[1] In addition, the Ontario Government recently announced that it plans to increase international student enrolment by another 50 percent over the next five years (Office of the Premier 2010) to approximately 86,000 international students.

In countries such as Canada, where immigration will soon account for all net population growth, international students are increasingly viewed as "designer immigrants" (Simmons 1999) who will be able to avoid the employment barriers regularly encountered by highly skilled immigrants by virtue of their Canadian education, integration, and work experience. While there is currently no conclusive evidence, preliminary research suggests that former international student status does provide some indication of better economic outcomes (Sweetman and Warman 2009). Furthermore, international students can be a creative immigration strategy to support the population and economic growth of less traditional immigrant destinations, such as the Atlantic region. Most importantly, international students who become connected to Canadian communities and well-integrated, are more likely to express a strong desire to stay and immigrate (Halifax Global 2005). If international students are indeed individuals that Canada wants to retain as immigrants, from a government policy perspective, there is a need for comprehensive settlement services and supports for international students to facilitate a smooth transition towards their full integration and participation in Canadian society.

Canadian Work Experience and Immigration Pathways: Retention through Policy Reform

To increase its edge in attracting international students, both as migrants and immigrants, Canada has introduced significant reforms to allow for Canadian work experience and clear immigration pathways. In 2006 international students were given the right to work off-campus during their studies for up to 20 hours a week during school and full-time on off-semesters (CIC 2011c). As of 2008 postgraduation work permits were revamped significantly to allow international students without a job offer to work anywhere in Canada in any field for up to three years (although the permit cannot be longer than the length of their educational program) (CIC 2011d).

Two clear immigration pathways from within the country now exist: the federal Canadian Experience Class (CEC) and the Provincial Nominee Programs (PNPs). Most of these programs represent a "two-step" approach to immigration, whereby migrants "earn" their permanent residency by working for a number of years in Canada. Given the current policies on international student tuition and access to settlement services, these programs also represent a shift towards immigrants who are self-funded in terms of education, skills development, and integration.

Announced in 2008, the CEC international student stream allows for international students with a Canadian degree from a recognized institution to apply for expedited permanent residency after completing one or two years of Canadian work experience in an occupation classified as managerial, professional, technical, or skilled trade according to the National Occupational Classification Matrix. In addition, the CEC requires proof of English or French language proficiency (based on the occupational classification) (CIC 2011a). While the volume of CEC applications has been lower than expected, the federal government projects granting permanent residency to up to 25,000 principal applicants, spouses, and dependents by 2014 for both international students and temporary foreign workers.[2] Based on the preliminary CEC data available for 2009, 869 of 1,176 successful CEC applicants were admitted through the international student stream,[3] suggesting that international students will make up the majority of CEC applicants in future years.

As a second new pathway to immigration, the federal government and the provinces negotiated PNPs designed to encourage skilled immigrants to settle in those provinces. Manitoba was the first to implement its PNP in 1999, followed by Saskatchewan, New Brunswick, Newfoundland, Nova Scotia, and Prince Edward Island. All provinces and territories except Nunavut now have a PNP, each designed differently according to provincial priorities—many with specified streams. Provinces nominate applicants for permanent residency who are then assessed and approved by Citizenship and Immigration Canada. All provinces except New Brunswick, Prince Edward Island, and the territories have specifically designed international student streams within their PNPs to provide an expedited pathway to permanent residency. For international students to qualify, some PNPs require Canadian work experience while others do not; some are employer driven (requiring job offers) while others are applicant driven; some require in-province education; and most only accept education from a publicly funded institution (see Appendix for a breakdown of PNP programs). While the volume of international students admitted through PNPs varies by province, use of the program has been growing. As the volume of permanent residents admitted through the CEC and PNP increases, the volume admitted through the Federal Skilled Worker Program will be decreased in proportion, which is a significant change to the functioning of the Canadian immigration system.

Settlement Services and Integration: A Need for Policy Reform

The number of former international students immigrating to Canada through all channels has almost doubled in the last five years, from roughly 5,500 in 2003 to more than 10,000 in 2008 (CIC 2009).[4] Yet successful immigration and settlement is not based solely on simplified and accelerated work permit procedures and permanent residency pathways. As explained by the Deputy Minister of Citizenship and Immigration (CIC) at the time: "Ultimately, the goal of integration is to encourage newcomers to be fully engaged in the economic, social, political and cultural life of Canada" (Dorais 2002). Integration into Canadian society is an enormously important component of the settlement process, and it is not a process that can be successfully undertaken solely by the (prospective) immigrant. Section 3 (1)(e) of the Immigration and Refugee Protection Act (IRPA) recognizes that "integration involves mutual obligations for new immigrants and Canadian society" (Government of Canada 2001). In order to fulfill this objective, the federal government funds a complex array of settlement services and support programs.

Unfortunately, the IRPA only considers the successful integration of permanent residents and convention refugees, and not international students, their spouses, and dependents (among others), until they have earned permanent residency which can easily take 10 years after first entering the country to study. Provincial governments also provide settlement services, and in most provinces international students are able to access these services based on more relaxed eligibility criteria. However, among all the settlement services, provincial settlement services tend to be a minority. For example, in Ontario, only about 20 percent of settlement services are funded by the province and 80 percent by the federal government.

While one of the attractions of international students to our governments is that they are self-funded, there needs to be a change in the settlement system to serve the needs of these migrants. Just as current policies recognize that different groups (e.g., refugees, women, highly skilled immigrants) require different support programs, there should be recognition of the needs of international students as a distinct group. As the literature review below demonstrates, it should not be taken as a given that international students will not encounter some of the same barriers to entering the Canadian labour market as skilled workers do, such as lack of Canadian work experience, poor networks, or language fluency.

Taking into account the intense competition for international students and skilled immigrants at an international level, the federal and provincial governments cannot take for granted that international students who study in Canada will choose to stay. Permanent stay rates in Canada stand at about 18 percent, compared to over 29 percent in Germany and 27 percent in France (OECD 2010). In addition, a New Zealand survey demonstrates that the intention to apply for permanent residency does not guarantee that an international student also intends to apply for citizenship (Butcher 2004). In Canada, the intention to stay is generally much higher than actual stay rates: a 2007 survey of Chinese international students at the University of

Saskatchewan found that 35 percent had a strong intention and 53 percent had a moderate intention to stay (Lu, Zong, and Schissel 2009). A 2009 survey of international students in Atlantic Canada found that 40 percent of all respondents intended to apply for permanent residency (Siddiq et al. 2010).

LITERATURE REVIEW

As international student migration has grown over the years, research on the integration and adaptation challenges and needs of international students has proliferated. However, there has been very little international research that considers the settlement and service needs specific to international students who intend to immigrate or enter their host country's workforce after graduation. While research findings related to other migrant groups, such as skilled workers and temporary foreign workers, may be applicable to international students, this literature review examines research focusing specifically on international students intending to immigrate. Much of the current research identified for this literature review was produced by Canadian organizations and Canadian graduate students and focuses on the factors influencing these students in choosing to stay after graduation to work and/or begin the immigration process. This literature notes that international students are a diverse group, with different locations of study and cultural backgrounds that influence their needs. As far as I could identify, there is no Canadian or international research that considers the differences in settlement needs between university and college students or between smaller and larger post-secondary institutions; the settlement needs of international students, beyond concerns over job opportunities and labour market integration, in the period between their graduation and the receipt of permanent residency; and the settlement needs of students' spouses and dependents.

The identified literature on service and support needs is divided up into the five following sections: job and career support, social and emotional support, academic and language support, immigration support and information, and international student offices.

Job and Career Support

Heike Alberts and Helen Hazen (2006) conducted a survey of 185 international students at the University of Michigan. They found that while personal and societal factors tend to influence international students in the United States to return home, economic and professional factors provide incentive to stay in the host country after graduation; 64 percent said that the prospect of better jobs and career opportunities compared to their country of origin was influencing them to stay after graduation (Alberts and Hazen 2006, 209).

The 2009 Survey of International Students, conducted by the Canadian Bureau of International Education (CBIE 2009), is considered the most comprehensive

Canadian survey of its kind. This study found that half of surveyed university students and three-quarters of college students choose to study in Canada because of postgraduate work opportunities (CBIE 2009, 19), and that 51 percent of university students and 57 percent of college students plan on applying for permanent residency (316). A 2006 survey of over 2,500 of Montreal's international students found that 49 percent cited available employment in their field of study as a reason to stay on after completing their studies (CROP 2006, 16). Similarly, a 2009 survey of Chinese international students at the University of Saskatchewan (Lu, Zong, and Schissel 2009) revealed a strong, positive association between working off-campus during studies and the intention to immigrate. These findings highlight the link between postgraduation and off-campus work opportunities and the desire to immigrate, and point to the importance of providing employment training and job opportunities as a settlement service.

Based on the responses of 900 international students participating in surveys, focus groups, and individual interviews, a 2007 report for the CBIE by Sheryl Bond provides insight into international student needs in preparing for the postgraduate work search. As Bond notes, it takes more than a degree to get a job: previous work experience, especially Canadian work experience, is essential. One respondent stated: "There are not many options for jobs for international students, as most employers need Canadian experience" (Bond 2007, 18). When asked what advice they would give new students, those respondents who were in or had recently entered the labour force stressed the importance of being connected, networking, volunteering, and gaining work experience. They also highlighted having a co-op or internship placement as part of their studies. Angela Bohonos (2009) makes the point that lack of experience and exposure to the Canadian workplace "often results in failure to understand the unwritten norms of behaviour, especially non-verbal behaviours" for international students (Bohonos 2009, 47). Having Canadian work or volunteer experience provides familiarity with workplace expectations and a smoother transition into the labour market.

Yet 70 percent of the respondents in Bond's study reported that getting involved in extra-curricular activities (including work) was difficult to varying degrees (Bond 2007, 22). Of the respondents who were still in school, only 34 percent had any work experience (23). Although changes to off-campus work permits have been introduced and expanded, the 2009 CBIE Survey of International Students reports that only 18 percent of university students and 22 percent of college students worked off-campus for pay. On a positive note, when considering on-campus work as well, the percentage increased considerably to 46 percent of university and 32 percent of college students (CBIE 2009, 50). A greater understanding of how to support and encourage international students in pursuing work and volunteer opportunities, especially off-campus where they increase their exposure to employers, is essential to their settlement. A recommendation by Bohonos (2009) is early career planning intervention (described later in the section Good Practices: Current Projects and Programs for International

Students Intending to Immigrate) so that international students are more likely to pursue work and volunteer experience.

Furthermore, international students experience unique challenges in entering the Canadian labour market and thus require targeted services. Bond's report by CBIE (2007, 18) found that due to real or perceived barriers, 68 percent of the international student respondents did not plan to stay in Canada to work. Nearly 80 percent of the respondents cited pessimism about job prospects and career opportunities as a concern.

Despite changes to work permit regulations in 2006 and 2008 (described above), significant employment concerns remain. In 2006 focus groups held as part of an International Student Post-graduate Employment Project in Halifax found that the most common difficulties or complaints identified by students included the lack of connections with potential employers, and difficulties in meeting employers; language barriers or perceived language barriers because of a distinct accent; lack of Canadian work experience; and lack of understanding on the part of employers regarding the process of would-be immigrants acquiring work permits and permanent residency status. Working with and educating employers is an important component of supporting international students intending to immigrate. Employers' lack of knowledge prevents international students from even being considered in the hiring process. While post-secondary institutions have an important role to play in reaching out to employers, the provincial and federal governments also have a responsibility.

Bohonos (2009) found additional barriers to employment, including the lack of knowledge of Canadian workplace culture and employer expectations; limited knowledge of job search resources available; poor communication skills, such as understanding non-verbal behaviour in a Canadian context; and low self-confidence. In her literature review, Bohonos notes that Canadian employers expect confidence expressed in the form of a firm handshake, good eye contact, and positive self-talk, which are dominant Canadian cultural and workplace norms that many international students are unfamiliar or uncomfortable with. Bohonos's empirical study indicates that the incorporation of activities and opportunities to practice interpersonal communication significantly increases job search confidence and job search knowledge, and that an increase in job search knowledge is related to an increase in confidence. She also found a significant relationship between participants' level of job search confidence and level of identification with Canadian culture, suggesting that an understanding of Canadian cultural norms and social expectations may have a significant impact on job search success and labour market outcomes. The implication of these findings is that Canadian-focused job search and career development support should be complemented with services that support international students intending to immigrate in understanding Canadian cultural norms and social expectations.

Social and Emotional Support

The research suggests that successful experiences in social and cultural adaptation will increase the likelihood that international students will develop ties with a community and choose to stay, and that social and emotional supports are also important in helping international students and graduates in beginning the settlement process. The authors of a study conducted in 2005 of 160 Chinese undergraduate international students at the University of Saskatchewan concluded that "social and emotional adaptations are [as] critical as economic adaptations in facilitating intentions to stay permanently" (Lu, Zong, and Schissel 2009, 307). They recommend, in addition to the labour-market-orientation policies, to pay special attention to accessible cultural orientation programs. Likewise, a survey of 949 Master's students in the United States and United Kingdom found that the adjustment process for international students was the most significant predictor of their intention to stay in the host country, and that social support, especially from fellow students, was central to this process (Baruch, Budhwar, and Khatri 2007).

Alberts and Hazen (2006) support the finding that the adjustment process is crucial to international students' decision about whether or not to stay. Just over half of the respondents reported that "feelings of alienation from US culture" were encouraging them to return home after their studies (Alberts and Hazen 2006, 212). The authors suggest:

> [F]eelings of discontent (sometimes even depression) associated with the challenges of an international move are often projected onto the host country, whether or not it is the shortcomings of the host country that have caused these feelings. (212)

Thus, providing the services to support international students through the cultural adaptation process, in addition to coping with and challenging discriminatory behaviour, is critical in positively influencing their immigration intentions.

In creating the Halifax Region Immigration Strategy, consultations with international students revealed that about half had not originally come with the intention of immigrating but subsequently decided to stay. All of these students had developed strong social and community roots within Halifax (Halifax Global 2005). Mandal (2009) found a strong relationship among kinship, friendship, and neighbourhood social capital and settlement intention among international students at the University of Manitoba. Of those students with high rates of kinship and friendship social capital, 89 percent indicated an intention to settle in Canada. Of those with high neighbourhood social capital, 89 percent intended to settle specifically in Manitoba (Mandal 2009). These results point to the importance of supporting links not just within the university community, but also with the wider community, when pursuing a regional immigration strategy.

An important factor in social and emotional support is the ability to make friends, both on and off campus, with other international students and Canadians.

For example the survey of 949 Master's students in the United States and the United Kingdom found that the most influential social support was that of host country students (Baruch, Budhwar, and Khatri 2007). Further indicating the importance of these social ties, the University of Saskatchewan study by Lu, Zong, and Schissel (2009, 306) found:

> Male students' migration intentions tend to be associated with friendship with Canadians and kinship in Canada, social network factors, and social activity participation which clearly facilitate adaptation into Canadian society. These factors have much less significance for female students who tend to be driven by feelings of emotional connectedness.

In addition to providing the social and emotional support, friendships and social interactions with Canadian students also support international students in developing an understanding of Canadian cultural norms, social interactions, and work attitudes, thus improving their conversational skills and potential to successfully navigate the Canadian labour market.

Yet, the literature speaks to the difficulty that international students experience in establishing friendships with Canadian students. A survey of more than 2,500 Montreal students found that 47 percent were unsatisfied with their welcome by other students and 49 percent were also unsatisfied with their success in establishing friendships with Canadian students (CROP 2006). The CBIE Survey of International Students (2009) found that only about one in three respondents reported "lots of success" in making friends with Canadian students. A discussion at a community-campus summit on international students, held at Monash University in Australia, found that lack of interaction with domestic students was, in addition to language barriers, one of the biggest challenges in campus community engagement (Monash University 2010). A study by Grayson (2007) found that low-self confidence in English language ability was often a barrier to making friends. Another report from Newfoundland and Labrador on strategies to retain immigrants mentioned homestay programs, which arrange accommodation for international students with local families, as helpful to the integration of international students into the wider community (Gilroy 2005). These research findings suggest that providing services that support international students in connecting with Canadian students, families, and society, including language support services, are an essential settlement service. While none of these studies specifically focuses on the issues of racism and discrimination, these issues are a significant barrier that continues to exist and requires an ongoing commitment by governments and university and college administrations to challenge and eradicate it.

Finally, employment experience is important in creating a socially and emotionally supportive environment for international students. The recommendations coming from the research and consultations carried out for the Halifax Region

Immigration Strategy made the interesting point that creating roots in the community is also achieved through co-op and summer jobs. Thus, supporting international students in understanding local hiring practices, searching for jobs, and other services are important components for developing and fostering community ties (Halifax Global 2005).

Academic and Language Support

There is a lack of research on academic and language issues in relation to international students considering immigration. The only reference was that of the University of Saskatchewan study by Lu, Zong, and Schissel (2009, 393) that found: "[A]ll students whose average is above 85 ... have either strong or moderate intentions to stay permanently" and "meeting the university's requirement of English proficiency increases the odds of strongly intending to immigrate in comparison with students who only have a basic or intermediate proficiency" (Lu, Zong, and Schissel 2009, 297). These findings suggest that actively supporting international students' academic performance and their English or French language proficiency can have an important influence on their decision to stay permanently.

There exists, however, a great deal of research on the academic and language challenges and support needs of international students in general. One issue needing to be addressed is the utilization rates of existing support services. The CBIE Survey of International Students (2009, 54) reports that only 21 percent of university and 32 percent of college students use study skills/learning support services, and only 12 percent of university and 23 percent of college students use language tutoring services. This underutilization is surprising in light of less than half of students reporting "a lot of success" in written assignments, and 6 out of 10 students reporting only "some success" or "little or no success" in speaking English or French (CBIE 2009, 46).

The 2006 First Survey of International Students in Atlantic Canada suggests one reason for the low use of support services is lack of awareness. Over 35 percent of international student respondents were unaware of the existence of both laboratories and mentor programs, and 26 percent were unaware of learning support services (Lebrun and Rebelo 2006). These findings suggest the need for better methods of distributing information about available services and facilities. In addition, Bohonos (2009) makes the crucial point that some cultures attach stigma to seeking assistance, especially from personal counselling services; this stigmatization needs to be taken into account when promoting programs and services.

Strong language skills are, of course, essential not only for academic success but also social integration and successful labour market entry. Having the ability to fully understand and communicate in English is key to success in Canada, and it goes beyond simple language competency to encompassing an understanding and utilization of accents, slang, jargon, idioms, and other cultural references. Research confirms that a major barrier for international students seeking employment in Canada is their limited fluency in English and resulting weak interpersonal communication skills

(Amsberry 2008). While post-secondary institutions require proof of a high level of English language proficiency, there is much anecdotal and documented evidence that many international students struggle with fluency (Bohonos 2009). Since language entrance requirements do not guarantee conversational fluency, language support remains an important settlement service for international students.

A review of services for international students at Memorial University noted that while English as a Second Language (ESL) support was available, more needed to be done to support the development of English language skills, such as "sheltered" or "adjunct" courses, which combine ESL teaching with attendance in regular courses (Burnaby 2002). In terms of struggling with language, differences exist between region of origin: the CBIE Survey (2009, 33) found that 51 percent of East Asian, 34 percent of North African and Middle Eastern, and 31 percent of South East Asian respondents reported having difficulty in passing their English language proficiency test. These differences suggest the potential need for targeted language support services.

In addition to language ability, communication and cultural learning styles can also act as barriers to academic success. For example, a number of studies conducted at the University of Melbourne from 1997 to 2003 confirmed anecdotal evidence of international students' disadvantage in the medical fields, in particular for those of Asian origin (Hawthorne, Minas, and Singh 2004). Issues with critical thinking, problem-based learning, English language ability, and communication styles were identified as the main barriers to academic success. In response to these barriers, the faculties of Medicine, Dentistry, and Health Sciences created a "faculty-specific concurrent support programme, designed to ensure that all overseas-born students … are provided with an exceptional level of linguistic and cross-cultural support" (Hawthorne, Minas, and Singh 2004, 153). The program recognizes the need for faculty-specific support programs for international students, and that "there is a genuine risk of the needs of individual international students being lost, with linguistic and cultural differences negatively impacting on academic performance" (158). This program pursues a comprehensive approach to supporting the language and academic needs of international students.

Immigration Support and Information

Immigration support and information for international students intending to immigrate is also an under-researched area. Heather Moore (2008) explores the experiences of three York University international students making the transition to permanent residency. One graduate explains the important role played by his campus community social network and the informal advice from others who had gone through the process. He indicated that this resource was important in dealing with the overwhelming anxiety associated with the immigration process—something he believes holds many international students back from pursing immigration.

A survey of Montreal students found that 30 percent had never received any information during their studies on immigrating to Canada (CROP 2006). The survey recommends that educating international students about immigration pathways at the beginning of their studies rather than nearing the end would help inform their study and work decisions. Research and consultations conducted in the Halifax region suggested that while all the information and forms needed for immigration are available online, access to an interactive process is lacking (Halifax Global 2005).

International Student Offices

To adequately meet their settlement needs, international students must have a clearly defined place to go to access settlement services. Thus, International Student Offices (ISOs) are an indispensable resource for international students. Bond (2007) reported that ISOs are the main point of institutional contact for international students when they seek academic and employment support, even when these services are provided in separate offices. "For the most part ... it is the staff at the ISO who carry the responsibility for institutional support" (Bond 2007, 25). The report notes that there were few programs targeted to international students in their last year of study (and thus planning their immigration pathway), but mentions a few instances of "good practice" such as a mentoring program linking international students with members of the business and professional community, and the distribution of an informational CD with advice on preparing for and getting a job in Canada. However, the report also acknowledges that many institutions are unable to offer such services due to a shortage of staff and resources, and that ISOs in general are working well over capacity. The report suggests that full-scale review of service requirements and current resourcing is past due. Furthermore, the CBIE (2009, 54) survey states that 54 percent of university students and 64 percent of college students report using the services of an International Student Advisor, which suggests room for improvement in reaching out to and engaging international students in the services currently available to them.

GOOD PRACTICES: CURRENT PROJECTS AND PROGRAMS FOR INTERNATIONAL STUDENTS INTENDING TO IMMIGRATE

In this section I provide an overview of current projects and programs across Canadian institutions and in the community, with a few international examples, whose *specific* goal is to support international students intending to immigrate. While this list is not comprehensive, it does represent the projects and programs that I could identify through a detailed Internet and literature review.

University of Manitoba: Job Searching for International Students Who Wish to Stay in Canada

Bohonos (2009) presents a detailed explanation of the program, its structure and activities. Recognizing the unique needs of international students in Canadian job searching, the University of Manitoba's Student Counselling and Career Centre introduced a pilot program in 2007, which was subsequently continued and expanded. The purpose of the program was to increase international students' knowledge, skills, and confidence in conducting a successful job search in Canada.

> [The program] was developed with the belief that providing opportunities to learn about Canadian workplace expectations as well as the practice of interpersonal communication in a supportive environment may alleviate the anxiety international student[s] experience [with] regards [to] their career search and enable them to be more competitive in the job market. (Bohonos 2009, 12)

The program is eight weeks in duration and is offered once a week for two hours to a closed group of 15 to 25 participants. While many other post-secondary institutions also hold special sessions for international students, they are usually single two-hour sessions. The longer format allows for more practical exercises.

Rather than employing a lecture-based format, the program is rooted in problem-based learning strategies to encourage students to integrate and apply what they learn by using small group work, hands-on practical activities such as role modelling, and one-on-one interaction. Because an informal survey of participants found that few of them interacted with their Canadian peers due to low self-efficacy with language fluency, providing opportunities to interact and practice their English fluency was a key component in course planning.

Program goals were determined in consultation with participants. Participants were mainly concerned with employment skills rather than decisions about career choice; therefore, the specific goals of the program included discussing Canadian culture and workplace norms, key skills required by Canadian employers, employer expectations, resumé and cover letter writing, job search strategies, and interview preparation advice.

Bohonos (2009) suggests that future programs should run for the duration of the academic term and offer ongoing advice and support upon completion of the program, with the possibility of a second program that provides job search support to students who have graduated. She also recommends early intervention, suggesting that students should be encouraged to enrol in the program much earlier in their studies to get them thinking about their career development, obtain Canadian work or volunteer experience, and build references and networks.

Halifax: HRDA International Students' Post-Graduate Employment Project

Funded by the Atlantic Association of Community Business Development Corporations and carried out by the HRDA Employment Centre in 2006, the International Students' Post-Graduate Project sought to help international students find employment in the Halifax region through a project implemented in three phases. The first phase consisted of focus groups with international students to identify their job search needs, including resumé and cover letter writing, interview skills, networking skills, work permit information, and general job search skills. Based on these needs, four workshops were held over a weekend, which constituted the second phase. The third phase of the project was a networking lunch. The event educated recruiters about the misconceptions and facts related to hiring international students and educated international students about the companies who were recruiting. A networking session followed the lunch, allowing the international students to meet and speak with recruiters, discuss areas of interest, and circulate resumés. The networking lunch allowed students to practice their networking skills, interview skills, and self-promotion, and to better understand the perspectives of the employers.

New Brunswick and l'Université de Moncton: *Destination Emploi pour Étudiants Internationaux*

Started as a pilot in 2008, the *Destination Emploi* project is funded by the provincial government and aims to retain francophone international students from l'Université de Moncton as immigrants to New Brunswick. Located in the university, the objectives of the project include helping international students enter the labour market during their studies and after graduation, providing additional coaching to students during their studies and assisting them with social integration into the community, encouraging New Brunswick businesses to hire international students, and educating students who are about to graduate about how to immigrate to the province.

To achieve these objectives, the project funds staff to meet individually with international students and discuss issues related to employment, hold employment workshops, provide ESL instruction, organize job fairs to connect international students with employers, and distribute fact sheets for employers explaining the process of hiring international students. Staff also provide information and support to international students interested in immigrating. The project has been very successful, placing 77 percent of participants in off-campus employment during their studies and 61 percent in postgraduate employment. In 2009 35 students stayed after graduation to work and 10 former international students gained permanent residency through the PNP, compared to no international students gaining permanent residency in 2008 through the PNP.

Speaking with an administrator of the project at l'Université de Moncton, I learned that the structure of the project has important benefits for both the provincial government and the university. From the perspective of the university, the active recruitment of international students as immigrants is not a university responsibility and is an ethically questionable practice contributing to "brain drain." Funding the employment services fully or partly through federal and/or provincial government can address the issues of responsibility and conflict of interest. Meanwhile, physically locating the employment services on campus increases their accessibility to international students and recognizes that employment services are an essential service for all international students regardless of whether or not they decide to immigrate.

Newfoundland and Memorial University: Career Development and Family Integration Support

As part of its strategy to retain international students as immigrants, the Government of Newfoundland and Labrador provided Memorial University with two grants to deliver the Professional Skills Development Program for International Students and the Family Integration Support Program. Launched in spring 2010, the Professional Skills and Development Program is provided through the Centre for Career Development and is a semester-long certificate program offered to all undergraduate and graduate international students. The program consists of seven weekly in-class sessions, one community/service learning initiative, and two networking sessions where participants meet employers. Participants must attend all sessions to receive a certificate. The in-class sessions focus on topics such as Canadian work culture, the Canadian job search process, the Canadian interview process, and intercultural communication (Memorial University 2011). In addition, participants must volunteer in the community outside the university to familiarize themselves with and make connections in the community.

The Family Integration Support Program supports those international students who have brought their families with them and provides integration support through information and referrals, social events to introduce families to the St. John's community as well as rural Newfoundland, and a support network. The program is based in part on the premise that students with families are even more likely to immigrate and settle and that supporting the integration and well-being of students' families will encourage this result.

A one-time special grant was also provided for a Rural Integration Tour. The tour took international students to rural Newfoundland where they were introduced to employers, with the aim of attracting them to these communities once they graduate. Finally, funding for a summer wage subsidy program has been approved. Starting in the summer of 2011, employers in the hospitality industry in rural Newfoundland have been provided with a wage subsidy for international students. The goal of this program is to create bonds between international students and rural Newfoundland, with the aim of attracting international students to this region after graduation.

In addition to the funding for these programs and projects, the Office of Immigration and Multiculturalism has a staff member dedicated to educating international students and employers about the PNP and promoting international students as prime candidates for employers. Informational sessions through the Office of Immigration and Multiculturalism are held on-campus to educate international students about the PNP and immigrating to Newfoundland and Labrador.

Conférence régionale des élus (CRÉ) *de Montréal*: A Regional Approach to Integrating and Retaining International Students

The *Conférence régionale des élus* (CRÉ) *de Montréal* is a provincial government agency that promotes regional development in the Montréal area. Each region of Quebec has a similar agency. Since 2006, in partnership with the City of Montreal, the universities and colleges of the region, the provincial student union, the Montreal youth forum, Montreal International, and the Board of Trade of Metropolitan Montreal, CRÉ has been coordinating research and promoting the recruitment, integration, and retention of international students as a source of immigration and cultural and economic development. A survey of over 2,500 Montreal international students provided information for the development of policy and program recommendations. Central to these recommendations is the recognition that supporting the integration of international students during their studies is a key component of retaining them as immigrants. The report notes the importance of adequately funding integration services, increasing interactions with Quebec students, and getting international students out into the wider off-campus community.

The first phase of the CRÉ's plan focused on student recruitment, with the development of a "Study in Montréal" website (www.studyinmontreal.info/en), which even includes an apartment and carpooling search board, and two welcoming kiosks at the Montréal-Trudeau Airport staffed by Quebec students (Accueil Plus 2011). The next phase will focus on international student retention. Once provincial funding has been secured, the proposed activities will target retention and organized events to bring international students and employers together. Finally, while not targeting international students specifically, the Montreal: For Your Life, for Your Career (2011) project provides free information and immigration counselling for temporary workers looking to gain permanent residency—and international students and graduates are eligible for this service.

Alberta, New Brunswick, and Newfoundland: Focus on Employers

While many universities provide information for employers on hiring international students, few provinces or cities are targeting employers to educate them about the value of hiring international students and the ease of doing so. The active promotion of international students as potential employees by federal, provincial, and municipal governments is key to an effective immigration strategy as their involvement will help increase employers' confidence in international students. It is extremely important to provide up-to-date, comprehensive information to employers. Surprisingly, many of the post-secondary institutions that do provide information have not updated their websites since the 2008 changes to the postgraduate work permit, which can mislead employers and discourage them from hiring international students.

In Alberta a 2006 collaborative campaign with the provincial and municipal government, the Edmonton Economic Development Corporation (EEDC), and post-secondary institutions was launched to promote international students as prime candidates for employers. The campaign included a page on the EEDC website (EEDC 2011) providing information and resources, brochures, media releases, and events such as a 2007 employer breakfast.

New Brunswick's SolutionsNB (2011) website endorses immigrants as a solution to labour needs, and prominently promotes international students. The site provides information on hiring graduates, co-op students, and students who are still studying, in addition to providing personalized contact information for staff at each post-secondary institution who can connect employers with international students.

As part of its immigration strategy launched in 2007, the Government of Newfoundland and Labrador created an *Employer's Guide to Hiring Immigrants and International Students* (Department of Human Resources, Labour and Employment 2011). The guide provides employers with suggestions on how to expand their recruitment process to target international students, how to interview candidates whose first language is not English, and how to assess qualifications and language skills. It also offers detailed information on the procedures for hiring international students. In addition to the guide, the Office of Immigration and Multiculturalism has a staff member dedicated to educating employers about the PNP and promoting international students as prime candidates for employment. Given that most employers are unaware of the PNP and do not have the time to research the process themselves, the project is based on active and direct outreach, working to dispel myths surrounding the perceived difficulties of hiring international students and to provide employers with information about where and how to recruit international students.

Ontario: Providing Immigration Support through Facebook

Launched in June 2010 the Opportunities Ontario Facebook group allows Facebook users to post detailed immigration questions related to Ontario's PNP that are answered by a staff member of the Ministry of Citizenship and Immigration. The Facebook format permits a high degree of interaction between the group members and the staff member answering questions. With 1,283 "likes" as of May 2011, the Opportunities Ontario Facebook group appears to be popular and useful.

University of Newcastle, Australia: International Post-Graduate Employment Pilot Project[5]

The International Post-Graduate Employment Pilot Project (IPEPP) is a joint project between the International Division of the University of Newcastle and the Hunter

Business Chamber. The IPEPP was funded by the university and received in-kind support from four supporting organizations: University of Newcastle Career Services, Northern Settlement Services, Australian Industry Group, and the Lord Mayoral Enriching Newcastle Diversity Working Group.

Organized into occupational teams, participating students attended a series of sessions to learn about Australian work culture, resumé writing, job search techniques, and interview skills. After finding that many of the students had language fluency problems, language training support was provided. One unanticipated discovery was loneliness and isolation among the students. As a result, social activities were developed to build the students' confidence. The students undertook a series of visits to local businesses aimed at improving their comprehension of how their occupation is practiced locally and to provide employers with a good sense of what skills the students possessed.

The coordinator position was central to the success of the project. In addition to organizing and facilitating training sessions for the students, the coordinator provided one-on-one support to place the student with an employer and continued to provide support to both the student and the employer after the placement. As the students neared the completion of their studies, the coordinator assisted them with organizing working visas or permanent residency and met personally with each potential employer. He briefed all relevant staff thoroughly about the project and gave a profile of the types of students they would be likely to encounter. This relationship with employers continued throughout the project to ensure that their expectations were met by the students and to gather feedback on ways to improve the project.

From the students' perspective, the project was enormously successful. In addition, from a public education perspective, the project increased employers' appreciation of the skills and experience of international students. The community partnerships, especially with the Hunter Business Chamber, were central to publicizing the project and creating awareness of international students as desirable employees. Unfortunately, funding for the pilot was discontinued.

MYSA International, Australia: Third-Party Service Provision

MYSA International is a new division of Multicultural Youth South Australia Inc., a not-for-profit non-governmental organization that is the state advisory, advocacy, and service delivery body for youth from multicultural backgrounds. TAFE South Australia, the Technical and Further Education sector administered by the state of South Australia, has engaged MYSA International to provide a range of services for its international students at no extra cost to students. MYSA International provides airport pickup and transfers, arranges accommodations, provides orientation and settlement support, and organizes a volunteer Buddy Program that offers bilingual language support (MYSA 2011). While the services provided are not structured to specifically integrate and retain international students as immigrants, they exemplify an alternate service delivery model, especially for smaller colleges and schools that are located in communities with more than one post-secondary institution.

KEY CHALLENGES AND RECOMMENDATIONS

In carrying out the research for this chapter, I identified a number of challenges that should be considered in the provision of support services to international students and the move towards recruiting international students as immigrants. Funding of post-secondary support services, access to settlement services after graduation, and jurisdictional responsibility are key challenges. Research gaps are another area I will consider.

Funding

With the exception of post-secondary institutions in Quebec and a few in the Atlantic provinces who charge Canadian fees to francophone international students, international students pay much higher tuition rates than Canadian students because the provinces do not provide operational funding for them. For many post-secondary institutions, international student services face funding and staffing challenges. Recent analyses suggest that adequate investment in international students is an issue, both in the context of their higher tuition fees and their economic contribution. For example, the Conférence régionale des élus (CRÉ) de Montréal found that Quebec non-francophone international students at both the college and university levels paid more in tuition than was invested in their education and support (CRÉ 2006). Siddiq et al. (2010) found international students in the Atlantic provinces spent $2.68 on average for every dollar spent on them by the Atlantic governments.[6]

Yet, as this chapter argues, high-quality services are essential in supporting international student integration and encouraging them to stay, work, and immigrate to Canada. The Siddiq et al. (2009) study suggests that, from a purely fiscal perspective, it makes economic sense for governments to increase their expenditures on international students. Furthermore, most of the services supporting potentially immigrating students are also essential for international students in general, and student services are becoming an important factor in international student recruitment and retention.

Another issue is the ability of smaller post-secondary institutions to fund high-quality international student services. The federal Standing Committee on Citizenship and Immigration (2010) states that ensuring effective delivery and achieving comparable settlement outcomes across Canada is a best practice benchmark. The federal government's jurisdiction over immigration and its promotion of international students as ideal immigrants, as well as the provincial governments' involvement in these areas, suggest that these levels of government should also play a role in ensuring these students have access to comparable services.

ACCESS TO SETTLEMENT SERVICES

The second key challenge relates to the second temporary worker phase that many international students must go through as they progress towards permanent residency.[7] While I was unable to identify research specific to international students that considers the impact of the settlement services available to them during this phase, the literature on immigrants, temporary foreign workers, and refugees shows that early intervention improves social and labour market integration. Thus, the ineligibility of international students and temporary foreign workers for federal and some provincial settlement services contradicts the stated desire to retain international students as immigrants. Many post-secondary institutions provide limited, if any, services to graduated students. Speaking anecdotally with international student support staff at various post-secondary institutions, I found that some universities are currently able to provide support to former international students even though it is not part of their mandate. However, the staff also noted that their ability to provide this support cannot continue with the increase in international students. In light of their current immigration objectives, the federal and provincial governments need to review the eligibility criteria for their settlement services and address international students' unique service needs.

Jurisdictional Responsibility

The general lack of a coordinated strategic approach to international student support and settlement services between the federal, provincial, and municipal governments, post-secondary institutions, and the settlement sector is a complex challenge that significantly influences the first two identified challenges. In a report on the internationalization of Halifax, Sinziana Chira (2009) explores the tensions between the differing mandates of the various stakeholders involved in international student support, specifically around job search support and immigration. At the federal level, Chira found that Citizenship and Immigration Canada (CIC) staff believed that the province and universities stood to gain the most from attracting international students as immigrants and should therefore provide most of the support. They also argued that the province and universities were in a better position to provide the required support and funds. Staff working for the province, however, indicated that the province did not provide job search support for international students and graduates because their policy approach was based on the desire to retain motivated, independent immigrants who already have all the required expertise to succeed. At the university level, ethical concerns around supporting the "brain drain" of less developed countries leads to a focus on international students as sources of diversity and revenue rather than potential immigrants. This narrative dictates an institutional focus on supporting academic success and day-to-day pragmatic issues rather than building ties with the local community, especially after graduation. Finally, Chira (2009) found that immigrant settlement agencies expressed interest in partnering with local universities to support international students, but ineligibility of international students for their services and the lack of provincial funds for international student settlement were recurring issues.

Although Chira's study was specific to the Halifax region, it reflects the general disconnect between many provinces' increasing focus on the PNPs as an immigration pathway and their lack of financial support for international students. In addition, her study speaks to the complex challenges in a coordinated approach when CIC appears to view international student settlement neither as a priority nor its responsibility. CIC's approach in the Halifax region towards international student settlement issues supports the argument that the federal government has been downloading the responsibility for immigrant selection and support onto the provinces, post-secondary institutions, and employers. Further discussion and coordination between the federal and provincial governments, post-secondary institutions, and the settlement sector on the issue of international student support and integration are required to ensure the success of international student immigration objectives and to support the internationalization of post-secondary institutions through a growing share of international students.

Research Gaps

International students as immigrants is an emerging research area, and as such a number of gaps and a lack of synthesis exist in the available research. Specific areas where little or no research exists specific to international students intending to immigrate include the different settlement needs of university and college students and between smaller and larger post-secondary institutions; the different settlement needs of undergraduate and graduate students; the settlement needs of international students beyond concerns over job opportunities and labour market integration in the period between their graduation and the receipt of permanent residency; the settlement needs of students' spouses and dependents; and international comparative research on approaches to supporting international students considering or intending to immigrate.

Most Canadian research on international students intending to immigrate comes from two regions that have historically had low rates of immigration: the Atlantic region and the Prairie provinces. Conducting more geographically focused research would contribute to a greater general understanding of immigrating international students' needs and how these needs are influenced by their cultural background and their location of study.

ENDNOTES

1. As reported by CIC Media Relations through correspondence, September 17, 2010.
2. As reported by CIC Media Relations through correspondence, April 19, 2010.

3. Ibid.
4. Many of these former international students immigrated through the Federal Skilled Worker Program, which required that they leave Canada and apply for immigration status from outside of the country. Others were sponsored as family members or immigrated through a PNP.
5. Information gathered through personal correspondence.
6. Individual government calculations: NB: $1.78; NL: $1.88; NS: $4.04; and PEI: $3.71.
7. However, some provinces have cut the requirement for a postgraduation work period for graduate students applying through their PNPs, meaning they can skip this phase (see Appendix).

ACKNOWLEDGEMENTS

I would like to thank World Education Services in supporting the research for this report as well as its ongoing commitment to exploring this policy area. I would also like to thank all the individuals in Canada and Australia who took the time to respond to my questions about their work or research, including: Josee Jaques of *Destination emploi pour étudiants*; Teeba Alsafar of Memorial University; Nellie Burke, Executive Director of the Newfoundland Office of Immigration and Multiculturalism; and Celia Smyth of Grant MacEwan University (BC). Finally, I would like to thank Ryerson University for the opportunity to present this research at the Migration and the Global City conference in 2010, and Harald Bauder for the opportunity to publish it.

REFERENCES

Accueil Plus, 2011. Accessed April 5, 2011. www.accueilplus.ca.

Adlain, S. 2006. "International Students Postgraduate Employment Project." Report submitted to HRSDC, Halifax. Accessed August 8, 2011. www.greaterhalifax.com/site-ghp2/media/Parent/International_Students_Postgraduate_Employment_Project.pdf..

Alberts, H., and H. Hazen. 2006. "Visitors or Immigrants? International Students in the United States." *Population, Space and Place* 12: 201–216.

Amsberry, D. 2008. "Talking the Talk: Library Classroom Communication and International Students." *International Journal for Educational and Vocational Guidance* 5: 91–99.

Baruch, Y., P. S. Budhwar, and N. Khatri. 2007. "Brain Drain: Inclination to Stay Abroad after Studies." *Journal of World Business* 42: 99–112.

Bond, S. 2007. "Northern Lights: International Graduates of Canadian Institutions and the National Workforce." Report presented to the Canadian Bureau for International Education. Accessed June 3, 2010. www.cbie.ca/data/media/resources/20071030_NorthernLights_e.pdf.

Bohonos, A. 2009. "Assessing the Effectiveness of a Career Program for International Students." Master's of Education Thesis, University of Manitoba.

Burnaby, B. 2002. "Where the Rubber Hits the Road: Services for International Students at Memorial University of Newfoundland." Report presented to Memorial University of Newfoundland.

Butcher, A. 2004. "Educate, Consolidate, Immigrate: Educational Immigration in Auckland, New Zealand." *Asia Pacific Viewpoint* 45 (2): 255–278.

Canadian Bureau of International Education (CBIE). 2007. "Canadian Universities and International Mobility of Students." Accessed May 29, 2010. www.cbie.ca/data/media/policy/20080617_CanadianPanoramaNAFSA.pdf.

———. 2009. "Canada First: The 2009 Survey of International Students." Accessed May 29, 2010. www.cbie.ca/data/media/resources/20091110_SurveyInternationalStudents_e.pdf.

Chaloff, J., and G. Lemaitre. 2009. "Managing Highly Skilled Labour Migration: A Comparative Analysis of Migration Policies and Challenges in OECD Countries." Employment and Migration Working Papers, No. 79, OECD Publishing. Accessed on August 8, 2011. www.oecd.org/dataoecd/32/25/46656535.pdf.

Chira, S. 2009. "From Internationalizing Atlantic University Campuses to Internationalizing Halifax, Nova Scotia?" Report commissioned by the Association of Atlantic Universities and the Atlantic Metropolis Centre.

Citizenship and Immigration Canada (CIC). 2009. "Facts and Figures 2008." Government of Canada. Accessed May 22, 2010. www.cic.gc.ca/english/resources/statistics/facts2008.

———. 2011a. "Canadian Experience Class." Government of Canada. Accessed April 3, 2011. www.cic.gc.ca/english/immigrate/cec/index.asp.

———. 2011b. "Fact and Figures 2010". Government of Canada.

———. 2011c. "Studying in Canada." Government of Canada. Accessed April 3, 2011. www.cic.gc.ca/english/study/work-offcampus.asp.

———. 2011d. "Work Permits for Students." Accessed April 3, 2011. www.cic.gc.ca/english/study/work-postgrad-who.asp.

Conférence régionale des élus (CRÉ) de Montréal. 2006. "Intensifier les Efforts pour Attirer et Retenir les Meilleurs Étudiants Internationaux à Montréal." Accessed June 3, 2010. www.credemontreal.qc.ca/Publications/Avis%20et%20Memoires/Avis%20-%20Attirer%20etudiants%20intern%20-%20131106.pdf.

CROP. 2006. "Enquête auprès des étudiants internationaux de Montréal." CRÉ de Montréal. Accessed June 3, 2010. www.credemontreal.qc.ca/Publications/Developpement%20Economique/Enquete%20-%20Etudiants%20Internationaux%20-%201006.pdf.

Department of Human Resources, Labour and Employment, Newfoundland. 2011. *Employer's Guide to Hiring Immigrants and International Students in Newfoundland and Labrador*. Accessed April 5, 2011. www.nlimmigration.ca/media/10909/employersguidetohiringimmigrants.pdf.

Dorais, M. 2002. "Immigration and Integration through a Social Cohesion Perspective." *Horizons* 5 (2): 4–5.

Edmonton Economic Development Corporation (EEDC). 2011. International Students. Accessed April 5, 2011. www.edmonton.com/moving-to-edmonton/international-students.aspx.

Gilroy, G. 2005. *Retention and Integration of Immigrants in Newfoundland and Labrador: Are We Ready?* Final Report St. John's, NL: Atlantic Canada Opportunities Agency and oordinating

Committee on Newcomer Integration. Accessed August 8, 2011. www.nlimmigration.ca/media/2854/immigrationstudyfinal.pdf

Government of Canada. 2001. "Immigration and Refugee Protection Act." Accessed June 23. laws.justice.gc.ca/en/I-2.5/.

Grayson, P. 2007. "The Experiences and Outcomes of Domestic and International Students at Four Canadian Universities." *Higher Education Research & Development* 27 (3): 215–230.

Halifax Global. 2005. *Halifax Region Immigration Strategy: Research and Consultation Findings.* Greater Halifax Partnership, 2. Accessed July 3, 2010. www.halifax.ca/council/mayor/documents/6.HRMImmigrationResearch.pdf.

Hawthorne, L. 2005. "Picking Winners: The Recent Transformation of Australia's Skilled Migration Policy." *International Migration Review* 39 (3): 663–696.

Hawthorne, L., I. H. Minas, and B. Singh. 2004. "A Case Study in the Globalization of Medical Education: Assisting Overseas-Born Students at the University of Melbourne." *Medical Teacher* 26 (2): 150–159.

Kunin, R., and Associates. 2009. *Economic Impact of International Education in Canada: Final Report.* Presented to Foreign Affairs and International Trade Canada. Accessed July 15, 2010. www.international.gc.ca/education/assets/pdfs/RKA_IntEd_Report_eng.pdf.

Lebrun, D., and S. Rebelo. 2006. "The Role of Universities in the Economic Development of Atlantic Canada: A Focus on Immigration." Atlantic Canada Opportunity Agency. Accessed on July 3, 2010. dsp-psd.pwgsc.gc.ca/collection_2010/apeca-acoa/Iu89-4-37-2006-eng.doc.

Lu, Y., L. Zong, and B. Schissel. 2009. "To Stay or Return: Migration Intentions of Students from People's Republic of China in Saskatchewan, Canada." *International Migration and Integration* 10: 283–310.

Mandal, S. 2009. "Settlement Intentions of Post-Secondary International Students in Manitoba." Master of Arts Thesis, University of Manitoba.

MYSA. 2011. MYSA International. Accessed April 5, 2011. www.mysa.com.au.

Memorial University. 2011. "Sessions and Workshops." International Student Advising Office. Accessed April 5, 2011. www.mun.ca/isa/employment/psdpworkshopsandsessions.php.

Moore, H. 2008. "From Student to Migrant: Migration Narratives of International Students in Canada." Master's Thesis, York University.

Office of the Premier. 2010. "Investing in Postsecondary Education." Toronto: Government of Ontario. Accessed April 3, 2011. www.premier.gov.on.ca/openOntario/index.php?Lang=EN#Postsecondary.

Organisation for Economic Co-operation and Development. 2008. "International Migration Outlook: SOPEMI." Paris, OECD. Accessed September 15, 2010. www.oecd.org/dataoecd/30/13/41275373.pdf.

———. 2010. "Education at a Glance 2010: OECD Indicators." Paris, OECD. Accessed September 17, 2010.

Siddiq, F., B. Holterman, W. Nethercote, A. Sinclair, and A. White. 2009. *The Economic Impact of International Students Enrolled in Nova Scotia Universities: An Expenditure Analysis.* Minister's Post-Secondary Education Research Advisory Panel. Government of Nova Scotia. Accessed July 15, 2010. www.ednet.ns.ca/pdfdocs/univ-colleges/International_Students_Final_Report.pdf.

Siddiq, F., J. Baroni, J. Lye, and W. Nethercote. 2010. *The EconomicImpact of Post-Secondary International Students in Atlantic Canada: An Expenditure Analysis.* Dalhousie University, School of Public Administration. Accessed September 21, 2010. www.camet-camef.ca/images/eng/docs/EconImpact_IntStud_AtlCan_2010_eng.pdf.

Simmons, A. 2010. "Economic Integration and Designer Immigrants: Canadian Policy in the 1990s." In *Free Markets, Open Societies, Closed Borders? Trends in International Migration and Immigration Policy in the Americas*, edited by M. Castro, 53–69. Miami, Florida: North-South Press.

SolutionsNB. 2011. Hiring International Students. Accessed April 5, 2011. www.solutionsnb.ca/content/215480.

Standing Committee on Citizenship & Immigration. 2010. Best Practices in Settlement Services. Government of Canada. Accessed August 8, 2011. ensemble.etablissement.org/sites/ensemble.etablissement.org/files/cimmrp02-e.pdf.

Suter, B., and M. Jandi. 2006. Comparative Study on Policies towards Foreign Graduates: Study on Admission and Retention Policies towards Foreign Students in Industrialized Countries. International Centre for Migration Policy Development. Accessed August 8, 2011. research.icmpd.org/fileadmin/Research-Website/Publications/REV_Comparative_Study_on_Graduated_Students_Final.pdf.

Sweetman, A., and C. Warman. 2009. "Temporary Foreign Workers and Former International Students as a Source of Permanent Immigration." CLSRN Working Paper. Accessed June 23, 2010. www.clsrn.econ.ubc.ca/workingpapers/CLSRN%20Working%20Paper%20no.%2025%20-%20Sweetman%20Warman.pdf.

Appendix A: Comparison of PNP International Student Stream Requirements

Province, Program	Min. Academic Program Length	Studies Completed in Province	Provincially Recognized Institution	Min. Post-Grad Work Period	Job Offer	Work Related to Field of Study	Fees
Ontario: International Student with Job Offer Stream	2 years	N/A	Required	N/A	Required, Skill Level 0, A, or B, permanent & full-time	N/A	$1,500
Ontario: International Masters Graduate Stream (Pilot)	1 year	Required	Required	N/A	N/A	N/A	$1,500
Ontario: PhD Graduate Stream	2 years	Required	Required	N/A	N/A	N/A	$1,500
BC: International Graduate Program	1 year	N/A	Required	N/A	Required, Skill Level 0, A, or B, permanent & full-time	Required	$550
BC: International Post-Graduate Pilot Project	Graduate degree in natural, applied, or health sciences.	N/A	No reference to completing studies in Canada	N/A	Helpful	Helpful	$550
Alberta*	2 years undergrad or 1 year graduate	N/A	Required	6 months	Required, permanent & full-time	Required	No fee
Manitoba*	1 year	Required	Required	6 months	Required, permanent & full-time	Required	No fee
Quebec*	1 year	Required	Required	N/A	N/A	N/A	$390
Nova Scotia*	1 year	Required	Required	3 months	Required, permanent & full-time	Required	No fee
Newfoundland and Labrador	2 years	N/A	Required	N/A	Required, or prove labour market attachment	Required if not working already	No fee

* Alberta accepts graduates from recognized private institutions, though only from its province. Manitoba accepts graduates from all recognized Canadian private post-secondary institutions. Quebec and Nova Scotia do not explicitly address private or public funding. All other provinces require degrees or diplomas from publicly funded institution.[5]

Source: Created by Author

Chapter 17

THE SETTLEMENT OF YOUNG NEWCOMER CHILDREN: PERSPECTIVES FOR POLICY AND PROGRAM DEVELOPMENT

JUDITH A. COLBERT

INTRODUCTION

The future of the global city will—in large measure—be determined by the young newcomers of today. Children of all ages will shape the society of tomorrow, but it is the youngest newcomers whose influence will extend farthest into the future and whose successful settlement may be of most critical importance. It is widely recognized that the provision of appropriate, quality early childhood programs—when early interventions are possible—is a positive investment in the future. What may need further consideration is the possibility that from both a policy and programming perspective, specific attention to the settlement of immigrant and refugee children from birth through kindergarten can yield even greater dividends.

Attention to the needs of the youngest immigrants and refugees will help governments achieve policy objectives associated with newcomer settlement. Initiatives that promote the settlement of young children will help ensure that they realize their potential as individuals and ultimately participate fully in the economic and social life of their communities. Researchers in many fields have already provided a knowledge base on which to build policies for future program delivery. Much work remains, however, to connect findings and secure the attention of researchers and policy-makers in areas most closely related to migration studies.

In the paragraphs that follow I will attempt to make the policy issues more visible by shedding light on the reasons why the needs of the youngest newcomers have received so little attention, why their needs are distinctive, why early childhood is a critically important period, and why settlement support is possible. In the next section, I establish the magnitude of the situation and its relevance to future outcomes. The second section addresses the question why the needs of the youngest newcomers have received so little attention, which is followed by a section on the distinctive needs of young newcomer children. Thereafter, I explore why early childhood is a critically important period, and why settlement support is possible. Finally, I present my conclusion.

WHAT IS THE MAGNITUDE OF THE SITUATION?

The importance of the youngest newcomers to the future of the global city is undeniable. Already, cities in receiving countries are welcoming large numbers of young children, and in many ways, newcomer children are the fastest growing population group. In Toronto, one of the world's most ethnically diverse cities, between 2001 and 2006, 19,000 or 7 percent of all immigrants were children 0 to 5 years of age. Another 16 percent were between 6 and 14 years of age (City of Toronto 2010).

In the United States, the Knight Foundation (MPI 2010) has provided an overview of young children (under age nine) of immigrants living in 14 communities, most of which are not traditional gateways for immigration. The numbers for the decade 1990–2000 are dramatic and point to a clear trend. In all 14 communities, the number of young children of immigrant families grew faster than the number of young children of non-immigrants. The population of young children of immigrants grew by a range of 41 percent (Miami, FL) to 242 percent (Charlotte, NC). In three cities, the number of young children of immigrants exceeded 100,000 by the end of the decade: Long Beach, CA (807,680), Miami, FL (235,901), and San Jose, CA (159,088). In contrast, the number of young children of non-immigrants grew in only six communities and growth was much slower, ranging from 18 percent (Charlotte, NC) to 5 percent (Columbus, SC). In eight communities, the population of native born children zero to nine years of age declined over a range of 34 percent (Wichita, KS) to 1 percent (Miami, FL).

That increasing numbers of very young children are migrating to or being born to immigrants in cities is likely a trend throughout receiving countries. Moreover, where the number of young children being born to immigrants is growing faster than the number of children being born to non-immigrant families, existing programs will by default be used by more and more young migrants. An emerging question, therefore, is whether existing policies and programs meet the needs of young immigrants and refugees. If they do not, it becomes important to ask whether policies and programs that largely fail young newcomers serve the best interests of the receiving country, and how they should be changed to meet the distinctive needs of young newcomer children.

In spite of evidence of increasing numbers of young newcomers, most migration research is concerned with adults. Debra Pressé and Jessie Thomson (2008, 97) note that while over half of the world's refugee population consists of children under the age of 18, "Little research has been undertaken to help us understand what happens to refugee youth once they are resettled." Their observation is valuable but seems expressed largely in relation to older children as the emphasis shifts to "youth." Indeed, as discussed below, when research attention turns to children it often centres on older children, and neglects the situation of younger children.

WHY HAVE THE NEEDS OF THE YOUNGEST NEWCOMERS RECEIVED SO LITTLE ATTENTION?

The reasons why children have not received more attention from researchers or policymakers are varied, and include: the way the term "generation" is defined; standard data collection methods and sources; assumptions about children and their ability to adapt over time; and the tendency to look at immigrants as homogeneous groups without seeing individual differences.

Defining "Generation"

The complexity involved in defining an immigrant (or refugee) based on generation has led to various interpretations of "first" and "second" generation, including an assumption that the first generation includes all newcomers 15 years of age and older as defined for labour force age requirements and other purposes. This assumption is unhelpful for understanding issues involving young children. For example, in its 2008 immigration overview, Citizenship and Immigration Canada (CIC) provides information for the immigrant population 15 years of age or older and includes a supplementary table for the permanent resident population showing the number of years of schooling for children less than 15 years old (CIC 2009). This table is of little value to researchers studying young newcomer children since it does not define what is meant by "one year of schooling" (which may include kindergarten).

The practice of collecting data for first-generation immigrants 15 years of age and over often results in assignment of all immigrant children between the ages 0 and 14 years either to the second generation (i.e., with immigrants born in the receiving country) or to a compromise status as the one-and-one-half (1.5) generation. Assuming that a child automatically belongs in the second generation denies the child's reality: the experiences of a child born in the receiving country are very different from those of a child who has had to cope with often vastly different circumstances in the country of origin and the receiving country, especially a child who has experienced trauma and violence or the privation of a refugee camp. The 1.5-generation status places children in an ambiguous category that acknowledges but may fail to disentangle their distinctive needs as young migrants.

Data Collection

Population definitions, data sets, and research are inextricably linked. Since data on first-generation immigrants is often only available beginning at age 15, studies like the Longitudinal Survey of Immigrants to Canada (LSIC) conducted jointly by Statistics Canada and Citizenship and Immigration Canada include only immigrants who were 15 or older at the time of arrival (Statistics Canada 2007). Similarly, the Programme for International Student Assessment (PISA), carried out under the auspices of the Organisation for Economic Co-operation and Development (OECD), measures the academic skills of students at age 15 (Gluszynski and Dhawan-Biswal 2008).

Use of administrative data from school systems also has limitations with respect to young children. It promotes a research focus on the elementary and secondary years, beginning with kindergarten, in spite of a growing recognition by the OECD and others of the importance of early childhood programming (OECD 2001). When mentioned, the importance of early intervention with preschoolers often merits only passing reference (e.g, Anisef et al. 2010, 13). Emphasis falls on recommendations to support older children, which can also be carried out within the same school systems that generate the data, even though they address issues at a much later stage of a child's life when problems are likely to be more complex and correspondingly more intractable.

Assumptions about Young Children and the Ability to Adapt Over Time

Technical issues aside, the underlying reasons why immigration research has not directly addressed issues related to young newcomers may lie in deeply felt assumptions about young children and their role in society. It was not until the late twentieth century that the rights of children were recognized in the *United Nations Convention on the Rights of the Child* (1989), including the right to be heard and to participate in decisions made about them (Article 12). These rights continue to challenge beliefs and practices in many cultures where children are generally unseen, and where they are considered less as individuals and more as appendages of their parents and other adults in the community.

Others dismiss the possibility that young children face distinctive settlement challenges. For example, it has been suggested that young children have been excluded from the first-generation category in the belief that settlement is easier for children because they are, "more likely to acquire receiving culture practices, values and identifications easily and fluidly" than people who migrate when they are older (Schwartz et al. 2010, 242).

The idea that children acquire new ways more easily is closely related to a theory of adaptation based on a belief that settlement, like progress, gets better over time. This "straight-line" or "linear" form of assimilation contrasts with a "segmented assimilation" which highlights different patterns. In contrasting these two forms, Paul Anisef and his associates (2010, 3) comment: "[T]he straight-line approach suggests that children who immigrate at a younger age will have better outcomes than those who arrive later." They cite research indicating that age of migration predicts academic achievement and that the 1.5 generation gets more education and may even exceed the academic attainments of second and third generation (Anisef et al. 2010). Such generalizations, however positive in outlook, neither offer insight into factors that account for academic achievement, particularly when it is uneven within a group, nor provide a basis for explaining what happens when a child does not succeed.

Focus on the Group

When young children are dismissed as a group there is no opportunity to explore differences in either the circumstances of their settlement or their individual and family characteristics. In supporting a more "segmented" approach to assimilation, Anisef et al. (2010) point to the increasingly diverse nature of the newcomer population and to the more complex and challenging socio-economic contexts in which newcomers are expected to assimilate. They identify a number of contextual factors, such as poverty, opportunities for accumulating social capital, and school experience. An examination of those factors reveals the complexity of the newcomer experience. Conclusions, such as Worswick's that "the children of immigrants perform, on average, at least as well as the children of the Canadian born" mask discrepancies, such as Gunderson's findings of "stark differences in the academic performance of different ethno-cultural groups" (cited by Anisef et al. 2010, 5).

These discrepancies point to the importance of unpacking the data and looking more carefully at specific groups, including age groups. In fact, findings of uneven achievement of children from various groups are reminders that when broad generalizations are accepted at face value, the specific needs of a number of individuals will not be addressed. Further investigation is needed to find out why some children are less successful than others and provide a basis for public policies that not only support such investigations, but also provide for programming that addresses the distinctive needs of young newcomer children, and thus, promotes positive, long-term outcomes for the newcomer community.

WHAT ARE THE DISTINCTIVE NEEDS OF YOUNG NEWCOMER CHILDREN?

To determine the distinctive needs of young newcomer children, it is important to look first at some of the barriers they face as they settle into a new society. For purposes of discussion here, children are not distinguished by generation. A young "newcomer" is any child who is making a transition from one culture to another, and whose experiences at home differ from mainstream expectations. Also, since acculturation occurs across the life span, it is assumed that the challenges of acculturation also begin at infancy.

Barriers

When needs are unmet they become barriers to acculturation and settlement. All newcomer children, but especially the youngest, face the dual challenge of simultaneously adjusting to life in their receiving country and developing as individuals. As a result, the settlement of young children involves developmental as well as cultural factors and is influenced by the fact that developmental milestones and competencies are likely to differ in the old and new contexts (Oppedal 2006; Rousseau, Measham, and Bathiche-Suidan 2008). At the same time, the very young are often asked to meet expectations in more than one environment, each with conflicting cultural practices. A young child learning to eat must not only achieve the developmental milestones involved in holding and manipulating utensils, but also distinguish when it is appropriate to eat independently (mainstream Western settings) and when it is necessary to wait to be fed (in many home cultures).

In making the transition to a new country and coping with change, young children are often without parental support. Parents may be literally absent because one or both have been killed, stayed behind by choice or by force, or returned to their homeland for urgent reasons. Parents who are physically present may be emotionally absent because they are distracted by trauma or issues associated with their own settlement, such as concerns about their legal status. Parents who are present and available may be unfamiliar with the needs of their children or with ways of helping them, especially if they do not speak the language of their receiving community and are not aware of local resources. Often, parents with the best of intentions do not have time to offer support to their children because they are working at multiple jobs.

A case vignette described by mental health professionals in Montreal illustrates how programming that respects cultural differences and supports the settlement of young children can have far-reaching implications for the children and for other family members (Rousseau, Measham, and Bathiche-Suidan 2008, 71–72). It also shows how policies directed towards the very young can reach adult newcomers who might otherwise never seek help or settle successfully. The vignette concerns M, an eight-year-old refugee child who was referred for psychiatric assessment by his neighbourhood school. He is described as being socially isolated, not progressing academically, and being disruptive in class. He came to the province of Quebec, Canada, with his mother when he was four years old. His father was killed before migration. As M's story unfolds it becomes clear that his ability to succeed in school depends in large measure on his mother's ability to provide effective support, but that her ability to provide that support only emerges after she begins to deal with M's issues and receives help from the professionals assisting her son. M's behaviour appears to have been challenging for some time (he had been "an active and agitated child since his toddler years"). Although it seems likely that his difficulties are associated with his refugee experience, his mother said that some family members thought his behaviour might be due to an evil spirit. She expressed resistance to suggestions from professionals that M receive further assessment and treatment.

In time, the professionals acknowledged the mother's concerns and with the assistance of a traditional healer, prayers were said on M's behalf, including by members of M's extended family in their country of origin. The mother began to take language lessons and help her son with his homework. Further assessment revealed that M had specific problems, including learning disabilities and fine and gross motor language delays, and a potential language disorder. Appropriate interventions were begun and the school organized a special play group to help M make friends. Ultimately, M's behaviour improved, and he did better in school. His mother resolved some of her own difficulties and began to participate more fully in life in Canada.

At an age when they are constructing their sense of identity, young newcomer children like M are also coping with separation. In many cases, they are also dealing with various degrees of trauma, arising from events before, after, and during migration. Note that M's father was killed in his country of origin, and as a refugee it is likely that he experienced acts of violence. A survey of immigrants from four ethnocultural groups in Montreal, found that 47 percent had "witnessed some form of organized violence" and 28 percent had "personally suffered persecution" (Rousseau and Drapeau 2002, cited by Measham, Rousseau, and Nadeau 2005, 68). An Iraqi psychiatrist helping Iraqi refugee children in Egypt estimates that 50 percent of the refugees who have fled their homes since 2003 are children who have experienced direct exposure to wartime violence and combat experience, separation from caregivers, and other traumatic experiences. The children in the Egyptian clinic, ranging in age from 3 to 18 years, had a variety of behavioural and emotional problems that resulted in numerous complaints (Al Obaidi 2010, 72).

Often previous experience of trauma is related to current health needs (Nadeau and Measham 2005). For example, for victims of violence, physical symptoms may be an expression of memories of trauma. Differing concepts of health and illness as well as appropriate responses to illness, even in the very young, make it imperative that resources be dedicated to helping professionals become more sensitive to cultural differences and acquire the knowledge and skills they need to resolve symptoms and help young newcomers participate more fully in the life of their new society.

Other barriers relate to language, not merely because very young children are just acquiring verbal language, but also because while learning the language of their receiving country, they must also retain their home language. Language policies for young children must therefore have a dual focus to ensure that while young children are learning to communicate in a new language on a daily basis, they are also strengthening their home language. The latter is important because knowledge of their home language provides a foundation for cognitive development and later academic achievement, maintains their ability to communicate with their parents, and supports links with their culture of origin (e.g., Genesee, Paradis, and Crago 2004).

WHY IS EARLY CHILDHOOD A CRITICALLY IMPORTANT PERIOD?

Although young newcomer children warrant the attention of policy-makers because of the special barriers associated with their newcomer status, they also have much in common with their mainstream peers. For young immigrants and refugees, as for other children, the early years constitute a critical period when experiences can have long-term consequences that determine future outcomes. For young immigrants and refugees, however, experiences in this critical period are also distinctive because of factors related to their situation as newcomers.

Early Experiences

Researchers and health professionals already know that the effects of separation and trauma can be devastating and long lasting. They also know that when addressed early between the ages of two and five, these effects can be mitigated and repaired (Hertzman 2002). Additionally, when early help is not available to young children who have experienced trauma, they know that the impact of the trauma multiplies and affects later development. If the brain is unable to process cognitive information as a result of trauma, children may be labelled as learning disabled when they are really suffering the effects of trauma. Traumatized children who are in a constant state of alarm have difficulty concentrating and may withdraw or behave impulsively (Perry n.d.).

Given the likelihood that newcomer children have experienced trauma in their past, the potential effectiveness of programs to support them at an early age seems obvious. Programs for children and youth offered through the school system thus come too late for many. Pressé and Thomson (2008, 97) have rightly called for a "more strategic" focus on individual needs, noting that the effects of war and trauma on the subsequent integration of refugee children and youth are not well understood, even though research suggests that surviving war and its related trauma can have "devastating social and psychological consequences." On the other hand, the key issue may not be that the effects of war and trauma on children are "not well understood," but instead, that what is known about those effects is not linked to the experience of newcomer children, especially young children, and thus is not available to inform settlement policies and programs for young children.

Future Challenges

In addition to coping with present or past experiences, young newcomers must prepare for future challenges, including racism and other obstacles to their settlement. In the end, newcomers who are equipped to cope with such challenges before they arise are likely to have better outcomes. Researchers have found that since "children two and three years of age can mimic thinking styles of primary caregivers," young children can develop resiliency skills when adults model resiliency in the face of adversity (Pearson and Hall 2007, 12). Programs already exist to help early childhood educators and others teach resiliency thinking and coping skills to young children (e.g., Reaching IN Reaching OUT relates to children from birth to seven years of age). Researchers have also developed measures to identify resilience factors in children, including the very young (e.g., the Devereux Early Childhood Assessment Program (DECA) for children two to five years of age [RIRO 2010, Appendix E: 1–2]). In a study of 1.5-generation newcomers ages 10 to 13, Arthur et al. (2008) challenged the perception that children adapt more quickly than adults as well as the assumption that they do not face adjustment issues in their everyday experiences. They found that the newcomer children who responded most successfully to acts of discrimination against them were the children with healthy resilience patterns. Research findings can, thus, point the way to policies and programs that, if implemented in the early years, can mitigate or prevent the consequences of negative settlement experiences.

Effects of Intervention in the Early Years

Decision-makers also need to recognize that programs for young children can be important avenues for reaching parents and other family members. In M's case, efforts to help him ultimately benefitted M's mother and connected both back to relatives in their country of origin. Intervention involving health care professionals, school officials, counsellors, teachers, and fellow students as well as family members had a widespread, positive effect on the eight-year-old child. According to the vignette, M came to Canada when he was four years old and he was "active and agitated" as a toddler. It may be worth speculating on the cost savings, in financial and human terms, that might have been realized if action had been taken when M was still a toddler. Given the extensive supports that are often needed to help older children, it is important to consider the benefits of earlier intervention to help young children cope with separation issues and perhaps become more resilient before facing the challenges of formal schooling.

Available Data about the Early Years

To inform public policy and provide a basis for program investments, research must be based on facts. Researchers need data and a solid knowledge base on which to build hypotheses and carry out further studies. To create this knowledge base requires collaboration between and among researchers in a number of disciplines. With respect to young children, for example, researchers working with the Early Development Instrument (EDI) have generated data for at least 10 years on the school readiness of young children across Canada and elsewhere (Janus et al. 2007). Developed at the Offord Centre for Child Studies at McMaster University in Hamilton, Ontario, the EDI is a population-based measure which assesses kindergarteners in five domains:

physical health and well-being, social competence, emotional maturity, language and cognitive development, and communication skills and general knowledge. Data can be analyzed according to whether a child's home language is the language of instruction (English or French) or whether a child has another home language and is or is not considered a second language learner (SLL). If home language is a proxy for newcomer status, it is possible to use findings to compare how well each group of newcomers is prepared for school and find out where a group may be vulnerable for negative outcomes later on. Since its introduction, the EDI has been validated and its accuracy as a predictor of later outcomes confirmed. It has also been used in company with neighbourhood data to assess the effects of local context on school readiness.

Recent analyses of EDI reveal diverse readiness patterns among children based on their fluency in the language of instruction, with scores divided into subgroups according to home language (Janus, Hughes, and Duku 2010). These analyses confirm earlier findings by others that some newcomers are doing at least as well as the children of Canadian born (who are monolingual in the language of instruction) and support observations that some ethno-social groups (as identified by home language) are doing better than others. Analyses have also shown that some groups of bilingual children whose first language is neither English nor French but who are not classified as second-language learners had better outcomes than the language control group with children who were monolingual in the language of instruction. Even so, the fact that some of these children had lower scores in the communication skills and general knowledge category, is perhaps an indication that in spite of their positive scores overall, they, too, would benefit from increased attention to their settlement.

Expanding Knowledge

Research continues to identify factors in the lives of young children that contribute to their ability to function successfully in society. For example, for Claudia Galindo and Bruce Fuller (2010, 579) evidence that the social competence and emotional health of young children are "predictive of early success in school" is insufficient. They want to know more about specific social competencies in relation to specific social practices as they are found, not just in Latino children, but also in children from specific segments of the Latino culture (i.e., subgroups from Mexico, Puerto Rico, Cuba, and Central and South America.). In building on eco-cultural theory, these researchers join others who wish to learn more about how children acquire competencies and practices within culturally bounded settings. Work in this area, which seeks to distinguish characteristics of the diverse participants in the segmented assimilation discussed earlier, has the potential to open doors to further understanding of newcomers and point to new knowledge that can be applied in the design of programs and strategies to help young children succeed better in the society of the future.

WHY IS SETTLEMENT SUPPORT POSSIBLE IN EARLY CHILDHOOD?

Research suggests that settlement is not just about economic success but also about competencies that contribute to the well-being of individuals (Houle and Schellenberg 2010; Phythian, Walters, and Anisef 2006). Ka Ying Yang, a resettled refugee, characterizes her settlement experience as a personal journey that leads to a sense of belonging and a commitment to participate in society:

> Integration is a very long and personal journey involving self-examination, acceptance in a new community and a sense of belonging. It requires a level of pride in one's identity, and a willingness to adopt aspects of the cultural practices of the host community. Integration is more than achieving self-sufficiency. It includes a commitment to participate fully in the receiving society and to expect responsible reciprocity from host communities. (UNHCR 2002, v)

On a conceptual level, the settlement journey may be described as a process of building social capital, including both bonding capital, which includes close family and friends with the same social, cultural, and economic backgrounds, and bridging capital, which includes networks of individuals with varying backgrounds including for newcomers, members of mainstream society (Anisef et al. 2010). Settlement thus emerges as a process that is highly relevant to the early childhood years, when individuals are developing personal identity and learning to relate to their families at home and others in the wider world in programs for young children and elsewhere.

Early childhood programming has been recognized as an important support to the settlement of young newcomers (UNHCR 2002, 266–267). On a global basis there is broad recognition of the key role that children's programs play in achieving a number of policy objectives. As Donna Berthelsen (2010) suggests, these objectives include an increase in women's labour market participation, a reconciliation of work and family responsibilities that is more equitable to women, recognition of demographic changes, and the need to address social and economic inequalities for children from economically disadvantaged and newcomer families. At the same time, the contribution of early childhood programs as valuable investments to society has also been widely recognized (Berthelsen 2010; Fairholm 2009).

More information is needed to formulate objectives and design programs. In calling for additional research, Berthelsen (2010) identifies a range of issues that influence early childhood policy, including arguments for early childhood programs as economic investments, the importance of providing quality programming with the capacity to benefit young children as foundations for lifelong learning and social mobility, the importance of women's income, and children's rights to participation and early education. When serving newcomer children, settlement issues present additional areas for investigation into the role of early childhood programming as a support to young newcomers in relation to both their own experiences as newcomers and their interactions in the communities in which they live.

CONCLUSION

Researchers and policy-makers have a rich field for further inquiry and program development. To begin, both must recognize that young immigrants and refugees have distinctive settlement needs that must be explored and addressed.

Researchers in migration studies should become more interdisciplinary, rethink terminology and attitudes, and collaborate with colleagues in the early childhood and related fields. Researchers in child studies need to pay more attention to settlement issues and reach out and participate with others in the pursuit of greater understanding. Researchers in all fields need to be concerned with expanding the existing knowledge base and developing new data sets to assess the needs of young newcomers. They need to take a segmented approach, and eschewing broad cultural generalizations, explore the diverse complexity of newcomer populations.

Policy-makers and decision-makers have a role both in promoting the creation of new knowledge and in using existing knowledge to develop policies and programs that will support the settlement of young children. They need to be aware of areas where early childhood programs can achieve policy objectives and be especially informed of the value of early intervention and programming in areas such as appropriate language development that have special relevance for newcomers. In doing so, they will not only improve individual lives but also ensure a positive future for the global society.

ACKNOWLEDGEMENTS

This chapter builds on ideas first expressed in my book, *Welcoming Newcomer Children: The Settlement of Young Immigrants and Refugees*. Guelph, ON: Judith A. Colbert, 2010. www.welcomingchildren.ca.

REFERENCES

Al Obaidi, A. K. S. 2010. "Iraqi Psychiatrist in Exile Helping Distressed Iraqi Refugee Children in Egypt in Non-Clinical Settings." *Journal of the Canadian Academy of Child and Adolescent Psychiatry* 19:72–73.

Anisef, P., R. S. Brown, K, Phythian, R. Sweet, and D. Walters. 2010. "Early School Leaving among Immigrants in Toronto Secondary Schools." *Canadian Review of Sociology* 47 (2):103–129.

Arthur, N., A. Chaves, D. Este, J. Frideres, and N. Hrycak. 2008. "Perceived Discrimination by Children of Immigrant Parents: Responses and Resiliency." *Canadian Diversity* 6:69–74.

Berthelsen, D. 2010. "Introduction to Special Issue: Research on Children under Three—Reports from Seven Countries." *International Journal of Early Childhood* 42: 81–86.

Citizenship and Immigration Canada (CIC). 2009. "Facts and Figures 2008—Immigration Overview: Permanent and Temporary Residents: Permanent Residents." Accessed August 25, 2009. www.cic.gc.ca/english/resources/statistics/facts2008/permanent/index.asp.

City of Toronto. 2010. "Toronto's Racial Diversity." Accessed December 16, 2010. www.toronto.ca/toronto_facts/diversity.htm.

Fairholm, R. 2009. "Literature Review of Socioeconomic Effects and Net Benefits: Understanding and Addressing Workplace Shortages in Early Childhood Education and Care (ECEC) Project." Ottawa: Child Care Human Resources Sector Council. Accessed August 9. www.ccsc-cssge.ca/uploads/WFS%20LitReview%20-%20Socio%20-%20FINAL.pdf

Genesee, F., J. Paradis, and M. B. Crago. 2004. *Dual Language Development and Disorders: A Handbook on Bilingualism & Second Language Learning*. Baltimore, MD: Brookes Publishing.

Galindo, C. and B. Fuller. 2010. "The Social Competence of Latino Kindergartners and Growth in Mathematical Understanding." *Developmental Psychology* 46:579–592.

Gluszynski, T., and U. Dhawan-Biswal. 2008. "Reading Skills of Young Immigrants in Canada: The Effects of Duration of Residency, Home Language Exposure and Schools." Ottawa: Learning Policy Directorate Strategic Policy and Research, Human Resources and Social Development Canada. Accessed December 17, 2010. www.hrsdc.gc.ca/eng/publications_resources/learning_policy/sp_849_06_08/sp_849_06_08e.pdf

Hertzman, C. 2002. "Leave No Child Behind! Social Exclusion and Child Development: Perspectives on Social Inclusion." Toronto: Laidlaw Foundation.

Houle, R., and G. Schellenberg. 2010. "New Immigrants' Assessments of their Life in Canada." Ottawa: Statistics Canada. Analytical Studies – Research Paper Series, Catalogue no. 11F0019M, no. 322. Accessed May 25, 2010. www.statcan.gc.ca.

Janus, M., S. Brinkman, E. Duku, C. Hertzman, R. Santos, M. Sayers, J. Schroeder, and C. Walsh. 2007. *The Early Development Instrument: Population-Based Measure for Communities. A Handbook on Development, Properties and Use*. Hamilton, ON: Offord Centre for Child Studies.

Janus, M., D. Hughes, and E. Duku. 2010. "Patterns of School Readiness among Selected Subgroups of Canadian Children: Children with Special Needs and Children with Diverse Language Backgrounds." Hamilton, ON: Offord Centre for Child Studies. Accessed June 04, 2010. www.offordcentre.com/readiness/files/2010_05_06_SR_subgroups_SN_Lang_CCL.pdf.

Measham, T., C. Rousseau, and L. Nadeau. 2005. "The Development and Therapeutic Modalities of a Transcultural Child Psychiatry Service." *The Canadian Child and Adolescent Psychiatry Review* 14 (3):68–72.

Migration Policy Institute (MPI). 2010. "Community Profiles of Young Children of Immigrants." Accessed December 16, 2010. www.migrationinformation.org/integration/knight_profiles.cfm.

Nadeau, L., and T. Measham. 2005. "Immigrants and Mental Health Services: Increasing Collaboration with Other Services." *The Canadian Child and Adolescent Psychiatry Review* 14 (3):73–76.

Organisation for Economic Co-operation and Development (OECD). 2001. "Executive Summary: Starting Strong—Early Education and Care Report on an OECD Thematic Review." CCRU Briefing Note. Accessed December 16, 2010. www.childcarecanada.org.

Oppedal, B. 2006. "Development and Acculturation." In *The Cambridge Handbook of Acculturation Psychology*, edited by D. L. Sam and J. W. Berry, 97–112. Cambridge, UK: Cambridge University Press.

Perry, B. n.d. "Principles of Working with Traumatized Children: The Threatened Child." Accessed August 09, 2010. teacher.scholastic.com.

Pearson, J., and D. Hall. 2007. "Resilience: Coping Effectively with Life's Challenges." *Interaction* Winter:11–12.

Phythian, K., D. Walters, and P. Anisef. 2006. "The Acculturation of Immigrants: Determinants of Ethnic Identification with the Host Society." Paper presented at the annual meeting of the American Sociological Association, Montreal, Quebec, August 8, 2006.

Pressé, D., and J. Thomson. 2008. "The Resettlement Challenge: Integration of Refugees from Protracted Refugee Situations." *Refuge: Canada's Periodical on Refugees* 25:94–99.

Reaching IN … Reaching OUT (RIRO). 2010. *Resilience: Successful Navigation through Significant Threat*. Report prepared for the Ontario Ministry of Children and Youth Services. Toronto: The Child & Family Partnership. Accessed May 14, 2011. www.reachinginreachingout.com/documents/MCYS%20Resilience%20Report%2011-16-10%20Dissemination.pdf.

Rousseau, C., T. Measham, and M. Bathiche-Suidan. 2008. "DSMIV, Culture and Child Psychiatry." *Journal of the Canadian Academy of Child and Adolescent Psychiatry* 17 (2):69–75.

Schwartz, S., J. B. Unger, B. L. Zamboanga, and J. J. Szapocnik. 2010. "Rethinking the Concept of Acculturation: Implications for Theory and Research." *American Psychologist* 65:237–251.

Statistics Canada. 2007. "Longitudinal Survey of Immigrants to Canada (LSIC) Detailed Information for 2005 (Wave 3)." Accessed on April 27. www.statcan.gc.ca/cgi-bin/imdb/p2SV.pl?Function=getSurvey&SDDS=4422&lang=en&db=imdb&adm=8&dis=2.

UN High Commissioner for Refugees (UNHCR). 2002. *Refugee Resettlement: An International Handbook to Guide Reception and Integration*. New York: The UN Refugee Agency. Accessed December 16, 2010. www.unhcr.org/4a2cfe336.html.

COPYRIGHT ACKNOWLEDGEMENTS

Table 5.1: "Temporary Labour Migrants in Canada by Occupational Skill Level (2006–2008)," from Citizenship and Immigration Canada (CIC) publication *Facts and Figures 2008 – Immigration Overview: Permanent and Temporary Residents* (Ottawa: Citizenship and Immigration Canada, 2009). Reprinted by permission of Citizenship and Immigration Canada.

Table 12.1: "Families Occupying their Home in Italy," from Census data from the Italian Statistical Institute documents "Free and Occupied Dwellings (1961, 1971)" and "Living Accommodations for Families (1981 - 2001)" (Italy: ISTAT, 2001). Reprinted by permission of the Italian Statistical Institute.

Table 12.2: "Social Housing on Total Housing Stock," *Housing Statistics in the European Union in 2004* (EU: National Board of Housing, Building and Planning, Sweden and Ministry for Regional Development of the Czech Republic, 2004): 82. Reprinted by permission of the National Board of Housing, Sweden.

Table 12.3: A. Menonna, "Immigrants' Homes," from *Il Mezzogiorno dopo la Regolarizzazione*, (eds.) G. Blangiardo and C. Farina (Milan: FrancoAngeli, 2006): 110-124. Reprinted by permission of FrancoAngeli.

Table 12.4: "Public Housing Tenants in Italy and Its Regions" (Italy: Italian Ministry of the Interior, 2007).

Table 15.1: "Funding for Refugee Community Organization Building," from *Portfolio Budgets for Australia's Department of Immigration and Citizenship, annual reports, 1999-2011* (Australia: Department of Immigration and Citizenship, former Department of Multiculturalism and Immigration Affairs, 2008). Reprinted by permission Australia's Department of Immigration and Citizenship.